Politics, poetics, and hermeneutics in Milton's prose

Lucas Vorsterman after Peter Paul Rubens, title-page from Franciscus van de Haer,
Annales Ducum seu Principum Brabantiae Totiusque Belgiae, vol II (Antwerp, 1623)
(reproduced by permission of the Syndics of the Cambridge University Library)

Politics, poetics, and hermeneutics in Milton's prose

Essays edited by

DAVID LOEWENSTEIN

and

JAMES GRANTHAM TURNER

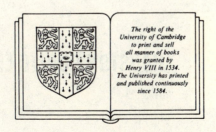

The right of the
University of Cambridge
to print and sell
all manner of books
was granted by
Henry VIII in 1534.
The University has printed
and published continuously
since 1584.

CAMBRIDGE UNIVERSITY PRESS

Cambridge
New York   Port Chester
Melbourne   Sydney

Published by the Press Syndicate of the University of Cambridge
The Pitt Building, Trumpington Street, Cambridge CB2 1RP
40 West 20th Street, New York, NY 10011, USA
10 Stamford Road, Oakleigh, Melbourne 3166, Australia

© Cambridge University Press 1990

First published 1990

Printed in Great Britain at the University Press, Cambridge

British Library cataloguing in publication data
Politics, poetics and hermeneutics in Milton's prose.
  1. Prose in English. Milton, John, 1608–1674 – Critical studies
  I. Loewenstein, David   II. Turner, James Grantham
  821'.4

Library of Congress cataloguing in publication data
Politics, poetics, and hermeneutics in Milton's prose: essays /
edited by David Loewenstein and James Grantham Turner.
    p.   cm.
Bibliography.
ISBN 0 521 34458 1
1. Milton, John, 1608–1674 – Political and social views.
2. Milton, John, 1608–1674 – Prose.   3. Great Britain – Politics and
government – 1642–1660.   4. Hermeneutics.   I. Loewenstein, David, 1955–
II. Turner, James, 1947–
PB3592.P64P65   1990
821'.4–dc20   89–7316   CIP

ISBN 0 521 34458 1

And now the time in speciall is, by priviledge
to write and speak what may help to the furder
discussing of matters in agitation. The
Temple of *Janus* with his two *controversal*
faces might now not unsignificantly be set
open.   (*Areopagitica*)

In words which admitt of various sense, the
libertie is ours to choose that interpretation
which may best minde us of what our restless
enemies endeavor, and what wee are timely to
prevent.   (*Eikonoklastes*, Preface)

Contents

Illustrations

Contributors

Lana Cable is Assistant Professor of English at the State University of New York at Albany. She has published articles on Milton and Phineas Fletcher, and she is completing a book provisionally entitled *Carnal Rhetoric: Image and Truth in Milton's Polemics*.

Thomas N. Corns was educated at Brasenose and University Colleges, Oxford, and at the Maximilianeum Foundation, Munich. He is the author of *The Development of Milton's Prose Style* (1982), co-author (with B. H. Rudall) of *Computers and Literature: a Practical Guide* (1987), and editor of *The Literature of Controversy: Polemical Strategy from Milton to Junius* (1987), and author of numerous essays and papers, mainly on Milton and on humanities computing. He has recently completed a study of the language of Milton's poetry, to be published in the Blackwell's Language Library. He is a senior lecturer at the University College of North Wales, Bangor.

Stephen M. Fallon is an assistant professor at the University of Notre Dame, where he teaches in the Program of Liberal Studies and in the English department. He has published articles on Milton in the *Journal of the History of Ideas* and *English Literary Renaissance*, and is currently finishing *Milton among the Philosophers*, a book on Milton's materialism and seventeenth-century metaphysics (forthcoming from Cornell University Press).

Stanley Fish is Arts and Sciences Distinguished Professor of English, Professor of Law, and Chairman of the Department of English at Duke University. His most recent publication is *Doing What Comes Naturally: Change, Rhetoric, and the Practice of Theory in Legal and Literary Studies* (Duke University Press, 1989). The present essay is from a forthcoming volume called *Milton's Aesthetic of Testimony, or It Takes One to Know One*.

Gary D. Hamilton is Associate Professor at the University of Maryland. He has written articles on Milton's epics and prose and has been particularly interested in studying shifts in theological and political discourse in the 1650s and 1660s.

Laura Lunger Knoppers, Assistant Professor of English at The Pennsylvania

State University, has published on Milton and Puritan views of marriage, and is currently working on a book on Milton and seventeenth-century covenants.

John R. Knott is Professor of English at the University of Michigan and the author of *Milton's Pastoral Vision* (Chicago, 1971) and *The Sword of the Spirit* (Chicago, 1980), and scholarly articles on Spenser, Browne, Bunyan, and Milton.

David Loewenstein is Assistant Professor of English at the University of Wisconsin-Madison. He is the author of *Milton and the Drama of History: Historical Vision, Iconoclasm, and the Literary Imagination* (Cambridge University Press, 1990), and is currently working on literary representations of rebellion in the age of Milton.

Janel Mueller is Professor of English and Humanities at the University of Chicago, and editor of *Modern Philology*. Her publications include *Donne's Prebend Sermons* (Harvard, 1971) and *The Native Tongue and the Word: Developments in English Prose Style, 1380–1580* (Chicago, 1984). She is currently at work on a volume of essays that bring various perspectives – contextual, generic, prosodic – to bear on *Samson Agonistes*, and on a book-length study of how patriarchy configures the relations of nature, culture, and gender in Milton's major poems.

Annabel Patterson is Professor of Literature and English at Duke University. She is the author of *Hermogenes and the Renaissance* (1970), *Marvell and the Civic Crown* (1978), *Censorship and Interpretation* (1984), *Pastoral and Ideology* (1987) and *Shakespeare and the Popular Voice* (1989). She has edited *Roman Images* for the English Institute, and is currently editing the *Milton* volume of the Longmans Critical Reader series.

Regina M. Schwartz, Associate Professor at Duke University, teaches Milton, the Bible, literary theory, and Renaissance literature. She is the author of *Remembering and Repeating: Biblical Creation in "Paradise Lost"* (Cambridge University Press, 1988). Her recent essays on Milton and the Bible include "From Shadowy Types to Shadowy Types" (*Milton Studies*, 28) and "Joseph's Bones and the Resurrection of the Text" (*PMLA*, 103). She is currently writing a book on biblical narrative and historiography entitled *Can These Bones Live?*

Nigel Smith is Fellow and Tutor in English at Keble College, Oxford. He has edited the Ranter tracts and is the author of *Perfection Proclaimed: Language and Literature in English Radical Religion, 1640–1660* (Oxford, 1989). He is currently writing a study of the transformation of literature during the Civil War and Interregnum periods for Yale University Press.

James Grantham Turner is Professor of English at the University of Michigan. He is the author of *The Politics of Landscape: Rural Scenery and Society in English Poetry, 1630–1660* (1979) and *One Flesh: Paradisal Marriage and Sexual Relations in the Age of Milton* (1987), and is currently working on libertinism and sexuality in England and France, 1650–1750.

Susanne Woods is Professor of English and Associate Dean of the Faculty at Brown University. She is the author of *Natural Emphasis: English Versification from Chaucer to Dryden* (1985), is finishing a book on freedom and tyranny in Spenser and Milton, and is principal investigator for an NEH-sponsored text recovery and full text database project, "Women Writers 1330–1830."

A note on citations and abbreviations

Milton's English prose will be cited from the Yale edition, *The Complete Prose Works of John Milton*, ed. Don M. Wolfe *et al*. (New Haven: Yale University Press, 1953–82), abbreviated where necessary as *CPW*. References (volume and page) will normally be added to the text in parentheses without further attribution.

Milton's Latin prose will be cited from the Columbia edition, *The Works of John Milton*, ed. Frank Allen Patterson *et al*. (New York: Columbia University Press, 1931–38), but an English translation and a *CPW* reference will always be provided. For ease of location, parenthetical references will always give the Yale first, followed after a semicolon by the Columbia.

"Prose concordance" refers to Laurence Sterne and Harold H. Kollmeier, eds., *A Concordance to the English Prose of John Milton* (Binghamton: Medieval and Renaissance Texts and Studies, 1985).

Other abbreviations are as follows:

Left Hand   Michael Lieb and John T. Shawcross, eds., *Achievements of the Left Hand: Essays on the Prose of John Milton* (Amherst: University of Massachusetts Press, 1974)

MCH I   John T. Shawcross, ed., *John Milton: The Critical Heritage* (London: Routledge, 1970)

MCH II   John T. Shawcross, ed., *John Milton, 1732–1801: The Critical Heritage* (London: Routledge, 1972)

Introduction: "Labouring in the Word"

DAVID LOEWENSTEIN AND JAMES GRANTHAM TURNER

Milton's prose works have always meant trouble. Are they essential achievements in their own right, or are they a pernicious diversion from his creative goal, violently partisan and tediously occasional? Bishop Warburton denounced their "abominable" virulence and "unnatural" forced grandeur, but extolled their "poetical enthusiasm" and sublimity, which at times excelled even that of the poetry (*MCH* II.90–2). Macaulay discovers in Milton's prose "the full power of the English language" –

> not even in the earlier books of the Paradise Lost has the great poet ever risen higher than in those parts of his controversial works in which his feelings, excited by conflict, find a vent in bursts of devotional and lyric rapture

– but he still represents Milton as a divided figure, struggling to reconcile the needs of "the statesman" and "the poet."[1] When critics try to isolate the sublime canonical bard from the vehement polemicist, the separated halves cling together again. When they try to abandon this critical separatism and to see Milton's work as a whole, conversely, the language of separation returns: the prose is assumed to be "left-handed," subliterary, a mere repository of ideas and gloss for the poems. In the unpremeditated language of Paradise, "Prose or numerous Verse" were interchangeable or indistinguishable (*PL* v.150). But for generations of interpreters, Milton's double career – as poet and as prose controversialist – has come to resemble the difficult marriage imagined in the divorce tracts and *Samson Agonistes*: a "cleaving mischief."

The separatist doctrine is often sustained more by faith than by evidence. One traditional scholar asserts the "*omnipresent* difference between Milton's poetry and Milton's prose," even though he himself demonstrates a number of similarities between the two. The same scholar claims that the poet described *all* his prose works as "labors of his left hand"; as Turner shows below, however, Milton's passing reference to having the use "but of my left hand" (I.807–8) is cancelled by its larger context, and should not be used as a universal principle to describe the achievements of the prose.[2] One progressive historian, who has made vast contributions to our understanding of Milton's prose and to the integration of his poetic and political career, still refers to the "left-handed prose propaganda" that interrupted his true vocation.[3] One psychoanalytic critic explores the deep connection between creativity and radical polemic, singling out the aggressive "Chariot of Zeale" passage in the *Apology* to show that Milton could indeed "hold the pen . . . in the right hand" in the prose, and yet maintains that Milton's "art could not survive amid these divisive passions," that he "severed himself" in the period of political activism.[4] Indeed, a major collection of essays on the prose, our only predecessor in the field, appeared under the title *Achievements of the Left Hand*, even though its best pieces, such as those by Joseph Wittreich and Michael Lieb, effectively abolish the dichotomy of poetry and rhetoric, performance and prophesy.

The current volume stresses precisely those elements and issues that allow us to break down this partitioning of Milton's career. The essays all focus on the prose, but they open up avenues to the major poems and to contemporary ideologies, theologies and interpretative practices. Most of them bridge the gap between the history-of-ideas approach (typical of much previous work on the prose) and literary/textual analysis. Our concerns are obviously conceptual and historical as well as literary: martyrdom, iconoclasm, prophesy, apocalypticism, biblical exegesis, supplementarity, monism, natural law, authority, performance, citation, defense, polemic strategies, "elective poetics," reception, the genres of autobiography and jeremiad, the status of prose itself. But these themes are reinterpreted dynamically and as it were amphibiously, revealing their double operation – as substantial ideas in seventeenth-century history, and as linguistic and aesthetic effects. Our contributors show not simply what was thought, but how; they do not limit themselves to summaries of content, but reconstruct performance or probe for underlying (often contradictory) hermeneutic processes. They are in no way homogenous in their approaches, however. With *Areopagitica* as a model, we have encouraged "neighbouring differences" rather than "forc't and outward union"; the result is a "mangl'd body," but one that may strive towards Truth.

Though none of the following essays is primarily theoretical, they do raise theoretical issues. The multiplicity of pieces on *Eikonoklastes* and the divorce tracts suggests that they speak directly to a decade concerned with representation, deconstruction and the politics of gender. The contributions of the two editors, wielding their "two-handed engine," call for a rethinking of the relation between creativity and polemic violence. Many of these essays deal with what Cable calls the "idolatry of words," the self-referentiality of the image, the self-authentication of discourse, the tautologies that lurk beneath the appeal to biblical authority. As Knott and Cable demonstrate, the poet/iconoclast was faced with the problem of distinguishing false and true martyrdom, false and true images – the false representation, embodied in Charles I, being that which bears witness only to itself. Many of us conclude, however, that all texts are false martyrs, and that all "assertions" usurp the authority they ostensibly obey.

These essays also propose a complex relationship between text and context, the aesthetic and the sociopolitical. David Norbrook has argued that Milton politicized the aesthetic in his early poetry; Keith Stavely, on the other hand, proposed that in his revolutionary prose Milton over-aestheticized the political, sacrificing *Realpolitik* to sonorous cadence and Utopian dreaming.[5] Stavely's polarity defines the political and the aesthetic too narrowly, we feel. The current volume highlights the aesthetic and literary dimensions of Milton's controversial writings, but its main concern is with the *interaction* between textual effects and the world of power – the ideologies of authority, the theological battles, or (less often) the political events that constitute "history." As our general epigraphs from *Areopagitica* and *Eikonoklastes* suggest, we are fascinated by those moments when significance is "set open" by war (like the temple of Janus), when revolutionary politics affect the act of interpretation itself. Our project implies, or moves towards, a dialectic and mutually constructive relation between text and context, rather than an inert background–foreground model. Thus, for example, placing *Eikonoklastes* against the background of radical Protestantism and revolutionary Puritanism may help explain the intellectual and social dimensions of Milton's iconoclasm; but treating the work as a literary text written by a poet-polemicist simultaneously fascinated by and deeply anxious about the power of an image explains even further Milton's ferocious attack on the spectacular representation of Charles I in *Eikon Basilike*. In Milton's demolition of the king's book and icon, the artistic and the political, the literary and the intellectual intersect: as a phenomenon, Milton's radical iconoclasm is simultaneously ideological and aesthetic.

Each individual essay explores a different aspect of this conjunction of literary and political discourse. As Mueller demonstrates, the bold transformation of the apocalyptic tradition in *Of Reformation* operates at a metaphorical level; in Milton's polemical use of body tropes, the "apocalyptic strain" stimulates an imaginative vision in which concept and image fuse together. Smith suggests that Milton's engagement with context may be creative and interpretive, as he appropriates and reworks the language of Parliamentarian apology and natural law to promote a new theory of ethics – the free trade of Truth expressed in *Areopagitica*'s numerous socioeconomic metaphors. Even in a text like the *Observations upon the Articles of Peace* – one of Milton's least studied and most disturbing polemics – we see him fashioning his polemical art to meet the political occasion: Corns shows how Milton supports the ethically dubious military operation in Ireland by exploiting an austere polemical style and by manipulating his audience's fears and prejudices. Fallon analyzes Milton's figurative imagination to show how his early monism develops in the divorce pamphlets. Drawing upon genre theory, Patterson considers how fictional narratives operate within Milton's divorce polemic, while Loewenstein stresses the mythopoetic dimensions of Milton's defense of the Protectorate in 1654; the *Second Defense* channels his poetic energies into a heroic vision of the new social order, while also responding with acute sensitivity to the fragile social realities of the historical moment. Focusing on *The Readie and Easie Way*, Knoppers demonstrates how boldly and self-consciously the polemicist appropriates and transforms the conventions of the jeremiad in order to challenge the ideology behind that prophetic mode – the notion that England would indeed remain elect.

To take Milton's prose seriously is to plunge into the vexed question of timeliness or occasionality. Our second epigraph applies not just to the revolutionary polemicist, but also to the literary critic: "in words which admitt of various sense, the libertie is ours to choose that interpretation which may best minde us of what our restless enemies endeavor, and what wee are timely to prevent" (III.342). According to separatist aesthetics, poetic achievement depends on withdrawal from the immediate processes of history, and particularly from the troubling pressures of political crisis. This withdrawal may be literal (Milton could only compose great works in the retirement forced on him by political failure), conceptual (literature transforms and transcends the specificity of the moment and the passions of commitment) or psychological (Milton may respond superficially to the changes of the times, but his real essence, the real "truth" of his literary power, lies in some perennial condition of his "ego" – as Fish argues below.) One problem of this position is theoretical: the opposition of the timeless/ literary to the local/political rests on a tautology, since this definition of the literary is obtained in the first place by subtracting the occasional and the political (which have, of course, already been defined to suit the hostile dichotomy). The timeless, far from being the source of artistic value, is thus a diminished category, a name without a thing, as Hobbes might have called it. Another problem is practical: it is difficult to read the essays in this volume without being aware of the vital interaction between Milton's creativity and the thrilling catastrophes of the Revolution. The fundamental change between the hermeneutic passivity of *Of Prelatical Episcopacy* and the activism of the divorce tracts – strikingly elaborated by Fish – reveals a deepening political crisis and personal involvement. Even a venerable Christian concept like martyrdom, as Knott shows, changed from year to year as the accelerated drama of the Revolution, and the reactionary events in France and the Piedmont, stirred the poet to new vehemence. Even in *De Doctrina*, Schwartz argues, questions of textual authority are inextricable from political questions. Discursive genres, such as the autobiographical romance studied by Patterson or the jeremiad studied by Knoppers, cannot be seen as fixed entities, since they gain new depth and meaning in the crucible of national and domestic politics. Milton's concerns were activated, concretized and so transformed by the developing stages of the crisis. His epistemology, his style, his self-presentation, his grasp of the relation between poetry and prose – all these alter profoundly between 1642 and 1644, or between 1654 and 1659. Like Truth itself, Milton was made, not found.[6]

One consequence of this activist conception of Milton is a new integration of the stages of his career. Fallon shows how Milton's heretical monism – central to the materialism of *Paradise Lost* – begins to emerge in the divorce tracts, while Woods argues that the concern with reader choice (what she calls "elective poetics") is as important for Milton's prose as it is for his poems. Such essays encourage us to see interrelations between the prose and the poems, and to reexamine the common assumption – the foundation stone of separatism – that the prose writings constitute a major period of interruption or diversion in Milton's poetic development.

Several essays stress the performative aspect of signification and self-presentation in the controversial writings. Milton's performance varies with the occasion, revealing (as Fish suggests) his uneasiness with the contradictions of interpretative authority. On the one hand, the danger of becoming a supplement to the Word encourages Milton to perform as minimally as possible; on the other hand, the pressure to reinterpret biblical authority in a text like the *Doctrine and Discipline of Divorce* provokes the bold supplementer to perform a series of dazzling hermeneutic maneuvers. Self-conscious of his performance in the divorce tracts, Milton negotiates, according to Fallon, between two audiences – the conventional dualists and the unconventional monists. In the *Second Defense*, as Loewenstein shows, Milton's self-dramatization reaches delirious heights, especially when he imagines himself receiving the applause of multitudes in Europe for his heroic deliverance of an exiled Liberty. Even in the *History of Britain*, Hamilton observes, Milton's self-presentation assumes heroic dimensions as he performs the difficult task of guiding his reader through the mazes of untrustworthy and contradictory historical authorities. Highly conscious of addressing a relapsing nation at the end of his revolutionary career, Milton transforms his jeremiad into a powerful "performative utterance" (as Knoppers shows) in which he dramatizes himself as the disregarded prophet facing personal danger from the misguided majority.

Concomitantly, he seeks to perform upon the audience. Turner shows how the imputed reader in *The Reason of Church-Government* changes to accommodate the sensuous as well as the rational response. Woods argues that, even in the relatively plain tracts of 1659, Milton employs such devices as repetition, litotes, and negative construction to promote active reader choice. Similarly, Hamilton stresses Milton's "art of indirection" in the *History*, which subtly prompts his reader – often through significant silences in the historical narrative – to scrutinize and question contemporary political issues. This is not the flamboyant, militant, and highly dramatic polemicist we encounter elsewhere in the prose writings; yet, as Hamilton's analysis suggests, the understated prose of indirection is quietly subversive, especially for the fit reader of Milton's historical work.

Our challenge, then, is to rethink Milton from the point of view of an all-embracing activism, a "labouring in the Word" through which he sought to gain the power and fervency he praised in the Apostles (1.715). Even in his earliest polemic Mueller finds an astonishing capacity to modify a providential perspective by valorizing human agency. Knott's emphasis on Milton's active and defiant conception of martyrdom confirms Mueller's observation, as does Loewenstein's consideration of Milton's dramatic assertion of himself in his state discourse, where he employs the power of mythopoetic vision to alter the ideological pressures of his age. Turner gives central importance to the anti-rational impulse of "Zeale," which promotes a heroic rhetoric obliterating the difference between Miltonic prose and poetry. Woods adds another dimension to this theme by transferring activism to Milton's reader, who finds herself negotiating – in both the prose and poetry – a multiplicity of meanings. As Knoppers observes, however, the notion of activism may reflect a crucial tension: the need for human action – expressed in Milton's own performative discourse – struggles with a sense of "its impossibility without divine aid." This leads him to a paradoxical position: "deferring to Biblical authority, Milton establishes his own."

Indeed, a number of these essays explore tensions and contradictions in Milton, establishing him as a figure divided, not by the cleavage of prose and poetry, but in every work and at every level. Focusing on questions of citation and authorization in *De Doctrina Christiana*, Schwartz (like Knoppers) shows Milton grappling with rival claims to authority – his own versus biblical authority. His emphasis on the plainness and clearness of scripture conflicts with his strenuous efforts at interpretation; as Schwartz suggests, this interpretive engagement can be competitive and aggressive – a confrontation between Milton and scripture, an act of dismembering and rearranging the sacred text. Patterson discovers in the syntax of the *Doctrine and Discipline* a tension between a disinterested self and a self-interested author, between an impersonal zeal for reform and Milton's "owne by-ends"; his use of myth – for example, the union of Eros and Anteros to express reciprocal love – conveys "both a generic and a gendered discomfort." Likewise, Fallon stresses a tension between blamelessness and responsibility in the divorce tracts, where the voice of the patriarchal and injured male repeatedly undermines Milton's more humane plea for no-fault divorce based on incompatibility. In *Areopagitica*, Smith detects a "creative tension" between political obligation and liberty, noting that Milton's ethics of virtuous choosing are not fully reconciled with ideas of natural law and contract. Even Fish, though he laments the attention given by left-wing critics to fissures and contradictions, takes obvious pleasure in demonstrating that Milton's argument is "everywhere divided against itself." Milton's contrary assertions about his achievements in prose reveal, as Turner suggests in the final essay, a

6

fundamental tension between the condemnation and the display of verbal splendor. His attitude towards textual authority is no less contrary; he yearns to liberate the spirit from imprisoning forms and to set truth flowing like a fountain, but also to freeze interpretation forever with the Gorgonian rigor of his gaze.

His critics inherit the same problematic dichotomy. Our motives in this volume are divided or "*controversal*," like the faces of Janus displayed in both our frontispiece and our epigraph from *Areopagitica*. We hope to stimulate fresh evaluation of the prose works, especially those that have been neglected, and to promote "what may help to the furder discussing of matters in agitation." At the same time, we want to refute the "separatist" or "left-handed" interpretation of Milton's life work, the tendency to disconnect and demote the prose and thereby to depoliticize the poetry. Faced with this persistent critical ideology, our impulse is to smite once and smite no more.

Notes

1 Thomas Babington, Lord Macaulay, *Literary Essays Contributed to the Edinburgh Review* (London, n.d.), pp. 25, 46–9.

2 C. A. Patrides, *John Milton: Selected Prose*, revised edn (Columbia, Mo., 1985), pp. 21, 43 (our emphasis). See, further, chapter 14 below, n. 12.

3 Christopher Hill, *Milton and the English Revolution* (Harmondsworth, 1979), p. 462.

4 William Kerrigan, *The Prophetic Milton* (Charlottesville, Va., 1974), pp. 170–3, and *The Sacred Complex: On the Psychogenesis of Paradise Lost* (Cambridge, Mass., 1983), pp. 64–5. More recently, Christopher Grose cites the "left hand" phrase as if it were spoken in the 1650s and referred to the whole of the prose, even though he goes on to argue that Milton's view of his own career changed significantly between the 1640s and the 1650s; *Milton and the Sense of Tradition* (New Haven and London, 1988), p. 10.

5 Norbrook, *Poetry and Politics in the English Renaissance* (London, 1984), pp. 235–85, Stavely, *The Politics of Milton's Prose Style* (New Haven, 1975), *passim*; *cf.* Kevin Sharpe, "The Politics of Literature in Renaissance England," *History*, 71 (1986), pp. 235–47.

6 This argument is intended to contrast the conclusion to Fish's essay in this volume with his powerful study of *Areopagitica* in Mary Nyquist and Margaret W. Ferguson, eds., *Re-Membering Milton: Essays on the Texts and Traditions* (New York and London, 1988), pp. 234–54. Fish argues in that essay that "historicist" criticism cannot be grounded in any truth outside itself; but in chapter 2 below, which explores the analogy (or, as he claims, the identity) between interpretive strategies and masculine neuroses, he assumes *in practice* – if not in theory – that the psychological is just such a realm of grounded truth.

Embodying glory: the apocalyptic strain in Milton's *Of Reformation*

JANEL MUELLER

No less in the New than in the Old Testament, times of crisis or upheaval evoke images of a transformation soon to be wrought by God on his people's behalf.[1] This Judaeo-Christian cast of mind finds its supreme referent in the figure of the Messiah or Christ, whose coming will spell the defeat of evil and bring a new order of beatitude and peace. From the biblical outlook, to struggle with the experience of history is also, necessarily, to seek the meaning of prophecy, for only in the light each casts on the other is there hope of humanly glimpsing the course of divine will in the world. Such a dual tension informs the visions of John of Patmos as well as Daniel. It underlies the expectations of cataclysm voiced by Isaiah and Jeremiah, Hosea and Amos, and the concern with the last days found in Paul the Apostle and Jesus himself. Fervently embracing scripture as their sole spiritual authority and rapidly setting themselves at odds with papal power, the first Protestants of the sixteenth century rediscovered the interdependence of received prophecy and lived history. They gave new thrust and currency to a medieval tradition of protest that had identified the Pope with Antichrist.[2] Soon after its origins, in a number of quarters more or less concurrently, the Reformation took on an apocalyptic significance. These were the last days; the end of the world drew near, and Christ would soon come in judgment and glory. Thus when Milton's first prose tract, *Of Reformation, and the Cawses that Hitherto Have Hindered It* (May 1641), climaxed by merging the Second Coming with the achievement of an English church discipline that would trace salient features to antecedents in Calvin, the vision that had shaped the outlook of early Protestantism recurred to launch the prose writer's career.[3]

The apocalyptic strain that figures in Milton's anti-episcopal tracts – most prominently in *Of Reformation* – deserves closer attention than it has yet received. Several recent book-length studies on the apocalypticism of sixteenth- and seventeenth-century English Protestants have facilitated the account I offer here.[4] It is now possible to chart Milton's location within a larger system of themes and emphases at the time he undertook the Smectymnuuans' defense as an outspoken advocate of the Root and Branch Petition that circulated in the optimistic first year of the Long Parliament, five months prior to the (anonymous) appearance of *Of Reformation* (1.976–84). I begin by characterizing a discernible Englishness of apocalyptic outlook – one whose sight-lines, already set by Lollardy, direct the use made of continental Protestant thought by later native writers. After indicating the degree of Milton's participation in this outlook, I discuss aspects of his text that identify a militant Presbyterian approach to the handling of apocalyptic materials. In decrying the Elizabethan Settlement as many others had and were to do, Milton stakes out a nonconformist but decidedly nonseparatist position toward the church of England before taking up the cry for root-and-branch extirpation of episcopacy that was pressed in 1641 by lay writers alone. Sensing himself "church-outed by the Prelats ... under whose inquisitorius and tyrannical duncery no free and splendid wit can flourish" – the charge lodged in *The Reason of Church-Government* early in 1642 (1.823, 820) – Milton urged a Reformation that would be a re-formation, a full relimning of the English bodies ecclesiastic and politic in which bishops would no longer have a place. Ideology and biography converge in this position, as Arthur Barker noted years ago: "The enthusiastic belief that the completion of England's reformation would bring with it the long-sought release of his poetical powers swept Milton into the ecclesiastical controversy."[5]

The intensely metaphorical apprehension of the dynamics of human collectivities registered in *Of Reformation* taps sources that lie deep in Pauline thought and in radical Presbyterianism as it builds on Calvin. At many points, antecedents and analogues can be found for Milton's apocalyptic strain, even for his revisions of the English outlook. Ultimately, however, his first prose tract is driven towards apocalyptic innovation by his vatic impressionability to glory, itself a symptom of his activist yearnings to fuse the polemical and rhetorical skills of the religious radical with the high ambitions of the poet.[6] He projects what among English thinkers in 1641, as far as I know, is an unprecedented role for human agency in and beyond history. Calvinist emphases on divine will and providential governance are made to accommodate a startling measure of human initiative as Milton pushes other, equally Calvinist, emphases to new limits. These include the incorporation – or what Calvin, as he glosses Paul, repeatedly figures as the ingrafting – of the elect into the body of Christ, who become that body on earth; the conforming of the elect more and more to Christ through the operation of the Spirit within them; and the completion of ingrafting at the Second Coming when the elect are invested in glorified bodies and united with Christ in the enjoyment of eternal glory. In its ultimate trajectory of vision and activism, *Of Reformation* proposes a functional equivalence of Christ with his members, intimating that they, once they rightly constitute themselves as his body by the Word and Spirit, may bring on the desired consummation of the last days and the final transcendence of time and history, the prophesied heavenly kingdom.[7]

I English apocalypticism in the making

Milton's first published prose tract, and his second intervention in religious controversy (after the attack on hirelings in *Lycidas* in November 1637), engages earlier English Protestant apocalypticism to work an eventual transformation upon it. In their studies of this native tradition, Richard Bauckham (pp. 14–21, 55–7) and Katharine Firth (pp. 1–7) stress how foundational the Augustinian view taken by Wyclif and his followers proves for later thinking about the relations of prophecy and history – a critical issue for the poet–prophet on the brink of a revolution. "Though the nature of the relation between Lollardy and early English Protestantism remains problematic in general," Bauckham remarks, "in the field of apocalyptic ideas there was real and important continuity" (p. 31). Augustine had championed a spiritual over a literal reading of scriptural passages on the end of the world, the Second Coming, and the Last Judgment. *On the City of God* casts human life in time as a conflict of the church with the world that will climax in the separation of the elect from the damned. Until this climax, at a time predestined by and known only to God, there will be a perpetual conflict of good and evil. Denying the reference of apocalyptic imagery to any historical situation, past or present, or to earthly fulfillments in the future, Augustine treated his two cities – Jerusalem and Babylon, the city of God and the city of the devil – as universal principles.

Potent implications for the appraisal of various prophetic texts of scripture attended this view of history. New Testament texts that undergirded Augustine's metaphysical and moral dualisms were invested with prime authority. These included the signs of his Second Coming given by Jesus in Mark 13 and Luke 21: the desolation foretold by Daniel as well as the rise of false Christs and false prophets seeking to seduce the elect with signs and wonders. Special prominence was given to warnings of a great apostasy, a man of sin, and a mystery of iniquity voiced by Paul in 2 Thessalonians 2 as well as the several allusions, in the first and second epistles of John, to preachers of false doctrine called Antichrists, who would arise in the last days. Further details on false prophets were culled from Matthew 24, 1 Timothy 4, 2 Timothy 3, and 2 Peter 2. Gradually, under the control of these declarative texts, some interpretation of the profusely visionary books of Revelation and Daniel could be ventured within the Augustinian mode. Fusing the connotations of falsehood, depravity, and violence that accrue to Antichrist in this collection of texts, Lollard authors make his figure a stark, recurrent epitome of all that opposes Christ or usurps his place.

Lollard thought struck a tenuous balance between an Augustinian search for enduring moral significance and a penchant for topical application that nevertheless remains true to Augustine by eschewing millenarianism. Firth instances a typical pronouncement from Wyclif: "It seemeth that the Pope is antichrist heere in erth, for he is agens crist bothe in life and in lore." If moral censure prompts the identification of the Pope with Antichrist, Wyclif may not be dealing here in historical interpretation at all. If, however, the identification points up the significance of papal corruption "at one time rather than at another" or uses it to mark "a new era in history," such functions would figure, in Firth's words, as "the first signs of the apocalyptic tradition in Protestant historiography." Since both or either of these functions might apply at any given juncture, she concludes that "the early reformers had trouble in making themselves clear."[8] The logic of Firth's distinction between ahistorical and historical applications of moral meaning is unimpeachable. But it does not seem true that the ambiguity that arose in practice gave the Lollards or the early English Protestants trouble in making themselves clear. On the contrary, since their interest in apocalyptic scripture sprang from their own involvement in historical conflict, these writers courted the ambiguity in their spiritual interpretations. At the very least, they did nothing to debar applications to their experience of opposition and oppression. Tyndale's dual gesticulations are typical. Characterizing Antichrist as "a spirituall thyng" that "shall (I doubt not) endure till the worldes end," he none the less insists on the unending historical interventions – "in the old Testament, and . . . also in the tyme of Christ, and of the Apostles" – of "one that preacheth false doctrine contrary to Christ." "Antechrist," asserts Tyndale roundly, "is now."[9]

Bauckham's perspective casts more light on the development of native apocalypticism. He notes the pervasive effects of its Augustinian legacy, which ensure that the focal images will be Christ and Antichrist, the church and the world; that thinking about the last days will use Jesus, Paul, and the John of the pastoral epistles to guide interpretation of such books as Revelation or Daniel; and that spiritual significance and moral application will always take priority. So potent, in fact, does this legacy remain among English Protestants that it delays the rise of millenarianism until the early seventeenth century – much later than its emergence among continental Protestants. For Bauckham the fusion of spiritual and moral significance with historical topicality does not figure as a source of trouble but, rather, as the start of an English tradition of apocalyptic thought. The English national history was the unique experience of the English.[10] After a span of prehistory in the late fourteenth century, apocalypticism peaks in the last decade of Henry VIII's reign, in Mary's reign, again in 1569–70, and again in 1588. A final high point, around 1641–4, coincides with the elation that accompanied the convening of the Long Parliament. The rise and repression of Lollardy comprise the prehistory. The first two accesses of Tudor apocalypticism coincide with the most severe heresy proceedings against English Protestants, while the latter two mark, on the one hand, the Northern Rebellion and the pope's excommunication of Elizabeth and, on the other, the defeat of the Spanish Armada. What these dates suggest about the formative role of circumstances is further borne out in the differential selection and shaping that English writers performed on the apocalyptic materials available to them in continental Protestantism.

Early English Protestant apocalypticism continues the tradition of Lollardy not only in its Augustinian emphases and its sensitivity to historical crisis but in its rhetorical practice as well – especially, its polemical virulence against Rome. In this vein, self-definition and self-vindication proceed through angry accumulation of differences hinging on the key concepts of Antichrist and the two churches. Such typical productions as Tyndale's *The Practyse of Prelates* (1530) or Bale's *Actes of Englysh Votaryes* (1550) heap phrases like "members of the devil" or "tail of Antichrist" into piles of what became stock epithets, while in larger units of discourse exemplum follows exemplum of lascivious monastics or duplicitous popes and archbishops who have brought ruin on princes. The notions of agency that accompany such denunciation and exposé may or may not be activist with respect to God. They certainly are activist with respect to humans, however, who should rise up to do his will and scourge such enormities. But though Tudor religious reformers practiced a rhetoric of active intervention, they could not agree on the political form such agency should take. Differentiating himself from Bale in this connection, Tyndale linked his polemic of Antichrist with trustful affirmations that the King would use his supreme authority to vindicate and uphold the true (Protestant) church of Christ in England – thus inaugurating what Paul Christianson terms "the imperial tradition" in native apocalyptic thought.[11]

Apparently Lutheran in derivation, the imperial tradition would not figure at all significantly in England before Elizabeth's accession, even though it counted such highly-placed early adherents as Thomas Cranmer and Thomas Cromwell. Indeed, in this formative period the imperial tradition established itself with no better success than apocalyptic polemics enjoyed. To consider why, it is important to recognize the reliance of both for their impact on the immediate political and religious context. Until Elizabeth there was no viable candidate for the title of Protestant champion on the English throne, and even she took a decade to establish herself. The precariousness of Tudor Protestantism also accounts for the sporadic character of apocalyptic polemics. Yet a different national history or a different era of Protestantism could yield a different story of apocalyptic virulence and calls for action by the crown or magistracy. Scotland witnesses as much under the sway of Knox's zeal.[12] So too, as we shall presently see, does an England whose Protestantism had fractured into warring parties by 1642. In the earlier English apocalyptic outlook, however, polemic and imperial strains alike remained subdued until the closing decades of the sixteenth century.

What, then, were the "strains" that distinguished English Protestant apocalypticism? The certainty of the church's sufferings under the fury of Antichrist for its profession of the gospel truth figured centrally from the start. The powerful image of the tormented and bleeding corporate body of Christ was focused sharply for English eyes by two indefatigable scholars and coworkers: Bale, in *The Image of Bothe Churches* (1548) as well as his compilations of Lollard history and testimony, and John Foxe, in the successive enlargements of his *Acts and Monuments* (Latin ed. 1559, English eds. 1563 *et seq.*). Bale and Foxe offered this image as an aid for interpreting the hostile circumstances in which early English Protestants found themselves and for achieving a larger Protestant understanding of the church history of past centuries. Although its appeal in the wake of Henry VIII's and Mary's repressive religious policies proved considerable, neither author went further in developing this image to argue for a special – or in any way separate – history of the true church in England. Reassessment of their work has shown that the idea of the "elect nation" postdates Bale and Foxe.[13] Their conception of the true church remained as internationalist as Protestantism itself was in their lifetimes. Within its larger sweep, however, this conception did admit of distinctively English emphases.

The excitement aroused in Bale and Foxe by the advent of the Reformation is conspicuous in their work. On the one hand, they share a general Protestant sense, born of crisis, that these are the last days; on the other, they claim a newness and firstness attaching to Wyclif and the Lollards as harbingers of the vital dissemination of vernacular scripture to the people. Foxe, for example, introduces the history of "John Wickliff, our countryman, and other moe of his time, and same countrie, whom the Lord ... raised up here in England" as that of "a valiant champion" on behalf of "the simple and unlearned people, being far from all knowledge of the holy Scripture." Then, when "pastors and sheepherds ... taught nothing else, but such things as came forth of the court of Rome," "this Wickliffe by Gods providence sprang and rose up: through whom the Lord would first waken again the world, which was overmuch drowned and whelmed in the deepe streames of human traditions."[14]

As the reiterative turns of this phrasing ("raised up," "sprang and rose up," "first waken ... the world") insist, priority distinguished England, if destiny did not. Accordingly, Bale and Foxe tended to bifurcate the true church's history into just two times, then and now. The present age of struggle and suffering would be different from all such former ages because the victory and release promised by God were at last near. Over against the pursuit of speculative allegory and elaborate chronologies that had begun to mark the Lutheran tradition, this binary periodization with its attendant spiritual emphasis aligned Bale's and Foxe's apocalyptic outlook with the Swiss Protestant thought of Heinrich Bullinger, Rudolph Gualter, and above all, John Calvin.[15] Believing that the Reformation was God's last great shaking of the world before the Second Coming, Calvin excluded Revelation from his magisterial series of New Testament commentaries as too abstruse a text to drive home the gospel truths required by the times. Instead, he stressed the prophetic centrality of 2 Thessalonians and its signs of the end – the great apostasy, the mystery of iniquity, the man of sin – all of which he saw fulfilled in the contemporary papacy and the Council of Trent.

For Bale, who did hazard a commentary on Revelation, priority also lay with the conjoint spiritual and historical meaning of Antichrist that had been central for Wyclif and lately reaffirmed by Calvin. As the shifting alignments of meaning and symbols show in parts 1 and 2 of *The Image of Bothe Churches*, Bale was not tempted into system-building by the paraphernalia of churches and angels, candlesticks and seals, trumpets and vials, and series of sevens. He took his challenge to be that of making the best matches he could between historical events and visionary images, judging, in Firth's words, "on moral or doctrinal characteristics and not on ... a suggestion of a hidden chronology in the mystic numbers" (p. 56). For his part, Foxe offered an affecting account of how he was driven by "the intollerable torments of the blessed Saints" to work out an eschatological time-scheme for the *Acts and Monuments*. Ransacking prophecy for a solution to the riddle of history, Foxe could find only a miserably inadequate measure of "the long continuance of these persecutions" in Revelation's "forty two moneths" until at last it dawned on him to "count these months by Sabbaths, as the weekes of Daniel are counted by Sabbaths. The Lord I take to witnesse, thus it was" (vol. 1, p. 129).

Although Foxe contented himself with his eschatological scheme and his numerical manipulations, they have proved more of an obstacle than an asset to understanding his work, both in his time and in ours. Deeply stirred by the suffering attested in large-scale martyrdom, he saw a special deliverance in Constantine's halting of persecution and adoption of Christianity as the official religion of the Roman Empire. This godly prince, in Foxe's view, became God's agent for a millennium of sorts – a thousand-year binding of Antichrist that enabled Christ's members to constitute themselves as the great body of the church. Otherwise, so the lesson of history seemed to run, the saints would have found no breathing space under the implacable fury of Satan. The next generation of English thinkers, however, would find insuperable drawbacks – both logical and historical – in Foxe's "millennium." More recently, such scholars as William Lamont and Paul Christianson have proposed to assimilate Foxe to the imperial tradition by construing his ideal Constantine as the prototype of an English monarch who would peaceably settle true religion.[16] But there is no warrant for this in the *Acts and Monuments*, where the enormously long narrative of Henrician and Marian persecutions breaks off at Elizabeth's accession, itself sketched against the backdrop of a religiously torn Europe. Remarking that Foxe's biblically-keyed apocalypticism has no place for "a second 'Constantinian' period of peace for the church on earth," Bauckham argues that Elizabeth figures as a blessed anomaly, not a universal savior, in Foxe's perspective on the last days (pp. 84–5).[17]

In fact, the most compelling reason for dissociating Foxe's work – and earlier English apocalypticism generally – from the imperial tradition and its trust in the agency of godly rulers is the glorification of suffering in the portrayal of its central subjects: the whole social spectrum of martyrs who are the tormented yet witnessing body of Christ. Foxe is utterly consistent throughout his huge compilation of narratives: evil is active, God's providence is active, and the saints keep faith with patience, awaiting the end. The underlying conception here – that of the true church under the Cross – figured in Reformation theology as a response to experience that involved a particularly literal extension of Pauline metaphor. By submitting in their own bodies to the violent self-sacrifice that Christ underwent in his earthly body, the members of his mystical body were being conformed by Christ to himself. For the present the glory of the elect was concealed from the world, as Christ's was, by a life of humiliation and suffering. In James Martin's words, "The theology of the Reformers was eschatologically oriented because it demanded faith in the *hidden* glory of Christ and His Kingdom along with a living hope of its future revelation."[18]

Here again, sixteenth-century English applications align with Calvin's handling of the theology of the Cross. Likewise eschewing any recourse to the agency of godly rulers, this theology develops under two aspects in his commentary on Thessalonians as authoritative scripture on the end of the world. Regarding the personal aspect, Calvin had a singular idea. He proposed equating the Second Coming with readiness for one's own death, a longing to be confirmed as an adoptive son of God (quoting Romans 8:14) and to possess the glory of Christ (quoting 2 Thessalonians 2:14) that can only find fruition in the life beyond this life.[19] By contrast, in its corporate aspect, Calvin's theology of the Cross mandated vigorous temporal activity on the part, at least, of true and faithful ministers. They were to attend closely to the ordering – or discipline – of the life of the church and its members, in keeping with Paul's many injunctions on the pastoral office, for their labors of love and severity could transform endurance like Christ's into expectation of Christ (pp. 413–23, expounding 2 Thessalonians 3). Traces of these Calvinistic formulations are easily recognized in Foxe's portrayals of the composed deaths of individual lay martyrs as well as the assiduous pastoral efforts that characterize his chief godly ministers – figures like Rowland Taylor, John Bradford, and John Hooper – until their dying breaths. Yet, although his expression became definitive, this apocalyptic outlook on the church as Christ's body under assault from Antichrist and his members is by no means only to be sought in Foxe. It is the dominant outlook until the close of the sixteenth century in England – one that left its stamp on the influential glosses of the Geneva Bible but, equally, on the views of the Elizabethan Settlement offered by apologists like Jewel, Fulke, and Whitgift.[20] In the seventeenth century, however, as "Antichrist" became a common label for Laud and other enforcers of English episcopacy, the image of the suffering body of

Christ underwent a dramatic contraction from international to national scope. The disestablished at home presented themselves as this body's true limbs. Foremost among these in number were the English Presbyterians – toward whom (and their Scots counterparts beleaguered by the recent Bishops' Wars) Milton evidently gravitates with his passionate, if often unspecific, yearnings after ecclesiastical "discipline" in the tracts of 1641–2.[21] Even so, as the next sections will show, Milton's apocalypticism does not reduce to a predictable version of the native tradition adjusted to Presbyterian ends. In relation to the tradition, his first tract starts as critique and ends as transformation.

II Milton's critique of English apocalypticism

Of Reformation opens by bidding for its readers' attention with some staples of native apocalyptic thought.[22] The standard linkage between Christ's body and the Reformation church is cast in terms of a no less standard spiritual adequation. "To consider first, the foule and sudden corruption, and then . . . the long-deferr'd, but much more wonderfull and happy reformation of the *Church* in these latter dayes" is nearly as "worthy" our "whole passion of pitty, on the one side, and joy on the other" as is "the story of our Saviour Christ, suffering to the lowest bent of weaknesse, in the *Flesh*, and presently triumphing to the highest pitch of *glory*, in the *Spirit*, which drew up his body also, till we in both be united to him in the Revelation of his Kingdome" (1.519). Except in its striking substitution of emphasis on the ultimate glory rather than the present suffering of the saints in Christ, this opening outlook seems to promise development along lines familiar from Bale and Foxe. Renewing their stress on providential agency with some stock phrases and imagery, Milton hails "how the bright and blissfull *Reformation* (by Divine Power) strook through the black and settled Night of *Ignorance* and *Antichristian Tyranny*." He also adopts their loosely evocative handling of apocalyptic images – here, the dragon of Revelation 12 – in a brief meditative replay of Bale's and Foxe's great themes. "I recall to mind at last, after so many darke Ages, wherein the huge overshadowing train of *Error* had almost swept all the Starres out of the Firmament of the *Church* . . . Then was the Sacred B I B L E sought out." Then, too, "*Princes* and *Cities*" came "trooping apace to the new erected Banner of *Salvation*" while "the *Martyrs*" held firm "with the unresistable *might* of *Weaknesse*, shaking the *Powers* of *Darknesse*, and scorning the *fiery rage* of the old *red Dragon*" (1.524–5).

Suddenly a glaring problem causes Milton to break off "the pleasing pursuit of these thoughts." How can his inherited English apocalypticism be made to fit current circumstances? The problem is focused sharply by the priority in reformation that Bale and Foxe had credited to England – "this *grace* and *honour* from G O D to bee the first that should set up a Standard for the recovery of *lost Truth*, and blow the first *Evangelick Trumpet* to the

Nations" through "our *Wicklefs* preaching," in Milton's rephrasing. The problem itself lies with the condition of the English church. "Albeit in *purity of Doctrine* we agree with our Brethren; yet in Discipline, which is the *execution* and *applying* of *Doctrine* home . . . we are no better then a *Schisme*, from all the *Reformation*, and a sore scandall to them" in retaining "sencelesse *Ceremonies*" and tying so vital a function as ministerial ordination to "the *pompe* of *Prelatisme.*" Milton mordantly registers the only sense native apocalypticism now has for him – a sense of irony: "Me thinkes the *Precedencie* which GOD gave this *Iland*, to be the first *Restorer* of *buried Truth*, should have beene followed with more happy successe, and sooner attain'd Perfection; in which, as yet we are amongst the last" (1.525–7). His irony lays bare a gripping anxiety. What if the great apostasy of Thessalonians, so stressed by Calvin as a sign of the world's end, should betoken not the Counter-Reformation papacy but the unfinished English Reformation? As Milton struggles with this "sore scandall" in the remainder of his tract, he subjects native apocalypticism to a reworking from the ground upward.

Milton's own apocalypticism is marked less by absolute originality than by an intensity that inseparably welds concept and image and by an always clear sense of what his ideological position requires him to retain or alter or expend.[23] The tribute to "Discipline" as "the *execution* and *applying* of *Doctrine* home" expressly signals his position as an advocate of a Calvinist church order.[24] The notion that the English Reformation would reach "Perfection" with the realization of such an order further signals that Milton is no separatist, but a would-be reformer from within the national church. This is exactly the position urged in the Root and Branch Petition of December 1640, five months before *Of Reformation* appeared, but it had much older roots in nonseparating radical Puritanism and its affiliated apocalypticism. The roots of this position – again, Milton's term "Perfection" is telling – lie deep in the primacy of the moral and spiritual meanings of history that characterizes English apocalyptic thought. Milton would cling to this primacy and attempt its wholesale renewal in his first tract. Reduced to outline, *Of Reformation* challenges three groups of English prelates on the grounds that their moral corruption makes them think wrongly and argue badly: the "Antiquitarians," a punning Miltonic coinage that subsumes appeals to tradition within 2 Thessalonians' mystery of iniquity; the "Libertines," who prove to be beneath argument; and the "Polititians," or the "no *Bishops*, no *King*" scarifiers (1.541, 570, 582).

But the inherited antitheses of native apocalypticism – the two churches, the body of Christ and the body of Antichrist – were not in instantly usable form for Milton in *Of Reformation*. Opposing a Roman, papal Antichrist was one thing; cleaving the English church was quite another. This realization had long kept Elizabethan advocates of Presbyterianism tarrying for the magistrate. Christianson (pp. 47–92) offers an absorbing account of the process by which the nomenclature of Antichrist, Babylon, and limbs of the devil got turned against English Protestant bishops first by separatist dissidents in the late 1560s, then by nonseparatists when Martin Marprelate Jr. wrote under cover of anonymity in the late 1580s. To internalize the defining antithesis of apocalypticism – the cosmic struggle of good and evil – within the church of England, to avail himself of such formulations for episcopacy as "the *spirituall* BABEL built up to the heighth of her Abominations" by Antichrist, "*Mammons* Son" (1.590), Milton had, at a minimum, to embrace the nonseparating reformism that sustained the militant Presbyterianism of such notable predecessors as Thomas Cartwright, Thomas Brightman, and Alexander Leighton and such a prominent contemporary as William Prynne. On the evidence left us in *Of Reformation*, he did so eagerly, with a first-hand knowledge of his major antecedents.

Thomas Brightman, an obscure clergyman–scholar of Elizabeth's time, leapt to posthumous fame with the publication of *A Revelation of the Revelation*. All of the early editions – Latin in 1609 and 1612, English in 1615 – were published on the continent, a symptom of the work's controversial character for a native audience. Brightman was in fact the first to break into print as an English exponent of millenarianism – understood as the thousand-year reign of the saints with Christ on earth – and discussion of his work and reputation has understandably centered around this aspect.[25] True, however, to the premium Milton lays on transmundane glory as the end of human activism, there is no room for millenarianism in *Of Reformation*. The glorified saints of the peroration are quite explicitly imaged in a heaven beyond time where "in supereminence of *beatifick Vision* progressing the *datelesse* and *irrevoluble* Circle of *Eternity*" they "shall clasp inseparable Hands with *joy*, and *blisse* in over measure for ever" (1.616).[26] Milton fastened on a less spectacular but no less troubling feature of Brightman's apocalypticism for a native audience: the peculiar wrath prophesied to lie in store for the English church as the first to begin a yet unfinished Reformation.

Like other later apocalypticists, Brightman worked to improve the fit between the times of prophecy and the times of history. For him, England's dilatoriness greatly complicated the stock bifurcation between all other thens and the now of Reformation. He purports to be certain enough when the new era dawned in earnest:

> The first entrance ... should be famous by this ... as it came to passe in our Kingdom of *England*: unto which *Christ sent our most gracious Elizabeth to be Queene* ... in the yeer 1558, and she againe gave her self, and her Kingdom to Christ, by way of thankfulnesse, which she shewed, by rooting out the *Romish superstitions* for the greater part of them, throughout all her Dominions.

But in very short order Brightman is found worrying:

> I hope, that he who hath begun this everlasting Kingdom, will make our Queen also to be the Type of this his eternall Kingdome ...

Only we must take heed, lest that we suffer his Truth to be corrupted, and his Majestie to be wronged and offended, by *Antichristian superstitions* ... We have made Christ angry against us already, in that we are so far off from coming to a full and due reformation; but if we shall return unto our vomit, with what fury will he burne out against us?[27]

Milton, noting "impeachments of a more sound rectifying the *Church* in the Queens Time," takes over Brightman's periodization along with his worries: "From this Period I count to begin our Times, which, because they concerne us more neerely ... will require a more exact search; and to effect this ... I shall distinguish such as I esteeme to be the hinderers of *Reformation*" (I. 531). He also characteristically seizes on Brightman's allusion to the dog that returns to its vomit – an image for impious folly in Proverbs 26:11, for chronic idolaters in 2 Peter 2:22 – and intensifies it as a figure for the "grossenesse" of Laudian prelates who "backslide one way into the Jewish beggery, of old cast rudiments, and stumble forward another way into the new-vomited Paganisme of sensuall idolatry" (I. 520).

Brightman's reformist alarm is localized in his lengthy defensive excursus on coming to realize that the church of England was prefigured by the church of Laodicea, rich and in need of nothing, but lukewarm in its works, which God threatens to spew out of his mouth in Revelation 3:16. Perhaps if Laodicea applies eyesalve, as she is commanded to do (verse 18), she will see her dangerous condition. This excursus caught not only Milton's notice, but that of numerous nonconformist readers and authors who took up "lukewarm Laodicea" as a contemptuous byword for the half-reformed national church under episcopacy.[28] Brightman begins by protesting earnestly that, as a minister of the church of England, he has the nation's good at heart:

God forbid that I should willingly distaine that church with any the least blot of infamy, which by the mercy of God ... doth sustaine me ... which before that I do by name specifie, I must put away from me by all earnest intreaty, the unjust suspicion which some men may raise against me, and the offense which they may take at my words.

Soon, however, he shifts emphasis to the prophetic call he feels to declare Christ's judgment on England.

I thought it my duty to cast my self rather upon whatsoever troubles, then to betray the salvation of that Church ... Truly ... I have not with dry eyes taken a survey of *Laodicea*. I could not but poure forth teares and sighes from the bottom of my heart, when I beheld in it, Christ himself loathing of us, and provoked extreamly to anger against us. (pp. 123–24)

How is Brightman so certain of having identified "lukewarm Laodicea"? "In our *Realme of England,*" he asserts,

> the matter is clear, where such a form of Church is established which is neither cold, nor yet hot ... It is not cold, in as much as it doth professe the sound, pure, and sincere doctrine of salvation, by which we have renounced that *Antichrist of Rome* ... But hot it is not, as whose *outward Regiment* is as yet ... *Antichristian and Romish, in the degrees of clergiemen, in elections and ordinations, and the whole administration of the Church-censures.*

This "tempering" or compromise between "*pure doctrine,* and *Romish Regiment,*" far from promoting a healthy religious body, inspires the most intense revulsion in God, who declares: "*It will come to passe that I shall spew thee.*" Brightman next moves from symptoms to spiritual diagnosis. "What other cause can we bring of our *lukewarmnesse,* then the love of riches and honours?" Elsewhere "the *Pastours of the Churche* are poore and of low degree ... neither have they any greater authority then their piety and their learning can purchase unto them," but in England "our *Bishops* are the *Peers of the Realme* ... equall to any of the highest and greatest *Earles,* for ... worldly pompe ... Where can ye see any Church, and Church-men, since the pope was turned out, so fat and flourishing in worldly prosperity?" At length Brightman urges upon the English church its sole hope of cure, the "true and heavenly wisdome" of scripture applied. "*Eye-salve* ... is prescribed against blindnesse; namely, that fleshly wisedom, and ignorance of spirituall things.... Do thou therefore hang upon *Christs mouth,* whence floweth that *that is profitable to teach, to reprove, to correct, to instruct in righteousnesse, that the man of God may be perfect, and prepared to every good work,* 2 Tim. 3:16, 17" (pp. 131, 133, 153–4).

The impact of this Laodicea excursus can be detected at several junctures in *Of Reformation.* Brightman provides the closest precedent I have found for the prayerful apologia that erupts from Milton as he turns to examine the early history of episcopacy. Like Brightman, he claims the most patriotic motives for anatomizing the ills of the English church:

> And heerewithall I invoke the *immortall* DEITIE *Reveler* and *Judge* of Secrets, That wherever I have in this BOOKE plainely and roundly (though worthily and truly) laid open ... faults and blemishes ... or have otherwise inveighed against Error and Superstition with vehement Expressions: I have done it, neither out of malice, nor list to speak evill, nor any vaine-glory; but of meere necessity, to vindicate the spotlesse *Truth.* (1.535)

Evincing a transcendental yearning that Brightman's millenarianism would meet in another fashion, Milton registers a touch of difference here in the concern with glory – or rather with its simulacrum, "vaine-glory," that might wrongly be imputed to him. Otherwise the proceedings of the two authors are quite consonant. Although Milton would not exclaim "O *Laodicaean*, how vainly, and how carnally dost thou boast of noblenesse, and precedency!" until he addressed Bishop Hall two months later in *Animadversions* (1.690), he infuses Brightman's interpretation of Laodicea with fresh currency here when he caps a list of charges against the bishops: "Their *devotion* most commonly comes to that queazy temper of luke-warmnesse, that gives a Vomit to GOD himselfe" (1.537). Brightman's multiple echoes of Pauline phrases in describing ministerial functions in the eyesalve passage may, moreover, provide a pattern for the recurring Miltonic catalogues of this kind in *Of Reformation* – for example, "brotherly equality, matchles temperance, frequent fasting, incessant prayer, and preaching, continual watchings, and labours in his Ministery"; "attributing to all men, and requiring from them the ability of searching, trying, examining all things, and by the Spirit discerning that which is good"; "to exhort all, to incourage the good, to admonish the bad, privately the less offender, publickly the scandalous and stubborn; to censure, and separate from the communion of *Christs* flock, the contagious, and incorrigible, to receive with joy, and fatherly compassion the penitent, all this must be don, and more then this is beyond any Church autority" (1.549, 566, 575).[29] For such specifically pastoral applications of Pauline catalogues, however, both Brightman and Milton had a ready precedent in Calvin, whose commentary on Thessalonians stresses the active preparation of the ministry for Christ's Second Coming by promoting discipline among his members in the church.

Against this backdrop of ideologically based affinities, the differences in Brightman's and Milton's eyesalve passages stand out the more sharply. Brightman equates seeing aright with repentance and submissiveness to Christ's just anger at Laodicean England. But Milton takes this eyesalve to be the apocalyptic energy of scripture, the special inspiration that will descend upon Christ's people in the last days (Acts 2:17) and make them as able as any minister to see and judge how to set England right:

> If we will but purge with sovrain eyesalve that intellectual ray which
> *God* hath planted in us, then we would beleeve the Scriptures
> protesting their own plainnes, and perspicuity, calling to them to be
> instructed, not only the *wise*, and *learned*, but the *simple*, the *poor*, the
> *babes*, foretelling an extraordinary effusion of *Gods* Spirit upon every
> age, and sexe.   (1.566)[30]

For Brightman, "their piety and their learning" forge a bond between ministers and people that validates clerical authority. For Milton, shared reason and plain scripture bind everyone in the church in effectual parity. Even though this resounding expression of a layman's confidence in the laity signals the limits of Milton's agreement with the ordained Brightman, *Of*

22

Reformation records no misgivings as yet about the clerical authoritarianism that imbued Presbyterianism as a movement.

From the vantage of native apocalypticism, surely the most radical single passage in Milton's first tract is the one that expressly sets aside a providential perspective to focus instead on analyzing and rehabilitating human agency: "Yet will I not insist on that which may seeme to be the cause on G O D S part; as his judgement on our sinnes, the tryall of his owne, the unmasking of Hypocrites ... But I shall cheifly indeavour to declare those Causes that hinder the forwarding of *true Discipline*, which are among our selves" (1.527, 528). I know of no analogue for such a summary dismissal of "G O D S part" in the interrelation of prophecy and history, although Milton has company enough in his activism and polemics. Bauckham and Christianson discuss the rise of these latter strains to prominence in Elizabethan apocalypticism, noting early incentives at the time of the Queen's accession by such establishmentarians as Fulke, John Aylmer, and Edwin Sandys, and recording a floodtide from every quarter in the "wonderfull yeare" of the defeat of the Armada. 1588 also ushered in the conception of England as an "elect nation," and the Gunpowder Plot prompted Jacobean prolongations of these strains.[31] While *Of Reformation* joins with this turn-of-the-century wave in rejoicing over the "proud Ship-wracks of the *Spanish Armado*" and the discovery of "conceal'd destruction ... in that horrible and damned blast" as well as sounding defiance to "the *great Whore*" of Rome and the Spanish "Tyrant that ... lies thirsting to revenge his Navall ruines that have larded our Seas" (1.615), the Miltonic margin of difference ultimately matters much more than these few common notes.

Of Reformation refuses to join in the late Elizabethan and Jacobean responsiveness to Tyndale's imperial theme of the godly prince who would settle true religion. At this era native apocalypticism sought to redirect providentialism along a militant internationalist course that would lead England, both monarch and nation, to war on behalf of continental Protestantism. As it pursued these aims the newer activism came to supplement rather than supplant Bale's and Foxe's image of the church as the suffering body of Christ. It proposed that God at his pleasure might raise up another Constantine to turn back the onslaughts of Antichrist and vindicate the blood of the martyrs. Milton would have none of this. He does credit Foxe as a historian, relying no less on him than on his other major sources – Holinshed, Speed, Stow, and Hayward – documented in the annotations of the Yale edition. Yet Milton also sets about demolishing several mainstays of the native apocalypticism that Foxe had labored to establish. In the first place, attacking certain politic actions by Cranmer, Latimer, and Ridley, he scorns the reflex of thought that equates a martyr with a true member of Christ in all things. "Saint *Paul* writes, that *A man may give his Body to be burnt*, (meaning for Religion) *and yet not have Charitie*: He is not therfore above all possibility of erring, because he burnes for some Points of Truth" (1.533). The veneration accorded such figures inverts the right relation of gospel and glory: "And for those *Prelat-Martyrs* they glory of, they are to bee judg'd what they were by the *Gospel*, and not the *Gospel* to be tried by them" (1.603). While pointing to failings in Foxe's sainted Marian bishops was a feature of nonconformist polemic by 1641, Milton takes an extra large step into new territory by challenging the automatic identification of martyrdom and the true church.[32]

Equally revisionary implications develop from his refusal to credit any authority but scripture on true discipline for the church. Not what "the Apostles sometimes did . . . but what they writ was of firm decree to all future ages," for what discipline "was in the *Apostles* time, that questionlesse it must be still" (1.550–1, 602). In itself, of course, this had been the quintessential English Presbyterian position since Cartwright engaged in controversy with Whitgift in the 1570s. But Milton parlays it into a sweeping repudiation both of the Foxean thousand-year binding of Satan and of the reverence for patristics that marked English Protestantism generally, as he asserts three large facts about the primitive church: "1. The best times were spreadingly infected. 2. The best men of those times fouly tainted. 3. The best writings of those men dangerously adulterated" (1.549). Milton proceeds to excoriate Constantine for murder, cruelty, heresy, injustice, superstition, and, above all, for corrupting "the simplicity, and plainnesse of Christianity" with "the gorgeous solemnities of *Paganisme*" – wealth, property, and temporal power (1.556). What, the reader asks, half-breathless, is the aim of all this ferocity? Even Brightman and the Smectymnuuans had paid Constantine the special respect due to an instrument of God.[33] Milton himself offers to explain his attack on Constantine as part of his rejection of the imperial tradition. He makes his point with a sardonic turn on a stock image for the interdependence of spouses in a marriage – here used to reflect on the unholy union of spirituality and temporality: "I am not of opinion to thinke the Church a *Vine* in this respect, because . . . she cannot subsist without clasping about the Elme of worldly strength, and felicity, as if the heavenly City could not support it selfe without the props and buttresses of secular Authoritie" (1.554).[34]

Closely examined, however, Milton's rejection of the imperial tradition in *Of Reformation* proves to be part of a larger apocalyptic design. This design embraces the setting aside of divine agency, the denial of authority to ancient ecclesiastical practice, and the critique of the model of martyrdom for the church. It makes equally for striking omissions. While the fairly recent establishmentarian claim to legitimize episcopacy *jure divino* drew much fire in other opposition writings of the time,[35] Milton's first tract, focusing on contemporary human agency and its potential for social transformation, does not even register the existence of the claim. Its author is otherwise engaged, his task nothing less than refounding and politicizing the concept of the church as Christ's body. "Why should not the Piety, and Conscience of *Englishmen* as members of the Church be trusted in the Election of Pastors," he demands, "as well their worldly wisedomes are priviledg'd as *members* of the *State* in suffraging their Knights, and Burgesses?" (1.600). Dispensing with transcendental and hierarchical sanctions, Milton stresses popular initiative and immediate action as he seeks to show the English what they may do to revitalize their own institutions by the plain light of scripture and their own intellectual rays, under the workings of the Spirit within them.

III England's bodies, England's glory

To impress on the English the potential for glory that lay within immediate reach in their own institutions, body imagery becomes the master Miltonic trope, attaining a density and nuance in *Of Reformation* that defy full analysis.[36] In introducing this imagery, Milton courts his readers with the received wisdom of conventional formulations: "A Commonwelth ought to be but as one huge Christian personage, one mighty growth, and stature of an honest man, as big, and compact in vertue as in body; for looke what the grounds and causes are of single happines to one man, the same yee shall find them to a whole state" (1.572).[37] Once anchored in truism, however, body imagery undergoes ever more strenuous extensions as the case against episcopacy mounts. Milton charges that the bishops have "hamstrung the valour of the Subject by seeking to effeminate us all," that they have "Two Leeches ... that still suck, and suck the Kingdome, their Ceremonies, and their Courts," and – "now heare how they strike at the very heart, and vitals" – that "they set at nought and trample under foot all the most sacred, and life blood Lawes, Statutes, and Acts of *Parliament*." Not content with the injury they have done at home, the bishops "seek to rouze us up to ... a cursed, a Fraternall *Warre*. ENGLAND and SCOTLAND dearest Brothers both in *Nature*, and in CHRIST must be set to wade in one anothers blood; and IRELAND our free Denizon upon the back of us both" (1.588, 589, 592, 595–6).

This polemical stretching of body imagery reaches its height when, in the first of several modulations that provide a reliable index to deeply felt concerns in his early prose, Milton resorts to narrative and offers "A Tale."[38] Brought in with a breezy by-your-leave to Livy's "*Menenius Agrippa*," the tale concerns a body troubled by "a huge and monstrous Wen little less then the Head it selfe, growing to it by a narrower excrescency," that claims "by due of merit" before the assembled members that "if the head should faile, none were fitter then himselfe to step into his place." Fortunately for the confounded members, they are able to summon "a wise and learned Philosopher ... that knew all the Charters, Lawes, and Tenures of the Body." He dismisses the Wen's fraudulent "Petition of right." "Wilt thou (quoth he) that art but a bottle of vitious and harden'd excrements, contend with the lawfull and free-borne members? ... Head thou art none, though thou receive this huge substance from it ... What good canst thou shew by thee done to the Common-weale?" The Wen's brazen reply, that "his Office was his glory," at once touches a raw nerve in this authorial *alter ego* and a recurrent theme of the tract. "Know," thunders the Philosopher, "that all the faculties of the Soule ... cannot part from ... their severall vessels, and *ventricles* ... without dissolution of the whole Body; and that thou ... art to the head a foul disfigurment and burden. When I have cut thee off, and open'd thee, as by the help of these implements I will doe, all men shall see" (I. 583–4).

Livy's part notwithstanding, Milton's negative elaborations of body imagery in this tale have a demonstrable source in the polemics of two other nonseparating Presbyterian agitators: Alexander Leighton, whose *Appeal to the Parliament, or Sions Plea against the Prelacie* was printed in Amsterdam "the year and month wherein *Rochell* was lost" (October 1628), and William Prynne, whose *Lord Bishops, None of the Lords Bishops* appeared in London in November 1640. That month Leighton, a physician, had just been released from eleven years' imprisonment in Newgate after he was convicted of sedition in the Star Chamber, whipped, and mutilated (nose slit, ear cropped). Prynne, a lawyer, had more notoriously suffered the same punishments for a sedition charge brought against him and Henry Burton and John Bastwick by Laud in the Star Chamber in 1637. The public carrying out of the mutilations, compounded subsequently by the triumphal release of Prynne and the other two men, also in November 1640, assured them the status of popular heroes (I. 36–7, 43–5, 62). Drawing on the same conventional conceptions of the bodies ecclesiastic and politic, both Leighton and Prynne depict the bishops as wens in grotesque analogies that Milton converts into a small, self-contained fable with an unmistakable program for political action. Here is Leighton:

> As a knob, a wen, or any superfluous bonch of flesh, being no
> member doth not onely overburthen the body, but also disfigureth the
> feature, yea killeth the body at length except it be cut; so these Bishops
> be the knobs and wens and bunchie popish flesh which beareth down,
> deformeth and deadeth the bodie of the Church, that there is no cure
> (as we conceive) but cutting off. (pp. 10–11)

And here is Prynne's salvo against Laud and the other English bishops who concur in the Romish identification of the "church" with its clergy:

> *Prelates* ... are not the Body it selfe of the Churche, but *wennes*, or
> *swellings* ... *Strumae*[,] great *swellings* like the Kings Evill, which are
> commonly next the Head ... Onely in this they will not be called the
> Kings Evill, because they claime their Originall from *Christ* ... though
> they be but certaine *Abscessus*, or *Apostemes* (and so indeed *Apostates*
> from the true *Church of Christ*) which not only deforme the Body, but
> greatly indanger the life thereof.

"Surely," Prynne concludes in ringing tones, "the *true Church of Christ* in *England* disclaims *communion* with such a *false Church*, as the *Hierarchie* calls it selfe" (sig. D1v).

Since a mere six months separate *Lord Bishops* and *Of Reformation*, other affinities between the two works are likely enough. Prynne's tract is especially valuable in relation to Milton's for the explicit evidence it gives of ties with Calvinist – and ultimately Pauline – apocalypticism. *Lord Bishops* starts right out by citing 2 Thessalonians 2:4 against the prelates for exalting themselves above other ministers of God: "And thus they participate of the Prelacie of the Great Antichrist, who is (as the Apostle styles him) *he that exalts himselfe, above all that is called God.*" Shortly thereafter, a marginal reference to "2 Thess. 2" compounds with one to "1 John 2" to drive home the point that Milton will make about the corruption of the church even in apostolic times: "Every thing that hath been in use in the *Apostles* times, and in the *true Church of Christ*, is not therfore *Apostolicke*. . . For we read, that the *Mistery of Iniquity* began to worke in the *Apostles times*, and even then there were many *Antichrists*, and that in the very midst of the Church." Tracking the history of unending corruption to present-day England, Prynne stoutly decries, much as Milton soon would, "the *Prelates* . . . that set their proud *feet* upon the *Kings* both Laws, which are the *sinews*, and loyall People, which are the *members* of the same Body Politick, whereof the King is the Head" (sigs. A1r, D2r).

When he seeks, however, in a long passage to elaborate positive connotations of body imagery, Prynne's emphasis falls decidedly more on the personal and spiritual than on the activist implications drawn by Calvin from the promised sending of the Spirit "to all and every particular member of *Christs* Mysticall body, whether Ministers or People." "It may truly be said," Prynne asserts, "that as we begin *Spiritually* to live by the *Holy Ghost* through *Faith* by the *Preaching of the word of God*: So this *Holy Ghost* in the severall graces and operations there of is preserved, and is as it were nourished in us by the continuall ministration of the food of the same *word* in our *Soules*." An extended analogy displays his assurance in treating spiritual process as physiological fact regarding the true members of Christ's body.

> Even as . . . the *Breath* goeth with the *voyce* or *word* spoken; or as the *blood* hath its course in the *veins*, or the *vitall Spirits* have their *Seat* in the *heart*; or as the *Animall Spirits* in the *braine*, when they are derived into all the parts of the *body* in the *Arteries* and *Veines*, so . . . all the members are thereby actuated and moved, [and] so this *Holy Ghost* is as it were, nourished and preserved in us.

Prynne reserves a last spiritualized application of this body imagery for his peroration. While it begins by sounding the newer imperial assurance that the King will be "*reconciled to God* in *reforming* the manifold and horrible abuses of the *Prelates*" and thus "united to his loving and loyall People, as the Head to the Body, in this Body representative, the *Parliament*," the peroration climaxes in a prayer that reverts to the inherited emphases of Foxean apocalypticism in the weight placed on spiritual concerns, the sufferings of Christ's true members, and divine deliverance:

> And lastly, the same *Lord Jesus Christ*, powre his Spirit of Grace and Supplication upon all the people of the Land, that being sensible of their own Sins, and of the Nationall Sins of the Land, as also of the heavy yoake of *Antichrist* . . . they may truly repent and reforme their lives, and cry alowd to the *Lord* . . . *Amen, Even so come Lord Jesus* and helpe thy poore *England*, and thy poore People therein. *Amen.*
>
> (sigs. F3v–F4r, H2v, L3r–v)

In aligning with Foxe at the close of *Lord Bishops*, Prynne finishes a good distance from Milton.[39] *Of Reformation* exhibits more appreciable affinities overall with *An Appeal to the Parliament*. Although Tyndale and Bale pioneered the strategy, it is Leighton who sets in motion – for this round of antiprelatical controversy – the scholarly heaping of historical examples and citations that looms so large in *Of Reformation*. As Milton would, Leighton surveys the reigns of English monarchs from Edward VI to James I, inquiring why Reformation was left imperfect; Leighton also anticipates Milton in learnedly discoursing on the unhierarchical notion of a bishop in apostolic times (pp. 69–80, 8–11).[40] Beyond discursive strategy, Milton seems clearly to pick up on Leighton's lead in elaborating and applying body imagery as a primary trope. Here is Leighton evoking the vital importance of Calvinist discipline to the weal of bodies ecclesiastic and politic:

> Can a body live without a *Sowle*? Ore a *sowle* insensate or activate a body without *Sinews*? As we have heard the puritie of Doctrine to be the *Sowl* of the Church, whereby it liveth, so also *Discipline* hath been shewed to be the *Sinews* of the Church . . . They who hinder Discipline, bring the State at length to an extreamly desperate point.
>
> (p. 194)

Convinced that England has reached just such a point of crisis, Leighton projects the hopes of the imperial tradition upon Parliament in spirited incitements to action – "you are the *Physitians* of state; up and doe your cure" – that ascribe to the members "the power of the whole Kingdome, yea both of the head and of the body" (p. 174).

Amplifying his trope with a prophetic stridency that glances back at Knox and ahead to Milton, Leighton exhorts:

> Awake and know this you great Senators, who are the *Sences* and *sowle* of the King and State . . . you are these Spirits that should carie vitall heat unto the head, and all the members: You must tell the King, that

... if he follow the Counsell of *Christs* enemies, as the *Prelates* and others, then *Christ* will be his enemie ... You must bouldly ... ask the King in plain tearmes, if the *evill* (yea this verie evill) be not removed, how he shall give an accompt when the destroyer cometh. (pp. 270–1)

While Leighton's urgings to root out episcopacy in England chiefly take the form of warnings, as do Brightman's, there is a move toward the close of *An Appeal to the Parliament* to offer positive incentives to godly activism within an apocalyptic framework. These, however, offer no foretaste of a Miltonic ardor for a glory that will carry him beyond time. Rather, they re-echo Brightman's tempered hopes that there may yet be time for England to set its house in order according to God's behest. "It is a great fault in men of place, both Ministers and Magistrats," says Leighton, "that they would have God to doe all the hard worke by himself ... but they who will raigne with God, even in the glory of any good work, must do for him, and suffer with him in the doing of the Work" (p. 170). "Yea," he affirms near the close of his tract, "if our *Laodicea* will be zealous and amend, the Lord ... will set his favour upon us; in stead of judgment we shall have mercie; in stead of ignominie glorie; in stead of want, plentie; valour and magnanimitie, for faintheartednesse: our Church shall be beutifull; our common-wealth floorishing, if we remove the drosse from the silver" (p. 248). While abounding throughout in warnings of the wrath to come, Leighton ends by muting his apocalyptic notes and clinging instead to reformist activism, expressed in this earthbound and timebound image of a beautiful church and a flourishing commonwealth graced by prosperity and civic virtues.

For all of the frequently substantive correspondences they offer, neither Prynne nor Leighton finally provides anything approaching a full precedent for the remarkably complex joint development of themes and images in *Of Reformation* – the programmatic argument for congruity in the English church and state that develops by extension of the body tropes and, in turn, extends itself into apocalyptic climax. In Leighton and Prynne, reformist activism eventually splits off from apocalypticism, or vice versa. While Prynne exults in Christ's promise to send the Spirit to dwell in his members, his final apocalyptic vision renews standard native emphases on the church's patient sufferings as it awaits deliverance at the Second Coming. The horrible mutilations sustained by Prynne probably account for his Foxean outlook, since his authorial self-consciousness openly trades on his scapegoating by Laud and his liberation by Parliament.[41] As for Leighton, his calls for drastic surgery and his denunciations of Laodicean lukewarmness are moderated, and somewhat undercut, by his bland vision of a tempered and temporizing church.

In all three writers – Prynne, Leighton, and Milton – the frequent recourse to body tropes bespeaks familiarity not just with Augustinian dualisms but with Calvin's repeated attempts to articulate the gospel and Pauline mystery "that we live with Christ, having entered by faith into the Kingdom of Christ." This, as he states in his commentary on 1 Thessalonians 5:10, citing Romans 8:10, is a relation by which "Christ Himself, into whose body we have been ingrafted, revives us by His power, and the Spirit who dwells in us is life *because of righteousness.*" Calvin's commentary on Romans 8:11, 10, 29 insists more vividly still on the systemic vitalism by which the power of Christ's person is transfused through his members, the body of the church:

> In the person of Christ there has been exhibited a specimen of the power which belongs to the whole body of the Church ... He lives and flourishes in us because He quickens us by His power, until He destroys our mortal flesh and at last renews us perfectly [vivit ac viget in nobis ... quia vivificat nos suo vigore, donec exstincta mortali carne perfecte demum renovet] ... Christ is placed in a state of pre-eminence, not only that He should excel in honour among believers, but also that He should include all believers within Himself.

In his commentary on 1 Thessalonians 5:10 Calvin further endows this language of incorporation with an apocalyptic dimension:

> Since Christ rose for the purpose of making us all at length partakers of the same glory with Himself, because we are His members, Paul intimates that His resurrection would be of no effect, unless He appears a second time as their Redeemer, and extends to the whole body of the Church the fruit and effect of that power which He displayed in Himself [fructumque et effectum eius quam in se exhibuit virtutis ad totum Ecclesiae corpus extendat].[42]

Here Christ raises – or "extends" – his body to a higher power, as its "fruit and effect" increase exponentially from vivifying to revivifying, and the church attains final incorporation in the glorified bodies of its resurrected human members.

The modulation from body tropes to apocalypticism in *Of Reformation* raises hard questions about Milton's relation to the Calvinistic figurations that he inherits as a professed Presbyterian. What does Milton make of Calvin's intimation that the perfecting of the glorified body of Christ and his members necessitates the Second Coming? And how does Milton arrive at a position beyond Calvin's in imputing to human agency a role in bringing about the Second Coming? I suggest two approaches to these questions: one textual, centering on the dynamism of the imagery in *Of Reformation*; and one inferential, concerned with Milton's search for a resolution of the problem that glory had posed for him in some of his recent poetry.[43]

The dynamism of the body tropes in *Of Reformation* begins to take on positive political overtones in a key passage, charged with patriotic fervor, that salutes the incomparable balance of monarchical, aristocratic, and democratic elements in "the Common-wealth of *England*: where under a free, and untutor'd *Monarch*, the noblest, worthiest, and most prudent men, with full approbation, and suffrage of the People have in their power the supreame, and finall determation of highest Affaires." Naturalizing the political as skillfully as any theorist of his time, Milton offers to explain the superiority of the English constitution by analogy with the "certaine mixture and temperament" of "the elements or humors in Mans Body," where each "partaking the severall vertues of each other . . . may keep up a steddy, and eev'n uprightnesse in common." Arguing from a mixed state as the condition that determines the health of institutions as well as persons, he next urges that this condition of health be extended in the nation. The English body ecclesiastic is to be made "parallel" and "uniform" with the English body politic by the institution of a national Presbyterian church, "when under the Soveraigne Prince *Christs* Vicegerent . . . according to *Gods Law*, the . . . Ministers in their severall charges have the instructing and disciplining of *Gods people* by whose full and free Election they are consecrated to that holy and equall *Aristocracy*" (1.599–600). Fortunately Milton's language is specific enough at this juncture to enable recognition of an operative prototype in the Scottish Presbyterian Kirk, which with the promulgation of the second Book of Discipline (1578) had vested in individual congregations the right to elect their ministers.[44]

Don Wolfe has characterized Milton's call "for members in each church to elect their own minister, as they do their own members in the House of Commons" as "one of the most original ideas in *Of Reformation*" (1.115). It is noteworthy, however, that the core analogy and its attendant argument had already been set out in converse form by Thomas Cartwright, the father of English Presbyterianism, in his *Replie* to Whitgift's *Aunswere to the Admonition* (1574). While Milton analogizes from the weal of the state to that of the church, Cartwright had analogized from church to state in contending for Presbyterianism as

> that kinde of government whiche the Philosophers that wryte of the
> best common wealthes affirme to be the best. For in respecte of
> Christe the heade, it is a Monarchie; and in respecte of the auncientes
> [elders] and pastoures that govern in common and wyth like authoritie
> amongste them selves, it is an Aristocratie, or the rule of the best men;
> and in respect that the people are not secluded but have their interest in
> churche matters, it is a Democratie, or a populare estate. An image
> whereof appeareth also in the pollicie of thys realme, for, as in respect
> of the Queene hir majestie, it is a Monarchie, so in respect of the most
> honourable councill, it is an Aristocratie; and having regarde to the
> Parliament, whych is assembled of all estates, it is a Democratie.[45]

Apart from logical form, there are other revealing differences between the projections of the ideal of a mixed polity by these two nonseparating English

Presbyterians across an interval of seventy years. Cartwright emerges as the more doctrinaire Calvinist. With him church government is primary – normative even for civil government. Cartwright also offers a much more acquiescent view of existing civil institutions, finding "Democratie" enough in England if the "interest" of "the people" is "not secluded" under sessional or parliamentary representation. In Milton, by contrast, a visionary aim transfigures the ostensible rundown of social facts. He bases all exercise of civil power and all warrant for civil institutions in the "full approbation, and suffrage of the People." He next analogizes from popular consent in the English political sphere to the election of ministers by congregations in the "Apostolicall, and ancient *Church*," terming monarchy grounded in popular consent "what is already Evangelicall as it were by a happy chance in our *Politie*" (1.600). Thus armed, as he represents himself, with the gospel truth on the founding of human institutions, Milton urges upon England the immediate fulfillment of the unique opportunity afforded by its historical development – the opportunity to bring its bodies politic and ecclesiastic into full congruity.

In forcing a trope to operate as an argument by analogy, Milton projects a systematic correspondence between the English bodies politic and ecclesiastic that has at least two intrinsic difficulties. One, hardly to be discounted as rhetorical excess, Milton seems to have decided to ignore, although he compromised his political acuity by doing so. It is the clear implication of his mixed state–body politic trope that not just the bishops in the House of Lords, but any organ constituted as the Lords were, would have to yield place to a popularly elected Commons as the only valid foundation for civil government. There is no independent reason to think, however, that Milton advocated a unicameral English Parliament. Judged as a formulation of the Presbyterian position and its practical ramifications regarding the key issue of episcopacy, *Of Reformation* shows itself inferior to the Root and Branch Petition. The second difficulty triggers Milton's move from politics into apocalypticism. It concerns the obvious asymmetry between the English bodies politic and ecclesiastic with respect to their all-important heads. While the body politic is complete and actualized by the king, Parliament, and people, the body ecclesiastic is to a significant degree incomplete and unactualized, since the king stands in as "*Christs* Vicegerent" over the ministers and people (1.600).

At first this asymmetry between the two bodies causes Milton no trouble. His prose resonates with a confidence in reformist activism that rivals even Leighton's: "Thus then wee see that our Ecclesiall, and Politicall choyses may consent and sort as well together without any rupture in the STATE, as Christians and Freeholders." "Here," Milton adds, "I might have ended" (1.600–1). But *Of Reformation* does not only not end here; it has great trouble ending for some while. What proves troubling is the power that the prelates must still be acknowledged as wielding, both in their polemics against

Presbyterianism and, above all, in their personal influence with Charles. Can the king – this king – substitute for Christ as head of the English church? As uncertainty builds on this point, Milton's almost unconditional earlier confidence in human agency begins to falter: "Let us not dally with God when he offers us a full blessing, to take as much of it as wee think will serve our ends, and turne him back the rest . . . lest in his anger he snatch all from us again"; "Let us not for feare . . . or else through hatred to be reform'd stand hankering and politizing, when G O D with spread hands . . . points us our the way to our peace" (1.602, 610).

At length Milton sheds his sunny optimism about the ease of achieving his proposed congruity of bodies while the bishops "threaten uproare and combustion, and shake the brand of Civill Discord." But he refuses to abandon faith in the capability of Christ's true members to constitute themselves as his body, and he calls out emotionally for this to take place:

> Were it such a desperate hazard to put to the venture the universall
> Votes of *Christs* Congregation, the fellowly and friendly yoke of a
> teaching and laborious Ministery, the Pastorlike and Apostolick
> imitation of meeke and unlordly Discipline . . . ? Were it such an
> incurable mischiefe to make a little triall, what all this would doe to
> the flourishing and growing up of *Christs* mysticall body?

At this juncture the text breaks quite self-consciously out of polemic into prayer, to open thereafter into apocalyptic vision:

> O Sir, I doe now feele my selfe in wrapt on the sodaine into those
> mazes and *Labyrinths* of dreadfull and hideous thoughts, that which
> way to get out, or which way to end I know not, unlesse I turne mine
> eyes, and . . . lift up my hands to that Eternall and Propitious *Throne*,
> where nothing is readier then *grace* and *refuge* to the distresses of
> mortall Suppliants.   (1.613)

This strange ejaculation offers a Miltonic translation of Calvin's personal understanding of the Second Coming – a readiness to be joined to one's divine head in which, however, vatic transport significantly substitutes for the dissolution of death.

Personal concerns merge with collective ones as Milton pursues his apocalyptic strain along Calvin's other axis, that of the redoubled efforts incumbent on all true ministers in anticipation of the "last days." Again there is a telling Miltonic adjustment. *Of Reformation* enlarges the role of godly activism in preparing for the Second Coming from the clergy to the laity, the church in all its members. Moving now to redress the asymmetry in his earlier formulation of the congruence of the bodies politic and ecclesiastic, Milton invokes Christ as "Omnipotent King, Redeemer of that lost remnant whose nature thou didst assume, ineffable and everlasting *Love*," with this appeal: "Now unite us intirely, and appropriate us to thy selfe, tie us everlastingly in willing Homage to the *Prerogative* of thy eternall *Throne*" (1.613–14, 615). Concept and image are inseparably welded by the force of Milton's imaginative vision. The English body ecclesiastic declares itself ready to receive its absent head, and this lay author duly communicates the church's readiness to King Jesus through the universal office of prayer. Replacing the imperial tradition with the power of the English people as exercised in their rights of assembly and direct appeal to the crown, Milton envisages human power as reaching to the throne of God and winning its appeal for incorporation with the divine. "Now wee knowe, O thou our most certain hope, ... that ... thou art with us" (1.615–16).

Milton indeed hinges not just the full Reformation of the church of England but the Second Coming itself on efforts by "this great and Warlike Nation." Two complementary verbs ("presse on hard," "open") placed in temporally convergent predicates ("at that day," "when") attest the ongoing dynamism of the body tropes as well as the vital factor of human agency. Milton assigns England to "presse on hard ... to be found the *soberest, wisest*, and *most Christian People* at that day, when" – here he shifts his address from the members to the head – "thou the Eternall and shortly-expected King shalt open the Clouds to judge the severall Kingdomes of the World." This Miltonic advent of Christ to join with his members in glory is also, in an orthodox enough fashion, the Last Judgment. But the vision breaks sharply with Calvin, and with Protestant orthodoxy as a whole, in two important respects.

First, Milton substitutes merit for election as the criterion of glorification. As a consequence, his meritorious nation exhibits no direct kinship with the providentially-steered "elect nation" that begins to figure conspicuously after Foxe. Lollardy – the earliest and, for Milton, the purest stage of English apocalypticism – would seem to offer the closest native analogue for the achievement system by which he calibrates godly activism with degrees of heavenly glory. Translation of the Christ–Antichrist duality into an opposition between spiritual advancement and worldly preferment is an especially notable shared feature of Lollard and Miltonic eschatology.[46] As formulated in *Of Reformation*, a higher order of merit qualifies for a higher ranking, "where they undoubtedly that by their *Labours, Counsels*, and *Prayers* have been earnest for the *Common good* of *Religion* and their *Countrey*, shall receive, above the inferiour *Orders* of the *Blessed*, the *Regall* addition of *Principalities, Legions*, and *Thrones* into their glorious Titles." A corresponding set of demerits incurs the reprobation – and consignment to deepest hell "after a shamefull end in this *Life*" – of those "that by the impairing and diminution of the true *Faith*, the distresses and serv.tude of their *Countrey* aspire to high *Dignity, Rule* and *Promotion* here" (1.616).

Milton, moreover, represents the condition for the Second Coming – the meritorious striving of the united godly nation – as depending in its turn upon the efforts of a solitary figure – the inspired poet himself. In *Lycidas*

Milton had struggled with the pain and perplexity brought on by the abrupt death of a virtuous young candidate for the ministry, as corrupt pastors continued to abuse the faithful and degrade the church. It is striking how absent the theme of suffering in patience – the enduring emphasis of native apocalypticism – is from any resolution broached in this elegy. Turning chiefly on the question of how "deed" relates to "meed," perplexity is somehow mastered and pain assuaged by relegating glory and reward to divine disposition in the hereafter while continuing to tie merit to human action in the here and now. Resuming this two-tiered perspective in *Epitaphium Damonis*, his elegy on the unexpected death of his closest friend in August 1638, Milton additionally adumbrated the prospect of earthly glory for a great poet of great English subjects. *Of Reformation* provides a fresh, vernacular redrawing of this figure in the "some one" who "may perhaps bee heard offering at high *strains* in new and lofty *Measures*." The future poet will energize the corporate body, readying it for its celestial Head with a work "whereby this great and Warlike Nation instructed and inur'd to the fervent and continuall practice of *Truth* and *Righteousnesse*, and casting farre from her the *rags* of her old *vices* may presse on hard to that *high* and *happy* emulation to be found the *soberest, wisest,* and *most Christian People*" (1.616). The strains heard in *Of Reformation* are of a higher mood than any that had yet sounded or would sound in Milton's poetry for years to come.[47] Not the least attraction of the Presbyterian position, the reformist hopes occasioned by the Long Parliament, and the new medium of prose for Milton in early 1641 must have been the challenge of forging better connections between history and eschatology, earthly endeavor and heavenly reward, human merit – especially literary merit – and transcendent glory. *Of Reformation* records his efforts to recast native apocalypticism as a unitary framework where a divine design finds realization in and through the struggles of the English people toward ever more perfect forms of individual and institutional life.

Notes

1 This essay has profited immensely from David Loewenstein's and James Turner's detailed critiques of an earlier draft. I thank them greatly for the generosity, wit, understanding, and assistance they have lavished on me. The responsibility for remaining inadequacies is, of course, my own.

2 The standard survey is John J. I. von Döllinger's *Prophecies and the Prophetic Spirit in the Christian Era*, trans. Alfred Plummer (London, 1873). On a powerful movement that, however, had limited impact in England, see Marjorie Reeves, *The Influence of Prophecy in the Later Middle Ages: A Study in Joachimism* (Oxford, 1969).

3 Several of my emphases – for example, on Milton's early activism and optimism and on the saliency of metaphor in his thought – have been adumbrated by David Loewenstein in chapter 1 of his study, *Milton and the Drama of History: Historical Vision, Iconoclasm, and the Literary Imagination* (Cambridge University Press,

1990), which I, unfortunately, read only after completing the first version of this essay.

4 The most helpful for present purposes have been Richard Bauckham, *Tudor Apocalypse* (Appleford, 1978); Paul Christianson, *Reformers and Babylon: English Apocalyptic Visions from the Reformation to the Eve of the Civil War* (Toronto and Buffalo, 1978); Katharine R. Firth, *The Apocalyptic Tradition in Reformation Britain, 1530–1645* (Oxford, 1979); and Christopher Hill, *Antichrist in Seventeenth-Century England* (Oxford and New York, 1971).

5 *Milton and the Puritan Dilemma* (Toronto, 1942), p. 17.

6 *Cf.* John Peter Rumrich, *Matter of Glory: A New Preface to "Paradise Lost"* (Pittsburgh, 1987), chapters 1 and 2.

7 As this preliminary characterization already shows, there are aspects of the apocalyptic fervor in *Of Reformation* that are, at best, tenuously contained by the thought forms of Calvinism, even though Milton explicitly recognizes no failures of fit as he writes this tract. For an incisive account of the progressively heterodox concepts of "Word" and "Spirit" that were developing in England in Milton's lifetime, see G. F. Nuttall, *The Holy Spirit in Puritan Faith and Experience* (Oxford, 1946); on the Puritan lineage of these terms, see John S. Coolidge, *The Pauline Renaissance in England* (Oxford, 1970).

8 Firth, p. 7, citing John Wyclif, "De Papa" (1379).

9 "Preface to the Reader," *The Parable of the Wicked Mammon,* in *The Whole Workes of William Tyndall, John Frith, and Doctor Barnes* (London, 1573), p. 60.

10 On successive correspondences between major national events and developments in English apocalypticism, see Bauckham, pp. 204, 208–27, 140, 162–84, Firth, p. 84; and Christianson, chapter 5.

11 Christianson, pp. 22–4, 29–36, 41–5; *cf.* Firth, pp. 24–6.

12 Firth, pp. 111–32, has a superb discussion of Knox's apocalypticism, especially the prophetic self-consciousness and the deep political involvement that distinguish him from English contemporaries. Milton pays tribute to Knox in *The Tenure of Kings and Magistrates* (III.223–5).

13 For critiques of Haller's argument in *Foxe's Book of Martyrs and the Elect Nation* (London, 1963), see Viggo Norskov Olsen, *John Foxe and the Elizabethan Church* (Berkeley, 1973), pp. 36–42; Christianson, p. 100; Bauckham, pp. 71–2, 86–7; Firth, p. 108.

14 John Foxe, *Acts and Monuments,* 8th printing of 3rd ed. (London, 1641), vol. 1, pp. 555–6.

15 Michael Fixler, *Milton and the Kingdoms of God* (Evanston, 1964), pp. 28–32; Firth, pp. 81–2; Bauckham, chapter 2.

16 On problems posed by the Foxean "millennium," see Firth, chapters 5 and 7. On Foxe and the imperial tradition, see William M. Lamont, *Godly Rule: Politics and Religion, 1603–60* (London, 1969), pp. 23–5; Christianson, pp. 41–5. Christianson does acknowledge that only the dedicatory letter addressed to Elizabeth in the 1563 edition of the *Acts and Monuments* compares her to Constantine, and that Foxe omitted this letter and its content from the 1570 and later editions, where he proposed dating Satan's binding to Constantine's reign.

17 Foxe's eschatology becomes explicit in his unfinished last work, a Latin commentary on Revelation entitled *Eicasmi,* posthumously published (London, 1587).

18 *The Last Judgment in Protestant Theology from Orthodoxy to Ritschl* (Edinburgh, 1963), p. 12.
19 *Calvin's Commentaries: The Epistles of Paul the Apostle to the Romans and to the Thessalonians*, ed. David W. and Thomas F. Torrance, trans. Ross Mackenzie (Edinburgh, 1960), pp. 406–10, expounding 2 Thessalonians 2:13–14. On the singularity of the personal aspect of Calvin's apocalypticism, see Heinrich Quistorp, *Calvin's Doctrine of the Last Things*, trans. Harold Knight (London, 1955), pp. 34–7, 111–14.
20 Bauckham, pp. 44–50, 113–22, 135–6; Firth, pp. 80–1.
21 "Discipline" was not merely a verbal badge for a Presbyterian outlook in popular parlance. The term had been singled out and stressed by Calvin himself as a key to his vision of church order and its societal ramifications as energized through the powers of the ministry. See Book IV, chapter 12, of John Calvin, *Institutes of the Christian Religion*, trans. Henry Beveridge, 8th printing (Grand Rapids, Mich., 1979), II.453, for discussion elaborating on this celebrated pronouncement:

> If no society, nay, no house with even a moderate family, can be kept in a right state without discipline, much more necessary is it in the Church, whose state ought to be the best ordered possible. Hence as the saving doctrine of Christ is the life of the Church, so discipline is, as it were, its sinews; for to it it is owing that the members of the body adhere together, each in its own place. Wherefore, all who either wish that discipline were abolished, or who impede the restoration of it, whether they do this of design or through thoughtlessness, certainly aim at the complete devastation of the Church.

22 On the historical circumstances and rhetorical implications of Milton's bid for a readership, see Thomas N. Corns, "The Freedom of Reader-Response: Milton's *Of Reformation* and Lilburne's *The Christian Mans Triall*," in R. C. Richardson and G. M. Ridden, eds., *Freedom and the English Revolution: Essays in History and Literature* (Manchester, 1986), pp. 93–110.
23 For cognate discussion, see Loewenstein, chapter 1.
24 See note 21 for the source, in Calvin, of the pronouncement on doctrine and discipline to which Milton's phraseology alludes.
25 The fullest is Firth's, pp. 164–76; *cf.* Bryan W. Ball, *A Great Expectation: Eschatological Thought in English Protestantism to 1660* (Leiden, 1975), pp. 59, 82–4, 116–19, and Christianson, pp. 100–6.
26 Incidental remarks (Christianson, p. 193 n; Firth, p. 233 n) affirming Milton's interest in the millenarianism of Brightman and of Joseph Mede, Milton's former tutor at Cambridge, in *Of Reformation* may have perplexed this otherwise evident matter.
27 *A Revelation of the Revelation* (Amsterdam, 1615), pp. 381, 382. I find extremely puzzling the claims advanced by Christianson (p. 102) and Firth (pp. 167–8) on behalf of Brightman as a shaper of the "elect nation" concept of reformation England. Wherever he singles out England for remark (pp. 128–9, 524–5, 532–3), he invariably strikes cautionary or qualifying notes.
28 See references in Christianson, p. 280, and Firth, p. 270.
29 The first passage echoes 2 Cor. 8:14, 1 Cor. 7:5, Luke 21:36, Rom. 12:10, 1 Thess.

4:9, 5:17, 2 Tim. 4:2, Rev. 3:3, and 1 Pet. 4:6. The second echoes 2 Cor. 3:2, Acts 17:11, John 5:39, 1 John 4:1–7, Phil. 4:8, 9, and 1 Thess. 5:21; the third echoes 2 Thess. 3:15, 1 Thess. 5:12–15, Rom. 12:7–19, and 1 Pet. 3:18. These verses largely occur in contexts that deal with the end of the world and the Second Coming. Regarding the densely scriptural weave of this prose, remarks made seventy years ago remain apposite: "There is no authority upon which Milton depends more in this pamphlet, or to which he more frequently alludes, than the Bible ... The words and ideas of Scripture are so closely interwoven with Milton's own that it may be said that he thinks in the language of the Bible" (Will T. Hale, ed., *Of Reformation* [New Haven, 1916], p. liv).

30 This catalogue elaborates Prov. 21:11, Ps. 8:2, Luke 4:18, and Joel 2:28, 29.

31 Bauckham, pp. 130–3, 146, 155, 173–80; Christianson, pp. 33–6, 45–6. Anthony Marten's *An Exhortation, to Stirre up the Mindes of All Her Majesties faithfull Subjects* (London, 1588) and Thomas Rogers' *An Historical Dialogue touching Antichrist and Poperie* (London, 1589) inaugurate the "elect nation" theme.

32 Naming no names, Brightman characterizes Laodicea's churchmen as "prudent and moderate men in the matter of religion, such as we call at this day *statists, or moderate and direct Protestants of State,* and which are commonly known to be *lukewarme professors*" (pp. 130–1). Christianson, p. 163, quotes John Bastwick's *A Letany* (London, 1637) on the low standards for Reformation held by the martyred Marian bishops. Robert Greville, Lord Brooke, similarly asperses Cranmer and Ridley in *A Discourse Opening the Nature of That Episcopacie Which is Exercised in England* (London, 1642), p. 195. On Milton's revisions of Foxe, see John R. Knott, Jr., "'Suffering for Truths sake': Milton and martyrdom," chapter 8 below.

33 Brightman, sigs. B1v–B2v; Hale, ed., *Of Reformation*, p. 121. For a fine rhetorical analysis of Miltonic polemics here, see Michael Lieb, "Milton's *Of Reformation* and the Dynamics of Controversy," in Lieb and John T. Shawcross, eds., *Achievements of the Left Hand: Essays on the Prose of John Milton* (Amherst, Mass., 1974), pp. 55–82.

34 *PL* v.215–17 famously attests Milton's later positive use of this image. Dispensing with imagery of any kind, Lord Brooke's *A Discourse of Episcopacie*, p. 50, would argue the same view of the church of England's independence of temporal authority the next year.

35 See Lamont's spirited discussion in *Godly Rule*, chapters 2–5.

36 I pass over, for example, the bestial dimensions realized in the superb play of allusion at the end of the first book (1.569), where the land and sea beasts of Revelation 13 merge with the behemoth and leviathan of Job 40:21, 41:1–2, to compound the expectancy voiced in Isaiah 27:1 that the Lord, in the day that he appears, will slay leviathan with his sword.

37 Pertinent discussions of the tradition include Ernst H. Kantorowicz, *The King's Two Bodies: A Study in Medieval Political Theology* (Princeton, 1957) and David George Hale, *The Body Politic: A Political Metaphor in Renaissance English Literature* (The Hague, 1971).

38 Compare the "Law case" of the rival gardeners in *Animadversions* (1.716–17) and the fable of Anteros in *Doctrine and Discipline of Divorce* (11.254–5). I discuss the latter in "'If True, Here Onely': Fabulation in *The Doctrine and Discipline of Divorce*" (forthcoming). To these passages should undoubtedly be added the

autobiographical reflections in *Reason of Church-Government* and *Apology for Smectymnuus* (1.801–23, 882–93).

39 For an account of the deep ideological indebtedness to Foxe that informed Prynne's Erastianism and nonconformity alike, see William M. Lamont, *Marginall Prynne, 1600–1669* (London and Toronto, 1963), pp. 16–27.

40 "Marginall Prynne" himself opened his scholarly vein two months after *Of Reformation*, when he saw his prison researches into print in the two-part *Antipathie of the English Lordly Prelacie* (July 1641).

41 For a characteristic expression, see Prynne's "Epistle Dedicatorie to the High Court of Parliament" that prefaces the *Antipathie*, sigs. qp3r–qp3v.

42 *Calvin's Commentaries on Romans and Thessalonians*, trans. Mackenzie, pp. 370–1, 165, 181, 340. For the Latin commentary on the respective verses, see *Ioannis Calvini in Novum Testamentum Commentarii*, ed. A. Tholuck (Berlin, 1831), vol. 6, p. 192; vol. 5, pp. 98, 109; vol. 6, p. 173. For discussion, see Quistorp, pp. 162–86; and on ramifications in later seventeenth-century English thought, see Ball, pp. 44–54.

43 The press report of one of the anonymous referees for this volume of essays raised the possibility that Milton's body tropes gradate toward apocalypticism following the lines of metaphorical extension attested for *kâbad*, a primary root in Hebrew. In glossing *kâbad*, item no. 3513 in the *Concise Dictionary of the Words in the Hebrew Bible*, p. 54, appended to his *Exhaustive Concordance of the Bible* (New York and Cincinnati, 1890), James Strong records a root meaning (to be heavy) that undergoes causative development (to make weighty) in both negative and positive senses. The semantic spectrum for *kâbad* thus encompasses, at one end, to lay (or lie) heavily, to afflict grievously, to be chargeable; and, at the other end, to abound, to be (or make) great, to bring honor (or be had in honor), to glory or glorify. I am grateful to this referee for a most suggestive speculation regarding the polylingual Milton. See also Rumrich, *Matter of Glory*, chapter 1.

44 On this new feature of the second Book of Discipline, see Ian B. Cowan, *The Scottish Reformation: Church and Society in Sixteenth-Century Scotland* (New York, 1982), p. 183.

45 *A Replye to an Answere made of M. Doctor Whitgifte, agaynste the Admonition to the Parliament* (London, 1574), p. 35. For discussion, see Brian Manning, "Puritanism and Democracy, 1640–1642," in *Puritans and Revolutionaries: Essays in Seventeenth-Century History Presented to Christopher Hill*, ed. Donald Pennington and Keith Thomas (Oxford, 1978), pp. 156–60.

46 See the suggestive discussions by Michael Wilks, "Reformatio Regni: Wyclif and Hus as Leaders of Religious Protest Movements," in *Schism, Heresy and Religious Protest*, ed. Derek Baker, Studies in Church History, no. 9 (Oxford, 1972), pp. 109–30, and by Christina von Nolcken, "Another Kind of Saint: A Lollard Perception of John Wycliff," in *From Ockam to Wyclif*, ed. Anne Hudson and Michael Wilks, Studies in Church History – 1 Subsidia, no. 5 (Oxford, 1987), pp. 429–43.

47 My perspective on *Of Reformation* in relation to Milton's search for self-understanding and an epic vocation in his early poetry differs on two key points from Michael Fixler's. I find in the prose tract the successful apocalyptic resolution that he ascribes to *Lycidas* (*Milton and the Kingdoms of God* [Evanston, 1964], pp. 60–3).

I also view Milton's apocalyptic activism a good deal more positively, as the following observation from Fixler shows: "By virtue of the fact that as a poet he had undertaken to celebrate the providential justice of God and the glories of his nation, Milton identified his vocation too precariously with the immediate fate of his country" (p. 73).

2

Wanting a supplement: the question of interpretation in Milton's early prose

STANLEY FISH

I

Very little has been said about Milton's second antiprelatical tract, *Of Prelaticall Episcopacy*, in part because there is not very much to say about a tract that is determined to say nothing at all. It does however say one thing, loudly and often: that scripture is "the only Book left to us of Divine authority, and not in anything more Divine than in the all-sufficiency it hath to furnish us" (*CPW*, 1.625). The important assertion here is not of scripture's divinity – that, after all, goes without saying and therefore in some sense to say it is to say nothing – but of the scripture's all-sufficiency; for that means not only that the scriptures are all we need, but that the scriptures themselves do not need anything, and most certainly they don't need us. To think otherwise, to think that the scriptures cannot convey their message without some intermediary aid, is to commit the impiety of thinking that the "divine Scripture wanted a supplement, and were to be eek't out" (1.626). The impiety is captured in one of the meanings of "eke," "to make good a deficiency" (*OED*): if the scriptures must be eked out, they are not all-sufficient, and if they are not all-sufficient they are not divine. Indeed, the case is even worse than that: if the scriptures are deficient, then they are not complete, are not, in some sense, themselves until their deficiency is supplied by some addition or supplement; and since that supplement can only be supplied by human agents – by the very men and women whose needs the scriptures supposedly furnish – the scriptures turn out to be fashioned, made into what they are, by those who look to them as an independent (free-standing, objective, acontextual) source of authority. Rather than providing a transcendent and self-declaring guide to human activity the scriptures become the product of human activity and, in Milton's "worst case scenario," become indistinguishable from the "devices and imbellishings of mans imagination."[1]

The supplement, then, is at once unnecessary and dangerous; it is unnecessary because the scripture is by definition sufficient and complete in and of itself, and it is dangerous because, as something added, a supplement may come to stand in place of, to overwhelm, that which it is brought in to

assist. But while they are linked in Milton's argument, these two charac-
terizations of the supplement finally strain against one another, for to insist on
the danger of the supplement is finally to call into question the all-sufficiency
and independence of that which can supposedly do without it. If the
scriptures can be threatened by a supplement, are they not more fragile and
less secure in their identity – in their fullness – than Milton claims? And if they
are so "perspicuous" (1.651) as to make any addition to them an "impiety"
(1.651), why do so many go to such lengths (a phrase intended literally) to eke
them out? Is there something about the scriptures that provokes such efforts,
and what could that something be except a deficiency that makes a supplement necessary? When Milton dismisses, as an obvious absurdity, the
possibility that "the divine Scripture wanted a supplement," is he denying
that the scriptures are in *need* of a supplement, in which case he would be
affirming their self-sufficiency, or is he denying that they lack a supplement,
in which case he would be affirming their incompleteness by identifying
them as the product of a supplement they already have?

These are not questions that Milton explicitly raises, although they are
certainly raised by the contemporary philosopher who more than any other
has made the question of the supplement or supplementarity his subject. I
refer of course to Jacques Derrida, who in a series of texts has explored the
long history in which the supplement has always been regarded as dangerous.
In the story Derrida tells, the supplement or supplementarity is another word
for what he calls "writing in general," not writing in the "vulgar" sense, but
writing as a name for the supposed exteriority of representation or signification in relation to the thing represented or signified. "Writing, the letter, the
sensible inscription, has always been considered by Western tradition as the
body . . . external to the spirit, to breath, to speech, and to the logos."[2] In that
same tradition (the tradition of "logocentrism") writing is that spacious
outside or conveying which by engaging and capturing our attention turns us
away from an interior reality; supposedly an aid to the presentation or com-
memoration of the real, it usurps the position of the real and seduces us into a
forgetfulness of its own secondariness: "Writing, a mnemotechnic means,
supplanting, supplanting good memory, spontaneous memory, signifies
forgetfulness" (p. 37). What is forgotten or lost sight of is the origin or logos
which "without writing . . . would remain in itself" (p. 37). In its movement
away from the full and immediate perception of the origin – of presence
before mediation has removed it – writing is the "original sin" (p. 35).

Writing in short is "that dangerous supplement" (the title, taken from
Rousseau, of a chapter in *Grammatology*), that "menacing aid," that "surplus"
or extra or addition that pretends to be in the service of plenitude (although
one might wonder why plenitude requires service), but, in fact, "adds only to
replace" (p. 145); and what it replaces is that which is entirely "other than it"
(p. 145); the supplement is that substitute "mediocre makeshift" which
insinuates itself into the heart of the "self-sufficient" of that which "ought to

lack nothing at all in itself," that which "does not have to be supplemented" because "it suffices" (p. 145).

It is hardly necessary to note the extraordinary similarity between Derrida's vocabulary and the vocabulary of Milton, but of course one notes the similarity only to remark on (what appears to be) the difference: while Milton endorses the distinction between the thing itself and the proposed supplement to it, Derrida rehearses it only to undermine it, or to reveal it undermining itself. His thesis is simple and, in its way, devastating: the condition of supplementarity – of an incompleteness that requires an addition to eke it out – is originary, and is itself the origin of that which is opposed to it in the name of purity and presence. The supplement or writing is not secondary, does not come after a plenitude it then threatens; rather it is "primordial" and names, and *thereby marks* the absence of, a plenitude that is not now and never was available in and of itself. The supplement does not offer itself as an addition to something already fully formed and complete; "it comes to *make up for* a deficiency . . . to compensate for a primordial nonself-presence."[3] That nonself-presence, that "so called" all and self-sufficient fullness, "can be filled up *of itself* [can become what it is] can accomplish itself, only by allowing itself to be filled [pieced or eked out] through sign and proxy";[4] and if writing or the supplement "must necessarily be added . . . to complete the constitution of the ideal object," of presence, it is because "'presence' had already from the start fallen short of itself."[5]

This does not mean, as Derrida hastens to add, that there is no such thing as presence, or the experience of presence, of immediacy, of total sufficiency, of ground; it is just that presence – whether it be of God or the world or the self – rather than occupying a realm independent of and prior to the articulations that strain to characterize it, is the product of those articulations, of systems of signification, of writing, of the dangerous supplement. Thus, while presence remains a category and an effect one can experience, it can no longer be posited as "the absolutely matrical form of being" but as a "determination" of that which is supposedly derivative of it.[6] And therefore in the strict sense, that is, in the sense in which these terms have always sounded in the logocentric tradition, "there never has been and never will be a unique word, a master name."[7]

This last pronouncement returns us forcefully to Milton and *Of Prelaticall Episcopacy*; for it is in the (master) name of a self-sufficient and self-generating and unique word that Milton speaks (or does he speak? that, as we shall see, is the question.) The scripture is, if anything is, "the transcendental signified . . . pure auto-affection . . . which does not borrow from outside itself . . . any accessory signifier, any substance of expression foreign to its own spontaneity."[8] On the very first page Milton is insisting that the scripture is "only able," by which he means both that among all things it only is able and that it is able "only," by itself without any aid; and twenty-three pages later he is still sounding the same note, urging us, as the tract ends, to give "ourselves up to be taught by the pure and living precept of *God's* word only, which without more additions, nay with a forbidding of them, hath within it selfe the promise of eternall life, the end of all our wearisome labours" (1.652).

As an assertion and a claim this statement would seem to be an obvious candidate for a deconstructive reading, an easy target for just the kind of analysis to which Derrida subjects Plato, Husserl, Saussure, Lévi-Strauss, Austin, and Rousseau. One can almost hear the questions: isn't a discourse that argues for the self-sufficiency of an ideal object a disconfirmation of that very argument? Doesn't the very fact of the tract's existence, the fact that someone felt compelled to produce it, belie its own message? How can so many words be expended in the service of something that requires no aids? If additions to the pure and living precept of God's word are forbidden, what is the status of this very effort? Isn't *Of Prelaticall Episcopacy* an impiety of just the kind it condemns? Isn't it the very thing it thunders against? Isn't it a supplement?

In some readings of a deconstructive kind, these questions would mark not the beginning but the end of the matter, for they would indicate that once again a discourse has been shown to stand on its putative ground only by forgetting or repressing the intuition that would unsettle it, by concealing from itself "a certain exterior" that it cannot name or describe without undoing its constitutive rhetoric.[9] In this case the rhetoric is the rhetoric of scriptural self-sufficiency, and what the discourse conceals and represses is the "scandal" of its own existence, all the more easy to "overlook" because it is so obvious. But we cannot stop here, because rather than being blind to the "problematic" of his own activity, Milton foregrounds that problematic and makes it the basis of a strategy. The question of the "status of his own discourse" is not one he evades or dodges or misses, but one he raises and raises with all of the rigor to which a deconstructionist might lay claim. I do not mean to suggest that Milton is a proto-poststructuralist; rather I mean to suggest that in the context of the position he self-consciously espouses, he is inevitably aware of the difficulties and "troubles" on which post-structuralism feeds.

My thesis, then, is that Milton, no less than his modern deconstructive reader, is uneasy about his performance, and for similar reasons. In a word, that performance is superfluous, and because it is superfluous, it is also, potentially at least, impious. If the scripture is fully able to satisfy us, there is no need to say anything else, and since the fullness of scripture is the tract's first assertion, it is over before it begins.[10] At the same time that the opening sentences promise to adjudicate between the respective claims of scripture and tradition, scripture is declared to be the judge of the dispute, and almost immediately the tract finds itself all dressed up with nowhere to go. Indeed going somewhere is precisely the error it wishes to avoid, as from the very first danger and impiety are associated with movement. Those who are "not contented with the plentiful and wholesome fountaines of the Gospell"

(1.626) are described as failing to "hold fast to the grounds of the reformed *Church*" (1.624); instead they "run to that indigested heap . . . which they call 'Antiquity'" (1.639); and when they are not running, they are "forraging" (1.627); they "stagger" and are "mislead" (1.627); they "gadder" (1.631) and "fondly straggle"; they "change" (1.632); they "fetch" (1.637); they "fall to searching" (1.639), they "truant" (1.642), they "creep by degrees" (1.650), they "labour" (1.652), they "deduce."

Deduce may seem a strange word to bring up the rear of this list, but in fact it captures in a precise and abstract way what is wrong with movement: deduction begins from first axioms and then moves away from them toward a conclusion; but the first axiom to which Milton is committed – that the scriptures are *all*-sufficient – contains its own conclusion and therefore expressly prohibits (nay, forbids) seeking for conclusions elsewhere. The act of deducing is a repeated target of scorn in the tract; it is by the degrees or steps of deduction that the prelates arrive at their claims of authority; "Episcopall men," Milton observes in accusation, "would cast a mist before us, to deduce their exalted Episcopacy from Apostolik times" (1.648). The (insubstantial) content of that mist is a "petty-fog of witnesses" (1.648) and "testimonies," two other words that reappear often and are always allied with deduction as the components of a suspect practice, a practice that leads men to seek in some external formula that which should reside within them. The practice is conceived of as a legal one, and in the course of it witnesses and testimonies are always found to be "grey," "bare," without "credit," "alleged" and "corrupt," inauthentic, broken, disfigured, and tainted. Implicitly opposed to this practice is another in which witness and testimony are (quite literally) redeemed because they have reference to an *interior* motion which is, in fact, no motion at all; one witnesses by holding fast to that with which you are already allied; and one testifies to the residence within of the "something holy that lodges in [your] breast" (*Comus*, 1.245). As Milton will soon put it in the *Apology*, "the testimony of what we believe in religion must be such as the conscience may rest on to be infallible, and incorruptible, which is only the word of God" (1.912); and since the word of God is inscribed on the fleshly tables of the heart, the *circuit* of testimony (and of witness) can (indeed must) be completed without moving an inch from the center of an illuminated self.

Significantly, this is exactly the circuit (or non-circuit) that Milton himself travels (by not travelling) when he speaks of what has "moved" him to the present occasion:

> . . . it came into my thoughts to perswade my selfe, setting all
> distances, and nice respects aside, that I could do Religion and my
> Country no better service for the time than doing my utmost to recall
> the people of God from this vaine forraging after straw, and to reduce
> them to their firme stations under the standard of the Gospell.   (1.627)

At first it seems that the impulse to action (exactly the wrong word) is external – "it came into my thoughts" – but then it turns out that the phrase "it came" means no more than "it occurred to me"; the origin of the thought is internal, as is the activity it prompts, "to perswade myself." What is described is a psychological process that is wholly self-contained, a process that occurs without ever taking a single step, and one that issues in a resolution to recall others from the steps they have taken imprudently, so that they can once again assume the posture Milton himself exemplifies, marching in place "under the standard of the Gospell."

II

This then will be the business of the tract – to retard and reverse movement – but to say as much is once again to encounter the tract's problematic, the fact that it will itself necessarily move through time, in a succession of propositions; and characteristically Milton chooses to foreground that problematic by providing the reader with an advance plan of what he intends: he will recall the "vain" foragers by "making appeare to them first the insufficiency, next the inconvenience, and lastly the impiety of these gay testimonies, that their great Doctors would bring them to dote on" (1.627). "Making appeare" would seem to name a very strong action, one that could hardly be prosecuted without engaging in the very activities – of reasoning, deducing, proving – Milton rejects and indicts; but "making appeare" can also name a softer action in which the actor's contribution is limited to the clearing away of film and debris. Such an actor would not be guilty of adding to the scripture, of covering it with his own writing, for he would merely be removing the coverings and addition of others so that the scripture can do what it must be allowed to do, speak for itself. Needless to say, this is a difficult strategy to execute since it is always in danger of turning into the very thing it opposes, of turning into a supplement. The trick is to do as little as possible, to perform in a way so minimal that it is not a performance at all; and that is why the first thing Milton tells us as he approaches his task is what he will *not* do: "in performing this I shall not strive to be more exact in Methode, then as their citations lead me" (1.627). That is, his movements will be dictated by the "gay testimonies" of the "great doctors," and therefore they will not be *his* movements; by being thus careless in his method, he will forsake method. Method, after all, is crucial only if the truth is not yet found; but for one whose truth is within, method is beside the point, because the point to which method would bring one is always and already achieved. Such a one "shall not strive" because he need not strive, and because he need not strive he should not strive.

Milton's (anti)method of (non)striving is on display in the very first sentence of the tract's main section: "First therefore concerning *Ignatius* shall be treated fully, when the Author shall come to insist upon some places in his epistles" (1.627). "First therefore" promises a reasoned sequence of deductions based on evidence marshalled and considered, but the sequence never even gets started because the evidence is withdrawn *before* it is placed on the table. Of course it is true that Ignatius' appearance is only postponed, but as we shall see even when he returns he will be treated no more "fully" than he is here. Meanwhile, Milton proceeds with a "Next" that has no proper reference since the previous event has not yet occurred. What occurs now is the apparent citing of "one *Leontius Bishop of Magnesia,*" but he too is dismissed before he can take the stand; for he is "but an obscure and single witness" who, for all we know, might be "factious and false" (1.628); and "how," asks Milton, "shall this testimony receive credit from his word, whose very name had scarce been thought on, but for this bare testimony" (1.628). That is, how can you accept as authoritative the word of someone whose authority is itself in question? Any reasoning based on such a bare testimony is obviously circular and self-vitiating. Of course Milton's reasoning (if that is the word) is also circular, beginning and ending in a word; but that word is God's and the testimony is authoritative *because* it is bare, because it issues from an unimpeachable source that has no need of the external validation lacking to Leontius and others. It is because such validation is lacking that Leontius' testimony (whatever it might be) is never heard, and Milton returns him to the obscurity from which he has not been allowed to emerge, saying only "I will not stand to argue" (1.628). This is more than a report on his present intention: it is a perfect description of his performance; he stands exactly in the position he had assumed in the beginning, and he has declined to move from that position by arguing, despite the appearance of phrases like "First therefore" and words like "Next."

In this sequence, which will be repeated again, we see the whole of Milton's minimalist strategy: he will not so much consider evidence as consider considering it; and in every instance he will find, *before* the evidence is even brought to light, that it is inadmissible, first because it is itself corrupt and second because the foundations on which it may be said to rest are similarly corrupt. As a result he will have managed the considerable non-feat of remaining always in the same position, of not moving at all, because every time it appears that he is about to make a move it is aborted. To say that the strategy is negative is in fact to give it more positivity than Milton allows it to have. He doesn't *discredit* the evidence; he discredits the possibility of either crediting or discrediting the evidence, and thereby saves himself both the labor and the possible presumption that would inhere in even the slightest of actions. In ways that find many parallels in the poetry, *Of Prelaticall Episcopacy* is full of moments when action of some kind seems imminent, but never quite occurs.

As Milton leaves Leontius (without ever having encountered him), he takes a few Parthian shots at some other arguments that will also not be heard. One could say that "he was a member of the Councell and that may deserve to gain credit with us," but such an argument will presume on the soundness of the councils, and as everyone knows, "nothing hath been more attempted, nor with more subtilty brought about ... then to falsifie the Editions of the Councels, of which we have none but from our Adversaries hand" (1.628–9). Not that Milton wishes to argue the point; he introduces the topic by dismissing it – "nor shall I need to plead at this time that..." – and he concludes it, without ever having raised it, by saying that he does not here "purpose to take advantage of" it, "for what availes it to wrangle about the corrupt editions of Councells" (1.629). "Much rather," he says, "should we attend to what Eusebius the ancientest writer extant of Church-history ... confesses" (1.630–7). For a moment it seems that Milton is about to accept an authority other than the Bible and risk the danger of becoming a supplement to a supplementer; but then it turns out that what Eusebius confesses is that the distinction between bishops and presbyters is not one that is made clearly in the Scripture. Eusebius is being invoked not so that he can give evidence but so that he can admit his inability to go beyond the evidence already available in the Bible. And if Eusebius, "a famous writer," is unable to find support for Episcopacy, "much more may we think it difficult to Leontius an obscure Bishop" (1.631). The logic here simultaneously employs and eviscerates the standards by which tradition and history determine authority: as the more ancient and the most famous, Eusebius deserves a hearing, but he is heard only so that he can disqualify himself in favor of an authority that knows no time and transcends history: "Thus while we leave the Bible to gadder after these traditions of the ancients, we hear the ancients themselves confessing, that what knowledge they had in this point was such as they had gather'd from the Bible" (1.631).

It is no surprise then when Ignatius, who had been sent away with the promise that he would later "be treated fully," returns to become the object of exactly the same treatment – that is, no treatment at all – he met with in the first place. Predictably, Ignatius' *Epistles* are disqualified before they can be examined; five of them, Milton points out, have been rejected as "spurious" (1.635) because they have been seen to contain "heresies and trifles, which cannot agree in Chronologie with *Ignatius*." Once again the "proof" supposedly provided by patristic authority is discredited by the same standards by which that authority would maintain itself; that is, the evidence is declared to be doubtful in its own terms; and here doubt is cast not only on the texts, known by even those who cite them to be "interlarded with Corruptions," but also on the author, who, on the "evidence" of those same corruptions, cannot be securely identified as Ignatius. This line of reasoning allows Milton to come to his favorite kind of conclusion, one that squeezes his opponent from opposite directions: either these epistles are not by Ignatius at all and thereby lose the authority of his name, or else Ignatius is their author but he is not the Ignatius of repute, not "a Martyr but most adulterate, and corrupt himselfe" (1.639). Ignatius, then, is not himself; rather he exists only in pieces

– in Milton's words, "disfigur'd," "interrupted," "broken" and "disjoynted" (1.639) – and he must therefore be put together by the very person who will then cite him as authoritative. "How," Milton asks, can we credit "such an author, to whose very essence the reader must be fain to contribute his own understanding?" (1.639) With this question Milton returns us to his opening paragraphs (which in fact we have never left): Ignatius, both as a person and as a text (there is finally no distinction), is not "all sufficient" and therefore cannot furnish us with that which we must ourselves supply. And moreover, the fact that there are some who are moved (a word whose spatial dimension should be stressed) to supply it indicates that they are themselves no less deficient than he is, and in the same way; they too have no "essence," no "all sufficiency" to which they are united and of which they are an extension, and it is their incompleteness which sends them in search of supplementary aids, a search which ends only in the discovery of bodies even more "broken and disjointed" than their own. Later Milton (or at least his Adam) will decide that "single imperfection" can be remedied by joining in "collateral love and . . . amity" with others of like defectiveness (*PL* VIII.423–6), but here in 1642 the mathematics are more severe; the union of imperfection only begets more imperfection. What is required is a union that need not be sought because it is a mode of being in which we have so completely "given ourselves up to be taught by the pure and living precept of *Gods* word" (1.652) that we are, quite literally, animated by that word. At that point we will have become what Milton claims he already is in the *Apology*, "a member incorporate into that truth whereof I was perswaded" (1.871), and what Christ declares himself to be in *Paradise Regained*, a "living oracle" (1.460). Rather than betaking our selves to the "scraps and fragments of an unknown table," we should feed on the "Evangelick Manna" (1.639) that God has placed on the fleshly tables of our hearts. He who has been nourished by that Manna will feel no need to seek elsewhere for something that is already his substance. Not "disjoynted" himself, but an incorporate member, he will immediately see the disjointed texts of Ignatius and others for what they are – "verminous and polluted rags dropt . . . from the toyling shoulders of Time" – and will disdain those rags in favor of "the spotlesse and undecaying robe of Truth," a garment in which he is already clothed.

In this opposition between truth and time the several components of Milton's position coalesce. Time is the medium of motion and process, of eking out, of adding, supplementing; it is, in a word, the medium of incompleteness, although its perpetual promise is that wholeness and illumination are only a step away. Truth, on the other hand, is what abides; it does not need the temporal dimension in order to emerge; like Milton's muse it was present "Before the hills appeared, or fountain flowed" (*PL* VII.8), and it remains fully present in every moment of what is no longer a succession of differences but an order of the same. As Milton puts it at the close of this amazing passage, "Truth is the daughter not of Time but of Heaven, only bred up ... in Christian hearts" (1.639). This declaration not only displays Milton's deepest convictions, but explains, if it does not justify, the curious structure of a tract which, in Donald Davie's words (he directs them at *Paradise Lost*), declines to take advantage of the fact that it is "a shape cut in time,"[11] a tract which refuses to move forward or even to take a first step, a tract which never adds anything to its opening pronouncement (a pronouncement that announces its own superfluousness), a tract which in its determination to avoid burdening the world with one more "needlesse tractat" (1.626) systematically withholds satisfaction of the needs felt by every reader of discursive prose, the need for argument, evidence, testimony, deduction. These are the needs of the distracted "multitude" who have somehow wandered and must be recalled "from this vaine forraging after strawe" and "returned to their firme stations under the standards of the Gospell" (1.627); must be recalled, that is, to the security and self-sufficiency of their own Christian hearts where everything they vainly seek is always and already found.

At this point it would seem that Milton surely could rest on his circular conclusion, but he has pledged himself to be led in his "methode" by the citations of his adversaries, and he proceeds doggedly, "marching up and down in the same place."[12] Ignatius is followed by Irenaeus and Tertullian who now take their turns, or rather, do not take their turns, as their authority and even their identities are impugned in what is by now a familiar manner. Irenaeus is dismissed twice, first because although he reports that he was present when "*Polycarpus was made Bishop of Smyrna by the Apostles*," he was at the time, by his own confession, only a boy; and therefore says Milton "we would be rash to rely upon" his "young observation" (1.640, 641). But lest we think that his youth is the only reason to distrust him, Eusebius is brought in to testify that in his maturity Irenaeus became "infected" with the errors of Papias, another eyewitness of the acts of the Apostles, but one who was known to be of "shallow wit" and incapable of understanding what he saw and heard. The infection Irenaeus receives is retroactive, casting further doubt on the accuracy of his youthful report and on eyewitness testimony in general. As a consequence Polycarpus too is infected, since his Apostolic bishopric is attested to only by the now thoroughly discredited Irenaeus. Only Eusebius escapes, but he is relied on only to point out the unreliability of the tradition of testimony of which he is himself a part.

Even the Apostles themselves are tainted, for although they are not directly attacked, there is a sustained attack on those who, like Irenaeus, Papias, and Polycarpus, attend to their *persons* rather than to what they had written (writing of course inspired by the Spirit). In a manner most un-Miltonic, Milton imagines the pilgrimages (error once again always associated with *movement*) of those who would make a shrine of any place or spot to which the Apostles were known to have repaired: "O happy this house that harbour'd him, and the cold stone whereon he rested, this Village wherein he wrought such a miracle, and that pavement bedew'd with the warm effusion of his last blood, that sprouted up into eternall Roses to crowne his Martyrdome" (1.642). This lyrically suspect apostrophe is followed (as similar moments of "indulgence" will be in *Paradise Lost*) by a stringent and devastating indictment as idolatry of everything that might have seemed attractive in such scenes:

> Thus while all their thoughts were pow'rd out upon circumstances, and the gazing after such men as had sate at table with the Apostles (many of whom Christ hath profest, yea though they had cast out Divells in his name, he will not know at the last day) by this meanes they lost their time, and truanted in the fundamental grounds of saving knowledge. (1.642)

The syntax here is double: "Many of whom" can refer either to "such men" or to the Apostles, and even though it is likely that we will settle on the former reading, the latter is available and even (given the juxtaposition of "*Apostles*" with the parenthesis) insistent. If only at a subterranean level the Apostles too become "infected" with the same kind of waywardness or truancy that characterizes those who idolize them; they become "disjoynted" and "interrupt" from the truth and text of which they are incorporate members; and once again that truth and that text stand alone as the only authorities in a landscape from which all other authorities – Leontius, Ignatius, Irenaeus, Polycarpus, Papias, the Apostles themselves – have been cleared.

But no sooner has the ground been cleared than another of that "petty fog of witnesses" thrown up by tradition and custom threatens to befoul it. "Tertullian," Milton announces, "accosts us next" (1.644), but he is turned away before he can speak because "his testimony . . . is of no more force to deduce Episcopacy, than the two former" (1.644). In the paragraphs that follow, the words "testimony" and "deduce" appear with increasing frequency, emphasizing at once everything that is being declared suspect (because unnecessary) and everything that Milton is ostentatiously declining to do. The only testimony he will offer is the testimony of his unwillingness to consider any testimony; the only deduction he will make is that the deduction is superfluous and dangerous since it involves a movement away from the truth that should already reside in "Christian hearts" (1.639). He has nowhere to go, nothing to do except to "prove the insufficiency of these . . . Episcopall testimonies" and point out the "inconvenience" we fall into if we allow ourselves "to be guided by these kind of testimonies" (1.650). If the Fathers are read in this spirit, with the purpose of marking "how corruption and Apostasy [have] crept in by degrees," they can do us no harm, and can by negative example provide us with materials with which to "stop the mouthes of our adversaries and to bridle them with their own curb" (1.650). This is of course a precise description of what Milton has himself been doing (insofar as he has been doing anything), and the key terms of that description – "stop," "bridle" and "curb" – capture perfectly the determined non-motion of a tract designed not to produce words, but to stop their flow, not to generate conclusions but to block them, not to initiate movement, but to bridle it, not to provide satisfaction – for that would be to arrogate to itself that which it denies to others – but to induce frustration and a longing for a Word that has no need of it or anything else.

That at least is Milton's thesis, the self-sufficiency of scripture, and, as we have seen, it is a thesis that provides him with a justification for the "minimalist" strategy of dismissing extra-scriptural evidence even before it is examined. So successful is that strategy that it obscures the even more basic strategy that lies behind it: by foregrounding his efforts to prevent us from looking at texts other than the scripture. Milton averts our attention from the fact that we are at the same time being prevented from looking at the scripture itself. The effect is something very much like a sleight of hand: so intent are we on following the ways in which the Fathers and their texts are being dismissed that we never even notice that the *scripture is nowhere cited*. On one level this can be seen as an extension of Milton's point: even to look at the scripture is to be at a distance from that which should be the very content of one's heart and mind; to hold the scripture at arm's length as if it were merely an object is to be "interrupt" from it, and to be, like Ignatius, in a "broken and disjoynted plight" (1.639). But on another level, Milton's disinclination even to cite scripture in a tract that everywhere asserts its self-sufficiency can be seen as an admission, probably inadvertent, that behind the assertion is a fear, a fear of what will happen if he allows himself or his readers the slightest of movements, even the movement of opening an eye and taking a look. That fear is made explicit in the final paragraph, when Milton says of the scripture that "if one jot be alterable it is ... possible that all shall perish" (1.652). Although the reference here is to biblical passages that proclaim the power and imperishability of the Word (the word authorizes itself) the context suggests a Word so vulnerable that every motion toward it carries the threat of alteration. At this moment what becomes clear (although perhaps not to Milton) is that the scripture's very uniqueness is the source of the danger posed to it by something so small as the glances of men. Unlike any other "word" the scripture (or so is the claim) is self-interpreting (this is just another characterization of its self-sufficiency), which means not only that it needs no interpretation but that *it cannot survive interpretation*: that is to say, as a self-reading text it cannot be read without being turned into something other than it is. Even to look at it is to mark it with the differentiating lines that are necessarily the content of any temporally bound vision. This is what Derrida means by "originary violence,"[13] a violence that does not occur after perception, but is another name for perception, for what happens when *within* a system of differences (and there is no perception apart from some or other system) an act of predication, an act of *demarcating*, takes place. The violence is originary because what becomes pick-outable or legible is the product of what points it out, of the differential system within which (to borrow George Herbert's words) "We say ... This or that is" ("The Flower," lines 19–20). The "this" or "that" which is thus constituted can never be grasped in its "pre-read" shape, in a shape that is entirely its own and has not yet been obscured or overlain by a fatal touch of representation.

The logic is at once inexorable and paradoxical: in order to preserve the sacred text it must be protected from being read, protected, that is, from the very condition of being a text, of being at once the object and the product of an act of interpretation. Milton's entire enterprise depends on two related attempts to avoid textuality; he labors to prevent his own text from achieving a substance that would make it an addition, a supplement; and he avoids giving a textual substance to the interior Word by averting his eyes from it. The assertion of the tract is that the scripture is complete in and of itself, but it is a completeness that is compromised by the slightest inspection, and indeed by *any* action more volitional than the unconditional surrender urged by Milton in his final paragraph. We must, he says, give "our selves up to be taught by the pure and living precept of God's word only, which, without more additions, nay with a forbidding of them, hath within it selfe the promise of eternall life, the end of all our wearisome labours" (1.652). The statement is a complicated one, simultaneously a warning, a promise, and the expression of a fear. The warning is the same as the one with which the tract began: do not look to and/or become an addition; the promise is that by ending the presumptuous and unnecessary labors of adding or supplementing we will gain eternal life; and the fear is that if we persist in such labors they will not only be wearisome, but fatal, since their effect will be "to open a broad passage for a multitude of Doctrines that have no ground in Scripture to break in upon us" (1.651). In this sentence, which ends the penultimate paragraph, the fear is nakedly and pointedly expressed: once the Word has been subjected to even the slightest scrutiny its bulwarks (the sense of a fortress under siege is unmistakable) will have been breached and all will be lost; and the way to forestall this disaster is to remain closed up within the fortress we ourselves become so long as we do not stir or move in any way. The "ground" which supports us will simply crumble if we so much as glance at it. The warning in its conspicuous anxiety recalls the warnings given to Orpheus and to Lot, but it is even more severe: not "don't look back," but "don't look at all."

III

It is therefore all the more extraordinary to realize that in less than two years Milton will aggressively violate every injunction he here lays down, and will not only look scripture full in the face, but will urge in the strongest possible terms the very activities he now forbids. In the *Doctrine and Discipline of Divorce*, the scripture is the object not only of direct scrutiny, but of an interpretation so strenuous that even the word "manipulation" is too mild to describe it. Reading, rather than being forbidden, is commanded, and is to take exactly the form which in *Of Prelaticall Episcopacy* poses the greatest danger. In order to read the scripture correctly, Milton announces, one must be "a skillful and laborious gatherer," and the reason that this is required, an amazing reason given the anti-prelatical tracts, is that in the gospel Christ nowhere gives "full comments or continu'd discourses" but rather "scatters the heavenly grain of his doctrine like pearle here and there" (II.338), a doctrine which must therefore be put together and made whole by an interpreter. In short, the scripture is neither complete nor self-sufficient but itself demands – that is, wants – a supplement. The reversal could not be more total: that which should supply our needs must be itself supplied by our labors. Milton has himself let loose the forces whose containment was so much the business of his earlier work. What has happened? What does this mean?

One answer to this question would center around Milton's domestic situation, which had presumably led him "naturally" to the question of divorce. Arthur Barker maintains that even before Mary Powell deserted him Milton had reached conclusions about the lawfulness of divorce, and that his personal problems served only to sharpen and focus arguments he had already prepared. As post-Freudians we may be properly skeptical of Barker's generosity, but we must certainly agree when he declares that Milton "found it impossible to believe ... that the opinion on divorce at which he had arrived could be contrary to the divine will."[14] That opinion can easily be shown to be continuous with his other opinions and especially with the insistence, from which he never wavers, on the primacy of conscience and internal illumination. In principle the argument for divorce – that it is a necessary relief from the merely formal bondage of a spiritual misyoking – is of a piece with many of the arguments Milton makes in the anti-prelatical tracts for the primacy of conscience and the inner light. What is different is that the argument cannot make its way in the company of a strenuous literalism because the chief support of the opposing argument is an apparently unequivocal verse from the Gospel of Matthew: "Whosoever shall put away his wife, except it be for fornication, and shall marry another, committeth adultery" (7:19). It is the fact of this verse and the impossibility of avoiding it that dictates Milton's strategy and makes unavailable to him the anti-interpretivism of *Of Prelaticall Episcopacy*. As Barker puts it, "instead of opposing the plain truth of Scripture to custom, he had now to reinterpret the precept on which custom seemed firmly to base itself."

Indeed, the case is worse than that. What Milton must do is somehow show that a verse that seems to everyone else to enjoin divorce except for one particular offense should be read as allowing divorce for any of the myriad offenses that might fall under the general and expandable rubric of incompatibility. He must show that when Christ *says* a man can put away his wife only for reason of fornication, he *means* that a man can put away his wife for any reason he likes. The logic of his position is clear: it is the logic employed by Paulus Emilius when he was asked "why he would put away his wife for no visible reason" and replied by pointing to his shoe and saying, "*This shoo . . . is a neat shoo, a new shoo, and yet none of yee know wher it wrings me*" (II.348). His point is Milton's point: the reality of an *internal* lack of fit (between foot and shoe or man and wife) is independent of any external manifestation, any "visible reason"; it is a matter not of outward behavior but of the "inward man, which not any law but conscience only can evince," where "evince" is a Miltonic joke since the argument is precisely that what is essential is what does *not* show.

But as Milton himself points out, no matter how cogent his reasoning may be (and how much it follows from the general Puritan arguments against vestments and set forms), someone might still object that the cogency is worth nothing "when as the words of Christ are plainly against all divorce, except in case of fornication" (II.281). By raising this objection himself Milton highlights the interpretive issue and glances backward to the reliance in his earlier work on the argument he is about to reject, the argument for the "plain and unaffected stile of the Scriptures" which are forever "protesting their plainnes and perspicuity."[15] This is an early instance of what becomes a characteristic Miltonic strategy, to think through a problem by revisiting and complicating an earlier treatment of it. Milton is continually in dialogue with himself, responding not so much to the external challenges of ecclesiastical and parliamentary debate (although of course these things also figure in his thinking) as to the challenge represented by his former selves to the position he would now espouse. In the *Doctrine and Discipline of Divorce*, the two Miltons, the old and the new, meet in the single word that becomes their battlefield, "plainly" and all its cognates. The considerable tension in the tract derives from the fact that the claim of plainness is central both to the stance he abandons and to the stance he proceeds to assume.

It is a tension Milton seems deliberately to exploit when he responds to his own devil's advocate question ("what are all these reasonings worth . . . when as the words of Christ are plainly against . . . divorce?") by offering a theory of meaning in which the sense of an utterance cannot be construed independently of the conditions of its production. If we are to understand what Christ says, we must attend to "the occasion which induc't [him] to speak of divorce." He did not speak in a vacuum but *to* someone in a particular situation with its own structures and emphases. In this case he was speaking to the Pharisees who had put to him a "tempting question," a question designed to reveal him as lax with regard to the Law. It is in response to that question that he gives an answer more severe than he would have given to questioners of a more generous spirit:

> So heer he may be justly thought to have giv'n this rigid sentence against divorce, not to cut off all remedy from a good man who finds himself consuming away in a disconsolate and uninjoy'd matrimony, but to lay a bridle upon the bold abuses of those over-weening Rabbies: which he could not more effectually doe, than by a countersway of restraint, curbing their wild exorbitance almost into the other extreme, as when we bow things the contrary way, to make them come to their natural straitness. (II.281-3)

That is, since this stricture was only meant for those of pharisaical temper, the freedom of men who are not Pharisees cannot properly be abrogated by invoking a prohibition that was not addressed to them. Therefore, while Christ might say to the Pharisees, "*You* can divorce only for reason of adultery," he says to us, "to *you* divorce is permitted if, in your judgment, your marriage is not a true spiritual union."

It is, to say the least, an ingenious argument in the course of which Christ's plain decree is set aside in favor of a "laboriously gathered" interpretation; but no sooner has that interpretation been fashioned than it is proclaimed to be "most evident," that is, plain, and indeed it is introduced as something "we may plainly discover" (II.282). It is in these sentences that the text sets its own problem: how can plainness at once be dismissed as an "obstinate *literality* and an *alphabetical* servility" (II.280) and then in the very next instant be claimed for a reading that no one else had ever thought of? The solution to the problem lies in a distinction (itself finally a problem) between the entities of which plainness can be predicated. For a literalist of the kind Milton was such a short time ago, it is the text, more or less self-construing, that is, plain; for Milton, in his new role as active interpreter, it is the stance of the speaker in relation to a particular situation that is, or can be, plain. Once that stance has been determined, once it is clear from what angle a speaker makes his intervention and with what purpose in mind, the words he produces acquire an obvious shape and can then be declared plain. That is why Milton can at once scorn plainness and claim it; he scorns it as a property of words and claims it as a property of the contextual conditions within which words are uttered. Indeed he says as much at the end of this sequence: "And that this was the only intention of Christ was most evident" (II.283).

It is the word "intention" that formally announces Milton's new theory of interpretation,[16] for it names the place where meaning has been relocated now that it is said no longer to reside in words; but even as it names that place the word presents us with a new problem: if words do not specify the intention with which they are produced but rather must be construed in the light of that intention, how is it that we determine what the intention is? How is *it* brought to light? The difficulty becomes apparent at the very moment when Milton declares his thesis:

> that we are not to repose all upon the literall terms of so many words many instances will teach us: Wherin we may plainly discover how Christ meant not to be tak'n word for word, but like a wise physician, administering one excess against another. (II.282-3)

It is Christ's intention, says Milton, to be understood intentionally and not word for word, but how do we know that intention? The immediate answer is that it will be known by examining other "instances" of Christ's speech – we should attend, Milton advises, to "his own words . . . not many verses before" – but presumably those words too are to be understood intentionally, and therefore the support they give as evidence of an intention must itself be supported by additional evidence that will in turn display the same deficiency (wanting a supplement). Once words have been dislodged as the repository of meaning in favor of intention, no amount of them will suffice to establish an intention since the value they have will always depend on that which they presume to establish.

The same circularity is on display in an earlier moment when Milton considers the verse on which his entire case is based:

> *It is not good . . . that a man should be alone; I will make him a help meet for him.* From which words so plain, lesse cannot be concluded . . . that in Gods intention a meet and happy conversation is the chiefest and the noblest end of marriage. (II.245-6)

Although the assertion is that interpretation proceeds from the words to the calculation of God's intention, the actual direction is the other way around; the language does not dictate Milton's reading, and it would be open to someone with a different view to argue (for example) that the remedy for loneliness is the interpenetrating oneness achievable only in the act of intercourse. In short, there is nothing plain about the *words*; what is plain, at least in the eyes of Milton, is the intention in relation to which the words could only have the meaning he stipulates for them. Still, the question remains, how is that intention determined, and finally the only answer Milton gives (by not giving it) is that intention is not determined but simply assumed, and that its assumption is supported by its own strength – the strength of *belief* – and by nothing else. That is to say, what is supposedly the end of the interpretive process – the specification of what a speaker means – is in Milton's "procedure" its beginning. He starts with a conviction that his God is of a certain temper and inclination, and therefore he knows in advance of the appearance of any of his particular words what they *must* mean.

Nowhere is this clearer than in those passages in which rival interpretations are dismissed because to accept them would be to accept the picture of a God who is cruel and deceptive.[17] Noting that a strict reading of the verse from

Matthew would entail assuming that the latitude allowed to divorcers by Mosaic law amounted to the sanctioning of sin, Milton says that this is a doctrine he will "ever disswade" himself from believing; for "certainly this is not the manner of God, whose pure eyes cannot behold, much less his perfect law dispence with, such impurity" (II.303–4). "Can we conceave without vile thoughts," he asks, "that the majesty and holiness of God could endure so many ages to gratifie a stubborn people in the practice of a foul polluting sin" (II.316). The "vile thoughts" would be the thoughts one would have to have about God, about the kind of person he was, in order to read that signification into his words. It is a matter, Milton says, of the "honour of God" which is "misreputed" if he is read as "dispencing legally with many ages of ratify'd adultery." We repute him correctly only if we read him as granting a permission that was never withdrawn (except in the very special case of the Pharisees), for only then will we "recover the misattended words of Christ to the sincerity of their true sense" (II.355). This statement is supposedly made on behalf of the words, as if sense and sincerity were properties that have somehow been taken away from them and are now to be returned by the interpreter's labors. But, in fact, sense and sincerity are what the interpreter *lends* to the words by bypassing them in favor of something that stands behind them, the immaterial (because inner) intention that, quite literally, informs them. It is by means of the intentional context that the interpreter is able to *construct* both sense and sincerity, but since that context is itself without visible form, it too must be constructed even as it is invoked as a support. It is hardly necessary to remark how different this is from the anti-prelatical tracts where, in a typical passage, Milton enumerates the "extrinsic" contexts from which the prelates derive their arguments and says, as he dismisses them in turn, "we shall tell them of Scripture,"[18] the same scripture which in another place is exalted above the insubstantiality of "unwritt'n traditions."[19] In the *Doctrine and Discipline of Divorce* the unwritten controls the written to the extent of rewriting it whenever its apparent sense is inconvenient. While in *Of Prelaticall Episcopacy* Milton dismisses with contempt the authority of an author "to whose very essence the Reader must be fain to contribute his own understanding" (I.639), this is precisely what he does when he supplies the essence of God by specifying for him an intention for which there is no evidence save the persuasiveness of its assertion.

IV

Of course, Milton would not assent to this description of his labors, for although he acknowledges that he is performing them, he continues to speak as if they made no contribution whatsoever to the text they explicated. He speaks, in short, as if the minimalist strategy of the anti-prelatical tracts were still in force, as if his incredibly manipulative exertions were nothing more than a bit of light house-cleaning:

I trust, through the help of that illuminating Spirit which hath favor'd
me, to have don no every daies work: in asserting after many ages the
words of Christ with other Scriptures of great concernment from
burdensom and remorsles obscurity, tangl'd with manifold
repugnances to their native lustre and consent between each other.

(II.340)

The sentence proceeds in alternate fits of self-assertion and self-effacement.
The fact that Milton does work is qualified in advance when it is attributed to
the Spirit. The fact that the work is assertive is qualified when the asserting is
said to be an action that removes rather than adds. What he asserts is nothing
of his own but "the words of Christ" and simply by doing this (that is, by
doing very little) he rescues Christ's words from the encrustations left by
interpreters less circumspect than he. The effect is double and simultaneous
and is captured in the unusual construction of "asserting *from*" which must be
read as "asserting *away* from": by performing the minimal action of allowing
Christ to speak for himself, Milton (or so is his claim) undoes the
presumptuous and "burdensom" actions of others, replacing their layers of
"obscurity" with the "native lustre" of a self-declaring text.

One is hard pressed finally to decide which is the more remarkable, the
discursive contortions by which Milton demonstrates (at least to his own
satisfaction) that Christ's words could not possibly mean what every one had
always taken them to mean, or his denial that in mounting this demonstration
he is doing anything at all (the same minimalist claim he makes in *Of
Prelaticall Episcopacy*). The incredibility of the argument is compounded by
the incredibility of the claim that it is not being made. It can hardly be an
authorial strategy unless one imagines Milton trying to see how much he can
get away with as he alternates between an audacious interpretive program
and an equally audacious disclaimer of any interpretive intention (except for
the intention of protecting the text from interpretation). But the issue is one
Milton feels so keenly that it is doubtful that he would make it the occasion of
a virtuoso rhetorical performance, and one is forced to the conclusion that in
some sense he doesn't know what he is doing, doesn't know that he has
opened wide the door he so firmly closed in *Of Prelaticall Episcopacy* and has
become exactly the kind of force against which he inveighed, a dangerous
supplementer.

The prose, however, knows, and at one crucial point, its awareness of the
contradictory doubleness of its claims (to be doing all, to be doing nothing) is
concentrated in a single word:

Having thus unfoulded those ambiguous reasons, wherewith Christ, as
his wont was, gave to the Pharises that came to sound him, such an
answer as they deserv'd, it will not be uneasie to explain the sentence
it self that now follows: *Whosoever shall put away his wife, except it be
fornication, and shall marry another, committeth adultery*.   (II.329)

The word is "unfoulded" and the question is, exactly what word is it? What action does it name, the unfolding of an argument, of an explication, of a gloss, or the removal of glosses so that one can say of the text that it has been "unfoulded," that is, cleaned up? The latter is, of course, the action Milton has been claiming all along, as when he speaks of "restoring" the text (II.326), "dissolving tedious and *Gordian* difficulties" (II.340), of bringing to light the "pure" Law that "the undiscerning canonist" had "bescribbl'd with a thousand trifling impertinencies" (II.316), of clearing "the purity of God . . . from foulest imputations" (II.226). But if these and other phrases argue strongly for reading "unfoulding" as the act of removing interpretive debris, there is an equal pressure for the alternative reading in which to "unfould" is precisely to interpret and thereby to dilate, to enlarge on, to fill in, to add to, to supplement. Moreover, it is the alternative reading that describes the process of which this very moment in the text is a conclusion. Although his argument is impelled by the verse from Matthew, Milton never allows it to appear, knowing full well that were he simply to present it, it would be heard within the interpretive context assumed by his opponents. It has been his entire effort to dislodge that context, not so that the verse can be shown in its "native lustre," but so that he can establish another context in relation to which the meaning he desires the verse to have will seem inescapable. Here, thirty-six pages into a forty-eight page tract, he is betting that the new context has, in fact, been established, and therefore he risks displaying "the sentence it self that now follows." But, of course, the "sentence it self that now follows" is no longer the sentence *itself* (it never was), but is now the sentence as it is (must be) given the assumptions (about Christ's nature, God's intentions, and the proper way to respond to Pharisees) that Milton has so laboriously put into place. If the sentence is now "clear," as Milton asserts that it is in the same paragraph ("It being thus clear that the words of Christ can be no kind of command, as they are vulgarly taken"), its clarity is not really its own, but is the result of its having been overlain by commentary. The text is cleared – revealed in its "native lustre" – by being covered over with additional words; rather than being *un*covered, as Milton continues to claim, it has been *re*covered, rescued from the impertinence of previous "bescribblings" in order that it might receive (and take on the shape of) the "bescribblings" of Milton's explication. It becomes harder and harder to tell the difference between "unfoulding" and "unfolding" even as both the word (whatever it is) and the argument insist on it.

The difficulty, along with the ambiguous characterization of the tract as an action, has been present from the very beginning, and as early as the title, which, if we turn to it now, will seem less innocent than it might have at first:

THE DOCTRINE AND DISCIPLINE OF DIVORCE:
RESTOR'D TO THE GOOD OF BOTH SEXES
FROM THE BONDAGE OF CANON LAW, AND OTHER MISTAKES,

TO CHRISTIAN FREEDOM, GUIDED BY THE RULE OF CHARITY.
WHERIN ALSO MANY PLACES OF SCRIPTURE, HAVE RECOVER'D
THEIR LONG-LOST MEANING...

Here too is the double claim, the claim to be performing the minimal action of refurbishing and the claim (or admission) that the refurbishing is in fact constitutive of the form it supposedly conserves; and here too the double sense is carried by single words, by "restor'd" and "recover'd." To restore is either to return to an original state of self-identity, or to make good a loss (to re-store) in the sense of supplying a deficiency and thereby putting something in place of what once was; and in the same way, something that has been "recover'd" has either been returned to open and unobstructed view or dressed in new clothes, covered *again*.

Let me be clear about what I am claiming and not claiming. I am not claiming that these double meanings are to be regarded as the product of Milton's intention, that they appear in his text by design. To be sure this particular spelling of "unfoulded" occurs only here; elsewhere in the prose we find "unfolded." On the other side, however, in the poetry "unfould" and "unfold" appear in equal numbers and without any apparent pattern; at any rate, one might point out, "unfoulded" in the sense of removing encrustations is not even a word, and had Milton wanted to convey that sense he would have written "having thus unfouled." But had this been Milton's intention, "unfouled," which means "not yet soiled," would not have done the job since the meaning he would have wanted is "made pure after first having been soiled," and in order to achieve that meaning he might well have taken an existing word and altered it so as to suggest a two-stage (a fouling followed by an unfouling) procedure. In short, the evidence is inconclusive, but to repeat my disclaimer, I am not here interested in what it would be evidence of – Milton's intention. My thesis, rather, is that the possibility of reading words like "unfoulded," "recover'd" and "restor'd" in ways that go in contradictory directions – the directions of allowing the text to speak for itself, of elaborating or dilating the text into a new shape – is a localized instance of a contradiction that fissures the entire tract. Far from being a sign of Milton's intentional control, these and other moments are signs of the extent to which he is the site of intentions that pull against one another. On the one hand he is clearly desirous of loosening the constraints on divorce, and he knows that in order to accomplish this he must avail himself of the very interpretive skills he had earlier condemned; but on the other hand he is not yet able to accept the conclusion implied by the exercise of those skills, the conclusion that once textual authority no longer constrains the interpretive process, but is a matter of contest *within* that process, authority is ever decentered and never can be securely – once and for all – reclaimed. What Milton wants is at once to put the force of interpretation into play and to arrest that play the moment it produces the configuration he desires.

That is why in a tract that repeatedly proclaims the necessity of interpretation – "there is scarce any one saying in the Gospel, but must be read with limitations and distinctions, to be understood" (II.338) – he repeatedly attempts to shut it down. He attempts to shut it down first by identifying a verse – "I will make a helpmeet for him" – that is somehow exempt from the general rule and can be the basis of the plainness he denies to every other saying; later he attributes that same plainness to God's intention, although the plainness of that intention is belied by the exertions required to establish it; and in the last section of the tract, plainness – always invoked as a stay against interpretation's incursions – is said to reside in the "all interpretive rule" of charity. The rule of charity (really a version of the argument from intention) tells us that God would not require more of his creatures than they are able to perform, and therefore he would not require that they remain joined to unsuitable partners. But the rule fails as a constraint on interpretation in the same way that intention fails; for the question of what charity means is, like the question of God's intention, an interpretive one. There is nothing to prevent Milton's opponents either from defining charity differently – so that, for example, it would be charitable of God to enforce strict divorce laws because he would thus provoke men to more virtue than they would otherwise achieve – or from declaring that the "rule of charity" should not be extended to the issue of divorce because, Milton notwithstanding, it *is* within the capacities of fallen natures to make something valuable out of a less-than-perfect choice. In short, the "all-interpreting rule" of charity must itself be interpreted in order to be applied, and if it is interpreted once, then it can always be interpreted again.

It is these further turns of the interpretive screw that Milton seeks to preclude by doing, or claiming to have done, the interpretive job once and for all. When he declares that he has "don no every daies work in asserting the words of Christ," the suggestion is that the work is now complete and need never be supplemented; but the suggestion is undermined by his very success (if, for the sake of argument, we grant it to him); for if *he* has been able to "assert" Christ's words by embedding them in a constructed context of intelligibility (the context of Christ's relationship to the Pharisees), then someone who comes after him will be able (like those who came before him) to re-embed the same words (which, of course, are never the same) and assert them just as "plainly," but differently. When Milton declares that the "sincerity" and "true sense" of Christ's words have been recovered with the key of charity, he seems not to realize that once that key has opened the door, it can't be shut. It is because he does not or cannot see this that *The Doctrine and Discipline of Divorce* is at once so like and so unlike *Of Prelaticall Episcopacy*. In the earlier tract interpretation is closed down even before the (non)argument begins; the scriptures are not exposed even to anything so glancing as a look. In the later piece interpretation is supposedly licensed, but the license is withdrawn whenever it threatens the meanings Milton would privilege; the look the scriptures receive is long and full, but it is finally a gorgon's look, freezing, or attempting to freeze, what it sees so that no one will ever be able to see it in any other way. Like so many interpreters before and after him, Milton wants to crown his efforts by declaring – in opposition to the evidence provided by those efforts – that interpretation stops here.

V

It may seem that in turning the *Doctrine and Discipline of Divorce* into a tract about interpretation, I have slighted what are after all its major and explicit concerns, marriage and sexuality; but in fact the problematics of sex and interpretation, far from being disparate, are, at least in the context of Milton's concerns, one and the same. When he warns us in *Of Prelaticall Episcopacy* against admitting external authorities into our hearts and minds lest "we open a broad passage for a multitude of doctrines that have no ground in Scripture, to break in upon us" (1.651), the language is the same as that with which he urges the divorcing of an "Idolatresse . . . lest she should alienate his heart from the true worship of God."[20] In both instances an internal purity must be maintained by pushing away the defiling touch of something alien and unholy. In one case it is the touch of an impiously supplementing interpretation, in the other of an "enticing" woman who "allures [her husband] from the faith"; but finally this is a distinction without a difference, for as Milton points out, the important thing is that in the end "God . . . loses him a servant." In both tracts the central image is of a vessel already informed by or "dedicate"[21] to God, a self-sufficient text on the one hand, a person "full of praise and thanksgiving" on the other, and in both the integrity of the vessel is threatened by a force that would first breach its boundaries and then scatter its contents, thereby robbing it of its potency. In *Of Prelaticall Episcopacy* that force is called "supplementing" or "adding," while in *The Doctrine and Discipline of Divorce*, it is called, simply, woman; structurally, "woman" and "interpretation" are one and the same, alike secondary to a purity that will be compromised if they are admitted into its holy place. Once commentary invades the fortress of the scripture and mixes with its substance, that substance is hopelessly adulterated; once the fortress of the "dedicate" soul opens itself up to female enticements, its manly vigor is dissipated and the firmness of its faith may be lost forever.

In making this equation between the dangers of interpretation and of pollution by women, Milton does nothing new; he merely avails himself of various strains in an established misogynist tradition, one that has already appropriated and marked the very texts on which his argument depends. Howard Bloch cites Philo Judaeus on the designation of woman as a helpmeet made *after* and in the service of man: "the helper is a created one for it says 'Let us make a helper for him'; and . . . is subsequent to him who is to be helped, for He had formed the mind before and is about to form its helper."[22]

"Thus," Bloch concludes, "woman, created from man, is conceived from the beginning to be secondary, a supplement," and as a supplement she must be kept in her place and not be allowed to substitute her own authority for the higher authority to which she is naturally subservient. This is of course exactly the vocabulary in which Milton declares the superfluousness and impiety of "additions" to the "pure and living precept of *Gods* word" (1.652). "What ever is plastered on is the devil's work," thunders Tertullian. "To superinduce on a divine work Satan's ingenuities, how criminal it is."[23] Whether the divine work be the pure word or the heart of a man wholly (purely) bent on serving God, the imperative is the same: that which is essential and prior must keep itself separate from that which is secondary and supplementary or risk the loss of its identity.

The extent to which this "Nazarite" way of thinking informs Milton can be seen in this passage from *The Reason of Church-Government*. The subject is the "reverence" men should bear "to their own persons":

> And if the love of God as a fire sent from Heaven to be kept ever alive upon the altar of our hearts, be the first principle of all godly and vertuous actions in men, this pious and just honouring of ourselves is the second, and may be thought of as the radical moisture and fountain head, whence every laudable and worthy enterprize issues forth. And although I have giv'n it the name of a liquid thing, yet it is not incontinent to bound itself as humid things are, but hath in it a most restraining and powerful abstinence to start back, and globe it self upward from the mixture of any ungenerous and unbeseeming motion, or any soile wherewith it may peril to stain itself.   (1.842)

The "liquid thing" of which Milton admits to speaking metaphorically is in fact a quite literal reference to sperm, which he identifies in the second edition of *The Doctrine and Discipline of Divorce* as "the best substance of [man's] body, and of his soul too," a substance that one must not improvidently "pay out" (II.271). The man who "starts back" from mixture and refuses to spend the "radical moisture" of his "fountainhead" remains in a "filial relation with God," while the man who gives himself up to an "unbeseeming motion" – either by leaving the Bible to "gadder after" supplements or by allowing a woman to "delay [his] duty to religion" (II.262–3) – exchanges that relation for marriage to an inferior, either in the form of a commentary that comes after or of a creature who is "subsequent." In *Of Prelaticall Episcopacy* the sign of one's fidelity to God is a virgin text, one that has not been opened up (and therefore emptied) by interpretation; in *The Doctrine and Discipline of Divorce* the sign of one's fidelity to God is a virgin marriage or the marriage of a virgin, of a man who keeps the proper distance from a helpmeet who must be prevented from breaking up the (male) union of a man and his Creator.

In the conflicted economy of *The Doctrine and Discipline of Divorce*, the notion of a helpmeet occupies the same structural (and ambiguous) position as does the notion of interpretation: both are at once valorized and resisted. The admission that the scripture must indeed be "eked out" by interpretation is precisely paralleled by the acknowledgment that man is radically incomplete and requires the supplement of a helpmeet; the introduction of interpretation as an activity *constitutive* of authority is accompanied by – is indeed the same thing as – the introduction of woman as a piecing-up of male imperfection. But while this notion of a "unity defective" that requires the remedy of "collateral love" is embraced by Milton in *Paradise Lost* (*PL* VIII.426–7), here in the divorce tracts he draws back from it by repeatedly subordinating the helpmeet to a masculine interiority that is no less a closed fortress than the text he is supposedly opening up. But of course he is *not* opening it up, or rather, after having opened it up (with the "help-meet" verse as his wedge) he moves to close it down again by claiming that all he has done is let the (still self-sufficient) text speak for itself. In both contexts – the context of interpretive theory and the context of marital politics – the promise of liberation (from "obstinate literality" and Pharisaical rigidity respectively) is not redeemed, as Milton moves, despite his pronouncements to the contrary, to re-impose the authority he was on the verge of decentering.

The result is an argument that is everywhere divided against itself (in a state, one might say, of divorce), always moving in a direction from which it is at the same time recoiling; moving toward interpretive freedom, yet reserving that freedom to itself, urging a generous (charitable) flexibility in marital relationships, yet reserving that flexibility for only one of the partners so that he can better preserve his status as a separate and inviolate being. ("If they . . . seduce us from the worship of God" we must respond with nothing "lesse than a totall and finall separation" (II.263).) And always the interpretive and sexual issues are indissolubly entwined: interpretive fecundity is finally refused for the same reason that the helpmeet must be prevented from helping too much, in order to keep the lines of authority firmly in place. Milton is no more willing to share the interpretive franchise than he is willing to share the government of a household; rigid boundaries – of interpretive procedure and marital relations – are denounced only until they can be re-established in a new form of patriarchy; the claims of the (female) body are acknowledged only so that after having been satisfied the (masculine) mind will once again be free to exercise its sway. Again and again, on every level (of structure, theme, imagery, argument) a self-sufficient and self-propagating male unity – of person and text – is defended against the encroachments of difference, woman, sexuality, interpretation, all forces that Milton has himself set in motion, but forces he feels compelled to deny when their subversive threat comes too close to home.

It has become a commonplace to note these contradictions in the divorce tracts and to attribute them to Milton's "deeply masculinist assumptions."[24] It is said (by Mary Nyquist, James Turner, Stephen Fallon, and others)[25] that these assumptions war with Milton's more radical sympathies, and that, at least in the case of the divorce tracts, radical sympathies lose out. There is more than a little to be said for this view of the matter, but I find it limited by its origins in a left criticism that offers us the dispiriting alternative of either chastising Milton for his bourgeois-capitalist sins or praising him for having foregrounded the tensions and fissures in an ideology from which he was unable to extricate himself. David Aers and Bob Hodge are, I think, closer to the truth when they observe that despite his gestures in the direction of mutuality and the decentering of authority and power, Milton "still deeply feared and resisted the dissolution of the ego."[26] Aers and Hodge term this a paradox, but if it is one it is hardly attached to a particular ideology or set of assumptions, masculinist or any other. The question is a perennial one, and it is posed by Belial when he asks, "who would lose, / Though full of pain, this intellectual being / Those thoughts that wander through Eternity, / To perish rather, swallow'd up and lost?" (*PL* II.146–9). One answer is that Milton would, at least at those times when he expresses a desire to lose himself in a union with deity: to join a heavenly choir in which no single voice is heard and one's identity (exactly the wrong word) is relational, conferred by the community (of saints) that defines the shape of action; to march in a perfect cube, in a configuration that prevents any one person from standing out, from being i-dentified, except as a component of a structure that gives him a being he cannot claim as *his own*. "I conceived myself," he declares in *An Apology*, "to be not now as mine own person, but as a member incorporate into that truth whereof I was perswaded" (1.871). It is a conception to which Milton returns often but this very formulation of it betrays the difficulty he can never remove: "conceiving" is itself an action of the consciousness that seeks its own absorption, and therefore to conceive oneself as a member incorporate is to have measured and thereby reinstituted one's distance from the state (of non-appearance) so conceived. Milton wants two contradictory things: he wants (in Aers' and Hodge's words) to dissolve his ego, and he wants to be the one (the ego) that announces and performs the dissolving; he at once seeks and resists dissolution; or rather, *in* seeking it, he is also (and necessarily) resisting it. "Who can think submission?" asks Satan (*PL* 1.661), a question that is precise in its articulation of a requirement that cannot be met. One can think *about* submission all day long, but with every thought submission will once again have been deferred; it is simply not possible to affirm the diacritical nature of one's being without betraying that affirmation in the very act of producing it.

This is the dilemma to which Milton's entire career is a response, a dilemma that informs and structures his consideration of every issue he confronts. One sees it in the *Nativity Ode* when the wish to "join his voice unto the angel choir" and thereby "lose ... this intellectual being" is accompanied by the need to be the "first" (l. 26) to do so, that is, to do so pre-eminently. One sees it in *Lycidas* when the first person voice struggles against the traditions that claim to have already spoken him. One sees it in *Paradise Lost* when the prospect of merging in an undifferentiated union with a God who shall be "all in all" (III.341) turns into the horror of a uni-verse in which all distinctions will have been effaced and the landscape will be reduced to a "universal blanc" (III.48). And one sees it here, in *Of Prelaticall Episcopacy* and *The Doctrine and Discipline of Divorce*, when the scattering touch of interpreta-tion and woman is at once courted and pushed away.

In saying this my intention is not to slight the historical nature of Milton's concerns, but merely to point out that they come to him already structured by habits of thought that persist through every vicissitude of his literary and political life. Surely the divorce tracts are about divorce, and surely in the early 1640s the issue of divorce is intimately related to debates about domestic and political authority that will lead in a few years to the execution of a king. But if one is interested, as I am, in the source of the energy that makes Milton's writing (on every subject) so powerful, that source will be found not in the historical particulars to which he responds – and responds in a way wholly committed – but in the abiding (although not transcendental) obses-sions of which his various and occasional responses are the transformations.[27] This is not to say that Milton's work is everywhere the same, only to suggest that the differences (some of which have been noted here) between his productions can perhaps be best understood as differences in the ways in which he manages, or avoids, or makes capital of, the anxieties to which his self-divided ambition – to lose his voice and to celebrate that loss ("my adventurous Song, / That with no middle flight intends to soar / Above th' Aonian Mount") – makes him subject, or, rather makes of him the kind of subject he is, forever split between the desire for absorption into deity and the desire to experience (and record) that desire as no one before him ever has.

Notes

1 *The Reason of Church Government*, CPW, 1.757.
2 Jacques Derrida, *Grammatology*, trans. Gayatri Spivak (Baltimore, 1976), p. 35.
3 Jacques Derrida, *Speech and Phenomena*, trans. David Allison (Evanston, 1973), p. 87.
4 *Grammatology*, p. 145.
5 *Speech and Phenomena*, p. 87.
6 *Ibid.*, p. 147.
7 *Ibid.*, p. 159.
8 *Grammatology*, p. 20.
9 Jacques Derrida, *Positions* (Chicago, 1981), p. 6.
10 As Thomas Kranidas puts it, in the only other full discussion of the tract, "the battle is won in the first twenty lines." "Words, Words, Words, and the Word:

Milton's *Of Prelaticall Episcopacy,*" *Milton Studies*, 16, ed. James D. Simmons (1982), p. 154.

11 Donald Davie, "Syntax and Music in *Paradise Lost*," in *The Living Milton*, ed. Frank Kermode (London, 1960), p. 84.

12 K. G. Hamilton, "Structure of Milton's Prose," in *Language and Style in Milton*, ed. R. Emma and J. Shawcross (New York, 1967), p. 329.

13 *Grammatology*, p. 106.

14 Arthur Barker, *Milton and the Puritan Dilemma* (Toronto, 1942), p. 71.

15 *Of Reformation*, in *CPW*, 1.568, 566.

16 In the *Divorce Tracts* the notion of "intention" acquires a new prominence in Milton's writing. Not only does it appear more frequently, but its appearances are more closely tied to interpretive issues.

17 In the *Christian Doctrine* Milton often begins a chain of reasoning by saying that we must "imagine nothing unworthy of God," and he often dismisses a position by decrying the image of God it implies. See *CPW*, VI.160, 177; Columbia edn XIV.72–4, 108.

18 *The Reason of Church Government*, *CPW*, 1.827.

19 *Areopagitica*, *CPW*, II.529.

20 *CPW*, II.260.

21 *Ibid.*, p. 259.

22 Philo Judaeus, *On the Creation* (London, 1929), p. 227, cited in H. Bloch, "Medieval Misogyny," *Representations*, 20 (1987), p. 10.

23 Tertullian, "On the Apparel of Women," cited in Bloch, *op. cit.*, p. 13.

24 Mary Nyquist, "The Genesis of Gendered Subjectivity in the Divorce Tracts and in *Paradise Lost*," in *Re-membering Milton*, ed. Mary Nyquist and Margaret W. Ferguson (New York and London, 1987), p. 106.

25 See James G. Turner, *One Flesh: Paradisal Marriage and Sexual Relations in the Age of Milton* (Oxford, 1987), pp. 188–229. See also Stephen Fallon, "The Metaphysics of Milton's Divorce Tracts," chapter 3 below.

26 David Aers and Bob Hodge, " 'Rational Burning': Milton on Sex and Marriage," in *Milton Studies*, 13 (1979), p. 19.

27 In their introduction to this volume, the editors suggest that I am here arguing for the timelessness of Milton's concerns, but as my parenthesis "(not transcendental)" indicates, I am talking about a structure of concerns that is historical, limited to the duration of Milton's life. Surely there can be nothing ahistorical in asserting as a thesis (which one might refute) the pervasiveness in a man's work of certain themes and conflicts. There are many ways to be historical, and one should be wary of labeling as ahistorical the analyses of those who offer a history different from one's own.

3

The metaphysics of Milton's divorce tracts

STEPHEN M. FALLON

For some time readers have seen the divorce tracts as pivotal works in which Milton redefines his thoughts on Christian liberty, freedom of the will, and church government, but they also reveal Milton experimenting with an early and not fully rationalized version of the monism informing *De Doctrina Christiana* and *Paradise Lost*.[1] While contemporary marriage-theorists write of the importance of companionship as well as of procreation and the marriage debt, Milton alone closely anatomizes the interrelationship of spirit and body, and alone argues that a union of minds is *essential* to the couple's becoming one flesh, a process that others describe in purely physical and sexual terms. The uniqueness of this position is evidenced by its absence not only from the tracts of Milton's contemporaries, but also and more significantly from Milton's own *Judgement of Martin Bucer*, a translation of writings on divorce that most closely mirror his own. Conventional body/spirit dualism and a monism anticipating the mature Milton's are juxtaposed and held in tension in the divorce tracts, and the dissonance between competing metaphysical systems threatens to break the harmony of the works. Recently, James Turner has discerned in the Milton of the divorce tracts both a moralist who "reinforced" the separation of "mental states and physical phenomena" and a natural philosopher who "entertained a more unified vision of mind and body"; Turner argues that Milton is "torn between materialist monism and hierarchic dualism."[2] I would modify this reading by suggesting that much of the dualism of the tracts is conscious and strategic, and that Milton, in his own mind, is less torn between monism and dualism than he is intent on separating his audience into wise monists and blind dualists. Milton invokes dualism to blast his contemporaries for acknowledging the body before the spirit in marriage; he invokes monism to hold out to the godly the prospect of an ideal sexual life. What might look like a failure in metaphysical consistency is a strategy for separating truth from error, a strategy, it turns out, modeled on the teaching practice of Christ as interpreted in the *Doctrine and Discipline of Divorce* and *Tetrachordon*.

Rhetorical practice mirrors theme in the divorce tracts. Dichotomies proliferate: body/soul, fault/blamelessness, necessity/freedom, grunting Barrow/gentle spirit, and so on. Writing about marriage and divorce, Milton relies upon union and separation. Milton the marrier unites body and spirit into one substance, and treats doctrinal and moral offense as aspects of a single error. Milton the divorcer, like the God of *Paradise Lost* and the *Doctrine and Discipline*, creates order by separation, by circumscribing a world for gentle, wise, and monist individuals and setting it apart from the chaos of disordered dualism. But in this last step lie the seeds of a radical instability in the tracts that measures the distance between Milton and his God as divorcing creators. Dualism resists being domesticated as a teaching strategy to counter monism; its own internal opposition of body and spirit threatens to reinvade the preserve of monism. The end of this essay will explore the traces of this surplus of divorcive energy in Milton's endeavors to "fadge together" in his tracts antipathetic arguments that, like individuals separated by "natural antipathies," refuse to be married.

I Strategic dualism

At first glance, the divorce tracts seem aggressively dualistic, intent on reordering mistaken priorities and placing the claims of the separable spirit over the claims of the body. Insisting that marriage properly is a union of fit minds rather than a conjunction of bodies, Milton attacks the inversion of the priority between mind and body institutionalized in the canon and English church law, which allowed for divorce only in cases of adultery, impotence, frigidity, and consanguinity. He remarks that marriage and "all human society must proceed from the mind rather than the body, els it would be but a kind of animal or beastish meeting," and he faults current definitions of marriage for placing the fitness of minds "beneath the formalities and respects of the body, to make it a servant of its own vassall" (II.275, 598). Physical desire hands us over to inner servitude or necessity; in the absence of love sexual need is a "bestial necessity" (II.259–60).

Milton's anxiety about the loss of freedom that he perceives in sexual desire accounts in part for a trait of his biblical hermeneutics described by Turner, the reading *into* rather than *out of* the text (*One Flesh*, p. v). The most obvious example from the tracts is Milton's reading of Paul's concession to physical desire ("it is better to marry than to be aflame with passion" [1 Cor. 7:9]) as a reference to a "rationall burning" for union with a "fit conversing soul" (II.251). This reading, in the light of the sexual horror palpable in the tracts, suggests Milton's flirtation with the idea of virgin marriage. He acknowledges in passing the possibility of a healthy though rarely or never consummated marriage: "where the minde and person pleases aptly, there some unaccomplishment of the bodies delight may be better born with, then when the minde hangs off in an unclosing disproportion, though the body be as it ought" (II.246). What began as an attempt to reorder the claims of mind and body comes to look like a retreat from the body, and a repudiation of sensuality.

Despite this strident and dualist attack on sexuality, we are given brief and incomplete indications of a more balanced view. Milton acknowledges the need for sexual release even among the godly, and criticizes St. Augustine and other fathers "who were much tak'n with a preposterous admiration of single life" (II.448); he calls the Catholic command of priestly celibacy a "diabolicall sin" and an affront to man's nature (II.595). More significant than the grudging admissions that sexuality is an unavoidable part of human nature are hints at a redeemed sex life for the godly. Milton suggests that a proper union of minds can lead to a better sex life: "the deed of procreation . . . it self soon cloies, and is despis'd, unless it bee cherisht and re-incited with a pleasing conversation" (II.740).

The conflict of perspectives on sexuality in the tracts does not betray incoherence; rather it results inevitably from Milton's decision to address two audiences. Earlier, in *The Reason of Church-Government*, Milton had divided his countrymen into those whose desires had been corrupted, on the one hand, and the "gentler sort," to whom he directs his autobiographical narrative (I.802, 808). Now he divides his countrymen but addresses both: conventional, unreflective persons are dualists, who find food for the soul outside of marriage and food for the body within marriage; unconventional men, almost invariably labeled "gentle," are monists, for whom there can be no merely physical sexual life. Milton will reorder dualism for the benefit of "grunting Barrows," but to "persons of gentle breeding" he will demonstrate that the claims of the body and soul are inseparable (II.747).

Milton ascribes to his opponents the "crabbed opinion" of Augustine that God would have given Adam a male companion if marriage had been instituted for intellectual companionship rather than procreation (II.596). This view, in Milton's eyes, erroneously divorces the bodily and the spiritual. He elliptically suggests the dualist nature of this error in the dedicatory letter to *Tetrachordon*, by associating the opponents of his views on divorce with ultra-dualistic Gnostics (II.579). He dismisses his opponents' focus on the body:

> As for those who still rudely urge it no loss to mariage, no desertion,
> so long as the flesh is present and offers a benevolence that hates, or is
> justly hated, I am not of that vulgar and low perswasion, to thinke
> such forc'd embracements as these worth the honour, or the humanity
> of mariage, but farre beneath the soul of a rational and free-borne
> man. (II.692)

Marriage, an institution of God, cannot be defined in purely physical terms, because purely physical relations are unknown to the gentle individual. Where there is no union of minds, "there all corporall delight will soon become unsavoury and contemptible" (II.246). This forced yoking is insupportable to the "gentle" spirit, who senses that sexual relations touch the soul as well as the body, and that loveless sexual relations brutalize and corporealize the soul. When there is no union of minds in marriage, all that is left is

> a displeasing and forc't remedy against the sting of a brute desire;
> which fleshly accustoming without the souls union and commixture of
> intellectual delight, as it is rather a soiling then a fulfilling of mariage-
> rites, so it is anough to imbase the mettle of a generous spirit, and sink
> him to a low and vulgar pitch of endeavour in all his actions, or,
> which is wors, leavs him in a dispairing plight of abject and hard'n'd
> thoughts.   (II.339)

As Milton discusses the plight of the gentle soul, the terms relating to body and soul interpenetrate. The "imbased mettle" of the soul and the "hardened thoughts" are more than metaphorical in a monistic world; the "soil" here and in a later reference to the "soiling" of souls (II.619) might suggest not only abstract stain but gross corporeal materialization.[3] When it finds no mutual love at home, "the *soule* wanders after that satisfaction which it had hope to find at home" (II.269; my italics). The interpenetration of terms climaxes in the suggestion that the soul is expended with the semen; it "is the most injurious and unnaturall tribute that can be extorted from a person endew'd with reason, to be made to pay out the best substance of his body, and of his soul too, as some think, when either for just and powerful causes he cannot like" (II.271). With the paying out of the soul, the individual is threatened with bestialization and loss of identity.

Given the ascetic polemic against the body and the insistence on the importance of spiritual union, Irene Samuel's judgment that the tracts are informed by a "Platonic dichotomy of the world into two realms," the material and the spiritual, is explicable; in light of the monist suggestions of the inseparability of body and spirit, however, it is inadequate.[4] While Milton writes dualism into his text, he imputes it as a scandal to his opponents. The strategy of dividing the audience into the fit and the unfit (and accommodating the teaching accordingly) that I am ascribing to Milton here is one that Milton, in his discussion of Matthew 5:31–2, ascribes to Christ. Christ's prohibition of divorce except in the case of adultery should be regarded, Milton writes, as directed only to the Pharisees. These men, who misinterpreted the Mosaic law of divorce in Deuteronomy in order to put away their wives for trivial reasons, are answered according to their evil life, and to their aim of tempting Christ:

> The occasion which induc't our Saviour to speak of divorce, was either
> to convince the extravagance of the Pharises in that point, or to give a
> sharp and vehement answer to a tempting question. And in such cases
> that we are not to repose all upon the literall terms of so many words,
> many instances will teach us: Wherin we may plainly discover how

> Christ meant not to be tak'n word for word, but like a wise Physician, administring one excesse against another to reduce us to a perfect mean. (II.282–3)

Milton argues similarly in *Tetrachordon*:

> No other end therefore can bee left imaginable of this excessive restraint, but to bridle those erroneous and licentious ... Pharises; not by telling them what may bee done in necessity, but what censure they deserve who divorce abusively ... And as the offence was in one extreme, so the rebuke, to bring more efficaciously to a rectitude and mediocrity, stands not in the middle way of duty, but in the other extreme. (II.668)

There are two audiences for Christ's teaching on divorce, the tempting Pharisees on the mountain in Galilee, and the wise and godly man instructed by the Spirit and represented by Milton himself. Milton, for his part, also writes to two audiences. Like Christ, he is a physician "administring one excesse against another." The extreme deference to the body over the mind in English church teaching on divorce is countered with the extreme denigration of body and emphasis on aphysical spiritual union. But for those who have eyes to see and ears to hear (and skin to touch?), Milton offers quietly and briefly an indication of the godly joy of sex (see, for example, II.597). In metaphysical terms, the "perfect mean" between the two "excesses" of disordered and reordered dualisms is monism; the disintegration of body and spirit that characterizes each extreme represents false consciousness. Milton imitates Christ by accommodating his teaching to those entrenched in dualism. The dead body of the dualist answers to the "dead letter" of the Pharisee (II.588). As the letter of the Bible cannot without disaster be separated from the spirit of charity, so the body and spirit of man cannot be separated. The monism of the mature Milton is nascent in the tracts of 1643–5.

II Monism and metaphor

The battle between monist and dualist perspectives can be followed in Milton's metaphors, which point to the inseparability of body and spirit, and animalize those who attempt to separate them and grant priority to the body. Milton carries this animalization to an extreme in *Colasterion*; his opponent is a "Pork," a "mongrel," who argues "like a Boar in a vinyard, doing nought els, but still as hee goes, champing and chewing over, what I could mean by this *Chimera* of a fit conversing soul, notions and words never made for those chopps" (II.737, 757, 747). Milton continues the animalization of his opponents in his second sonnet on the reception of *Tetrachordon*, "I did but prompt the age to quit their clogs," rhyming "Dogs," "Frogs," and "Hogs" with the initial line, and throwing in "Owls and Cuckoos, Asses, [and] Apes" for good measure.

The attempt to separate body from spirit is absurd from a monist point of view; it results paradoxically in the despiritualization of the one substance. If there is only one substance, and if body is conceived as separate from spirit, then the body must be dead and spiritless. "Who," Milton asks in *Tetrachordon*, "that is not himselfe a meer body, can restrain all the unfitnes of mariage only to a corporal defect?" (II.711). The answer will be those like the "Pork" of *Colasterion*. And while Milton exploits the emotive force of this bestial characterization, he hints in a deceptively simple passage of *Tetrachordon* that these "meer bodies" are below animals: "the Soul as much excells the body, as the outward man excells the Ass and more; for that *animal* is yet a living creature, perfet in it self; but the body without the Soul is a meer senseles trunck" (II.624). The "outward man" or body excels the ass as we begin, but it is inferior to the ass as we conclude. To be a meer body is to be dead and senseless, to be a despiritualized lump. This passage, with its opposition of soul and body, is rooted in the dualism that Milton is in the process of questioning in the divorce tracts. But lest it seem an uncomplicated affirmation of dualism, we should note its echoes in a passage from *De Doctrina Christiana*, written after his unambiguous commitment to monism: "Where 'body' is spoken of as a merely physical trunk [*truncus*], 'soul' [*anima*] may mean either the spirit [*spiritus*] or its secondary faculties, such as the vital or sensitive faculty" (VI.318; XV.40; I have modified Carey's translation). On the same page appears Milton's affirmation that man is "not, as is commonly thought, produced from and composed of two different and distinct elements, soul and body. On the contrary, the whole man is the soul, and the soul the man: a body, in other words, an individual substance, animated, sensitive, and rational." Milton struggles here, as we must struggle, to articulate a monist conception of human nature with a vocabulary colored by dualism. If all substance is both vital and tangible inseparably, it can nevertheless be spoken of as one or the other in turn.

Milton picks up on the conception of the dead and senseless mere body when he describes the Answerer as a "fleamy clodd" (II.740). The vital spirits are refined from the blood, one of the two elements missing from this combination of phlegm and earth. Interestingly, the terms of this denunciation echo precisely a description of the errant wife: the virtuous man can find himself "bound fast to an uncomplying discord of nature, or, *as it oft happens, to an image of earth and fleam*" (II.254; my italics). The conflation of errant wife and controversial opponent suggested by this juxtaposition of images is typical of the tracts, as the rage directed against the wife echoes the rage against the opponents. In any event, the wife, like the Answerer, is dismissed by implication as a mere body; in the *Doctrine and Discipline* she is a "mute and spiritles mate" (II.251).[5]

It is also significant that the unfit wife is an "*image* of earth and fleam."

Milton, who would attempt to shatter the king's image at the end of the decade, peels away the image of the wife in the tracts.[6] Behind the image of the errant wife lie alternative possibilities: 1) a repulsive and diseased interior and 2) emptiness. The first possibility, which anticipates Sin in *Paradise Lost*, has been anatomized by Turner (*One Flesh*, pp. 194–203). My interest here lies in the second possibility, the image as veil of nothingness, which gives rise in the tracts to a series of metaphors having in common outsides-without-insides, metaphors that press upon us the metaphysical implications of the metaphorical mode. If in metaphor a physical sign points to an immaterial signified, then from the monist perspective every object is metaphorical, because external manifestation and internal significance are inseparable (or looked at another way there can be no metaphor, because the ontological distance required for its two-termed relations disappears). Milton's metaphors of outsides-without-insides embody the monist's view of dualist matter: dead, inert, cut off from its vivifying force. Behind the "veile" of the "appearance of modesty" in a virgin, a husband may find, "if not a body impenetrable," a mind "uselesse and almost liveles" (II.250). The "liveles" mind is almost no mind at all; one can penetrate the body, but one will find it empty. More to the point, a marriage without union of minds is "but the empty husk of an outside matrimony" and "the meer carcas of a Mariage" (II.256, 603). Again, these veils, husks, and carcasses might seem to be the metaphors of a dualist, rather than metaphors attacking dualism. But that even the monist Milton thinks still in terms of outsides and insides is evident from his emphasis in *Paradise Lost* on the "paradise within." The Father's comment to Adam that in naming the animals Adam has expressed "well the *spirit within* thee free" is typical of Milton's usage of the image of interiority for spirit despite his monism (VIII.440; my italics).[7] Lady Anne Conway, a neglected philosopher whose *Principles of the Most Ancient and Modern Philosophy* influenced Leibniz and offers the closest contemporary analogue to Milton's vitalist monism, argues against the dualists that "a Body is nothing but a fixed and condensed Spirit, and a Spirit nothing but a subtile and volatile Body."[8] Conway attacks Hobbes' substance as well as Cartesian *res extensa*, charging that Hobbes and Descartes

> have never proceeded beyond the Husk or Shell, nor ever reached the Kernel, they only touch the Superficies never discerning the Centre, they were plainly ignorant of the noblest and most excellent Attributes of that Substance which they call Body and Matter, and understood nothing of them. (p. 225)

These attributes, according to Conway, are "Spirit, or Life, and Light." Conway helps to unravel the paradox of Milton's images of outsides without insides. For the monist, the one substance is both outside and inside; it is only those who attempt to separate body and spirit who create the illusion of a "mere body."

The most striking image of an outside without an inside comes in the allegory of Error and Custom in the letter prefacing the second version of the *Doctrine and Discipline*. Custom, a "meer face," "count'nances" Error, a "blind and Serpentine body without a head" (II.223). The Yale editor notes a resemblance to Spenser's Error here, but it recalls as well Spenser's Orgoglio, a puffed up and empty bladder, and False Florimell, a form without interior substance. Like a bad marriage, which Milton elsewhere calls "a most unreal nullity... a daring phantasm, a meer toy of terror" (II.666–7), the monster is all show and no substance. Another notable "image" in the divorce tracts is the cloud given to Ixion by Jupiter in place of Juno, which gave him "a monstrous issue... the fruits of a delusive marriage" (II.597). The renounced interiors of the metaphors of outsides-without-insides resurface as metaphors of insubstantiality. The cloud given to Ixion and the "unreal nullity" and "daring phantasm" of a bad marriage shimmer in the tracts like the separated spirits of the dualist, spirits that have left behind in their flight hard crusts and "empty husks." The dualist barters his living body and substantial soul for a hardened, lifeless body and an insubstantial soul. In place of and opposed to these images of outsides-without-insides and of phantoms, Milton constructs images of Truth in which inside and outside are inextricably involved. As Custom provides a face for Error, so Milton, with his unconventional argument, will be the face of "discount'nanc't truth" (II.224). On the same page of the letter to Parliament, truth is both a mother and child, both a womb and that which is born from the womb. The womb is both the inside of the woman and the outside that contains the child.[9] If we can place the two metaphors together, truth is the solid interior of the living exterior. Yet, in apparent opposition to these gestative metaphors, truth is something intangible: "Truth is as impossible to be soil'd by any outward touch, as the Sun beam" (II.225). It is simultaneously body, interior of the body, and incorporeal substance; the divisions cherished by the dualist are obliterated in the figurative economy of the letter. In metaphors such as these, we can witness Milton working intuitively toward the monism that he will lay out discursively in *De Doctrina Christiana*.

Sexual relations in a fit marriage, like the metaphors for truth in the letter prefacing the *Doctrine and Discipline*, involve a seamless interpenetration of inner and outer. The gentle spirit might not place priority in marriage on genital union, but he can achieve greater intimacy than the crude dualist. In *Colasterion* Milton writes that the "*Metaphorical* union of two bodies into one flesh, cannot bee likn'd in all things to... that natural union of soul and body into one person" (II.734). The loveless but sexually active couple "grind in the mill of an undelighted and servil copulation" (II.258); with this metaphor Milton suggests that such relations amount not to a union of bodies but to a friction of surfaces. To overcome this impediment to bodily union Milton offers his own metaphysics of sexuality, which can be pieced together from the tracts. The union of minds is more than metaphorical. He writes in

Tetrachordon that "the unity of minde is neerer and greater then the union of bodies" (II.606). The union of minds can be taken as generating a true union of bodies:

> Wee know that flesh can neither joyn, nor keep together two bodies *of it self*; what is it then must make them one flesh, but likenes, but fitnes of mind and disposition, which *may breed a Spirit of concord*, and union between them. (II.605; my italics)

The child of a fit couple is a "Spirit of concord," a spirit that fills the husk and enlivens the carcass of an otherwise empty matrimony. This "Spirit" can help us to gloss the enigmatic claim in the *Doctrine and Discipline* that "the fit union of their souls be such as may even incorporate them to love and amity" (II.326). The spirit of concord is incorporated, made flesh, in the sexual union of the fit couple.

While it is one of the inescapable and disturbing facts about the divorce tracts that Milton does not seem concerned about and indeed rarely mentions children, the issue of procreation is not so much ignored as displaced. The birth of the spirit of concord can be read as a metaphysical obstetrics. A similar expropriation of gestation and birth informs the metaphors of the truth as womb and as newborn. One might add Milton's constant invocation of persons of "gentle breeding," with the emphasis on the second word. On the other hand, Error/Custom produces only flatulence, and Ixion's cloud only "a monstrous issue."

III Residual dualism

As I remarked at the outset, strategy echoes theme in the divorce tracts, which proceed by a process of separation or divorce and commingling or union. Despite the show of dualism in arguing for marriage as a union of spirits rather than bodies, the tracts insist on the union of body and spirit. Like Christ in Matthew, Milton divides his audience; like God in Genesis, Milton has created order by separating antipathies. But Milton is not God. Even readers sympathetic with what they perceive as Milton's modern and liberal sentiments on marriage cannot avoid recognizing the instability of Milton's arguments. He brings together in his tracts antithetical arguments that refuse to be reconciled, and the fault line between these arguments threatens to wrench apart the painfully constructed order of the tracts.

As noted earlier, the monism of the divorce tracts is marshalled against what Milton perceived as the enthrallment of the spirit to physical desire. When body is treated as separate from the soul, it inexorably destroys a man's freedom. A man married to an unsuitable wife seeks sex in his own bed or another's under the compulsion of what Milton calls with punning force "a prone and savage necessity" (II.733). Enslavement to unfit marriage is interchangeable with enslavement to the woman and to the body. Milton invokes his new conception of Christian liberty to untie all of these knots.[10] The man transformed in a good marriage is free from the letter of the law in that he follows willingly the prime institution of marriage (Milton bridled at the suggestion that this position allied him with the Antinomians [II.749–50]). In a fit marriage, the godly husband is no longer enthralled to a wife but joined "in conjugall fellowship [with] a fit conversing soul," with whom he freely shares "the mystery of joy and union" (II.251, 258). Milton hints at a kind of Christian liberty of sexuality through which one desires what one rationally should desire, instead of being compelled to satisfy brutish instincts.

Although the gentle spirit can find freedom in union with a fit mate, the fitness of the match lies beyond the control of either spouse, depending as it does on their immutable natures. Ironically, the monism that delivered Milton from the "prone and savage necessity" delivers men over to a different kind of necessity. Now that the distance between body and soul has been collapsed, humoral physiology in part determines whether one can love or not. Love is subject to "the venerable and secret power of natures impression" (II.238). If antipathies are founded in "natures unalterable" or "the immutable bent of nature" (II.249, 328), then nothing one can do will foster mutual love and thus true marriage. The immutability of natures is one of the most insistent themes in the tracts. In *Paradise Lost*, by which time Milton has come to repudiate the kind of necessity he introduces here, the outer man expresses the inner man, but there is no indication that the outer man determines the inner. In the divorce tracts, one is subject to one's own humoral "bent of nature." Milton objects to the Answerer's sarcastic suggestion that diet and medication could right the discord of humors in a failed marriage, not because he does not think love subject to the humors, but because the medical technology is inadequate (II.737). He scorns the stupidity of forcing love against nature: "what folly is it still to stand combating and battering against *invincible causes and effects*" (II.272; my italics). We might as easily force digestion as attempt to love where nature bids hate (II.605–6). Milton's wavering between liberty and necessity is illustrated by his conflicting claims: on the one hand, sexual appetite can be controlled by diet and exercise; on the other hand, one must be "supernaturally gifted" to live a celibate life; even godly men will be forced to find sexual satisfaction if frustrated at home (II.251, 269, 595).

Milton uncharacteristically embraces determinism in an attempt to shield those seeking divorce from moral censure. But this serves only to highlight a further irreconcilable tension in the tracts, that between blamelessness and responsibility. Milton's argument takes an ugly turn here. At the risk of making nonsense of his own arguments for natural antipathy, he consistently finds the man blameless and the woman guilty. Milton marshals his argument for the insurmountability of natural and therefore innocent antipathy against those who view divorce as a moral offense. But his humane plea for no-fault divorce for incompatibility is yoked by violence with violence, with the rage of the injured male against the wife who will not be a wife: "let her be a meet help, a solace, not a nothing, not an adversary, not a desertrice" (II.605). Blameless nature is forgotten as grossness, vulgarity, and bestiality arise from the woman's wilful refusal to conform to the man. The tension is epitomized in the well-known and grisly description of a failed marriage: "two carkasses chain'd unnaturally together; *or as it may happ'n*, a living soule bound to a dead corps" (II.326; my italics). The first half reflects the mutuality of Milton's liberal argument, the second the patriarchal Milton who sees man as a God to woman. He ascribes to the unfit wife in *Colasterion* "outrages . . . defraudments . . . injuries and vexations as importunat as fire" (II.731). The following passage from *Tetrachordon* jars with his argument for the separation of blamelessly antipathetic natures:

> But to binde and mixe together holy with Atheist, hevnly with hellish, fitnes with unfitnes, light with darknes, *antipathy with antipathy*, the injur'd with the injurer, and force them into the most inward neernes of a detested union, this doubtles is the most horrid, the most unnatural mixture, the greatest confusion that can be confus'd!
>
> (II.635; my italics)

The italicized phrase, by its mutuality, stands out in this catalogue of offended and offender. Blamelessness remains, but only for the offended (read "male") party in the marriage. Straining our credulity, Milton presents the spectacle of a man blamelessly falling into despair and atheism (II.260).

The shifting of Milton's position is recorded in the complementary physiological myths of marital incompatibility in the *Doctrine and Discipline* and *Tetrachordon*, that of the "twofold Seminary" and the "radical heat" of good and evil. In developing his argument for mutual blamelessness, Milton argues for the operation of a natural hatred:

> There is a hidden efficacie of love and hatred in man as wel as in other kinds, not morall, but naturall, which though not always in the choyce, yet in the successe of mariage wil ever be most predominant . . . That every woman is meet for every man, none [is] so absurd as to affirm . . . There is indeed a twofold Seminary or stock in nature, from whence are deriv'd the issues of love and hatred distinctly flowing through the whole masse of created things, and . . . Gods doing ever is to bring the due likenesses and harmonies of his workes together.
>
> (II.271-2)

Milton acknowledges the fact that all men and women are not potentially compatible, and suggests that the process by which compatible spouses are attracted to each other participates in the principle by which God orders the universe. Harmony is broken, however, when two incompatible persons of "just and honest intentions" enter matrimony after having their "sleeping discords and enmities of nature lull'd on purpose" by "error, or som evil Angel" (II.272). Such a couple cannot love, Milton argues in the *Doctrine and Discipline*, because of natural antipathy between their "radical and *innocent* affections of nature" (II.345; my italics). But by the time of *Tetrachordon*, what is "radical" in nature has taken on moral implications: "There is an intimat quality of good or evil, through the whol progeny of *Adam*, which like a radical heat, or mortal chilnes joyns them, or disjoyns them irresistibly" (II.606). Whereas earlier Milton specified that "naturall" hatred is "not that Hate that sins" (II.253), he can hardly say that this evil is "not that evil that is evil." The moral transformation of the physiology overcomes the contradiction between blamelessness and guilt by separating blameless good from blamable evil. That which separates is not the natural and blameless antipathy of complementary opposites, but the flight of good from evil, or more accurately the purging of evil from the good, anticipating the divorcing creation (II.273) of *Paradise Lost*:

> on the wat'ry calm
> His brooding wings the Spirit of God outspread,
> And vital virtue infus'd, and vital warmth
> Throughout the fluid Mass, but downward purg'd
> The black tartareous cold Infernal dregs
> Adverse to life; then founded, then conglob'd
> Like things to like, the rest to several place
> Disparted. (*PL* VII.234–41)

The reader of the divorce tracts cannot miss the fact that Milton compounds wife, sullen mass, and cold infernal dregs.

The final and most metaphysically pregnant tension arises in the course of Milton's attempt to debrutalize and redeem sexuality. The sensitive man faces real spiritual and physical danger in the sexual relations of a loveless marriage. These relations, as we have seen, will vulgarize, brutalize, enslave, and perhaps even kill him (II.273). Worse, as we have seen, he might lose his identity. The conduit for the draining of the identity is the penis, when marriage becomes the draining of "an impetuous nerve" into a "channell of concupiscence" or "the furrow of mans nativity" (II.249, 270). But if monism means that sexual relations can brutalize and corporealize the couple when there is no love, it also means that mutual love can spiritualize sexual relations. The anatomical intractability and harshness of the uncomfortably graphic images for the genital union of bodies is countered by the softened and spiritualized but also sexually charged images for the union of souls: instead of a discharging of semen from nerves into furrows or channels, true lovers intermix an "*influence* of peace and love" from the "fountain" of the "souls lawful contentments" (II.249; my italics). The insistence on lawfulness, from an author intent on separating technically legal but illegitimate sexuality from technically illegal but legitimate sexuality, underlines the sexual freight of this passage. Sexual relations become a mutual bathing in the waters of peace. To balance the many "anatomically correct" images of debased copulation Milton can summon only this indirect and sublimated image of godly sexuality, one from which the distinction of gender is washed away together with the harshness. If, as I suggested earlier, loveless sex is only a friction of bodies, this projection of godly sex is *not even* a friction of bodies. Although Milton has made "legitimate and good the carnal act," he avoids in the tracts the frank eroticism of *Paradise Lost*, partly for reasons of genre, but also because in the 1640s he still finds "somthing of pollution in it" (II.326). The collapsing of gender distinctions attendant upon this retreat from graphic detail is prophetic of the Spirit who is both cock and hen in the act of creation in *Paradise Lost*, and prophetic even more so of the genderless but physical relations of the epic's angels.[11]

With the refining of the "quintessence of an excrement" into a "fountain" of peace and love, one leaves Gnostic dualism for Neoplatonist emanationist monism, with all of that system's characteristic tensions. According to R. J. Zwi Werblowsky, "almost all historical manifestations of Neoplatonism are caught between the horns of th[e] same dilemma: their ontological monism (the world as a chain of emanations and thence divine) and their axiological dualism which equates the radical contrast between good and evil with that between Spirit and matter or Soul and Body."[12] For Christian Neoplatonists this axiological dualism is authorized by St. Paul's dualism of the flesh and the spirit. But Paul's dualism is moral rather than metaphysical; it depends not on a distinction between material and immaterial substance but on the orientation of the person toward or away from God. Paul's Hebrew monism has been obscured by the Greek philosophy that the Greek language of his letters misleadingly evokes.[13] (Milton, who knew Hebrew, was well situated to recognize this.) As St. Augustine explains in the *City of God* (XIV.v), one can be carnal even by living ascetically if one considers the soul rather than God to be the highest good. Notwithstanding such disclaimers, the use of the terms "flesh" and "spirit" to denote the wicked and holy orientations of the soul has exerted on Christian metaphysicians a powerful and dualist drag, from which Milton, despite his monism, is not exempt. This is the dilemma of the divorce tracts. Milton attacks both dualist complacency about the legitimacy of a loveless but consummated marriage and dualist repudiation of the separable body for an unnatural asceticism. But when physical sexuality is redeemed by a monist conception of the union of minds, it is spiritualized beyond recognition. The dualist and Gnostic horror of the body is countered by a monism designed in part to validate the body, but which associates virtue with the spiritualization and vice with the greater incorporealization of the one substance. Milton's intention to separate himself from dualism is thwarted, not by the strategic dualism of his arguments for spiritual union, but by a moral dualism secreted at the heart of his ontological monism.

Milton's first essay in matter–spirit monism is finally incomplete. If he intended the administration of one extreme dualism (spirit over body) to counteract and balance another dualism (body over spirit), his medicine has proved too strong. The monist physician must still heal himself.

Notes

1 See Christopher Hill, *Milton and the English Revolution* (New York, 1977), p. 125; John Halkett, *Milton and the Idea of Matrimony* (New Haven, 1970), p. 1.
2 James Grantham Turner, *One Flesh: Paradisal Marriage and Sexual Relations in the Age of Milton* (Oxford, 1987), p. 200; Turner's book anticipates my argument that the tracts contain elements of both dualism and monism (chapter 6).
3 Henry More uses the term "soil" for the degenerative materialization of the soul in a letter to Anne Conway (23 October 1660): "excess of passion voluntarily yielded to, addes some soile to the soule" (*Conway Letters: The Correspondence of Anne, Viscountess Conway, Henry More, and their Friends, 1642–1684*, ed. Marjorie Nicolson [New Haven, 1930], p. 169).
4 Irene Samuel, *Milton and Plato* (Ithaca, N.Y., 1947), p. 157.
5 Milton's description of the wife as a "sullen masse" in *Tetrachordon* illustrates a stress point in his argument (II.670). The noun suggests the inertness of the mere body, but the adjective grants the wife animate nature (though not animated personality), as Milton must do if he wishes to make her an opponent and not merely a piece of furniture. The paradoxical phrase is embedded in a paradoxical passage: "This word [wife] . . . does not signify . . . an intolerable adversary, not a helpelesse, unaffectionate and sullen masse whose very company represents the visible and exactest figure of lonlines it selfe. Such an associate he who puts away, divorces not a wife, but disjoynes a nullity which God never joyn'd." The wife is simultaneously overbearingly present and absent; she crowds the husband and leaves him alone. The paradox is compounded in the disjoining of a "nullity"; in legal terms this phrase signifies the separation of parties to a voided contract, but in metaphysical terms it suggests the non-existence of the wife. Divorce thus becomes a non-act.
6 For Milton's response to the King's image, see David Loewenstein, *Milton and the Drama of History: Historical Vision, Iconoclasm, and the Literary Imagination*, forthcoming from Cambridge University Press, and Lana Cable, "Milton's Iconoclastic Truth," chapter 7 below.
7 See also, for example, III.194; IV.20; VI.158; VII.204; VIII.221; IX.96, 121; X.220; XII.101, 488, 523, 587.
8 Ed. Peter Lopston (The Hague, 1982), p. 217 (Lopston prints the 1690 Latin translation of the English manuscript of *c.* 1676 along with the English retranslation of 1692). I demonstrate the close parallels between Milton's monism and Conway's in a book in preparation on Milton and seventeenth-century metaphysics, where I also demonstrate the centrality of metaphors of hollowness in *Paradise Lost*.
9 For another discussion of the allegorical narratives of *The Doctrine and Discipline*, and for an alternative reading of the birth metaphors contained in them, see Annabel Patterson, "No meer amatorious novel?", chapter 4 below.

10 See Arthur Barker, "Christian Liberty in Milton's Divorce Pamphlets," in *Modern Language Review*, 35 (1940), pp. 153–61.
11 On the sexual relations of Milton's angels, see William Kerrigan, *The Sacred Complex: On the Psychogenesis of Paradise Lost* (Cambridge, Mass., 1983), pp. 212–15, and Turner, *One Flesh*, pp. 279–80.
12 R. J. Zwi Werblowsky, "Milton and the *Conjectura Cabbalistica*," *Journal of the Warburg and Courtauld Institutes*, 18 (1955), p. 199.
13 John A. T. Robinson, *The Body: A Study in Pauline Theology* (London, 1952), pp. 11–33.

4

No meer amatorious novel?

ANNABEL PATTERSON

I By-ends

In June 1643, a recently abandoned husband published the first edition of his *Doctrine and Discipline of Divorce*, and about six months later the second edition, "revis'd and much expanded," followed. With the advent of feminist criticism there is renewed interest in these two works, which the Yale edition of Milton's prose allows us to read superimposed, without defining which text is, as it were, on top. Both title-pages declare that the institution of marriage in England at the time demands revision for "the good of both sexes," a claim easily refuted by today's readers of both sexes, who quickly discover the passages of masculinist bias that, no matter what happened later in *Paradise Lost*, cannot be explained away.

Similarly, the return of a critical climate in which (given certain caveats about the social construction of the self) recourse to biography is once again respectable permits inspection of the motives that led Milton to turn private domestic embarrassment into public polemic. The result can be a reading of the divorce pamphlets that deals sceptically with Milton's claims to objectivity, both within the pamphlets and later in the autobiographical section of the *Second Defence*. In this atmosphere of creative suspicion, the focus of inquiry becomes less the arguments for divorce themselves and the dubious logic by which Milton made the biblical texts on marriage serve his purpose, and more the structure of personality and the shape of the career.

While I am highly sympathetic to both of these approaches, and will inevitably implicate both of them in what follows, this essay attempts rather to locate the *Doctrine and Discipline of Divorce* at the point of intersection between psychobiography and a resurgent genre theory that, in the demise of structuralism, now seems possible. This pamphlet holds interest for genre theory because it hovers on an undrawn boundary between polemic and narrative, a boundary whose uncertainty Milton himself discerned and attempted to stabilize by declaring, in a crucial passage to which we shall return, that this was "no meer amatorious novel" (II.256). In fact, this statement was made in reference not to the pamphlet as a whole, but to the myth of Eros and Anteros that Milton inserted into it as an image of the reciprocal love and need that was central to his redefinition of marriage. Yet in making the defensive comment, Milton showed self-consciousness about the presence of fictional narrative *within* his pamphlet, and used a term (*novel*) whose past and future were both problematic in the emergent poetics of narrative fiction. As a derivative of the Italian *novella*, the term referred back to the brief erotic tales of the late Middle Ages, as in Burton's 1621 allusion to "Boccaces Novels,"[1] and as Milton apparently employed it when, in the *History of Britain*, he related "another story . . . of Edgar, fitter for a Novel then a History" (v.327), a tale of mistaken (though fortuitous) bedding and concubinage. Yet in its own denotation of the new, or novelty, *novel* also had affiliations with the French *nouvelles*, literally news, or scandalous journalism, which by 1663 was so well established as a genre that it produced its own satire, the *Nouvelles nouvelles* of Donneau de Vizé.[2] While Milton's own primary term for fiction was *romance* (and this too, as I have argued elsewhere, was an increasingly disturbing category for him)[3] the prophetic mobility of *novel* to displace *romance* as term preceded its paradigmatic victory. *Clidamas, or the Sicilian Tale* (1639) was a Heliodoran romance whose semi-anonymous author (J. S.) offered it to the reader as a "little Novel . . . which though in it selfe be nothing yet . . . may prove something" (f. A2). And, as Michael McKeon observes in his magisterial *Origins of the English Novel, 1600–1740*, "by the time 'the novel' was beginning to be accepted as the canonic term for prose fiction in the modern age, the epistemological transformation that is vital to its constitution as a genre had already proceeded very far."[4] No one was more alert than Milton to the epistemological dilemmas inherent in story-telling; and, as we shall see, the narrative impulse would drive him up against the frontiers, such as they were, that divided the romantic past from the novel (and novelistic) future.

For the myth of Eros and Anteros is only one of the interpolated narratives that Milton inserted into the *Doctrine and Discipline of Divorce*, and about the others he was apparently less self-conscious. These include a miniseries of allegories with sexual plots ending with the Eros/Anteros myth but beginning with the liaison, added to the second edition of the pamphlet, between Custom, who is female, and Error, who is male; and a disguised autobiographical account of Milton's own courtship and the early days of his marriage, told prophetically in the style of the domestic fiction that would shortly replace the fashionable, pseudo-historical romances imported from the continent.

These two types of narrative are distinguished both from each other and from the polemical frame by an oblique relationship to truth or the real. The allegories operate by forcing into painful visibility allegory's structural paradox, that it tries to give language incarnational force, to provide imaginary bodies for disembodied abstractions. By their shared sexual emplotment, Milton's allegories in the *Doctrine* reveal the perversity of this enterprise in general, and particularly the unspeakable agenda which required him to resort to allegory when legal or theological vocabularies failed him. In the first two in the series of three, also, the distortions that Milton introduces into familiar symbolic plots anticipate the grotesque family romance between Satan, Sin, and Death in *Paradise Lost*, itself often noted as a problematic shift of generic gears.

The concealed autobiographical novel, by contrast, registers its presence with a naive realism that predicts Defoe or even Richardson in its mundane vocabulary and social setting, but differs from early novelistic technique primarily in reversing the fictional use of personal pronouns. That is to say, where Defoe creates utterly convincing first-person narrators who appear to relate their biographies, Milton conceals his own by the use of the third person. This stratagem is, however, often subverted by the emotional investment that prose itself candidly registers. And there may be a third story told only, as it were, in occasional slips of the lexicon, a lapsarian tale of Milton's delayed and painful sexual coming of age, visible momentarily in metaphors and euphemisms for sexual process and parts of the body, a form simultaneously of linguistic precision and avoidance.

If so, all three types of narrative are, finally, different versions of the same story, the tale of what Milton called his "owne by-ends." The phrase occurs in the supplementary address to the Long Parliament that Milton added when he also added his name to the pamphlet, and it stands as one of those disclaimers that proclaim the presence of that which is stated to be absent. "Who among ye," Milton wrote to the parliamentarians, "hath not been often traduc't to be the agent of his owne by-ends, under pretext of Reformation" (II.225). A few sentences later, that "traduc't," or falsely accused, is *almost* replaced by the notion that there may be something in the accusation, something that can be turned to everyone's advantage: "Yet when points of difficulty are to be discusst, appertaining to the removall of unreasonable wrong and burden from the perplext life of our brother, it is incredible how cold, how dull, and farre from all fellow feeling we are, without the spurre of self-concernment" (II.226). This statement certainly encourages us to read Milton in a way that defies the depersonalizing and antianthropological premises of postmodernism, denying us for nearly two decades the commonsense categories of author, *œuvre* and intention; yet without such categories we cannot even begin to see how interesting is the *Doctrine and Discipline of Divorce*. It is *most* interesting precisely in the relation between intended and unintended meaning, in the textual presence of those "by-ends" that Milton knew he would be accused (if not traduced) of having allowed into the deep structure of his text. And if there is currently any subject on which light might be thrown by the "spurre of self-concernment" it might very well be what Milton called "Reformation," the process by which the mistakes we made in the past are carried in the psyche, represented in forms of consciousness, and converted into recommendations for the future. Who among us, one might therefore ask, can afford to cast the first stone of condescension at the narrative stratagems I am about to illustrate, the ruses of a self in process of sexual and social reconstruction, with more of both to follow?

II The eloquent "he who"

I start with the suspected presence in the *Doctrine* of the domestic, autobiographical "amatorious novel," as the most conceptually demanding, if not the most shocking, of Milton's narrative modes; and with two recent proposals about the novel's origins in autobiography, specifically the spiritual autobiography associated with English religious radicalism. Each of these proposals abuts on Milton, the first more directly than the second, but the second more richly. In Leopold Damrosch's *God's Plot, Man's Stories*, the claim is made that one of the cultural formations that led to the emergence of the English novel as a distinct genre was the "radical analysis of the self" that minority Protestantism necessitated and for which autobiography was the natural expression.[5] Damrosch's chapter on Milton, however, deals only with *Paradise Lost*, without recourse to the explicit and implicit autobiography that readers of Milton have for years recognized as embedded in the work of the left hand; and it is less concerned with the domestic psychodrama within the poem than with the theological struggles to which it bears witness. For Damrosch, the novelistic moment (which Bakhtin found recurring in many cultures and centuries apart) occurs only at the Fall, when Adam and Eve become the complex characters that the novel demands. Paradoxically, they thereby *lose* the freedom of choice in action that Angus Fletcher regards as the dividing line between the novel's characters and the bound agents of allegorical narrative.[6] They are thereby distinguished from the narrator of *Paradise Lost*, who has supposedly regained that freedom by his superior vision and alignment with Providential pattern.

In McKeon's *Origins of the English Novel* there is a similar claim that fiction, as it evolves in this period, demonstrates the tension between "individual life and overarching pattern" (p. 91). But McKeon offers a more complex genetic model for the novel, in which spiritual biography is only one of the progenitors, along with criminal biographies and travel narratives; and he locates the matrix of narrative instability from which the novel emerged as an epistemological problem rather than a theological one. Too subtle to argue that the novel replaces the romance by making a stronger claim to believability, McKeon posits a continuous interplay between the critique of romance conducted by what he calls "naive empiricism" and a sceptical critique, carried on more or less simultaneously, of "naive empiricism" itself. These terms can certainly illuminate Milton's lifelong struggle to evaluate fictionality under the category "romance." But more precisely to the point here is McKeon's account of how spiritual autobiography stages a dialectic between different versions and historical phases of the self or writing subject.

In this type of narrative, the basic dynamic between individual life and overarching pattern (which Christianity calls Providence) is reenacted, he argues, by the interplay of Character and Narrator, the first by historical, chronological standards necessarily unrepentant, the second possessed of the powers of atonement that will eventually register the autobiography generically spiritual: "As the plot unfolds horizontally, the dangerous gap between Character and Narrator gradually diminishes through vertical narrative intrusions, until the two finally are one, the latter consciousness having subsumed the former in what might be seen as the narrative equivalent of atonement" (p. 95).

McKeon compares this narrative principle to Milton's famous description in *Areopagitica* of the process of learning by one's mistakes, or of "knowing good by evill . . . the scanning of error to the confirmation of truth." For McKeon, however, Milton functions only as a theorist of this "scanning of error," not as a writer himself of spiritual or secular autobiography. The insights so brilliantly encapsulated here are worked out not in relation to Milton's poetry or his prose, but in relation to Defoe's *Robinson Crusoe*, whose relation to spiritual autobiography is clear and direct.

I propose that the *Doctrine and Discipline of Divorce* also introduces the "scanning of error" as a narrative principle, in a story in which Character and Narrator have at least as complex a relation. The theme of error in the *Doctrine* was, of course, foregrounded on both title-pages. Its symbolic form appears in the allegory of Custom and Error added to the second edition. Its realistic content, or what McKeon would call its grounding in naive empiricism, is found later, in Book 1, chapter 3, where Milton seeks to refute the argument that divorce would be unnecessary if people carefully considered the "disposition" of their intended mates beforehand. "But let them know again," Milton responded to this unheard objection,

> that for all the warinesse can be us'd, it may yet befall a discreet man
> to be mistak'n in his choice: *and we have plenty of examples.* The
> soberest and best govern'd men are lest practiz'd in these affairs; and
> who knows not that the bashfull mutenes of a virgin may oft-times
> hide all the unlivelines and naturall sloth which is really unfit for
> conversation; nor is there that freedom of accesse granted or presum'd,
> as may suffice to a perfect discerning till too late: and where any
> indisposition is suspected, what more usuall then the perswasion of
> friends, that acquaintance, as it encreases, will amend all: And lastly, it
> is not strange though many who have spent their youth chastely, are
> in some things not so quick-sighted, while they hast too eagerly to
> light the nuptiall torch; nor is it therfore that for a modest error a man
> should forfeit so great happiness, and no charitable means to release
> him. Since they who have liv'd most loosely by reasoning of their
> bold accustoming, prove most succesfull in their matches, because

their wild affections unsetling at will, have been as so many divorces to teach them experience. When as the sober man honouring the appearance of modestie, and hoping well of every sociall vertue under that veile, may easily chance to meet, if not with a body impenetrable, yet often with a minde to all other due conversation inaccessible, and to all the more estimable and superior purposes of matrimony uselesse and almost liveles. (II.249–50)

Here Milton, rejecting Fielding's thesis in *Tom Jones* that allowing a young man to sow his wild oats will unite him at last with his true Sophia, introduces a century earlier a far less allegorical story than Fielding's, a story in which the style of naive empiricism is supposedly explained by the phrase added in 1644 (*"and we have plenty of examples"*) – that is to say, social analysis as the basis for generalization. But the sociological force of "plenty," along with "oft-times," "usuall," "many," "often," is undermined by the corrective nature of the argument, which requires the "sober man" to be perceived as the exception to the carnal rule of the double standard. And where is this sober man to be found, the reader may well ask? The answer, along with a corroborative style and certain exact matches of detail, exists in Milton's early biographies.

The extreme specificity of the contrast between a chaste youth and a sudden haste to light the nuptial torch correlates all too precisely with the story of Milton's sudden marriage in the summer of 1642. "After Whitsuntide it was, or a little after, that he took a journey into the country; nobody about him certainly knowing the reason, or that it was any more than a journey of recreation; after a month's stay, home he returns a married man, that went out a bachelor." So wrote Milton's nephew Edward Phillips, who also recorded the temperamental mismatch between the "philosophical life" of the husband, and the young wife who had "been used to a great house, and much company and joviality."[7] These are, of course, the alternatives Milton had explored for himself in *L'Allegro* and *Il Penseroso*, now given a still more realistic and social form.

Let us pause for a moment on the question of social form. Another aspect of coincidence between Milton's supposedly impersonal narrative of failed courtship and Phillips' admittedly personalized one is the role that friends play in the marital negotiations. Milton described how "the perswasion of friends" worked on the sober young man of small experience to believe that a suspected "indisposition" would disappear on better "acquaintance." The phrase reappears in Book I, chapter 12, where he describes those who do not have the "calling" for marriage, "but by the perswasion of friends, or not knowing themselves do often enter into wedlock" (II.274). Edward Phillips mentions no persuasion in the making of the original match; but his account is remarkable for its emphasis on "the strong intercession of friends of both sides" in effecting the reconciliation. Both texts, therefore, read as a gloss on each other, speak to the specifically social, economic and sociopolitical interests behind the marriage, since the poor financial circumstances of the Powells (including an uncollectable debt to John Milton Sr.) and the changing fortunes of the King's party in the war (which worsened in 1645, suggesting the wisdom of recovering a republican protector) were undoubtedly stronger motives on at least one side of the bargain than the emotional argument Milton, in the *Doctrine*, was attempting to make supreme. It need hardly be said that these were the conditions in which social historians of marriage have become increasingly interested, and which have long been posited as the base of the eighteenth-century domestic novel. It is almost too good to be true that another of Milton's biographers, perhaps John Phillips, perhaps Cyriack Skinner, refers to the campaign for divorce as "the mending of a decay in the superstructure" (p. 1040), a term that perfectly mandates, if mandate were necessary, our reading of these stories in terms of their socioeconomic and political coordinates.

But (to return to the contest between L'Allegro and Il Penseroso in Milton's story) the *Doctrine and Discipline of Divorce*, itself a severely titled work, operates solely under the sign of the latter. The would-be divorcé, invariably referred to as male, is not only sober but melancholy to a fault, even to aberrancy. Having mischosen his mate, Milton remarked earlier (Book I, chapter 3) that he is far worse off than the single man, for "here the continuall sight of his deluded thoughts without cure, must needs be to him, if especially his complexion incline him to melancholy, a daily trouble and paine of losse in some degree like that which Reprobates feel" (II.247). We find here, in other words, a Character whose psychological profile distinguishes him from those "plenty of examples" who share his marital fate. And in the same passage Milton emphasizes his individuality, by arguing that he shall "doe more manly, to be extraordinary and singular in claiming the due right whereof he is frustrated, then to piece up his lost contentment by visiting the Stews, or stepping to his neighbours bed, which is the common shift in this misfortune" (II.247).

One might be tempted to assume, given the actual biography, that the mischosen mate might have been represented as a young and hence permissibly joyous Allegra. Not so. Instead, the question of female Character is ambiguated by two alternative hypotheses of feminine unacceptability. One appears in the narrative of unwise courtship, when the "bashfull mutenes of a virgin" conceals the "unlivelines and naturall sloth which is really unfit for conversation" (II.249). The other appears much later in the pamphlet (and in its chronological development), when Milton is confronting the argument made by Béza and Pareus, that the Mosaic dispensation for divorce was awarded for the protection of wives against the cruelty of husbands. "Palpably uxurious!" exclaimed Milton at this point (Book II, chapter 15), in one of the most dramatic utterances of the entire work:

> Who can be ignorant that woman was created for man, and not man
> for woman; and that a husband may be injur'd as insufferably in
> mariage as a wife. What an injury is it after wedlock not to be belov'd,
> what to be slighted, what to be contended with in point of house-rule
> who shall be the head, not for any parity of wisdome, for that were
> something reasonable, but out of a female pride. (II.324)

He then inserts a scriptural anecdote from the book of Esther (1:10–22), of
"the cours which the Medes and Persians took by occasion of Vashti, whose
meer denial to come at her husbands sending lost her the being Queen any
longer." It is surely no coincidence that the language of the "divine relater,"
as Milton here refers to the holy Word, matches that of Edward Phillips, who
related how "Michaelmas being come, and no news of his wife's return,"
Milton

> sent for her by letter; and receiving no answer, sent several other
> letters, which were also unanswered; so that at last he dispatched down
> a foot messenger with a letter, desiring her return. But the messenger
> came back not only without an answer ... but ... reported that he
> was dismissed with some sort of contempt ... [which] so incensed our
> author that he thought it would be dishonorable ever to receive her
> again (p. 1031)

The hidden autobiography, in other words, here carries the story of Milton's
marriage from the hasty courtship through early days of contention "in point
of house-rule" and eventually to the repulse that defined the wife as not
passively resistant but actively rebellious against her lord and master.

Here, then, both the spoken and the unspoken biography suggest that
Milton did not know precisely what he wanted in a wife, docility or
liveliness, an ambiguity that his own text records with less candor than that of
his nephew, who reported that Milton "found his chief diversion" while his
wife was away and *before* her "deniall to come at her husbands sending" in
visiting Lady Margaret Lee, "a woman of great wit and ingenuity." Indeed,
whether or not he realized the implications of the admission, Edward Phillips
remarks of this phase of the marriage that Milton was "now as it were a single
man again"! Since the characterization of the female as insubordinate was
added to the 1644 edition, as was the biblical anecdote of Vashti's refusal, we
might speculate that the intense anger that Phillips reported was still seeking
an outlet even as Milton was doing his utmost to place his arguments in the
respectable and impersonal framework of the thought of the continental
reformers.[8]

But there is a more intimate part of the story still, which will take us from
Character, male and female, back to the Narrator. In McKeon's account of
spiritual autobiography and its successors in the novel, it is the Narrator who
supposedly controls the realist or empirical "scanning of error" on the
horizontal axis of narrative by exerting the vertical pressure of atonement.

One could reformulate this in Milton's own words as the tension between one's own "by-ends" and a genuine, impersonal zeal for "Reformation," a tension which, it should by now be clear, is far from resolved in the *Doctrine and Discipline of Divorce*. This tension is most clearly recorded in the terrain of syntax, which is also the terrain in which Character and Narrator meet at the closest quarters. Recall, in the Narrator's attack on feminine insubordination, the exclamation "What an injury is it after wedlock not to be belov'd," which in this context would make more sense if it had read "What an injury is it after wedlock not to be *obeyed*." But its full significance in the pamphlet as a whole may be understood if we hear in it an uncontrollable echo of an earlier passage in which Milton introduces the paradox that the would-be divorcer is actually the best upholder of marriage: "for to retain still," he wrote,

> and not to be able to love, is to heap up more injury ... He therfore who lacking of his due in the most native and humane end of mariage, thinks it better to part then to live sadly and injuriously to that cherfull covnant (for not to be belov'd and yet retain'd, is the greatest injury to a gentle spirit) he I say who therfore seeks to part, is one who highly honours the maried life, and would not stain it. (II.253)

We can see, perhaps, a powerful Freudian slippage from the high-minded "to retain still and not to be able to love" to the elegiac (and soon to be echoed) "not to *be* belov'd and yet retain'd." Who, this syntax asks, is doing the divorcing, and at what moment does it occur? At the failure of love, or at the formal separation? Who injures whom? Does the chiasmus indicate a moment of gender parity in Milton's thinking, or rather the hideous recognition that when he thought he was in control (retaining, but unable to love) he was in fact himself to be retained, but not to be beloved?

In a much later passage (Book II, chapter 20), Milton reassumed command over this situation, reworking the paradox about injury so as to apply only to the woman:

> The law can only appoint the just and equall conditions of divorce, and is to look how it is an injury to the divorc't, which in truth it can be none, as a meer separation; for if she consent, wherin has the law to right her? or consent not, then is it either just and so deserved, or if unjust, such in all likelihood was the divorcer, and to part from an unjust man is a happines, and no injury to be lamented. But suppose it be an injury, the Law is not able to amend it, unless she think it other then a miserable redress to return back from whence she was expell'd, or but entreated to be gon. (II.349–50)

So "not to be retained" has become, simply, "expell'd," and the story of the wife who refused to return has been exorcised in another, occluded finale, the miserable opportunity imposed by law to "return back from whence she was expell'd," the worst punishment that Milton can imagine.

But there is another syntactic symptom of distress in the passage of revealing chiasmus. The point at which Character and Narrator meet most clearly is in the use of personal pronouns. "He therfore," wrote Milton, "who lacking of his due . . . he I say who therfore seeks to part . . . is one who highly honours the maried life." It is in deference to the late Joan Webber that this part of my argument is subtitled "The eloquent 'he who'", for it was in contemplating how much was accomplished for the study of seventeenth-century prose in *The Eloquent "I"* that I realized how much more might still be said, not least because Joan Webber's account of Milton's "I" restricted itself to the pamphlets on church reform. In that context, she was able to argue that Milton's use of the first personal pronoun, along with other syntactical constructions such as passive verbs and ethical datives, indicated a devout striving after impersonality, a wish to express the subordination of his talent to his calling:

> Milton's muting of the "I" in passages wholly taken up with himself makes his desires seem to rest on God. And often where the "I" does make itself aggressively felt, an overarching periodic sentence prevents the collision of personal with impersonal simply by encompassing both in a larger order.[9]

This idealized reading of Milton's egotistical sublime anticipated McKeon's tension between the "individual life and the overarching pattern," which in spiritual autobiography brings Character and Narrator into continuous negotiation; but it could not, I suggest, have been maintained at this ideal level had Webber turned her meticulous investigation to the divorce pamphlets.[10]

For the *Doctrine and Discipline* introduces a new twist to the syntactical device developed in the church reform pamphlets for distinguishing an ideal and disinterested self from a confessedly self-interested author. The ideal "he who" appears as the heroic agent of reform, "hee who shall indeavour the amendment of any old neglected grievance in Church or State" (II.224), or "he who wisely would restrain the reasonable Soul of man within due bounds" (II.227). Both of these are built into the new address to Parliament added in 1644, and contrast with the modest ethical dative: "For me, as farre as my part leads me, I have already my greatest gain, assurance and inward satisfaction to have done in this nothing unworthy" (II.232). More clearly heroic, participating in the structure of epic and chivalric metaphor with which Milton enlivened his attacks on prelacy, is the "He therefore who by adventuring shall be so happy as with successe . . . to light the way of such an expedient liberty and truth as this . . . [and] shall deserve to be reck'n'd among the publick benefactors of civill and humane life" (II.239–40). Here, in fact Milton changed the "He that" of 1643 to "He who" in 1644, one of those miniscule alterations that would seem to carry no significance unless perceived as structural.

But alongside these heroic personae exists another, who belongs rather to the world of error and mistaken choice that Milton entered for the first time in the *Doctrine and Discipline,* and for which, paradoxically, the humility of ethical datives could not serve, because of the need to conceal his "own by-ends." So the new preface introduces also the figure of "He who marries" and "intends as little to conspire his own ruine, as he that swears Allegiance" (II.229). He will reappear as the anonymous "sober man" who appeared in the story of unwise courtship, and who reappears in the subsequent lament for the failure of love: "He therfore who lacking of his due . . . thinks it better to part then to live sadly and injuriously . . . (for not to be belov'd and yet retain'd, is the greatest injury to a gentle spirit) he I say who therfore seeks to part, is one who highly honours the maried life, and would not stain it." Especially in that remarkable construction, "he I say who," the grammar of self-division is painfully audible.

III Grinding in the mill

The three myths or allegorical narratives differ from the "amatorious novel" we have just been reading by virtue of their uncomfortable blend of high abstraction with an emphatic sexuality, which goes well beyond the in-carnational protocols of allegory as a narrative procedure. In Milton's retelling of Plato's myth of the union of Plenty and Poverty (a pagan version of the story of Ruth and Boaz) everything that was happy or high-spirited in the original is erased. In the *Symposium,* Plenty, having overindulged at Aphrodite's birthday party, lies down in the garden of Zeus and falls asleep, whereupon Poverty, "considering her own straitened circumstances, plotted to have him for a husband, and accordingly she lay down at his side and conceived Love."[11] For Milton, Poverty is recognizable in that loneliness of which Adam complained in the garden, but the myth has gone awry; Plenty vanishes from his text, Penury cannot "lay it self down by the side of such a meet and acceptable union . . . but remains utterly unmaried . . . and still burnes in the proper meaning of St. Paul" (II.252–3). An awkwardness about gender, one might suspect, shows in the conversion of Penury from feminine to neuter, and in the revised genealogy. Instead of the birth of Love, "Then enters Hate, not that Hate that sins, but that which is onely a naturall dissatisfaction and the turning aside from a mistaken object." In this version of the myth the sexual engagement (which represents the spiritual or emotional one) either does not occur at all, or, if it does, is so unsatisfactory that it leads to that familiar image of the domestic bedroom, the "turning aside."

The myth of Custom and Error with which the 1644 pamphlet begins is also a myth of generation gone askew. Here Custom is the aggressive female ("being but a meer face"), and, like Penury, is seeking a mate who has what she lacks, namely a body. She "rests not in her unaccomplishment, untill by secret inclination, shee accorporat her selfe with error, who being a blind and Serpentine body without a head, willingly accepts what he wants, and supplies what her incompleatnesse went seeking" (II.223). Lana Cable noted in 1981 the sexual content of this striking opening to the *Doctrine*; but possibly the conventions of academic discourse did not then permit her to say what she meant by the "obvious . . . implications" of this representation of Error as male.[12] The appropriate gloss, I think, comes from Yeats' late poem, *The Chambermaid's Second Song*, where the blind and serpentine body is identified as "his rod and its butting head / Limp as a worm, / His spirit that has fled / Blind as a worm."[13] This myth, too, issues in an allegorical birth, although it is emphatically not an offspring of Custom and Error, but rather a birth they would prevent, crying "Innovation," "as if the womb of teeming Truth were to be clos'd up" (II.224). Mysteriously (or perhaps we should say carelessly), a few moments later Truth is no longer the rightful mother, but the child: "Though this ill hap wait on her nativity, that shee never comes into the world, but like a Bastard, to the ignominy of him that brought her forth: till Time the Midwife rather then the mother of Truth, have washt and salted the Infant, declar'd her legitimat, and Churcht the father of his young Minerva" (II.225). The editors of the Yale *Prose Works* remark on this "grotesque" mingling of classical myth with the Anglican service of churching women after childbirth, a relic of the Hebrew purification rites and Old Testament emphases on female uncleanness. But still more unsettling is Milton's distortion of the familial structure of several stories at once, so that Time becomes not Truth's male father, a commonplace of Renaissance thought, but her female midwife; while the role of the father is now usurped by the author of the *Doctrine and Discipline of Divorce*, who both claims the Olympian privilege of paternity *without* the assistance of a woman (the birth of the brainchild *through* the brain) and confesses, by way of the metaphor of churching, to an uneasy physicality that requires some ritual (verbal) exorcism.

Cable also proposed that the "accorporation" of Custom and Error functions as a grotesque parody of the longed-for union of Eros and Anteros (Book I, chapter 6). Perhaps; but what I notice rather is the peculiar misappropriateness of the Eros/Anteros model, literally a tale of passionately incestuous love between brothers, as an image of human *marriage*, whose oddness in this context is only underlined by Milton's disclaimer that "of matrimoniall love no doubt but that was chiefly meant." Before attempting to erase this problem by recourse to learned commentary, it might be well to ask whether Milton *needed* to invoke this young all-male image of desire, when he might have just as easily remembered the union of Cupid and "his eternal Bride" Psyche that concludes the published versions of *Comus*. *That* myth would indeed have stood in pure contrast to the two distorted unions and genealogies that precede it, not least because in that earlier, ideal moment Milton could contemplate the "blissful birth" of twins, Youth and Joy. Not so young now, he apparently could not bring himself to recall that particular shape of desire, and the myth he chooses belongs rather to the mindset of Adam after the Fall and before reconciliation with Eve:

> O why did God,
> Creator wise, that peopl'd highest Heav'n
> With spirits Masculine, create at last
> This *novelty* on Earth, this fair defect
> Of Nature, and not fill the World at once
> With Men as Angels without Feminine,
> Or find some other way to generate
> Mankind?
>
> (x.888–95; my italics)

Without the "novelty" of the female, there could be, need be, no "amatorious novel." Milton's framing of the Eros/Anteros myth as a divine fiction sung to him by his "Author," and his denial that it belongs in the genre of domestic or romantic fiction, registers both a generic and a gendered discomfort.

Such a reading can only be reinforced by the language Milton employs to denote human and heterosexual activity in the *Doctrine and Discipline of Divorce*. In 1978 Edward Le Comte, in two terse pages, collected some of these metaphoric phrases, concluded that they registered Milton's "disgust or scorn," and suggested that if the divorce pamphlets "reflect a sexual refusal, they reflect one, or an inclination to one, far more likely to have come from the husband."[14] He noted that Milton equates heterosexual activity not only with animalism – "a bestial necessity," "bestial burning," "animal or beastish meeting," "a brutish congress" – but also with physical labor and slavery. Central to this perception is a sentence Milton added to the 1644 edition: "that to grind in the mill of an undelighted and servil copulation, must be the only forc't work of a Christian mariage, oft times with such a yokefellow, from whom both love and peace, both nature and Religion mourns to be separated" (ii.258); and Le Comte showed how this image proleptically alludes to the story of Samson, who in rabbinical tradition was doubly enslaved by the Philistines, combining toiling at the mill with enforced service as a stud.[15] The sexual pun derives also from the discourse of common bawdiness. Le Comte cites the couplet from a 1647 popular rhyme: "Digby's lady takes it ill, / That her lord grinds not at her mill."

But we can now see more clearly how and why the sexual distress in the *Doctrine and Discipline of Divorce* is entangled with Milton's ideology of work. Thanks to Anthony Low's exploration of georgic as a theme among social reformers both prior to and during the English Revolution, and without accepting at face value, as Low does, Milton's repeated claims that the work of the intellect may count as socially useful labor,[16] we can see that the *Doctrine and Discipline* evinces the same intuition of social and economic instability, expressed in terms of agricultural practice and the politics of landowning, as do the early poems.[17] This intuition had become, apparently, less capable of repression as the Civil War developed. Yet the *Doctrine and Discipline* issues it in so confused a register as to make the question of self-consciousness, or of the priority of the social versus the sexual in the construction of the self, as unanswerable as always.

We should group around the grinding in the mill the following phrases from elsewhere in the pamphlet: "bondmen of a luckles and helples matrimony" (II.240); "the work of male and female" (II.240); "sowe the furrow of mans nativity with seed of two incoherent and uncombining dispositions" (II.270); "an improper and ill-yoking couple . . . the disparity of severall cattell at the plow" (II.277); and especially "God loves not to plow out the heart of our endeavours with over-hard and sad tasks . . . by making wedlock a supportless yoke . . . to make men *the day-labourers* of their own afflictions" (II.342; my italics). This allusion to day-labor connects the pamphlet to the crucial sonnet on the parable of the talents ("Does God exact day-labor, light denied?"); but here it reveals more sharply its coordinates in a socioeconomic analysis that Milton has and has not completed. Perhaps he meant to avoid its conclusions by appropriating its discourse to what he thought was his topic, by relegating it to the status of metaphor. "I spake ev'n now," he wrote on the question of whether the Mosaic dispensation could possibly be interpreted as a license or escape-clause given to a hard-hearted people, "as if sin were condemn'd in a perpetual *villenage* never to be free by law, never to be *manumitted*: but pure sin can have no tenure by law at all, but is rather an eternal outlaw, and in hostility with law past all attonement" (II.288). But in the deep structure of Milton's imagination the socioeconomic consciousness is now inseparable from the erotic drama that the pamphlet is staging, *because* Milton has now himself entered the terrain of mistakenness, and is no longer luckily excluded from the curse of labor. Under this curse, which has always connected agricultural labor with genital pain, Milton cannot distinguish the body from the body politic, the master from the slave, the grinder from the ground. He has found himself expected to plow and "sow the furrow of man's nativity," and, worse still, to spend in the process, "to be made to pay out the best substance of his body, and of his soul too, as some think" (II.271), becoming indistinguishable in this metaphoric exchange from day-laborers, villeins, or even oxen and asses. Milton shares the yoke. Sex is hard work when the heart is not in it; and it would be unkind of his readers to give him the same advice that thousands of mothers gave their daughters: "Shut your eyes and think of England."

Yet in a sense he did just that, stylistically. He turned to euphemism. If writing is, as some think, the art of *not* saying what one means, the most profound avoidance, some of Milton's finest writing occurs in the effort to conceal from his readers and probably from himself the precise effect on his psyche of the long-delayed induction into heterosexual experience. Le

Comte's formula of "disgust or scorn" cannot account fully for this language, too lapidary to allow disgust to register on the reader's sensory scale or to permit the moral distancing of Narrator from Character that scorn requires. In fact, it is not always clear whether it is the Narrator or the Character of this story who is responsible for reimagining the physical events that the Narrator must repudiate precisely because, as Character, he had so deeply invested in them. Especially in chapter 3, where Milton excoriates canon law for its focus on adultery, his language ricochets between what in *Paradise Lost* he would later register as (divine) "distance and disaste" (IX.9). The admonitory distance is invoked by archaic moral allegories of the body (complete with alliteration), in the "vessell of voluptuous enjoyment," or the "fountain" "from whence must flow the acts of peace and love," or "the channell of concupiscence" (II.248–9). But the embarrassing carnal knowledge (which is only half-acknowledged) is written in a libidinal narrative that confuses success and failure and is marked by a compulsion to repeat. "The impediment of carnall performance," the "stopt or extinguisht veins of sensuality" and the "disappointing of an impetuous nerve" alternate with the "impatience of a sensuall desire . . . relieved," and the "prescrib'd satisfaction of an irrationall heat." Even the surrounding vocabulary is contaminated by the story of tumescence and detumescence; so the canon law prescribes that "the contract shall stand as firme as ever" however "flat and melancholious" the emotional relationship may be. Above all, in the notorious "quintessence of an excrement" Milton rather highlighted than solved the problem of distance and distaste, as abstract thought and philosophical idealism (expressed in a classicizing and pseudoscientific vocabulary) reveal their connections to a venerable tradition of misogynistic disgust. As Freud observed in his case-history of "Dora," "the Early Christian Father's 'inter urinas et faeces nascimur' clings to sexual life and cannot be detached from it in spite of every effort of idealization."[18]

Each of Milton's allusions to sexual process, then, is a micronarrative, with a different ending, of the search for satisfaction, of the structure of desire, which modern and postmodern criticism, itself responding to Freudian theory, has made synonymous with the novel as a category of thought, as a genre. In Tzvetan Todorov's *The Poetics of Prose* the quintessential novel must articulate the shared paradoxes of desire and narrative, that "we desire at the same time desire and its object." When we get what we thought we wanted we no longer want it. The story is over. And he also suggests that one of the novel's essential moods, in the grammatical sense, is the optative, of which the renunciative is a special case.[19] The *Doctrine and Discipline of Divorce* is, I suggest, a special case of the renunciative novel, announcing its genre through the paradox of Milton's statement: "he I say who therfore seeks to part, is one who highly honours the maried life, and would not stain it" (II.253). If his story remains carnal, for all his attempts to allegorize it, if the individual life breaks through the generalizing and impersonalizing impulse, if the Narrator fails to control the Character and effect the atonement, and they remain yoked together in the ambiguous lexical territory of euphemism, the "by-ends" that criticism is unfairly equipped to notice, we need not, I think, today be embarrassed, either for Milton or ourselves.

Notes

1 Robert Burton, *Anatomy of Melancholy*, IV.ii.2.
2 See Erica Harth, *Ideology and Culture in Seventeenth-Century France* (Ithaca, 1983), pp. 174–5.
3 See "Paradise Regained: A Last Chance at True Romance," in Richard Ide and Joseph Wittreich, eds., *Composite Orders: The Genres of Milton's Last Poems, Milton Studies*, 17 (1983), pp. 187–208. See also Barbara Lewalski, "Milton: Revaluations of Romance," in *Four Essays on Romance*, ed. Herschel Baker (Cambridge, Mass., 1971), pp. 57–70.
4 Michael McKeon, *Origins of the English Novel, 1600–1740* (Baltimore, 1987), p. 27.
5 Leopold Damrosch, *God's Plot, Man's Stories* (Chicago and London, 1985), p. 21.
6 *Allegory: The Theory of a Symbolic Mode* (Ithaca, 1964), p. 66.
7 See John Milton, *Complete Poems and Major Prose*, ed. M. Y. Hughes (New York, 1957), p. 1031. Subsequent citations from early biographers (in the text) will also be from Hughes.
8 See also Book II, chapter 18, where Milton redefines fornication as a series of obstinacies derived from Theodosius, which included the "lying forth of her hous without probable cause" (II.334), and is illustrated by Judges 19:2, where "the Levites wife is said to have playd the whoor against him; which Josephus and the Septuagint . . . interpret only of stubbornnes and rebellion against her husband" (II.335). "And this I shall contribute," added Milton, "that had it ben whoordom she would have chosen any other place to run to, *then to her fathers house*" (my italics).
9 *The Eloquent 'I': Style and Self in Seventeenth-Century Prose* (Madison, 1968), p. 197.
10 Webber actually argues that the intrusion of self into Milton's church reform pamphlets constitutes "the same kind of spiritual autobiography that other Puritans wrote, except that it is translated into literary terms" (p. 217).
11 *Dialogues of Plato*, trans. Benjamin Jowett, 4 vols (Oxford, 1871), vol. I, p. 519.
12 "Coupling Logic and Milton's Doctrine of Divorce," *Milton Studies*, 15 (1981), pp. 147–8.
13 *Collected Poems* (London, 1950), p. 346.
14 *Milton and Sex* (London, 1978), pp. 29–30. This swift-moving and often reckless account of Milton's conscious and unconscious responses to sex and marriage has now been replaced by James G. Turner's *One Flesh: Paradisal Marriage and Sexual Relations in the Age of Milton* (Oxford, 1987), which judiciously recognizes Milton's concept of sexuality as "many-layered" (p. 203), and places the misogyny of the divorce pamphlets in the context of other seventeenth-century theorists of marriage, as well as the "virginal philosophy" of *Comus* (p. 222) and the attacks on female rule in the political pamphlets and *History of Britain*.

15 The point originated with Samuel Stolman, " 'To Grind in the Mill ...' ", *Seventeenth-Century News*, 29 (1971), pp. 68–9.

16 *The Georgic Revolution* (Princeton, 1985), contains a section on "Milton and the Georgic Ideal," tracing ideas of work, and of intellectualism as labor, throughout Milton's *œuvre* (pp. 296–352).

17 See my "Forced Fingers: Milton's Early Poems and Ideological Constraint," in Claude Summers and Ted-Larry Pebworth, eds., *The Muses Common-Weale* (Columbia, 1988), pp. 9–22.

18 *Dora: An Analysis of a Case of Hysteria* (1905), ed. Philip Rieff (New York, 1963), p. 47. Compare Turner's argument that it was precisely the extent of Milton's idealization of marriage that produced, by its failure to be realized, the disgust. My reading of Milton's sexual vocabulary, however, differs from Turner's emphasis on "physical particularity" and "medical precision" (*One Flesh*, p. 198) by attempting to recognize the element of euphemism or self-protective intellectualism that Milton's vocabulary exhibits. All these strategies Milton shares with Freud, whose equally notorious passage in *Dora* about the difficulties of discussing "such delicate and unpleasant subjects" as "bodily organs and processes" asserts the distance achievable by "dry and direct ... technical names" (p. 65), only to detour into (unintentional) *double-entendre*: "J'appelle un chat un chat." (Only Jane Gallop has been bold enough to translate this; see her "Keys to Dora," in Charles Bernheimer and Claire Kahane, eds., *In Dora's Case* [New York, 1985], p. 209.) And it is worth noting that without the prurience by which genitalia were themselves rendered euphemistically in Viennese culture at the turn of the century (as in the famous "Schmuckkästchen," jewel-case) Freud's repertory of dream-symbols would have been much impoverished.

19 Trans. Richard Howard (Ithaca, 1977), pp. 105–6, 114.

Areopagitica: voicing contexts, 1643–5

NIGEL SMITH

The Luddites, Rimbaud, the Communards, wildcat strikers, the movements of May '68 – in every case the revolution does not speak indirectly; they are the revolution, not concepts in transit. Their speech is symbolic and it does not aim at an essence. In these instances, there is speech before history, before politics, before truth, speech before the separation and the future totality. S/he is truly a revolutionary who speaks the world as non-separated. There is no possible or impossible ... Utopia wants speech against power and against the reality principle which is only the phantasm of the system and its definite reproduction. It wants only the spoken word; and it wants to lose itself in it.

> Jean Baudrillard, *The Mirror of Production*, trans. Mark Posner
> (St. Louis, 1975)

Baudrillard's remarks were invoked in the first issue of the *New Statesman* of 1988, in a feature on the workers' and students' "revolution" in France during May 1968. Baudrillard's sense of the moment of revolutionary speech sits well with *Areopagitica*, that most elusive of pleas for liberty of conscience and freedom of the press, a plea which both understands and misunderstands itself, which invokes utopia seemingly to deny it, and which so readily occupies itself with itself that it is difficult to locate it in its historical context, as if the orator were lost in a sea made of his own sound-waves.

Consequently, most previous accounts of *Areopagitica* have ignored the way in which Milton's text uneasily internalizes various stated positions from the Parliamentarian and Puritan spectrum. It will soon become apparent that any attempt to demonstrate this necessitates some revision of the way in which the context itself is understood. *Areopagitica* interprets its context as it attempts to put forward nothing less than a new theory of ethics, a substantial revision of Plato's *Republic*. The orator's voice binds together, as if it were an emulsifying agent, different concerns which are so many fragments of the truth. These elements – the matters of audience, ideology, public debate, censorship and publication, speech in Parliament, republicanism, natural law, and Italian perceptions of the English – are the fragments of knowledge across which the orator slides in his exemplary demonstration of the new ethics: the exercise of choosing in a virtuous way.

The most intelligent and incisive comment made about the purpose of *Areopagitica* is Ernest Sirluck's remark that Milton had to appeal to the Erastians (those who believed that the state should control the church), whose support against censorship would be necessary if the Presbyterians in the House of Commons (the source of support for the Licensing Act of June 1643) were to be defeated (II.170–8). It is difficult to refute this insight into Milton's motivation, but we are still left wondering about the textual consequences of this aim.

The politics of 1643 and 1644 were confusing. Despite the victory over the Royalist army at Marston Moor in July, 1644, Parliament did not seem to be winning the war by the end of the year. The leadership and the two Houses themselves were increasingly divided, not least over the shape of the nation's religious future. The regicide arguments of the later 1640s had not even been dreamt when *Areopagitica* was published.[1]

In this context, Milton's first extremely radical statements were made, between 1643 and 1645. With the effective abolition of episcopacy, and the debate over a future form of national church government in the Westminster Assembly of Divines, the mid-1640s saw the appearance of several publications which challenged the fundamentals of most Puritans, Presbyterian, Independent or otherwise. Mortalism (the notion that the soul remains with the body until the general resurrection), the denial of scriptural literalism, claims that individuals could have God within them, and Milton's own contribution, divorce for spiritually incompatible partners, were given voice from 1643 onwards, and were vigorously controverted in the writings of the (usually Presbyterian) heresiographers.[2]

Milton's position in this field of heresy has always been seen as problematic, if not anomalous.[3] There is little direct evidence to help us. On the one hand, the divorce arguments brought down the full weight of Presbyterian denunciation (II.142). On the other hand, the poet was not associated with the most extreme radicals, dissociated himself from them in print, and presented himself not so much as a Puritan humanist but as a gentleman poet.[4] If Milton had provided a substantial and unambiguous statement regarding church discipline in this period, scholarship would be relieved of a burden. The earlier antiepiscopal tracts present no clear preference for any kind of church discipline, beyond a rejection of Roman and episcopal religion, and a generally favorable glance at the sects – at the time a necessary polemical stance. Milton seems to have written *Areopagitica* partly in response to the hostile reception of his first divorce treatises. As he said in the *Second Defence*, since so many people were addressing reform in the realm of church government and politics, he intended to look at the domestic realm, that is, marriage, education and freedom of publication (*CPW*, IV.i.624; Columbia edn, VIII.130, 132).

I Education not toleration

Milton's purpose in writing *Areopagitica* is entirely consistent with the educational program which he had been pursuing since 1640, both as a tutor and as a reinterpreter of the scripture and legal or theological tradition for the sake of final reform. The constituency of radical reformers to which Milton specifically attached himself, the circle of scientific reformers around Samuel Hartlib (to whom *Of Education* was addressed), is a clear example of the milieu with which Milton associated himself.[5] In this circle, radical religion, politics, and natural philosophy went hand in hand in an excited international correspondence over the nature of final reform. Though Hartlib was somewhat wary of the prodigious Milton, *Areopagitica* is best understood in the context of the learned exchange of ideas.[6]

The primary argument of *Areopagitica* is concerned not with toleration at all, but with the necessity of freedom of the press for the better circulation of knowledge, so that the reformed "truth" may be reconstituted. The arguments advanced by most sectarians and radical Puritans are framed in terms of the nature of spirit and conscience.[7] The image of the "gathered church," the way in which believers were expected to "ingraft" into the Word or Christ (the figurative expression of their fellowship), presents a notion of debate, practice and existence entirely other to the worldliness of Milton's tract. The Independent tolerationists employed a symbolic language of devotion, rather than the terms of power and action stressed by Milton. Roger Williams' *The Bloudy Tenent of Persecution* (London, 1644) was one of the most advanced forms of discourse produced by a radical in these years in which total toleration was advocated and grounded in the premise of a complete separation of church and state.[8] Though Milton had moved towards Williams' position in the antiepiscopal tracts, and though he spoke in *Areopagitica* of the *"unity of Spirit"* and the *"bond of Peace"* (II. 565), he did not express in the mid-1640s the notion of a complete separation between church and state. Neither did he express himself in Williams' terms. God's "beam," enlightening His church for the further discovery of truth (II. 566), is suggestive more of education than of ecclesiology. In *Areopagitica* and the divorce tracts, Pauline language did not predominate as it did for Williams:

> no man denies a double ministry. The one appointed by Christ Jesus in his Church, to gather, to govern, receive in, cast out, and order all the affairs of the Church, the house, city or kingdom of God (Eph. 4; I Cor. 12). Secondly, a civil ministry or office, merely human and civil, which men agree to constitute, called therefore a human creation (I Pet. 2.[13]), and is as true and lawful in those nations, cities, kingdoms, &c., which never heard of the true God.[9]

Unlike Williams, Milton argues initially from a position assuming the value of books in the enhancement of virtue. Books are living men, embodying a divine image (II.492). To suppress or destroy them is to fracture that divinity. Truth lies in the choices made available to the individual in the course of acquiring knowledge, that is, reading. Where Williams describes the relationship between divinity and congregation, Milton explores a pattern of education which would aid the collective recovery of lost and scattered divine truth.

Milton's argument is not based upon a notion of the Truth or knowledge as something which is separated, like the Spirit, from the world. Rather, it is a property argument based partly upon the limitation of monopoly to the author's ownership of his copy. Men need to live from the sale of their books, as much as others need to "feed" on books when they read them. The link between the latter and the former, life and copyright, is one of the first examples of the unusual yokings in the text. At the same time, the retention of copyright by the author (which Milton says should be assured by the signing of each book) signifies the name, honor and virtue of the author and allows those qualities to be disseminated publicly. In other words, *Areopagitica* is based partly upon a notion of property and engages obliquely with the terms of the political dispute between King and Parliament. But these terms are "bent" or refracted in Milton's tropology to set forth through the language of oratory a version of Athenian democracy. This involves a revision of the utopian image to produce a further image of the virtuous individual in the republic. Only when this image is established does Milton offer a defence of specifically religious toleration.

Areopagitica is a speech made to Parliament, though printed, in imitation of Isocrates' habit of writing political pamphlets in which he posed as a speaking orator.[10] In addition, the speeches of several influential Parliamentarians, such as John Pym, Sir Edward Dering, and Sir Henry Vane, had been published in the early 1640s, so the oratical scene of Parliament had already reached out into the book market. As we have already seen, Milton's address is commonly and correctly seen as an attempt to win the support of the Erastian party in Parliament away from the Presbyterians in the Assembly of Divines, who were the major voice in favor of press censorship. It is therefore fitting that Milton should make courteous reference to the Erastian leader, legal theorist, and Parliamentarian, John Selden. In fact, Milton cites Selden's *De Jure Naturali et Gentium juxta Disciplinam Ebraeorum* (1640) on the importance of the voicing of all opinions in order that the truth be reached in the speediest way:

> Wherof what better witnes can ye expect I should produce, then one of
> your own now sitting in Parlament, the chief of learned men reputed
> in this Land , Mr. *Selden*, whose volume of naturall & national laws
> proves, not only by great autorities brought together, but by exquisite
> reasons and theorems almost mathematically demonstrative, that all
> opinions, yea errors, known, read, and collated, are of main service &
> assistance toward the speedy attainment of what is truest.   (II.513)

What has not previously been realized is that Milton appears to echo Selden's Latin: "ea quae sic imperata sint nec unquam sint non observanda, sicut et in demonstrativis principia ac theoremata, indicentur et fiant manifesta."[11] Significantly, "theorem," "mathematical," and "demonstrative" occur rarely in the prose, and then only in *Areopagitica* and the divorce tracts, where other ideas of Selden are also used.[12] Milton is using Seldenic language. In doing so, he seems to be voicing allegiance to an interpretation of nature in which man's natural reason helps him to arrive at the truth through *proairesis*.[13] "Heresy" has its origins in this same root: "*hairesis*" – "choice."

Selden seems to have regarded this perception of man's rational capacity to determine matters with a God-given light of nature ("intellectus agens") as part of the Baconian movement, and Milton, by means of echo, appears to be following him.[14] Natural law itself was variously described as the principles which God had given to man, and which existed prior to the positive laws which man invented in society:

> The natural and positive divine right differ in this: that the positive is mutable and various according to God's good pleasure (for that which was heretofore in the Judaical church is different from that which is in the Christian church); but the right natural is always the same and like itself, and for this reason also it is called the law eternal.[15]

At the root of natural law is a vision of the principles which govern man after the Fall. In the state of nature, division, will, and lust threaten to destroy mankind. Natural law exists to protect mankind from these consequences of the Fall. The Mosaic law is consistent with natural law: "That Judaical Law which was given by Moses to the Israelites as proper only to them, was a most exact determination and accommodation of the law of nature unto them."[16]

For Selden in particular, failure to comply with the law of nature should be met by punishment from God. On this point of obligation, Selden is markedly forceful. At some points in *De Jure Naturali*, Selden argued that a contract which was made in the positive sphere was binding upon the participants even if natural law was offended.[17] This was but one step away from Hobbes' notion of sovereignty and obligation, quite unlike Milton's later statements on political obligation. But Selden remained more ambiguous overall, still offering an older view of natural law in which individual citizens behaved virtuously through nature, a view which would have been attractive to Milton.[18] For Selden, obligation and liberty existed side by side. As we shall see, Milton fails to reconcile the two views, and forces a creative tension precisely from their conjunction.

II Natural law troped

Selden's work and Milton's use of it constitute one aspect of a much wider concern which exists in this particular version of natural law theory. Selden's text includes a detailed and extensive exploration of the laws and customs of the Israelites, and the transmission of that culture through Antiquity and the Middle Ages in Rabbinic literature.[19] The reader is presented with a complete representation of Hebrew society, the *republic* (in the sense of a state or commonwealth) of the Hebrews. Such a topic was not uncommon in the later Renaissance. Humanist apologists for the independent Dutch Republic saw similarities between their state and the original republic of the Hebrew people.[20] Selden's scholarship had serious consequences for English politics. For instance, tithes could be shown, in Hebrew society, not to have their origins in a divine or natural law for the maintenance of priests, so providing a powerful argument against the economic foundations of the established church in England.

Indeed, in a series of works on Hebraic customs and traditions, Selden went on to disprove the moral authority of the churches, thereby enhancing the strength of the Erastian argument.[21] In *Areopagitica*, London becomes a Hebraic "City of refuge" (II.553; Numb. 35), part of a "Nation of Prophets, of Sages, and of Worthies" (II.554; Numb. 11:27–9) who fashion justice, or discover laws natural and national to revive and protect truth. The rewriting of the history of natural law, in Hebraic and Byzantine society, is a parallel movement of both Selden and Milton in his divorce tracts, where the "republic" is rediscovered in enormous juridical detail.[22] Where Selden remained ideologically uncommitted, however, Milton saw his part as one of scholarship in the cause of Reformation.

Such an interest in the Hebraic seems largely absent from the writings of other radicals in the toleration debate. Of course, even as extreme a Pauline spiritualist as Roger Williams still uses the Old Testament, but with an emphasis upon unsurprising typologies – the journey to the Land of Israel, for instance.[23] He focuses upon the necessity for consciences to be left unhindered, since through Grace and Reason, the need for restraint is diminished. Again, Williams' specific context is church discipline and organization, and the need for spiritual democracy to prevail, rather than the wider educational argument adopted by Milton. Moreover, society in *Areopagitica* is a mosaic of individual activities, enhancing the "republican" perspective: even if Milton would have had a king in his ideal state at this point (kings are simply not mentioned in the tract), the roles played by private citizens and legislators are the focus of the reader's attention.

The natural law interest was by no means confined to Selden, nor even to the Parliamentarians. After all, the Royalists could argue that there was no inconsistency between divine right kingship and natural law. Concepts used in apologetic arguments were marked in the mid-1640s by their circulation among all parties. For Royalists, monarchy was there by nature as much as it was there by divine right. Natural law was for the Parliamentarians a justification of its case, not an argument for the abolition of monarchy. *Areopagitica* reflects a fluidity of public exchange in which arguments and their modes of articulation were slowly and indistinctly taking shape.

The most significant Parliamentarian apologies were those of Henry Parker, whom Milton also echoes in *Areopagitica*.[24] If Milton did want to win over the Parliamentary centre, it would have been an astute persuasive move to adopt the vocabulary (though not exactly the opinions) of this acclaimed Parliamentarian. Parker argued that the King was offending nature by harming his subjects since *salus populi suprema lex esto*: "'Twas never beleev'd before that any but God could work contrary to nature, but now it must be beleeved."[25] Though Selden openly ridiculed this argument in his *Table-Talk*, it is reflected in *Areopagitica* by the peculiar presence of some of Parker's vocabulary, words which do not appear with frequency in Milton's other prose works. One instance which may have attracted Milton is Parker's discussion of the origins of government and prelapsarian nature. There is no final proof that Milton was using Parker's language in this way, but the incidence of references in each context, and Parker's prominent use of the marital analogy in constitutional argument, make it unlikely that Milton did not have Parker in mind. The important word is "sublime."[26] Explaining the origins of laws, Parker writes in *Jus Populi* (London, 16 October 1644) that:

> If *Adam* had not sinned in Paradise, order had been sufficient alone
> without any proper jurisdiction: it may well be supposed, that
> government, truly so called, had been no more necessary amongst men
> on earth, then it is now in Heaven amongst Angels ... We may then
> acknowledge that order is of a *sublime* and celestiall extraction, such as
> nature in its greatest purity did own; but subjection, or rather servile
> subjection, such as attends humane policy amongst us, derives not it
> self from Nature, unless we mean corrupted nature.   (p. 3, my italics)

In Milton, the usage of "sublime" is twisted round, so that it becomes associated with the virtue which allows mankind to regain that which was lost at the Fall. Freedom of the press will lead to healthy minds and brave bodies "to bestow upon the solidest and sublimest points of controversie, and new invention, it betok'ns us not degenerated" (II.557). Milton envisages a return through virtue to that state of perfection in which nature and governance are harmonized, and true creativity is possible.

If "sublime" represents an education into the greatest benefits of nature, the figural construction of *Areopagitica* raises a problem in the process of consumption which it envisages as education. Milton represents natural law by that most fundamental of processes for production and consumption – eating – the central animating metaphor of the tract. Here, in Milton's figurative language, a contradiction appears between books as food and books as men. Books are living men to be "eaten" by other men – a crisis of production and consumption which remains unresolved in the imagistic subtext of the tract. There is no element which serves to protect, so that it is possible to say that a contract or obligation theory is missing. Milton's imagery has attempted to root virtue in natural law, but in doing so it fails to define the liberty of the virtuous subject. Being virtuous is a self-constituting act of citizenship, but it was not a very useful tool with which to resist arguments for royal supremacy.

As for the Licensing Act of June, 1643: "I am of those who beleeve, it will be a harder alchymy then *Lullius* ever knew, to sublimat any good use out of such an invention" (II.507). The alchemical meaning of sublimation, to purify, has affinities with the meaning of sublime adopted by Parker: "of the most exalted kind."[27] The Licensing Act will never be able to encourage the standard of collective virtue which prevails in Milton's tract. In addition, such a repressive piece of legislation will not allow that which is repressed in unreformed society to come to the top and manifest itself in the public forum which decides truth and virtue.

Areopagitica not only promises a return to the image of sublimity envisioned by Parker, but takes the word from its political context in Parker, and puts it to work for the sake of "invention" (including rhetorical *inventio*) and tolerance, without entirely shedding the political connotations. Justifying the Parliamentary recourse to arms in 1642, Parker wrote that

> Reason of State is something more sublime and imperiall then Law: it may be rightly said, that the Statesman begins where the Lawyer ceaseth ... *To deny to Parliaments recourse to reason of State in these miserable times of warre and danger, [is] as to deny them self-defence.*[28]

Parker appears to be saying that a recourse to arms is an extreme measure and associated not merely with austere republican masculinity (as opposed to effeminate monarchical courtliness) but with the grandeur of empire. By 1650, "sublime" was definitely a republican word. The usages here by Parker and Milton are examples of the generation of republican vocabulary in the 1640s: the concern is with the well-being of virtuous citizens.[29] Again, Milton can be seen repeating Parker and at the same time subtly revising his message. The famous image of the dragon's teeth in *Areopagitica* is usually assumed to be taken from Ovid's stories of Cadmus and Jason.[30] But the image is also used by Parker:

> The maine Engineers in this Civill Warre are Papists, the most poysonous, serpentine, Iesuited Papists of the World. And the Papists in *Europe* either pray for the prosperity of the design, or here contributed some other influence and assistance to it. This warre was not the production of these last two yeares, nor was England alone the field wherein the Dragon's teeth were sown.[31]

In Milton, this becomes the image of the active republic, full of vibrant, energetic individuals. By permission of the simile, people fight and create: "I know they are as lively, and as vigorously productive, as those fabulous Dragons teeth; and being sown up and down, may chance to spring up armed men" (II.492).

III Italy, heresy, and sexuality

As with Parker's writing, a large amount of *Areopagitica* is rooted in continental, specifically Italian history. The significance of the Council of Trent was known to most educated English people, but Milton makes specific use of the imaginative patterns in Paulo Sarpi's histories of the Council of Trent and of the Inquisition. Indeed, the genealogy of censorship in Milton's tract has its origins most convincingly in Sarpi. It is too early to talk of a widespread Italianate republicanism among Parliamentarians in 1644, but, as Blair Worden has shown, the experience of visiting the Italian states and of reading Italian political writing had a profound effect upon English discussions of power and virtue.[32] Milton imbibes the Italian anti-Papal perception of persecution and uses it to expand his notion of the necessity to discuss vice or heresy before rejecting it. Indeed, Milton goes beyond Sarpi, who maintains that there is a natural law (though not an ecclesiastical one) against the reading of bad books.[33] This usage is best seen when it works in both positive and negative ways for Milton. An interesting example is the use of Bernardo Davanzati's *Scisma d'Inghilterra* (Florence, 1638). Davanzati was a Florentine antiquarian, who dedicated this work to the Duke of Tuscany.[34] The end of this piece provides the imprimaturs which Milton brings to life satirically as the bobbing priests and friars: "Sometimes 5 *Imprimaturs* are seen together dialogue-wise in the Piatza of one Title page, complementing and ducking each to other with their shav'n reverences" (II.504). But is Milton attacking the content of the work, or the fact that it had to succumb to Papal licensing?

Milton uses Davanzati's attack on the immorality of Henry VIII's court in a negative way, making it behave in the opposite way to Davanzati's intentions: "I name not him for posterities sake, whom *Harry* the 8. nam'd in merriment his Vicar of hell" (II.518).[35] Milton says that smutty foreign literature like Davanzati's can creep into England uncensored, while decent English publications are gagged by an Inquisitorial censorship. Yet the very use of Davanzati allows Milton to let licentiousness exist in his text as an expression of the toleration which the *scisma* so berated by Davanzati permitted. Likewise, Milton turns Sarpi about: where Sarpi's genealogy of censorship was at pains to show that the church should be in charge of censorship in religious matters, and the state in secular matters, Milton is against both forms of press censorship. Licensing will not prevent license as long as men can read foreign books which cannot be licensed (II.503). By citing libertines like Aretino, *Areopagitica* presents that moral choice to the reader which should be informed by virtue.[36] This is curious, for it puts pressure upon the very limits of Milton's toleration. Davanzati is repeating a story which was written by an English recusant as an attack upon the English Reformation of Henry VIII.[37] The Reformation and its intimate connection with the sexual life of the King and his wives was a perfectly legitimate way of attacking Protestantism (with official sanction) in Italy, just as the hordes of references to the sexual perversions of monks and nuns were legitimate attacks upon Catholicism in England. Would Milton have objected to the circulation in Italy of a scurrilous and obscene English attack upon mendicants? The closing sentences of the tract refute the claim of the Stationers that censorship will enhance the escape of "malignant books" abroad. In whose eyes are these books malignant – Milton's, the censor's or those who live abroad (II.570)? Milton's refusal to comment here becomes an affirmation of the final absence of any justly imposed censorship. There is no escape from the degree of legitimacy which regimes give to certain publications, but there are ways of using the ammunition of the opposite side in one's own cause. In *Areopagitica*, toleration does not supersede the claims of religious and national polemic, and neither does it preclude the possibilities for creative engagement with the life-blood spirits of enemy nations.

The very citation of Davanzati creates in Milton what has been aptly (though for the wrong reasons) called a "libertine syntax," a language which appropriates the voice of other, sometimes opposite speakers, in order to challenge one's own moral order, or to mock the order of the appropriated voice itself.[38] Milton's words are libertine because they refute intentions of propriety, making the achievement of virtue an act of verbal muscularity and masculinity. Such an achievement is partly a consequence of Milton's inability to think beyond continuing religious difference in Europe, and of the awareness that this situation will necessarily involve the mutual generation of hostile codes and images by each side.

Areopagitica thus recognizes the uses which a state might make of intolerance. Had he been prepared to tolerate even Catholics through an ideal of love in society and governance, as did William Walwyn (who was to become a Leveller, and who was in 1644 an extreme tolerationist), Milton's attitudes to knowledge and power would have been fundamentally different. For this reason, Sirluck's suggestion that Milton was condensing Walwyn's arguments for toleration in *Areopagitica* is probably erroneous (II.87).[39] Walwyn is prepared to see the love of and from God as that which should ensure the toleration of all, provided they do not endanger the civil peace, including Catholics. It is because Milton cannot imagine Catholics who are not politically intransigent that he argues for their exemption from toleration. Milton's Janus-faced conception of the need for choice, and his notion of education through contraries, of learning good through evil, is rooted partly in an awareness of the perpetual existence of evil – in international terms, Rome. The "libertine syntax," shot through with contrariness in the motions of its own construction, admits to itself the possibility of committing violence on the enemy, and of being strong enough (it is, after all, compared to an army) to resist attacks on its own virtue.

The genesis of Milton's sentences admits this ambivalence of invention and militant strength. In the same sentence as the Dragon's teeth is an echo from Sarpi that words can cause wars. Milton begins the sentence with the image of the "vigorously productive" society, but he ends it with Sarpi's indication that books can help cause destruction. The syntax is libertine in the literal sense that it is apparently out of control. The impression given is that Milton is unable to free the text from its connotations in Sarpi. Milton's orator is unable to free his words from Sarpi's printed text. And at the beginning and end of the paragraph in which this sentence occurs, the notion that books live is broached not primarily because of their virtue, but because they live with "the pretious life-blood of a master spirit," so they should be prone to punishment if dangerous or malicious. The syntax manages to express opposites by means of the mode of appropriation of its source texts, behind which lie the very acts of reading which Milton would have the censors leave unhindered. But at the sight of the licenser in the imprimatur, the muscular reader tosses ("dings" – II. 553) the book away from his virtuous person, in a sinewy rebellion against bondage. It is almost as if Milton has picked up in his echo of Sarpi the Venetian's opinion that man was finally in control of himself, not Providence.[40] This hint of individual power makes *Areopagitica* even more radical through the presentation of a form of secularism, at odds again with the terms of the tolerationists.

IV Hijacking the Spirit

At the point where *Areopagitica* appears to borrow from Walwyn's exposition of freedom of conscience in *The Compassionate Samaritane*, Milton's tract turns from nature to grace, from the capacity of the virtuous man to order and choose from natural ability, to the power of scripture to edify. This has been seen as an ironic turn in the tract, a Pauline reversal in which Christ's sacrifice is seen to legislate charity and therefore toleration. Under this dispensation, natural perception is dignified:

> God then raises to his own work men of rare abilities, and more then common industry not only to look back and revise what hath bin taught heretofore, but to gain furder and goe on, some new enlightn'd steps in the discovery of truth. For such is the order of God's enlightning his Church, to dispense and deal out by degrees his beam, so as our earthly eyes may best sustain it. (II. 566)

In this spirit, Milton refers to Lord Brooke's popular plea for toleration, no doubt a pragmatic gesture in the direction of a respected Parliamentarian, but also indicative of the framework in which the rest of a specifically republican endeavor should be exercised (II. 560).[41] Milton appears to regard the Puritan argument for, and language of, toleration as another fragment of truth to be gathered up in the greater whole. The effect of this treatment is to give the religious imagery of toleration the status not of an uncomplicated mediator of divine truth (as it was for most Presbyterians, Independents and separatists), but as a set of tropes which are to be deployed when necessary. The highly-wrought nature of the metaphors in *Of Reformation* (1641) gives a similar impression.

In *Areopagitica*, the language of congregational unity and toleration (*"the unity of Spirit"* and *"the bond of peace"*) is made to function on behalf of the republic. Spiritual and political liberty (according to Milton's restrictions) are identified here through a pun. Milton identifies the popular assembly of Athens addressed by Isocrates, the *ecclesia*, the "Parliament." Clearly, open speaking ("plain advertisement") and virtuous thinking through free choice, benefit both church (*ecclesia*; Sarpi's "congregation") and state, however separate they are, and however we might doubt Milton's religiosity because of his entertainment of secular arguments or sentiments. Parliament, it is implied, should outlaw calumny (*ad hominem* attack, as opposed to reasoned disagreement with an argument [II.494]), a republican version of a standard and orthodox Puritan objection. Nevertheless, this should not prevent personal censorship: the Cynics are implicitly derided because they uttered "impudence," even though they remained, rightly in Milton's view, uncensored by the Athenian laws (II.495).

But the Cynics took from their leader Antisthenes the complete sufficiency of virtue and wisdom, and contempt for pleasure and ostentation – the usual source for their sharp rebukes.[42] In a similar reliance upon personal perfection, Milton appears to signal Antinomian affiliations in *Areopagitica*, through his reference to the text of Paul, "To the pure all things are pure" (Titus 1:15). But there is no theology of grace such as we find in the Antinomians proper.[43] *Areopagitica* is built upon the notions of inner control and courage central to the Greek and Roman idea of virtue. Hence the large degree of body imagery in the tract. The Spartans (II.496) become images of warlike and disciplinarian Parliamentarians and Puritans, who have yet to learn the uses of learned and sophisticated verse for the betterment of law and civility. The fact that the Spartans did not have this, until Thales sought to convert them, made simple but virtuous battle songs prone to degeneration into lewd chorusing and promiscuous behavior – libertinism.[44] Burning one's books (killing life-blood) is legitimate so long as one owns them. This is a voluntary act, similar to that self-discipline exercised by Origen when he interpreted scriptural injunctions for holiness as an instruction for self-castration.[45]

Censorship of the sort disliked by Milton had its causes beyond the ethical realm and in a fractured moment in the history of Rome, just after the transition from Republic to Empire. Octavius did not censor the pro-Republican history of Livy, while Ovid was banished for "some secret cause." Exile (erasing the person from presence in the state) for endangering the security of the state, Milton seems to be saying, is justifiable, though suppressing an exile's writings is not. Yet, as we have already seen, exiling a book or a man is no help to the cause of censorship: ideas outside the "city of refuge" always find a way of seeping back inside.

Along with the presence in the text of the city state, *Areopagitica* is also permeated with references to trade and commerce. Milton is concerned to safeguard the copyright of authorship (a monopoly of one over one) – that part of a censorship should certainly remain (II.491). The notion of monopoly receives severe criticism in the mercantilist-flavored pamphlets of Henry Robinson, another voice for liberty of conscience. Robinson's understanding of toleration grows directly out of his experience of the English trade in the Mediterranean. He regards monopolies as restrictive on trade, and was later to speak on behalf of trade and legal reform during the Interregnum. In *Liberty of Conscience* (1644), Robinson recounts how English merchants in Italy and Spain protected themselves from the Inquisitorial gaze by sending "their eyes a gadding after beauty" (either church architecture and decorations, or women), so putting their souls in danger: far better to have a tolerant society where people will not be forced to dissemble and to cultivate lust.[46] Persecution threatens to force out English religious radicals who are also her "manufactors," just as the Moors were expelled from Spain and the Jews from Portugal. Though Milton remained implacably opposed to Catholicism, where Robinson would have it tolerated for the sake of trade, the implications of Milton's textual practice in the use of Davanzati and Sarpi is that *proairesis* must necessarily engage with cultural otherness for the sake of its own vigorous productivity.

In addition, Milton differed from Henry Parker on this issue. Whether Milton knew it or not, Parker had written a defence of the Licensing Act on behalf of the Stationers Company on the grounds that censorship protected the Stationers' monopoly.[47] In a later work on free trade, Parker argued against *laissez-faire*, in favor of a regulation which kept the trading balance in the hands of English merchants.[48] Milton's version of the free trade of truth demands that individuals, though wealthy in the truth, do not make others do their work, thereby converting the truth into a mere commodity (II.544). Rather, they should resist all controls on the exchange of knowledge (II.545), and participate in the struggle to gain (that is, read) "our richest Marchandize, Truth" (II.548; see also the "spiritual factory" of 1.802). Being virtuous through self-control and *proairesis* makes the citizen the highest resource, above normal exchange relationships.

Nevertheless, Milton does not stress in *Areopagitica* the desirability of every man having his own access to the moving power of the Holy Spirit, something which would have been far more in tune with the religious radicals of the early 1640s.[49] Rather, *Areopagitica* becomes a compelling statement of a variegated Renaissance republicanism, a productive but confused yoking together of the forces which were coursing through England at the time. This is not, of course, the regicide republicanism of the late 1640s and early 1650s, but the image of a society in which individual virtue can flourish, in which divine grace and civic virtue combine in individual acts of intellectual labor (the prime end to which Milton's tract is dedicated [II.554]).

In the dangerous books or the books which propose censorship, Milton is able to see a way of reading which benefits the free republicans. So the constraints in Plato's *Republic* are seen as parts of a fiction designed to inculcate standards of virtue rather than as the literal truth of how things should be. This makes *Areopagitica* compatible to some extent with the Erasmian and Morean view of the function of utopian literature.[50] It would seem to be the "natural laws" which Milton sees in the "*Atlantick* and *Eutopian* polities": "those unwritt'n, or at least unconstraining laws of vertuous education, religious and civill nurture" (II.526). Significantly, education is seen to enable a discovery of natural law principles. The aspersions which Milton casts upon utopias here are typical of the Janus-faced modes of apprehension which *Areopagitica* comes to recommend.[51] Because they are ideal the Utopia and the New Atlantis are unattainable, but with the light of nature and of the "streaming fountain" of scripture, they point to "the better and exacter things, then were yet known" (II.543). As with all of *Areopagitica*, possibilities and limitations are simultaneously indicated. At the same time, very little is offered here which mitigates Baudrillard's claim (see above, p. 103) that *a priori* speech fulfils itself before attaining "essence." The "essence," the "politics" and the "history" are in the "better and exacter things" to come which are offered but never laid open. *Proairesis*, through unrestricted reading, thinking and writing, remains a textual effect.

Still, *Areopagitica* represents one moment in J. G. A. Pocock's "language" of republicanism.[52] The well-known praise of the English nation is made in terms of a republic of poets and musicians, all of whom "create" the republic in a collective manifestation of superlative style, unlike Plato's call for a society in which such artistic freedoms are suppressed (II.523). The Puritan Reformation of Manners, we are shown, needs some limits to the degree of restraint which discipline imposes upon or generates within individuals. England itself becomes the Roman Eagle, rising in the "midday beam" and the "fountain . . . of heavn'ly radiance" (II.558). Even if the republic was a vision, part of the knowledge of political theory, rather than a separate program at this stage, the principles existed in political imaginations in the early 1640s.[53] The republic exists as a series of images, perhaps as broken and shattered as Milton's images of Truth themselves. Just so, *Areopagitica* is but one version, and a complete reversal of Plato's idea of a state which banished its poets, though one which needs the image of Plato's utopia and his version of virtuous self-control in order to define itself (II. 522–6). Milton refuses Plato's analogy between city and soul, thereby freeing the individual for action from Plato's rigid hierarchies.[54]

In this way, *Areopagitica* transforms the modes of learning by which truth is discovered into aesthetic forms, simultaneously frozen yet in motion, sometimes severed from their context in the process of public debate, but isolated, pleasing and perpendicular in their seeming wholeness. The conformity of the Presbyterians would "freeze" intellectual endeavor as if it were a "January," but the name of the first month points to the image of the two-faced god: there is more than one way of reading "unity" (II. 545). Likewise, sin remains our "provoking object," a "huge heap increasing under the very act of diminishing" (II. 527). The English are "forc't and frozen" into obsession with the strict division between visible congregations, whereas they should simultaneously apprehend similarity or sameness and difference: indifferency should allow the visible churches and the invisible church to coexist in a perpetual truth-revealing tension (II. 564).[55]

By using the trope of books as men, Milton finds an apt metaphor of many collaborating bodies, healthy in their active juxtaposition, as opposed to the dominant royalist image of the body politic.[56] The almost pervasive spectacle of the state with the King as its head, the people as the body and limbs is entirely displaced, while any risk of an oblique mention of body politic is suppressed by the absence of the image of Christ as head of the body of the church. In this way, both royalist and Presbyterian *jure divino* arguments are avoided, and the question of magisterial authority is largely postponed for the sake of a greater concentration upon personal responsibility and collective energy.

As is well known, *Areopagitica* is constructed as a piece of rhetoric with Milton's speaking *persona* adopting the stance of a republican orator in a righteous "passion" against the vacuous wind of courtly flattery and hypocritical "mystical pluralists." Once again, the origins of Milton's language lie in Parliamentarian apology. Parker is quite clear about the value of learned oratory:

> the Kings interest will be the more hopefully pursu'd when Schollars second it with their Arts, and the Schollars Interests will be the easier gained, when the King seconds them with his Armes. But of all kindes of Learning Oratory is most relyed on: and of all kindes of Oratory, that is most made use of, which is most wantonly painted and dressed.[57]

As Milton reformed the masque and Puritanized the pastoral in the 1630s, so he sought to redirect oratory to the matter of edification through virtue and tolerance. It is the very imitation of Athenian oratorical sound in print which communicates affectively the ideal of political life as it should be – supposedly democratic, liberal, able to comprehend more than one point of view – not the very different sounds of the Puritan sermon: "To which if I now manifest by the very sound of this which I shall utter, that wee are already in good part arriv'd, and yet from such a steepe disadvantage of tyranny and superstition grounded into our principles as was beyond the manhood of a Roman recovery" (II.487).

Areopagitica closes with an image of the English before 1640, the vocabulary of which points towards the state of slavery as much as episcopal government: "brutish, formall, and slavish" (II.559). The Parliament is rediscovering the original liberty of the English people, consistent with the principles of natural law. This is the meaning of the "revolution" (II.493) taking place, and Milton is telling the Parliament that freedom of the press is a vital part of this liberty. The primary image of virtue is one drawn from classical republicanism. Natural law, in various guises, becomes the chief creative presence in the tract, creative in that Milton wants to be seen honoring Parliament and in that he makes natural law language attempt the work of toleration. Yet, as we have seen, the orator introduces no notion or argument which is consistently maintained without contradiction or heavy qualification. Milton's ethics are finally incompatible with natural law and contract. In the vision of free choice perspectives are raised, and oratorical gestures made, which could never be accommodated by the tolerationist positions. *Areopagitica* delivers a methodology for Reformation, a series of aestheticized exemplars of how to think properly. The tract is an abstraction from the interpretative procedures of the divorce tracts, and it prepares the reader to read, to think, and to write in similar terms. The tract is inconclusive because of the need to show how truth is to be gathered, while the texts and voices which make up *Areopagitica* reveal disparate *ideologemes*, bits and pieces of the value systems which Milton presents as the components of what was to become the "good old cause."

Alas, neither the concerns nor the rhetoric of *Areopagitica* weighed heavily upon contemporaries. As is well known, the work was largely ignored in its own time. Curiously, a Bodleian Library copy of a late 1640s English translation of the German mystic, Jakob Boehme, has as an end-paper a page of a dismembered copy of *Areopagitica*.[58] Perhaps the original owner had more than one copy. Whether he did or he did not, the seventeenth-century binding is a clear indication of the spiritual concerns which predominated by the late 1640s, which were far different from the blend of educationally-slanted virtue theory, republicanism and natural law which prevails in Milton's tract. *Areopagitica* did exert an influence upon the republican apologists of the early 1650s, especially John Hall, but in 1644, in the attempt to persuade Parliament of the cause of virtue, in terms which the Parliament would have understood and been honored by, Milton's text consumed itself in a surfeit of its own passion.

Notes

1 For the most enduring narrative account of the events, see Samuel R. Gardiner, *History of the Great Civil War 1642–1649*, 3 vols (London, 1889), vol. II, pp. 1–47.

2 See Thomas Edwards, *Gangraena*, 3 parts (London, 1646). For specific discussions of mortalism, see Norman T. Burns, *Christian Mortalism from Tyndale to Milton* (Cambridge, Mass., 1972).

3 See Christopher Hill, *Milton and the English Revolution* (London, 1977), pp. 93–116.

4 See Thomas N. Corns, "Milton's Quest for Respectability," *Modern Language Review*, 77 (1982), pp. 769–79.

5 Milton and the new science receives a thorough discussion in Charles Webster, *The Great Instauration: Science, Medicine and Reform 1626–1660* (London, 1975), especially pp. 144, 190. See also *CPW*, I.288–306.

6 References to Milton occur in the correspondence of the Hartlib Circle: Sheffield University Library, Hartlib Papers, 3/2/43–4; 13/121–2; 59/9/1–9; 60/14/2–39; 62/30/1. *Of Education* is particularly praised by John Hall: MS Hartlib, 3/2/43–4.

7 The major work on Puritan spirituality is G. F. Nuttall, *The Holy Spirit in Puritan Faith and Experience* (Oxford, 1946). For Milton's contribution, see pp. 35, 67, 98, 114.

8 For Roger Williams, see Edmund S. Morgan, *Roger Williams: The Church and the State* (London, 1967), and W. C. Gilpin, *The Millenarian Piety of Roger Williams* (London, 1979). *The Bloudy Tenent* should always be read beside *Experiments of Spiritual Life and Health* (London, 1652), to gain a balanced perspective of Williams' thought.

9 Roger Williams, *The Bloudy Tenent of Persecution* (London, 1644) in A. S. P. Woodhouse, ed., *Puritanism and Liberty*, new preface by Ivan Roots (London, 1986), p. 276.

10 See J. A. Wittreich, Jr., "Milton's *Areopagitica*: Its Isocratic and Ironic Contexts," *Milton Studies*, 4 (1972), pp. 101–15, though the argument in this article is not entirely faithful to the complexities and contradictions in Milton's text. The point has been made often enough that the Areopagus was a council which imposed censorship.

11 John Selden, *De Jure Naturali et Gentium juxta Disciplinam Ebraeorum* (London, 1640), p. 109.

12 *A Concordance to the English Prose of John Milton*, edited by Laurence Sterne and Harold H. Kollmeier (Binghamton, 1985) lists the following instances of vocabulary in addition to the usages in the quotation: "theorems" (*CPW*, II.613); "theory" (*CPW*, I.933, II.222); "mathematical" (*CPW*, II.392, 393, VII.476); "demonstrative" (*CPW*, II.309, 582, 612).

13 See *CPW*, II.396. The origins of the term – voluntary action based upon reasoning – are Aristotelian (*Nicomachean Ethics*, II.vi.15).

14 Selden, *De Jure*, p. 116; see also the parallel account in Jeremy Taylor, *Ductor Dubitantium*, 2.1.1.39, in *The Whole of the Works of the Right Reverend Jeremy Taylor, D.D.*, 10 vols (London, 1851), vol. IX, p. 298. See also *ibid.*, p. 295: "The law of nature is a transcript of the wisdom and will of God written in the tables of our minds . . . not a product of experience, but written with the finger of God, first in the tables of our hearts." "Intellectual" in Milton's prose has a similar kind of

incidence to the other "Seldenic" words: Sterne and Kollmaier, *Concordance*: "intellectual[ls]" (*CPW*, 1.566, II.230, 505); "intellective" (*CPW*, II.374, 609); "intellect" (*CPW*, 1.664, II.492).

15 William Ames, *Cases of Conscience* (London, 1639), in Woodhouse, *Puritanism and Liberty*, p. 187.

16 Ames, in Woodhouse, *Puritanism and Liberty*, p. 191.

17 See Richard Tuck, *Natural Rights Theories* (Cambridge, 1979), pp. 90–6.

18 Tuck's opinion has been qualified by J. P. Sommerville, "John Selden, the Law of Nature, and the Origins of Government," *Historical Journal*, 27 (1984), pp. 437–47. For a succinct and brilliant demonstration of the coexistence of positive and negative notions of liberty, see Quentin Skinner, "The Idea of Negative Liberty: Philosophical and Historical Perspectives," in Richard Rorty, J. B. Schneewind and Quentin Skinner, eds., *Philosophy in History* (Cambridge, 1984), pp. 193–221, esp. pp. 203, 207, 209–13 for applications to Milton.

19 See for instance John Selden, *The Historie of Tithes* (London, 1618), pp. iii, 1–24, 49–56.

20 The most popular work was probably by Peter Cunaeus, translated in English (London, 1653) as *Of the Common-wealth Of The Hebrews*. Of relevance here is p. 43: "We confess indeed the land of *Palestine* was the favourite of Heaven, and much indebted to the divine influence above other Lands; yea, things went there sometimes contrary to the Law of Nature."

21 Selden, *The Historie of Tithes*, pp. iii, 1–24, 49–56.

22 See Selden, *De anno civili & calendrio* (London, 1644); *Uxor Ebraica* (London, 1646); *De Synedris & praefecturis* (London, 1650).

23 Williams, *The Bloudy Tenent*, original edition, sig. a2v.

24 For Parker's career and popularity, see W. K. Jordan, *Men of Substance: A Study of the Thought of Two English Revolutionaries* (Chicago, 1942), pp. 142–3, 148.

25 Henry Parker, *The Contra-Replicant* (London, 1642), p. 4.

26 Sterne and Kollmaier, eds., *Concordance*, lists one use of "sublimat," five uses of "sublime," two uses of "sublimest" and one use of "sublimities." In the poetry, apart from one occurrence in *Comus*, "sublime" occurs only in the later poetry: nine times in *Paradise Lost* and one each in *Paradise Regained* and *Samson Agonistes*.

27 In *An Apology Against A Pamphlet* (London, 1642), Milton uses this definition of sublime as a means of ridiculing Joseph Hall: *CPW*, 1.890, 892.

28 Parker, *The Contra-Replicant*, p. 19.

29 "*Democracie* is the best *Nurse* of *high* Spirits," wrote John Hall in his 1652 translation of Longinus' *On the Sublime* (p. 53), noting also the necessary meeting of "Experience" and "*vivacity* of Invention" for sublime expression (p. 11), a suitably Miltonic prescription. The language and imagery of classical republican- ism remained a powerful presence in the West European Renaissance memory, despite the rise of seigneuries and monarchies. More needs to be known about Parker's understanding of republicanism. For Milton and classical republican values, see Z. S. Fink, *The Classical Republicans: An Essay in the Recovery of a Pattern of Thought in Seventeenth Century England* (Evanston, Ill., 1945), pp. 45, 82, 90, 91, 93, 107, 116. See also David Norbrook, "Marvell's 'Horatian Ode' and the Politics of Genre," in Jonathan Sawday and Thomas F. Healy, eds., *Literature and the English Civil War* (Cambridge, forthcoming).

30 Ovid, *Metamorphoses*, III.101–30; VII.121–42.

31 Parker, *The Contra-Replicant*, p. 9.
32 "Classical Republicanism and the Puritan Revolution," in *History and Imagination: Essays in Honour of H. R. Trevor-Roper*, ed. H. Lloyd-Jones, V. Pearl and B. Worden (London, 1981), pp. 182–200.
33 See Paulo Sarpi, *The Historie of the Council of Trent*, trans. Nathanael Brent (London, 1620), p. 472.
34 Davanzati's works in this volume, besides the *Scisma*, include "Notizia de' Cambi," "Lezione della Moneta," "Orazione in Morte del Gran Duca Cosimo I," "Due Orazione ò vero Azioni Accademiche," "Coltivatione Toscana Delle Viti, e d'alcuni Arbori." The imprimaturs which Milton quotes (II.503–4) follow the latter work and not the *Scisma*. John Toland, Milton's biographer, published a translation of the treatise on money as *A Discourse Upon Coins* (London, 1696).
35 It is not unlikely that Davanzati was drawing upon Nicholas Saunders, *De Schismate Anglicano* (Rome, 1586), if not replicating it and not acknowledging the author of the original work. Saunders certainly refers pointedly to Sir Francis Bryan, the figure of interest to Milton. If this is the case, Davanzati's practice provides another irony for Milton and an attack on Milton's own principle of the author's retention of his copyright.
36 For a brief association of Milton with the tradition of Renaissance (and republican) virtue, see Quentin Skinner, *The Foundations of Modern Political Thought*, 2 vols (Cambridge, 1978), vol. I, p. 218.
37 See n. 35.
38 See Christopher Kendrick, *Milton: A Study in Ideology and Form* (London, 1986), p. 33.
39 Similar strategies of ridicule to those used in *Areopagitica* may be seen in the works of another Leveller, Richard Overton, notably *The Araignment of Mr. Persecution* (London, 1645) and *Martin's Eccho* (London, 1645). Overton's plea for toleration is markedly more pro-sectarian than either Milton's or Walwyn's. None the less, Overton shares with Milton a recourse to works by Selden and by Sarpi, while Walwyn's reading (albeit only in English translations) represents precisely that form of "trying all things" recommended by Milton: see Nigel Smith, "Atheism, Scepticism and Perfection in Radical Religious Writing, 1640–1680," in M. Hunter and D. Wootton, eds., *Atheism in Early Modern Europe* (Oxford, forthcoming). The Bodleian Library uncharacteristically acquired the quarto editions of Milton and Overton, along with Selden: Gwen Hampshire, "An Unusual Bodleian Purchase in 1645," *Bodleian Library Record*, 10 (1982), pp. 339–48.
40 The echo is from Paulo Sarpi, *The History of the Inquisition*, trans. Robert Gentilis (London, 1639), p. 69. See David Wooton, *Paulo Sarpi. Between Renaissance and Enlightenment* (Cambridge, 1983), pp. 134–5.
41 See Robert Greville, Lord Brooke, *A Discourse opening the Nature of that Episcopacie, which is exercised in England* (London, 1641). Brooke emphasizes indifferency and the importance of individual right reason. Milton might be pointing back to his own antiepiscopal tracts here, which included statements in support of extreme sectarians, like Familists, remarks he qualified in the mid-1640s.
42 *CPW*, II.495n.
43 See Nigel Smith, *Perfection Proclaimed: Language and Literature in English Radical Religion, 1640–1660* (Oxford, 1989), pp. 315–18.
44 Milton is engaging here with Plato's argument in *The Republic*, 607a, that the only

permitted poetry should be "hymns to the gods and praises of good men."

45 Origen's self-inflicted castration arose from his interpretation of Matt. 19:12: "Some make themselves Eunuchs for the kingdom of heavens sake."

46 Robinson, *Liberty of Conscience* (London, 1644), pp. 6–7.

47 [Henry Parker], *To the High Court of Parliament: The Humble Remonstrance of the Company of Stationers* (London, 1643). Milton is probably answering this tract in kind: both speak ultimately for the advancement of learning.

48 Henry Parker, *Of A Free Trade* (London, 1648).

49 For instance, see John Saltmarsh, *Dawnings of Light* (London, 1645), p. 1.

50 See M. A. Screech, *Erasmus: Ecstasy and the Praise of Folly* (London, 1980), chapter 2, for a treatment of this aspect of utopian and folly literature. In "*Areopagitica* and *Areopagiticus*: The Significance of the Isocratic Precedent," *Milton Studies*, 21 (1985), pp. 49–69, Paul M. Dowling is right to draw the distinction between the Puritans who would impose a rigid "reformation of manners" and Plato (see above, pp. 116–17), but he is incorrect in arguing that Milton follows Plato who would have laws which were consistent with the "customs" and "manners" of people (*Laws*, 788B). Milton regards censorship as a piece of bondage which must be removed so that the "laws of vertuous education" can remove the "custom" left by a historical condition of bondage. The relationship between externally-imposed and internally-known laws of regulation is left uncertain.

51 For Selden's contribution here, see Selden, *The Reverse and Back-Face of the English Janus* (London, 1682). Janus' two faces represents the dual potential of seeing matters from more than one viewpoint, of censorship and speech, and of the way in which Milton "turns round" images of repression.

52 J. G. A. Pocock, *The Machiavellian Moment: Florentine Political Thought and the Atlantic Republican Tradition* (Princeton, 1975), esp. pp. 3–80.

53 For instance, see C. M. Williams, "The Anatomy of a Radical Gentleman: Sir Henry Marten," in D. H. Pennington and Keith Thomas, eds., *Puritans and Revolutionaries* (Oxford, 1978), pp. 118–38. See also above, n.29.

54 See Plato, *The Republic*, 415de, 432a, 435a5–7; 443ab; 441de. See also above, n.50.

55 The stressing of "unity of spirit," despite differences in church discipline, was the particular province of a number of Independent divines and laymen, notably, in the mid-1640s, the Antinomians John Saltmarsh and William Sedgwick: see Smith, *Perfection Proclaimed*, pp. 229ff.

56 There is also the potential for the portrayal of violent persecution in the mutilation of these bodies: Michael Wilding, "Milton's *Areopagitica*: Liberty for the Sects," in Thomas N. Corns, ed., *The Literature of Controversy: Polemical Strategy from Milton to Junius* (London, 1986), pp. 7–38, esp. pp. 12–13.

57 Parker, *The Contra-Replicant*, p. 1.

58 Jakob Boehme, XL. *Questions Concerning the Soule* (London, 1647), Bodleian 4° B. 41. Th. Seld.

6

Milton's *Observations upon the Articles of Peace*: Ireland under English eyes

THOMAS N. CORNS

Hardly anyone has looked critically at Milton's *Observations upon the Articles of Peace*.[1] We may speculate about this silence among the numberless infinities of Milton critics. In part, no doubt, the text has been ignored for stylistic reasons. Much of it is the reproduction – as a prelude to refutation or comment – of dry and drossy stuff by Milton's enemies, though I shall explain later the strategic importance of this copious and dull documentation. *Observations* represents Milton's prose at its least flamboyant. No striking and elaborate imagery etches the memory of its readers, no lofty *sententiae* are transcribed from this tract to grace a book-plate or the walls of public libraries. Yet this austerity of style, I shall demonstrate, serves well the polemical moment.

Perhaps most significantly, Milton's pamphlet embarrasses his supporters. He wrote it on instruction from the Council of State as part of their preparations for the Cromwellian expedition to Ireland. In a sense he wrote it for hire – a fortnight before the commission, he had been appointed "foreign secretary," coincidentally at the same meeting at which Cromwell had been named as "the commander-in-chief of the troops for Ireland."[2] Critics of a more genteel age perhaps felt uneasy about this mercenary aspect, though, as I shall show, the tract accords well with that radical vision he had developed elsewhere. Milton's pamphlet works as a preemptive justification for that Cromwellian ruthlessness manifest in the storming of Drogheda, where the garrison of 2,600 were given no quarter, and of Wexford, where, in almost indiscriminate slaughter, about 2,000 people were killed by the victors. By 1653, the last resistance had been overwhelmed and the conditions prepared for the wholesale confiscation of the property of Irish landowners and its transfer to London financiers and parliament's supporters in arms.[3] To praise Milton's skill perhaps feels uncomfortable, a little like enthusing over the technological accomplishment of a morally dubious military operation.

Yet though we approach the text through a maze of ethical and historical problems, approach it we should. Milton's complicity in this dark chapter of Anglo-Irish relations defines the complexities and limitations of his political radicalism. Moreover, *Observations* exhibits his writerly genius more starkly than those more likeable tracts that speak the language of freedom. My purpose in this essay is to demonstrate the potency of Milton's polemical skill, how brilliantly he represents his enemies and plays upon his readers, how argument suits situation, how he adjusts his style to the exigencies of debate, and, most significantly, how, albeit through a process of close refutation and invective, he produces a voice and vision to match the spirit of the new republic of England.

Observations is a child of crisis. Problems posed by the newly configured alliance of the Catholics, associated with the Confederacy of Kilkenny and in rebellion since 1641, with the Marquis of Ormond, the royalist Lord Lieutenant, who had been engaged in suppressing them, had been compounded by the defection from parliamentary allegiance of Baron Inchiquin and his hitherto fiercely antiCatholic army and by uncertainties about the loyalties and intentions of the newer settlers of predominantly Scottish ancestry and of predominantly Presbyterian faith. Troops loyal to the regicide Rump were confined to Dublin and its environs (under the command of Colonel Michael Jones) and to several coastal enclaves in the north (under the command of George Monck). The necessity of the expeditious despatch of a relieving force was clearly apparent, and Milton's tract shares that sense of urgency.

The Council of State instructed Milton "to make some observations on the complication of interest which is now amongst the several designers against the peace of the commonwealth, and they to be made ready to be printed with the papers out of Ireland, which the House has ordered to be printed" (*Calendar*, p. 57). The format of the resulting volume, though an unusual one, satisfies the terms of the commission: roughly forty-four of its sixty-five quarto pages are taken up with documentation and the reproduction of, for the most part, writings unqualifiedly inimical to the Rump Parliament, chiefly the Articles themselves, Ormond's letter to Colonel Jones, and the attack of the Belfast Presbytery on the new English regime. That England's new political masters should subvent the dissemination of the works of its enemies may seem curious. Yet the intention, I suspect, was to repeat the achievements of quite the most successful propaganda coup of the mid-1640s, Long Parliament's publication of *The Kings Cabinet Opened: or Certain Packets of Secret Letters & Papers, Written with the Kings Own Hand, and Taken in His Cabinet at Nasby-Field, June 14, 1645* (London, 1645). As in *Observations*, most of the tract consists of documentation, in that case, copies of letters by and to the King captured at the battle of Naseby, followed by "Annotations" by government civil servants which point up their significance. Again, as in the case of *Observations*, the principal import of the tract was to demonstrate that Stuart duplicity extended to a readiness to tolerate popery and to use an Irish army against the English people. As Gardiner notes, the "effect of [the] publication was enormous," and Milton drew heavily upon it in his *Eikonoklastes*.[4] The same strategy underpins the whole conception of *Observations*: a reading public, conditioned to interpret evidence of royalist and papist conspiracies, is presented once more with documentation of the same readiness of the Stuarts, in the words of the preface to *The Kings Cabinet*, to assail the godly English with "all the Papists in *Europe* almost, especially the bloody Tygers of *Ireland*" (sig. A3v).

Like the authors of *The Kings Cabinet*, Milton in *Observations* is playing the Catholic card, and, though the tract serves in some ways to validate the expedition to Ireland at a time when more radical voices were recommending the soldiery of the New Model Army to resist embarkation,[5] his primary concerns, I shall argue, are much less with Irish affairs than with a crucial phase of English domestic politics, the attempts by the Rump to discredit Presbyterian leaders while retaining at least the acquiescence of the rank-and-file supporters of Presbyterian persuasion. The curious proportioning of Milton's comments on the texts reproduced in *Observations* suggests something of his priorities. In the edition of 1649, while the thirty-three pages of the Articles receive four and a half pages of Milton's comment, Ormond's two-and-a-half-page letter to Colonel Jones gets as much, and the four and a half pages of the Representation of the Scotch Presbytery is met with a full eleven pages of refutation. What Milton has to say about Catholics, Ormond and the Ulster Presbytery has powerful implications for the images which he produces of both the English government and its enemies and which constitute the principal achievements of the tract.

Milton conducts his dismissal of Ormond's treaty with a curt ferocity. He seems to assume that he addresses himself to an audience already convinced – no doubt by the pamphlets and newsbooks of the early 1640s – of the demonic cruelty of the Irish Catholic rebels.[6] The now familiar anecdotes of the insurrection, those lurid accounts of babies tossed on pikes, of strippings, rapes, exotic disembowellings, desecrations, and miscellaneous massacres that had constituted the common stuff of the London press in previous years, seem taken as read. Milton's response curiously eschews documentation, explicitly assuming his readers' familiarity:

> We may be confidently perswaded, that no true borne *English-man*, can
> so much as barely read them [the Articles of Peace] without
> indignation and disdaine, that those bloudy Rebels . . . after the
> merciless and barbarous Massacre of so many thousand *English* . . .
> should be now grac'd and rewarded with such freedomes and
> enlargements, as none of their Ancestors could ever merit.   (III.301)

Milton assumes all right-thinkers know about the "bloudy Rebels" and concur. Moreover, he deftly plays upon what he assumes to be his readers' sense of national superiority. He singles out article 22 of the treaty, which had rescinded earlier legislation forbidding the practice of ploughing by affixing the plough to the draught-horse's tail (III.278). Such a practice, besides being cruel (not a point Milton makes), could be perceived as evidence of primitivism: who but a savage couldn't manufacture a functional collar, especially after he'd seen one being used? And proof, too, of idiocy: who but a fool would ruin a good horse by mistreating it in this way?[7] With apparent confidence of assent Milton concludes that the Irish demonstrate

> a disposition not onely sottish but indocible and averse from all Civility and amendment, and what hopes they give for the future, who rejecting the ingenuity of all other Nations to improve and waxe more civill by a civilizing Conquest, though all these many yeares better shown and taught, preferre their own absurd and savage Customes before the most convincing evidence of reason and demonstration: a testimony of their true Barbarisme and obdurate wilfulnesse to be expected no lesse in other matters of greatest moment. (III.304)

Milton is laying the ideological foundations for the Cromwellian settlement of Ireland, a settlement premised upon the belief that the Irish Catholics cannot be improved enough to make their free coexistence with British settlers safely feasible, and so must be controlled, subordinated, transported or destroyed: "true Barbarisme and obdurate wilfulnesse" cannot be treatied with.

Building on a sense of racial superiority, Milton persistently invokes a tradition in Anglo-Irish relations which the Rump is represented as maintaining and which the royalists place in jeopardy. English interest in Ireland rests on rights of conquest, a conquest provoked by the necessity of suppressing Irish piracy and raids on coastal Britain, a policy constituting the "long prescription of many hundred yeares." Moreover, English conduct towards those "justly made our vassalls" has been humane and decent. The English have nothing to apologize for in their conduct towards Ireland. Milton takes special issue with article 2, which repeals Poyning's Law, the legislation dating from the 1490s whereby "no Parlament could be summond there, no Bill be past, but what was first to be transmitted and allowd under the great seale of *England*" (III.264, 303). Thus Milton suggests that the republican government acts in an orthodox defence of English interests, whereas the Articles of Peace constitute a dangerous and unprecedented deviation from traditional practice. Moreover, on behalf of the late King, Ormond and the royalists are giving away Englishmen's time-honored rights in Ireland, "disallieg[ing] a whole Feudary Kingdome from the ancient Dominion of *England*," and, as such, the act constitutes treason, the betrayal of *national* interest – Ireland belonged, not to the King, but to the country (III.302–8).

Milton demonstrates the unacceptability of the Articles of Peace with a savage élan that works upon his target readership's shared sense of horror of Catholicism in general and Irish Catholic rebels in particular; probably in no other polemical context had he enjoyed such advantages, nor would he again. In writing his antiprelatical pamphlets, he had carried the burden of meeting stereotypical representations of the narrow and self-seeking puritan. The divorce tracts had to negotiate the taint of sectarian extremism so easily levelled by Presbyterians and their allies against more radical puritan groups.[8] Milton's defences of republicanism and regicide necessarily engaged that respect for a tenacious notion, that kingship constituted a bulwark against anarchy, which more then a century of state ideology had worked to engender. Yet in manipulating his readers' fear and loathing of Catholicism Milton, for once, had his audience's prejudices and assumptions advantageously oriented towards his own argument. Somewhat more demanding of his skills – and, I feel, more important in terms of the ideological problems facing the republican government in its early years – are the arguments to be constructed against Ormond's letter and in response to the Belfast Presbytery.

Ormond's letter, contrived to seduce Colonel Michael Jones from his loyalty to the Rump, offers Milton a relatively weak example of a royalist appeal to past and present supporters of parliament. Though Ormond was an astute politician with a distinguished record and a significant future in Irish affairs, he knew little about the requirements of Civil War polemic – he had written none – and in any case he was tailoring his address as a private letter to an individual, not a public appeal designed for publication. Had it worked, and had Michael Jones gone over to the royalists, presumably the letter would not have come to light. So Milton has at least the advantage of a certain slackness of style and presentation on Ormond's part.

He builds deftly upon the anti-Irish sentiment he has worked to arouse. Ormond is shuffled into the pack with the rebels of the Confederacy:

> The Letter ... had pass'd heer without mention, but that the other
> part of it ... roves into long digression of evill and reproachfull
> language to the Parlament and Army of *England*. Which though not
> worth their notice, as from a Crew of Rebells whose inhumanities are
> long since become the horrour and execration of all that heare them,
> yet ... to give the world all due satisfaction of the present doings, no
> fit opportunity shall be omitted.   (III.308)

Heretofore, and more usually throughout *Observations*, the word "rebel" had been reserved for the Irish Catholics, nor can it straightforwardly be applied to a royalist Lord Lieutenant who held his office from the crown which he continued loyally to serve: "malignant" is the usual Parliamentarian term of opprobrium for such figures.[9] But perhaps Milton's trick just succeeds: maybe English readers do overlook the distinction between Irish Catholics and Irish royalists adherent to the Protestant Church of Ireland, such as Ormond, regarding them all as an execrable and inferior race. Certainly, when Drogheda fell, no distinctions were observed in the subsequent massacre.[10] Milton's claim to speak for "the Parliament and Army of *England*" and his assiduous reiteration of Ormond's Irishness serve the same ends of provoking English national sentiment and obscuring crucial distinctions between the Irish forces now allied against the republic. Thus, Ormond's charge that the Rump contained only "the dregs and scum of the House of Commons" is met with

> this reproach and in the mouth of an *Irish* Man concernes not them onely, but redounds to apparent dishonour of the whole *English* Nation. Doubtless there must be thought a great scarcity in *England* of persons honourable and deserving, or else of Judgement, or so much as honesty in the People, if those whom they esteem worthy to sit in Parlament be no better then Scum and Dreggs in the *Irish* Dialect.
>
> (III.292, 315)

Milton, then, is working to secure an *English* response to *Irish* criticism. An English electorate had, after all, with unquestionable constitutionality elected to Long Parliament the MPs who remained in the Rump (though the constitutionality of events since Pride's Purge would not admit much scrutiny).

Milton persistently implicates Ormond with the Irish Catholics by simplifying the political configuration and thus offering a simple binary opposition between "rebels" and Parliament's friends; surely, no *real* Protestant would cross that divide:

> All men who are true Protestants, of which number he gives out to be one, know not a more immediate and killing Subverter of all true Religion then Antichrist, whom they generally believe to be the Pope and Church of *Rome*, he therefore who makes peace with this grand Enemy and persecutor of the true Church, he who joynes with him, strengthens him, gives him root to grow up and spread his poyson . . . he of all Protestants may be calld most justly the Subverter of true Religion, the Protector and inviter of irreligion and atheism, whether it be *Ormond* or his Maister.
>
> (III.309)

Ormond had played the familiar game of suggesting that the republic, primarily the work of revolutionary Independency, encouraged both heresy and irreligion (III.291).[11] Milton can offer, instead, the image of the republic as bulwark against popery, an evil most respectable Protestants could be relied on to regard with more hostility than the most extravagant of the sects. Moreover, Milton anticipates events. Throughout 1650 the Rump, as part of securing the acquiescence of Presbyterian opinion, launched a series of legislative and propaganda initiatives against the wilder sectaries and particularly against the Ranters.[12] Milton foreshadows the strategy with his assurance that "The Parlament, I think, professes not to tolerate such [the outrageously blasphemous], but with all befitting endeavours to suppress them," a point he reiterates in a later pledge that the republic will "not tolerate the free exercise of any Religion, which shall be found absolutely contrary to sound Doctrine or the power of godliness" (III.311, 325). Reformed religion is safe with the Rump: it is not safe with Ormond, who is the "Ringleader" of "that horrible Conspiracy" with the Irish rebels (III.316).

Milton dismisses Ormond with a jibe at his style – "There will not need more words to this Windy Railer, convicted openly of all those Crimes which he so confidently and yet falsely charges upon others" – which suggests a distinction between the wildness of his enemy's dialectic and the conclusive sobriety of his own. He had written a little earlier of "his . . . lavish pen," of his loosing of "the reines of discretion" as he "rambles . . . beyond all Soberness and Civility" in a "Torrent" of ill-conceived hectoring (III.315–16). Ormond, indeed, shows a clumsy exuberance of style. But, more important, the comments point to Milton's own stylistic choices. As I have elsewhere demonstrated, *Observations*, like *The Tenure of Kings and Magistrates* and *Eikonoklastes*, his other pamphlets of 1649, exhibits a new stylistic austerity, as unusual collocations become much rarer than formerly, his incidence of imagery falls quite sharply, and the imagery he does use sheds the luxuriance that had characterized it before.[13] The polemical implications of that shift in style become clear: Milton produces, for his defence of the republic, the voice of sober responsibility, which can be set in opposition to the excesses of its enemies. Political innovation must be transformed into a new orthodoxy, commanding wide assent, through the rapid assumption of the style of authoritative and businesslike control.

That tone pervades the third and longest of the major sections of *Observations*, Milton's stricture on the Representation of the Scottish Presbytery at Belfast. They, too, write "in frenzie," by

> throwing out a sudden rapsody of Proverbs quite from the purpose; and with as much comliness as when *Saul* propheci'd. For casting off, as he did his garments, all modestie and meekness wherewith the language of Ministers ought to be cloath'd, speaking especially to thir supreme Magistrate, they talke at random. (III.332–3)

Unrestraint, abandon, even a suggestion of immodesty are made to adhere to the Belfast Presbyterians, characteristics stereotypically associated with the sectaries, and properties deprecated by the solid middle ground of conventional puritanism. Artfully, Milton is easing the authors of the Representation away from their intended constituency.

His strategy emerges more clearly when viewed in the context of other campaigns of the early years of republican government. Blair Worden has charted the process whereby the Rump sought to achieve at least the acquiescence of its rivals and former allies among Presbyterians, who were newly "kingified" or adherent to a new sympathy for the Stuart monarchy. Parliament assured its financial backers that the Irish campaign "would be conducted on behalf not merely of the Rump's interest but of the united Protestant interest, in which presbyterians of all kinds were involved." Cromwell saw the confrontations with the Irish (and the Scots) as a means of uniting the majority of Englishmen against "barbarous races" which were "the enemies of the nation rather than merely the Rump, and campaigns against them offered the government its best hope of securing the tolerance, if not the support, of presbyterian opinion in England" (pp. 191–2).

Milton's own attack fits within this general scheme. Though the Rump found it possible to procure "passive sufferance" from most Presbyterians, it "had less success with presbyterian clergymen."[14] What Milton does in *Observations* is to discredit would-be leaders of Presbyterian opinion in terms calculated to carry weight with the Presbyterian rank and file. In effect, he builds upon the distinction he had first made in *The Tenure of Kings and Magistrates* between the leaders and the led: "As for that party calld Presbyterian, of whom I believe very many to be good and faithfull Christians, though misledd by som of turbulent spirit, I wish them earnestly and calmly not to fall off from thir first principles" (III.238). His tactics are to hive off the leadership "of turbulent spirit" while leaving an avenue of reconciliation open to their followers.

Just as Ormond's letter represented a relatively easy target for Milton's attack on die-hard loyalism, so, too, the Belfast Presbytery in its foreignness and polemical incompetence constitutes a disadvantaged version of Presbyterian royalism; nor does Milton hesitate to exploit its handicaps. Now himself at last close to the seat of power, he emphasizes the marginality of the Presbytery. Belfast, "a small *Town* in *Ulster*," "a barbarous nook of *Ireland*," is "a place better known by the name of a late Barony, then by the fame of these mens Doctrine or Ecclesiastical Deeds" (III.317, 327). Yet the Ulster Presbyterians, though contemptible, remain dangerous because of the complexities of the Irish problem and the succor they give to the enemies of reformed religion and English interest,

> the Sympathy, good Intelligence, and joynt pace which they goe in the North of *Ireland*, with their Copartning Rebels in the South, driving on the same Interest to loose us that Kingdome, that they may gaine it themselves, or at least share in the spoile: though the other be op'n enemies, these pretended Brethren. (III.317)

The "us" of "loose us that Kingdome" seems to embrace not only the Rump and its republican supporters, but Englishmen generally, to all of whom Ireland is rightly subordinate. Moreover, as in the case of Ormond and his Church of Ireland royalists, Milton extends the term "Rebel" to a new category, or so the epithet "Copartning" implies.

The Representation of the Presbytery had concluded with an injunction to its supporters against "swerving in their judgements to Malignant principles" and against joining with "Papists, and other notorious Malignants." Milton brushes this gesture aside as impractical, naive, or dishonest. Opposing the English Parliament and its army in Ireland, in 1649, effectively linked arms with the Catholic rebels of the Confederacy. Nothing "for the present can adde more assistance or advantage to those bloudy Rebels and Papists in the South" than the Presbytery's "seditious practises against us," a point which Milton can substantiate with the fresh news that the Ulster Scots have besieged Londonderry, bottling up "those Forces which were to have fought against *Ormond*, and the Irish Rebels" (III.299, 325, 322).

The actions of the Scots Presbytery in Belfast have implications for the political crisis facing the republican government in England. Quite simply, their decision defines starkly the options facing English Presbyterians: the latter may either reconcile themselves to a Puritan republic or else confederate with malignants and Catholics. The Ulster Presbyterians have chosen wrongly, linking with Parliament's foes, "against whom, though by them-selves pronounc'd to be the enemies of God, they goe not out to battell, as they ought, but rather by these thir doings assist and become associats." In sharp contrast, the Rump has acted and, it is implied, will continue to act to protect and nurture the freedom of Presbyterians to worship as they please, wherever such doctrine and discipline are desired (III.334, 326).

Worden has depicted the early years of the English republic as charac-terized by conservative and cautious government, contriving to draw in neutrals, to foster connections wherever possible with Presbyterians, and to offer itself as the guardian of order, decency and a sober, wide-spectrum Puritanism. I have demonstrated how Milton's *Observations* endorses that general strategy. But there is another voice to be heard, both in Milton's tract and elsewhere: the voice of republican commitment confidently asserting the values of a new age. David Norbrook has written recently on the ideological implications of Marvell's "Horatian Ode upon Cromwels Return from Ireland," interpreting it as a celebration of such new values.[15] Marvell's poem works towards the establishment of a postmonarchic ethos, founded on different loyalties, embodying different priorities and serving radically new political imperatives. Milton's Irish tract anticipates the ode in attempting to engender the spirit of the new republic, and it does so rather more straightforwardly.

Ormond had written of the republican "intentions to change the Monarchy of *England* into Anarchy, unless their aime bee first to constitute an elective Kingdome, and *Crumwell* [*sic*] or some such *John* of *Leiden* being elected" (III.291). Milton, far from apologizing for Cromwell, aggressively meets personality attack with personality cult:

> [Ormond] proceeds to the contemptuous naming of a person, whose
> valour and high merit many enemies more noble then himself have

both honour'd and feard, to assert his good name and reputation, of
whose service the Common-wealth receaves so ample satisfaction, tis
answerd in his behalf, that Cromwell whom he couples with a name
of scorne, hath done in few yeares more eminent and remarkable
Deeds whereon to *found* Nobility in his house, though it were
wanting, and perpetuall Renown to posterity, then *Ormond* and all his
Auncestors put together can shew from any record of thir *Irish*
exploits, the widest scene of their glory.   (III. 312)

Of course, Milton makes a racial point, about the obscurity of Irish achievement. But, more striking, comes the unmistakable rhetoric of the new men
of a new age, the assertion that claims based on the achievements of ancestors
are as nothing compared with the triumphs of the present: Cromwell, it
seems, may remark, like the Napoleonic Marshall Junot, "Moi je suis mon
ancêtre."

Again, while *Observations* certainly addresses the problem of neutralizing
Presbyterian opposition to the new regime, it does so in terms much less
conciliatory than those generally adopted by Milton's political masters.
Milton evidently – and with good reason – felt that Presbyterians and their
associates had treated harshly his divorce treatises of 1643–5.[16] In his
unpublished political poems of the mid-1640s he had rehearsed his enraged
anguish at the "barbarous noise . . . Of Owls and Cuckoes, Asses, Apes and
Doggs," and at the ignorance of his age (Sonnets XI, XII). He railed, too,
against the cupidity of Presbyterian divines:

> you have thrown off your Prelate Lord,
> And with stiff Vowes renounc'd his liturgie
> To seise the widdow'd whore Pluralitie
> From them whose sin ye envi'd, not abhorr'd.
> ("On the new forcers of Conscience")

In *Observations*, while he is careful not to reproach too closely the rank and file
of Presbyterian laity, Milton rehearses against the clergy, as represented by
the Belfast Presbytery, those same charges of ignorance and greed, and he
does so with a new air of Independent triumphalism. Thus, of "these illiterat
denouncers" he writes, "We may then behold [their] pittiful store of
learning, and theology." Again, in a comment which seems to embrace all
Presbyterian divines, he asserts, "we put down Bishops, and put up
Presbyters, which the most of them have made use of to enrich and exalt
themselves," and, with a phrase which shares the assumptions of his brilliant
retort, "*New Presbyter* is but Old *Priest* writ Large," he dismisses them, with
all priests, from the agenda of history: "But wherefore spend we two such
pretious things as time and reason upon Priests, the most prodigal mis-
spenders of time, and the scarcest owners of reason?" (III.328, 322–3, 318,

329). Such impatience manifests, perhaps, a Cromwellian ring. At the dawn of a new age, Milton has briefly broken pace to dignify such throwbacks with a refutation: later, he perhaps hints, he and fellow-republicans may be less considerate of such opposition.

Observations remains, of course, the least considerable of the three contributions Milton made to the polemical exchanges of 1649, that climactic year in English political history, and a comprehensive explanation of the changes we encounter in all three, changes in tone and style and in the relationship the author defines with his readers, must await a thorough account of *Eikonoklastes* and *The Tenure of Kings and Magistrates*. I would contend that this new Miltonic voice, a voice for the new age, is heard distinctly in his Irish pamphlet. In the unflamboyant engagement of his enemies, in the purposeful manipulation of documentation, and in his uncompromising, unapologetic tone, Milton, speaking for the revolutionary government, offers an appearance of unashamed republicanism, assured in its new values, proud of its achievements, and confident in its ability to complete the political – and cultural – transformation of England.

Notes

1 Apart from Merritt Y. Hughes' generally excellent introduction to his edition (*CPW*, III.168–89) and a scattering of stylistic observations in my *Development of Milton's Prose Style* (Oxford, 1982), the tract has attracted little critical attention, though, of course, it figures in most biographical accounts of Milton.

2 *Calendar of State Papers, Domestic Series, 1649–1650*, ed. Mary A. E. Green (London, 1875), pp. 40–1.

3 For the historical context, see Patrick J. Corish, "The Cromwellian Conquest 1649–53," *New History of Ireland*, vol. III, edited by T. W. Moody, F. X. Martin, and F. J. Byrne (Oxford, 1986), p. 336; Richard Bagwell, *Ireland under the Stuarts and during the Interregnum* (1909–16; reprinted London, 1965), vol. II, pp. 179–343; and S. R. Gardiner, *History of the Commonwealth and Protectorate, 1649–1660* (London, 1901), vol. I, pp. 79–177. Karl S. Bottigheimer, *English Money and Irish Land: The "Adventurers" in the Cromwellian Settlement of Ireland* (Oxford, 1971), offers the fullest account of the economic motivations behind the conquest and settlement. For particularly instructive maps of the scale of the expropriation, see J. G. Simms, "The Restoration, 1660–85," in the *New History of Ireland*, vol. III, p. 428, and Bottigheimer, *English Money and Irish Land*, p. 215. I am indebted to Dr Mary O'Dowd of the Queen's University, Belfast, for a number of comments.

4 S. R. Gardiner, *History of the Great Civil War* (London, 1889), vol. II, pp. 223–4. See footnotes to *CPW*, III.397, 449, 484, 526, 537–44.

5 For a consideration, in a literary context, of the Leveller case, see Michael Wilding, "Marvell's 'Horatian Ode upon Cromwell's Return from Ireland,' the Levellers, and the Junta," *Modern Language Review*, 82 (1987), pp. 3–4, and *Dragons Teeth: Literature in the English Revolution* (Oxford, 1987), pp. 119–21.

6 George Thomason, who himself had a financial interest in the reconquest, collected nearly forty items, mostly of news, concerning Ireland, in the last three

months of 1641 alone. See G. K. Fortescue, *Catalogue of the Pamphlets Collected by George Thomason* (London, 1908), vol. I, pp. 35–50 and vol. II, "Index," see under "Ireland." For some contemporary accounts of the rebellion, see Sir John Temple, *The Irish Rebellion* (London, 1645), *passim*, and elsewhere, such as Thomas Morley, *A Remonstrance of the cruelties committed by the Irish Rebels* (London, 1644), Anon., *Ireland* (London, 1647), Anon., *A Prospect of bleeding Irelandes miseries* (London, 1647). I am indebted to Ms Dawn McHale for a number of these references, and to Dr Pat Coughlan's paper on the perception and representation of Irish issues in the seventeenth century read to the conference on the literature of the English Civil War, held at the University of Southampton, 1987.

7 See *CPW*, III.303, n.11 and Keith Thomas, *Man and the Natural World: Changing Attitudes in England 1500–1800* (1983; reprinted Harmondsworth, 1984), p. 189 and n.46.

8 See my "Milton's Quest for Respectability," *Modern Language Review*, 77 (1982), pp. 769–79.

9 See *OED*, s.v. "Malignant," sb. b.; compare the Ulster Presbytery's use of the term, *CPW*, III.299.

10 It is uncertain how many of the garrison were English rather than Irish; the town had never at any time been in the hands of the Catholics of the Confederacy, and there was no real reason for assuming any direct guilt on the part of the townspeople included in the general slaughter for the earlier atrocities attributed to the Confederate rebels; see Corish, "Cromwellian Conquest," pp. 339–40, and Bagwell, *Ireland under the Stuarts*, vol. II, pp. 92–194.

11 See T. N. Corns, J. A. Downie and W. A. Speck, "Archetypal Mystification: Polemic and Reality in English Political Literature, 1640–1750," *Eighteenth-Century Life*, 7 (1982), pp. 1–27.

12 Blair Worden, *The Rump Parliament 1648–1653* (1974; reprinted Cambridge, 1977), p. 233.

13 Corns, *Development*, pp. 67–79, 83–101.

14 Worden, *Rump Parliament*, p. 81.

15 In a paper read to the Southampton conference, 1987.

16 Corns, "Quest," pp. 770–3.

7

Milton's iconoclastic truth

LANA CABLE

When Henry VIII first displaced the roodloft crucifix of a medieval English cathedral with his own coat of arms, his pointed act of iconoclasm shattered a symbolic and powerfully felt material connection between the worshiper's sense of divinity and the earthly spiritual prerogative of Rome.[1] By the same manipulation of material signs, Henry expropriated and transferred to the English monarchy Rome's spiritual claims over the individual worshiper. Now free to reinterpret the character of that which he would defend, the Defender of the Faith could exploit the worshiper's sacramental habit of using icons as a bridge between sensory experience and spiritual truth. Divine right monarchy could now claim its divinity not only by the traditional means of ecclesiastical sanction, but also by the monarch's symbolic presence amid, and iconic participation in, the activity of ordinary religious worship. Reiteration of Henry's skillful image-management by subsequent Tudor and Stuart monarchs habituated the sacramentally-inclined worshiper to iconic associations of Christian symbol with English head of state. Owen Felltham's extravagant epitaph for Charles I must be recognized not as a singular or blasphemous outburst but as the emotionally predictable response of a devout believer: "Here Charles the First and Christ the Second lies."[2] Yet as royal advisors had uneasily sensed at least as early as the reign of Edward VI, icon-manipulation entails great risks. On a purely practical level, once the iconoclast succeeds in rupturing primitive or naive belief in the icon, no rationale and no substitute icon can be assumed to recapture the same quality of belief. If the worshiper can witness demolition of the crucifix, he can conceive as well destruction of the King's sign, and ultimately, destruction of the King himself.

But this practical risk is only a concrete extension of the ambiguity inherent in any dealing with icons. As reformist inquiries into the question repeatedly demonstrated by their inconclusiveness, the truth or falsehood of icons cannot be found in their external characteristics. Instead, we must look to the purposes for which the icon is intended, and to the spirit in which the icon is interpreted or received. Herein, of course, lies the ambiguity, for both intention and interpretation are subjective, ultimately unknowable qualities – qualities not of the icon but of the icon-user.[3] Moreover, the iconoclast is as much an icon-user as the iconophile: creation of images and destruction of images testify alike to imagery's power over human consciousness. To break an old icon is to create an affective vacuum into which new meanings and responses the more readily may enter; to create a new icon is to lay claim to affective responses hitherto elicited by a different icon. Thus iconic destruction and creation are inextricably interwoven by the affective power both command. That power was wittingly tapped by Henrician and Edwardian reformers as they symbolically and literally quarried the ecclesiastical edifice to reinforce the monarch's secular one; it was tapped by Elizabethan and Jacobean portrait artists as they converted the symbolic two-dimensional medieval icon into a dazzling, emblematic, and allegorical costume-piece that heralded its subject's supremacy.[4] It was also tapped by the Caroline publicists who saw to it that the frontispiece of *Eikon Basilike* emblematically identified Charles I with Christ. And the affective power of images is simultaneously attacked and exploited by John Milton as he carves out his own ideas on the relations between language and truth.

I Representation and polemical truth

To go about justifying the ways of God to men by writing a poem is surely to argue that the relations between language and truth cannot be formulated by rules of logic or comprehended in humanly rational terms. The task Milton sets himself in *Paradise Lost* is both impossible and, for the devout Christian poet, compellingly necessary. With mortal human words he would express the inexpressible divine: "May I express thee unblamed? . . . Or hear'st thou rather pure ethereal stream, / Whose fountain who shall tell?" Neither himself nor anyone else shall tell the fountain, but Milton believes that the stream proceeding from it feeds the stream of words that shape his own poetic truth. Such a belief and truth may for many readers be made the more acceptable by Milton's chosen form, and by the qualification implicit in phrases like the one I have used here: to speak of truths as "poetic" is to signal a suspension of rigor in the veridical standards we ordinarily apply to rational exposition. But even Milton's ostensibly rational, unabashedly human and worldly prose polemics represent truth as untellable. *Areopagitica* reminds us that "Truth is compar'd in Scripture to a streaming fountain; if her waters flow not in a perpetuall progression, they sick'n into a muddy pool of conformity and tradition" (II.543). Originating in the fountain of light, eternal and inexpressible, truth once expressed immediately corrupts into mortality. Essentially elusive yet absolute, paradoxical truth depends for human realization on those affective and sensory aspects of language – imagery, symbol, metaphor – whose capacity to inspire but also to delude, to seduce, to appeal to man's irrational nature has from Aristotle onward generated apprehension and mistrust among philosophers, rhetoricians, moralists, and even poets.[5] For the poet invoking the truth of holy Light, this inherited sense of peccability in any human discourse on truth gives special poignancy to his entreaty: "May I express thee unblamed?"

The rhetorical status of truth can be distractingly ambiguous in Milton's earliest polemical writings.[6] His antiprelatical tracts demonstrate an idealistic notion that truth-speaking is sacred and therefore to be kept apart from the grimy political logomachy that entails "clubbing quotations" with his left hand. At the same time, Milton's most impressive displays of conviction – his manifest instances of truth-speaking – owe their force not to rational argument but to the affective appeal of his imagery. Several distinct sets of polarities – eternal truth versus temporal necessity, rational debate versus affective compulsion, divine revelation versus empirical history – produce an argumentative double bind. Neither dispassionate prose nor inspired poetry, the rhetorical hybrid of Milton's attacks on episcopacy pit reason uncomfortably *against* truth.

The tensions caused by Milton's ambivalence toward the expressibility of truth are never fully absent from his polemics. Indeed, it is his skillful manipulating these tensions rather than resolving them that accounts for the rhetorical power of his prose. But whereas the affective "truth-bearing" dimension of the antiprelatical tracts virtually overwhelms his rational argument, subsequent writings show him maneuvering comparable tensions into a dialectical asset. In the divorce tracts, human need and divine law are interpreted along with a number of other tensively paired issues – the relation of body and soul, the letter and spirit of the law, the Old Testament and the New, outward signs and inward realities – in such a way as to elevate each pair to a vital union in truth that can be achieved *only* by means of the generative potency of reciprocal tensions.[7] That such an account of truth also describes the dynamics of healthy sexual union is fundamental to the effectiveness of Milton's rhetoric in *Doctrine and Discipline of Divorce*: coupling imagery distinguishes wholesome, productive, spiritually fulfilling relations between the sexes from poisonous, barren, and debilitating ones. Both rationally and affectively in the divorce tracts, polemical argument and truth are united.

But this is not to say that for Milton either rational or affective expressions of truth actually contain truth or can be equated with it. *Areopagitica* represents mortally apprehensible truth with an image not of the thing sought, but of the activity of lively seeking.[8] The strenuous and varied efforts required to build the "mansion house of liberty" – learning and disputing, vigorously defending beliefs or yielding to even better arguments – demonstrate that for human beings, truth, like the "book" that comprises all our experience, requires never-ending and rigorous interpretation.[9] The thousand pieces of absolute Truth, like the torn and scattered body of Osiris, lie beyond mere human capacity to regather: "We have not yet found them all . . . nor ever shall doe, till her Master's second comming" (II.549).

As the foregoing brief survey suggests, Milton's polemical truth inheres at least as much in the impossibility as in the possibility of its representation. His truth can live neither within nor without the verbal icon: it both depends on and eludes, abandons or destroys the icons that give it shape. But it is not until Milton makes his assault on the King's icon that the problems intrinsic to representation of truth become an explicit political, moral, philosophical, and rhetorical issue. By adducing and manipulating the tensions of truth's unrepresentability, Milton taps the rhetorical force specific to iconoclasm. In *Eikonoklastes*, Milton equates truth with the energetic destruction of every human claim to represent it.

II Breaking the verbal icon

Perhaps the sliest form such tension-manipulating takes is Milton's expropriation, literalization, and consequent explosion of *Eikon Basilike*'s own carefully selected affective building-blocks – the king's metaphors, images, and symbols. For instance, when the King defends his intrusion on the House of Commons as justified by such "motives and pregnant grounds" as the Parliamentarians had no knowledge of, Milton first spends five paragraphs countering the justification point by point.[10] But before moving on to the next argument, he reaches back to the seemingly innocuous metaphor, almost forgotten by the reader, that the king had used to lend weight and seriousness to his concerns – "pregnant." Charles *"wanted not such probabilities (for his pregnant is come now to probable) as were sufficient to raise jealousies in any Kings heart*. And thus his pregnant *motives* are at last prov'd nothing but a Tympany, or a Queen *Maries* Cushion" (III.379). Milton's literalizing extension to an actual pretended pregnancy of the King's metaphoric "pregnant" makes the King's jealous motives appear not only false and mistaken but, because of the derogatory historical associations with Mary Tudor, simultaneously insidious, ludicrous, and vaguely pathetic. The effect is to expose the King's "jealousies" as paranoiac delusion and his rhetoric as incompetent. In an argument designed to sabotage *Eikon Basilike*'s triumph of style over substance, it is the latter charge that wounds.

When Charles later employs the trope of a storm-tossed ship to embellish his withdrawal from Westminster, Milton derides the "Simily" as "a garb somwhat more Poetical then for a Statist," but then he connects it "with many straines of like dress" to cover the entire work: "I begun to think that the whole Book might perhaps be intended a peece of Poetrie. The words are good, the fiction smooth and cleanly; there wanted only Rime, and that, they say, is bestow'd upon it lately" (III.406). Since Milton's metaphors "garb" and "dress" convert Charles' entire metaphoric effort to mere costuming, the King's book seems suddenly an insubstantial show, easily reducible to rhyme.

But few of the King's figurative passages are taken so lightly. When Charles observes, on the militia's having seized his military power, that the "chiefest Armes" left him had been only his "Praiers and Teares," Milton fires back, with an oath, a vivid recitation of the King's material acts:

> O sacred Reverence of God, Respect and Shame of Men, whither were yee fled, when these hypocrisies were utterd? Was the Kingdom then at all that cost of blood to remove from him none but Praiers and Teares? ... Were they Praiers and Teares that were listed at *York*, muster'd on *Heworth* Moore, and laid Seige to *Hull* for the guard of his Person? Were Praiers and Teares at so high a rate in *Holland* that nothing could purchase them but the Crown Jewels? Yet they in *Holland* ... sold them for Gunns, Carabins, Morters-peeces, Canons, and other deadly Instruments of Warr. (III.452)

Since "Praiers and Teares" effectively summarizes the wide-reaching pathetic appeal exercised by *Eikon Basilike*, it is easy to see why these words should provoke Milton to obliterate the figurative "chiefest arms" by maneuvering into position the arsenal of real arms, the weapons deals, and the military exercises by which the King had provoked the seizure. As Milton had argued in *Areopagitica*, "Books are not absolutely dead things" (II.492). He must now see to it that the "efficacie and extraction of that living intellect" that bred the King's book is publicly exposed as an intellect to which "arms" really meant *arms*, not a deluding piece of imagery.

But some of the metaphoric arguments in *Eikon Basilike* run aground almost of their own accord: Milton merely narrates their self-destruction. When Charles characterizes parliamentary government as a Hydra-headed monster, he starts off promisingly enough: if we admire such a government because it has more eyes to see, we must also acknowledge that it has more mouths to feed. As he continues, however, the body metaphor starts to flounder: parliamentary government "hath rather a monstrosity than anything of perfection beyond that of right monarchy, where counsel may be in many, as the senses, but the supreme power can be but in one, as the head" (*EB*, 49). With these words, Milton drily remarks, Charles "grounds his argument upon two or three eminent absurdities: First by placing Counsel in the senses, next by turning the senses out of the head, and in lieu therof placing power, *supreme* above sense and reason; which be now the greater Monstrosities?" Whether, in this case, bad style leads to nonsensical thinking or vice versa doesn't interest Milton: "Furder to dispute what kind of Government is best, would be a long debate, it sufficeth that his reasons heer for Monarchy are found weake and inconsiderable" (III.455). "Reasons" whose validity depends solely on metaphor require only destruction of the metaphor to be refuted.

Some of the King's metaphors require only a shade of literalizing for Milton to expose the supercilious thinking that lies underneath: "*But he must chew such Morsels as Propositions ere he let them down.* So let him; but if the Kingdom shall tast nothing but after his chewing, what does he make of the

Kingdom, but a great baby" (III.468–9). Thus, the line between the King's incompetent metaphor and his deliberate malice grows fine indeed.

But argument by metaphor, especially organic metaphor, carries other risks as well. When metaphor tempts Charles to claim seriously the intellectual and political magnificence implied in the trope of the King-as-sun, Milton carries his logic to a grotesque conclusion. Charles considers "*the concurrence of his reason . . . necessary to the begetting,* or bringing forth of any one *compleat act of public wisdom as the Suns influence is necessary to all natures productions.* So that the Parliament, it seems, is but a Female, and without his procreative reason, the Laws which they can produce are but wind-eggs." The vague generative beneficence of the King-sun's necessity to "all nature's productions" Milton aborts by bringing forth instead a Rabelaisian travesty, legislative "wind-eggs." And if Charles, eyes on the sun, overlooks the explicitly sexual reproductive implications of "begetting" and "bringing forth," Milton doesn't. Since the King claims his right by law, itself no more than the "Counsel of a Nation," then by Charles' own metaphor, he must acknowledge Parliament not conventionally as the King's wife, but rather as the entity who gave monarchy birth: "He ought then to have so thought of a Parliament, if he count it not Male, as of his Mother, which, to civil being, created both him, and the Royalty he wore." By probing the imagerial dimension of Charles' conflicting statements on Parliament, Milton traces the King's authoritarianism to origins he compares with the perversions of Nero: "And if it hath bin anciently interpreted the presaging signe of a future Tyrant, but to dream of copulation with his Mother, what can it be less then actual Tyranny to affirme waking, that the Parlament, which is his Mother, can neither conceive or bring forth *any autoritative Act* without his Masculine coition." From this portentous explication of the lesser metaphors "beget" and "bring forth," Milton derives the material he needs finally to explode the King's major symbol, the sun: "Nay that his reason is as Celestial and life-giving to the Parlament, as the Suns influence is to the Earth: What other notions but these, or such like, could swell up *Caligula* to think himself a God" (III.467). The unconscious and overt impulses toward tyranny Milton finds in the King's lesser metaphors reveal Charles' use of the sun-symbol as no elegant rhetorical device but malignant self-exaltation.

Hypothesizing from the above examples, we might be tempted to conclude that *Eikon Basilike* sets itself up for Milton's attack by its careless use of metaphor. But we would be mistaken on several grounds. First, the book's metaphoric language was calculated to achieve specific emotional effects to broaden its appeal. Its multiple editions testify to the strategy's resounding success: it not only got rhymed, it actually got set to music (III.360, n.33). Second, Milton is perfectly capable of using the same metaphors in much the same way. Charles' hackneyed storm-tossed ship, for example, shows up again only two paragraphs after the point at which Milton had ridiculed it as "poetical garb": "he left the City; and in a most tempestuous season forsook the Helme, and steerage of the Common-wealth" (III.408). Notwithstanding his critique of Charles' claim to the sun-image, Milton attacks the King elsewhere for applying it to an inferior personage: "with Scolastic flourishes beneath the decencie of a King, [he] compares [the Earl of Strafford] to *the Sun*, which in all figurative use, and significance beares allusion to a King, not to a Subject" (III.372). Moreover, despite the regard for rules seemingly acknowledged by his phrase "in all figurative use," Milton's own figuration answers to little rule beyond what will achieve *his* desired effect.

In an imagerial *tour de force* near the end of *Eikonoklastes*, we can watch Milton's metaphoric construct rise literally from nothing, shift mediums, collapse, and reconstruct itself with the breathtaking fluidity of Mulciber's Pandaemonium. The occasion is one of many concluding statements by the King, complacent in tone, but otherwise not intrinsically offensive: "Nothing can be more happy for all than in fair, grave, and honorable ways to contribute their counsels in common, enacting all things by public consent without tyranny or tumults" (*EB*, 168). With the rational substance of his refutation behind him, Milton arbitrarily converts Charles' claim to a negative and then proceeds to build variations on the theme of "no." First, the negation:

> The conclusion therfore must needs be quite contrary to what he
> concludes; that nothing can be more *unhappy*, more dishonourable,
> more unsafe *for all*, then when a wise, *grave*, and *honourable Parlament*
> shal have labour'd, debated, argu'd, consulted, and, as he himself
> speakes, *contributed* for the public good *all thir Counsels in common*, to be
> then frustrated, disappointed, deny'd and repuls'd by the single whiffe
> of a negative. (III.579)

Milton's arbitrary conversion of the King's "happy" to "unhappy" waits suspended by a sequence of tension-building participles, "frustrated, disappointed, deny'd and repuls'd" before at last revealing its cause in the vaporous "whiffe of a negative." From this synesthetic fragment, the very ghost of an image, Milton shapes a complex and changing scenario.

> Nothing can be more *unhappy* [than to be repulsed] by the single
> whiffe of a negative, from the mouth of one wilfull man; nay to be
> blasted, to be struck as mute and motionless as a Parlament of Tapstrie
> in the Hangings; or else after all thir paines and travell to be dissolv'd,
> and cast away like so many Naughts in Arithmetick, unless it be to
> turne the o of thir insignificance into a lamentation with the people,
> who had so vainly sent them. (III.579)

From the immaterial sound-scent "whiffe of a negative" proceed devastating effects. At the mere breath of a King whose book promotes and depends on iconic omnipotence, a counselling Parliament is not just silenced but trans-

formed to a purely decorative icon, a "Parlament of Tapstrie." But even that
identity evaporates numerically as their no longer countable substance
dissolves to wordless lamentation. Then permutations of volatile nothing
gradually shape a palpable image of evil:

> For this is not to *enact all things by public consent*, as he would have us
> be perswaded, this is to enact nothing but by the privat consent and
> leave of one not negative tyrant; this is mischeif without remedy, a
> stifleing and obstructing evil that hath no vent, no outlet, no passage
> through: Grant him this, and the Parlament hath no more freedom
> then if it sate in his Noose, which when he pleases to draw together
> with one twitch of his Negative, shall throttle a whole Nation, to the
> wish of *Caligula* in one neck.   (III. 579)

The "nothing" enacted by a "not negative tyrant" takes multiple forms, all
patterned on the "O" that had transformed parliamentary insignificance to
lamentation. Remediless mischief, the negative whiff from the tyrant's
mouth, stifles and smothers by stopping the "O's" of even wailing mouths,
allowing "no vent, no outlet, no passage through." As its final transformation, the "O" shapes a Caligulan hangman's noose, empowered to throttle an
entire nation by the ultimate synesthetic potency, "one twitch of his
Negative."

Milton's tactical metaphor-demolition and reconstruction, only a few
instances of which I have pointed out here, shows his iconoclasm operating at
language's most elemental level. As recent studies of Renaissance iconoclasm
demonstrate, the iconoclastic spirit of the Protestant reformers was seldom
merely negative. Secular and religious power-structures alike were forced to
respond creatively to the needs of changing human consciousness. In the
hands of the greatest poets of the era, iconoclasm became a vital artistic
principle that released the imaginative energies required to build anew.[11] In
passages like the ones examined above, the dynamics of Milton's creative
iconoclasm can be traced in vigorous action. His aims in *Eikonoklastes*, of
course, reach far beyond the individual verbal icon, but these examples
demonstrate one aspect of a truth that both depends on and destroys the icons
that give it shape.

III The self-witnessing idol

The idols *Eikonoklastes* pulls down with the King's image include prayers and
covenants, liturgical forms and governmental policies, clerical offices and
political reputations. In the context of *Eikon Basilike*, what these all have in
common – what in Milton's view makes them idols – is the way they are used
and intended to be received: in every case, their words, pictures, and outward
forms are proffered and accepted as actual truths, requiring implicit faith in
their claims to truth rather than supporting inquiry into truth or bearing

witness to it. The reciprocal complacencies of the proffered idol and the accepting idolater make a self-serving parody of the generatively reciprocal tensions that characterize Milton's polemical truth.

For Milton the principle of distinguishing between a true image and a false idol had never depended on the icon's mere external or sensible character-istics. We have seen how readily he can appropriate for his own purposes icons whose use by others he criticizes. But his satirical jibe at Charles' "poetical garb" hints at one aspect of imagery that can lead to idolatry – the image's capacity to delude or mislead through costuming or impressive shows.[12] Theatrics alone won't make an image into an idol, however. Shows by their very nature may indeed lend themselves to exposing falseness: Milton credits "the general voice of the people" with "almost hissing [King Charles] and his ill-acted regality off the Stage" (III.355). For an image to become an idol requires above all a credulous worshiper. Any image may thus become an idol, Milton notes in *Christian Doctrine*, even if it is an image of God: "Idolatry means making or owning an idol for religious purposes, or worshipping it, whether it be a representation of the true God or of some false god" (VI.690–1; XVII.134).

If idolatrous "purposes" are what determine religious idolatry, the same is true for what Milton terms "civil idolatry." Since *Eikon Basilike*'s spectacular shows demand worship, not applause, any distinction it may be assumed to make between true and false gods becomes a meaningless pretense. At the same time, Milton's portrayal of the King's book and style as a gallimaufry of religious sentimentalism and gaudy theatrics is complemented by his disdain for those who let themselves be manipulated by impressive shows: "Quaint Emblems and devices begg'd from the old Pageantry of some Twelf-nights entertainment at *Whitehall*, will doe but ill to make a Saint or Martyr. . . But the People, exorbitant and excessive in all thir motions, are prone ofttimes not to a religious onely, but to a civil kind of Idolatry in idolizing thir Kings" (III.343). The King's book appears as a "Tragedie" containing an "Anti-masque," his prayers are deceitful "trumpery" and "painted feathers," the King himself is a weak player in a "Saints vizard" whose courtiers and prelates strive to "imitate him exactly" (III.362, 533, 364–5, 408, 361, 351). But the "miserable, credulous, deluded . . . vulgar" fare even worse: their king "presumes a more implicit Faith in the people of *England*, then the Pope ever commanded from the Romish Laitie; or els a natural sottishness fitt to be abus'd and ridd'n" (III.426, 355). A presumption of "implicit Faith" exposes the King's spiritual arrogance, but "a natural sottishness" places the burden of idolatry on English backs "fitt to be abus'd and ridd'n" because of the willing servility of their king-worship. It is not doctrinal identification with Rome that makes an icon into an idol for Milton; it is the believer's own proneness to idolatry that stamps his worship Roman, regardless of its accidental components: "If the People resolve to take him Sainted at the rate of such a Canonizing, I shall suspect thir Calendar more then the Gregorian"

(III.343). Milton's doubts about the faith of the English people arise less from what they might call their religion (be it "Protestant," "Presbyterian," "Episcopal," or "Roman") than from what, by their conduct and demonstrated manner of receiving icons, they conceive religion to *be*.

Still, from the perspective of the image-worshiper, the image must somehow satisfy the desire to worship worthily. As Florence Sandler points out, the sacrificial and sacramental character of Charles' piety readily led to associating his imprisonment and death with the suffering and death of Christ.[13] It is an association *Eikon Basilike* fully exploits. The King regrets that he should be sold off to Parliament by the Scots at a rate higher than that earned by Judas; he compares his settling with Parliament to Christ's permitting himself to be tempted by the devil on the pinnacle; he asks God to forgive the people, for "they know not what they do"; in his frontispiece portrait, the kneeling King forsakes his earthly crown, gazes toward his heavenly crown, and in his right hand grasps the crown of thorns (*EB*, 137, 23, 46; Fig. 1). Even if the people were not predisposed to a "civil kinde of Idolatry," *Eikon Basilike* expropriates from an iconically charged style of Christian worship a sufficient quantity of verbal and visual images to ensure that the idolatrous habits of unthinking minds will automatically transfer to Charles. In Milton's view the intentionality of such martyrdom corrupts it:

> If I beare witness of my self, saith *Christ*, my witness is not true. He who writes himself *Martyr* by his own inscription, is like an ill Painter, who, by writing on the shapeless Picture which he hath drawn, is fain to tell passengers what shape it is; which else no man could imagin: no more then how a Martyrdom can belong to him, who therfore dyes for his Religion because it is *establisht*. (III.575)

Because they are manifestly designed for purposes of civil idolatry, the elements of the King's defense bear witness only of themselves. But by doing so, they inevitably betray their cause. For, to defend the King, *Eikon Basilike* uses strategies that mirror the wrongs for which the King has already been condemned.

A case in point is the King's expressed regret for having consented to the execution of the Earl of Strafford. The legitimacy of the charges against Strafford, which historians agree are questionable at best, is not for Milton an issue. He clearly agrees with Parliament's finding of treason. But what is at issue is *Eikon Basilike*'s exploitation of the dramatic Strafford case to create a public *perception* of royal remorse over one death that can in turn deflect perceptions of royal remorselessness over many others. As the King's "facile conscience" had first rejected and then later agreed to the treason charge against Strafford for reasons of policy, now his display of sorrow for the act of agreeing to it also has a political motive: "And we may well perceave to what easie satisfactions and purgations he had inur'd his secret conscience, who thaught, by such weak policies and ostentations as these, to gaine beleif and absolution from understanding Men" (III.376). The belief and absolution acquired by such "ostentations" neatly separate the *image of the act* of agreeing from the agreement itself, thus placing the act's meaning, its claim to "truth," not in what actually happened, but in how it is made to appear. The image thus bears witness only of itself. Moreover, the King bewails

> the blood of one man, his commodious Instrument ... that we might think him too tender to shed willingly the blood of those thousands, whom he counted Rebels. And thus by dipping voluntarily his fingers end, yet with shew of great remorse in the blood of *Strafford*, wherof all men cleer him, he thinks to scape that Sea of innocent blood wherin his own guilt inevitably hath plung'd him all over. (III.376)

Now since the King's "shew of great remorse" depends on the credulity of the dazzled gazer for success, the calculated stagework of blood-dipped fingers might have been simply exposed by Milton as sensationalist propaganda. But the King's intended audience is not only the English public: "*He hop'd it would be som evidence before God and Man to all posteritie that he was farr from bearing that vast load and guilt of blood* layd upon him by others" (III.376). By offering to prove his innocence before God with the same display of "evidence" as depends on credulous men and posterity, the impressive show bears witness to its own idolatry.

But the key to success in strategic ostentation is the "image-doting rabble" who fail to see that the image they worship requires their credulity. Milton argues this point explicitly as he rejects the King's claims to protection under the Solemn League and Covenant. As Merritt Hughes points out, exclusive adherence to the covenant's clause providing for protection of the King's person would have meant neglect of other more important provisions. Moreover, the covenant had already been variously broken by both King and Parliament; and in any case, the King himself had never agreed to the covenant's terms (III.80–8). The strategy of *Eikon Basilike* therefore consists in requiring that the covenant be honored not for the sake of its terms (which demands inquiry into whether the terms have been met) but for the sake of its *being a covenant*. Thus, in Milton's words, it "shall prevaile at last, over men so quell'd and fitted to be slaves by the fals conceit of a Religious Covnant" (III.595). Since a covenant by definition exists only according to its terms, to detach it from these is to make it no covenant: thus it operates for, bears witness of, only itself. And this, too, is politically convenient: instead of demanding from men a reverence they might have doubts about granting a secular ruler, it simply expropriates to the ruler a reverence with which well-meaning but uncritical men tend to invest covenants:

> For so long as a King shall find by experience that do the worst he can, his Subjects, overaw'd by the Religion of thir own Covnant, will

only prosecute his evil instruments, not dare to touch his Person, and that whatever hath bin on his part offended or transgress'd, he shall come off at last with the same honour as for well doing, he will not faile to finde them worke. (III. 595)

The "religion of their own covenant" empowers a people's tyrant. The King's showy book could not by itself make an idol of the Solemn League and Covenant; it could only exploit the idol covenanters had already made by worshiping the image of their own universally forsaken agreement. By making their covenant into a religious idol, they cancel its capacity, and their own reasoning capacity, for witnessing truth.

IV Such easy literature

Milton shatters the King's icon not only because it is a bad king's, but because it is a debased icon, an idol exploited and adored for purposes not necessarily apparent in the image itself. But idolatry thrives as well on materials not overtly iconic. In its defense of personal chaplains, set prayers, and the liturgy, in the manner of its scriptural quotation, and most spectacularly in its plagiarism of Pamela's prayer from Sidney's *Arcadia*, *Eikon Basilike* makes a showcase for what Milton could only regard as idolatry of words. Words exploited for purposes alien to their original intent, words devitalized and dispirited by rote recitation, words distanced from the tensive impulses of thought and feeling that generated them, become, like their exploiters, slaves to idolatry. By their misuse made the sign not of human meaning but of its cessation, self-witnessing dead words travesty their vital origin in the divine Word.

That words may be the object of the most pervasive and subtle idolatry is suggested by Milton's remarks in the preface to *Eikonoklastes*. For *Eikon Basilike* to gain wide public approval, it is enough that it be merely inscribed with the King's name, "the gaudy name of Majesty . . . his Regal Name and Authority . . . a name, then which there needs no more among the blockish vulgar, to make it wise, and excellent, and admir'd, nay to set it next the Bible" (III. 339). Under the aegis of the King's name, the King's book can be judged by "faction and the easy literature of custom and opinion," such easy literature as persuades its readers that they, too, may become "wise, excellent, and admir'd" by exerting as little imaginative, critical, and intellectual effort in reading it as had gone into the writing (III. 339). Like self-witnessing idols, easy literature depends on the cooperative servility, or more appropriately the cooperative indolence, of credulous readers and writers, word-speakers and word-hearers.

Of the many offenses *Eikon Basilike* commits, none elicits from Milton more contempt than its intellectual and spiritual laziness. The King "had it not in him to make a prayer of his own, or at least would excuse himself the paines and cost of his invention" (III.367). He should "endeavour to have more light in himself: And not to walk by another mans Lamp, but to get Oyle into his own" (III.552). Milton's own strenuous religious and intellectual discipline made prayer one of a Christian's "Ecclesiastical duties," a vigorous "exercise of that Heav'nly gift" that is our "freedom of speech to the Throne of Grace" (III.506–7). The King's book, on the other hand, "unhallow'd, and unchrist'nd" prayer by facile borrowing, while the sweet prayers of the King's divines have the sickly sweetness of unexercised morbidity: their "honycomb devotions" are supplied from the "rheume of thir Mellifluous prayers and meditations" (III.362, 365–6). For Milton, it is precisely the *effort* of original prayer, an effort subverted by liturgical forms, that at least partially constitutes prayer's worth: "He who prays, must consult first with his heart; which in likelyhood may stirr up his affections" (III.506). For the worshiper who uses set prayers, on the other hand, "having both words and matter readie made to his lips, which is enough to make up the outward act of prayer, his affections grow lazy, and com not up easlie at the call of words not thir own." Lazy affections present God not with prayer, but only with dispirited and meaningless forms, "a sett of stale and empty words" (III.506–7). And yet, for the believer with stirred-up, vigorous, and well-exercised affections, the effort of prayer becomes in fact supremely effortless. Vital words are like manna in the wilderness: "God every morning raines down new expressions into our hearts." But, like reserved manna, words idolatrously hoarded "will be found rather *to breed wormes and stink.*"

If spiritual indolence is the ultimate cause and effect of easy literature, it is not the only contributing influence, however. To the combination of "ease" and "little . . . Christian diligence, or judgement" Milton attributes the imitative patchwork of *Eikon Basilike*'s devotional style, but he also tellingly links such ease to the consequent augmentation of the book's market value:

> And this is the substance of his first section, till wee come to the devout of it, model'd into the form of a privat Psalter. Which they who so much admire, either for the matter or the manner, may as well admire the Arch-Bishops late Breviary, and many other as good *Manuals,* and *Handmaids of Devotion,* the lip-work of every Prelatical Liturgist, clapt together, and quilted out of Scripture phrase, with as much ease, and as little need of Christian diligence, or judgement, as belongs to the compiling of any ord'nary and salable peece of English Divinity, that the Shops value.   (III.360)

"Till we come to the devout of it" captures exactly the compartmentalizing effect created by *Eikon Basilike*'s division of each of its twenty-eight rather brief chapters into a section of political argument followed by a section of devotional meditations and prayer. The readily grasped, almost liturgical rhythms of the book's structure thus join its "clapt together, and quilted" devotions to make it a suitable shelf-companion to those other "as good

Manuals" whose easy acquisition in the shops matches the easy "lip-work" of "the whole rosarie of his Prayers" (III. 364).

Milton's association of easy literature with bought prayers is characteristic. From the beginning of his polemical career, his irony has targeted the business side of facile religion. In *Of Reformation*, the prelates would make spiritual relief a burgeoning enterprise by having us "commit to their dispose the whole managing of our salvation" (I. 548). *Areopagitica*'s implicit believer gladly pays the caparisoned priest to mind his religion for him, because he finds it "to be a traffick so entangl'd, and of so many piddling accounts, that of all mysteries he cannot skill to keep a stock going upon that trade" (II. 543–4).

But here, vendible ease is carried several steps further. The King in time of dire spiritual need discovers in himself such a "bankrupt devotion" that he is compelled not only to have "sharkd" his prayers "from the mouth of a Heathen worshipper" but to have "sould them to those that stood and honord him next to the Messiah" (III. 367). The moral wrong in *Eikon Basilike*'s plagiarism of the Pamela prayer lies not just in its being inappropriately heathen, despite Milton's scathing characterization of it as "the polluted orts and refuse of *Arcadia*'s and *Romances* . . . an ethnic Prayer" (III. 364). Neither is it precisely in the plagiarism itself, which Milton treats ironically as an ingenious form of revenue enhancement: "Many Princes have bin rigorous in laying taxes on thir Subject by the head, but of any King heertofore that made a levy upon thir witt, and seisd it as his own legitimat, I have not whome beside to instance" (III. 365). For a spiritual bankrupt to steal prayers might in itself be almost an object of pity: "he who wants a prayer to beseech God in his necessity, tis unexpressible how poor he is; farr poorer within himself then all his enemies can make him" (III. 366). This bankrupt, however, steals prayers not to fill spiritual emptiness, but to pawn the prayers "for hopes no less vain and presumptuous . . . then by these goodly reliques to be held a Saint and Martyr in opinion with the cheated People" (III. 367). Proffered as a sign of Charles' piety, the prayer's success depends on thoughtless and spiritually indolent readers to buy up the sign as their truth: "How unhappy, how forsook of grace, and unbelovd of God that people who resolv to know no more of piety or of goodnes, then to account him thir cheif Saint and Martyr" (III. 367). Like the credulous and cheated worshiper, the would-be saint's impoverishment is both spiritual and intellectual: he "thought no better of the living God then of a buzzard Idol, fitt to be so servd and worshipt in reversion . . . *without being able to discern* the affront rather then the worship of such an ethnic prayer" (III. 364, my italics). Thus Sidney's prayer, in its fictional context the sign of a pagan character's piety, becomes in *Eikon Basilike* a sign of Christian piety's bartered demise.

Besides the test of intellectual and spiritual vitality, an additional test may be brought to bear on easy literature. It is the simple test adduced by the life of the word-user himself. Throughout *Eikonoklastes* Milton challenges the King's words by pointing to the King's deeds:

> But if these his fair spok'n words shall be heer fairly confronted and laid parallel to his own farr differing deeds, manifest and visible to the whole Nation, then surely we may look on them who notwithstanding shall persist to give to bare words more credit then to op'n deeds, as men whose judgement was not rationally evinc'd and perswaded, but fatally stupifi'd and bewitch'd. (III. 346–7)

As with other truth-tests, the test of deeds against words implicates those who read the words as well as those who write them. Any who would not be "fatally stupifi'd and bewitch'd" must rely on their vital reason and senses to discern that which is "manifest and visible to the whole Nation."

But it is the King's effort by words to expropriate the moral and spiritual justification of someone else's life that Milton finds most absurd. Charles seems to regard his suffering as itself sufficient claim on the mercies granted King David: "I come far short of David's piety; yet since I may equal David's afflictions, give me also the comforts and the sure mercies of David" (*EB*, 149). Just as sufferings cannot themselves make a martyr, in Milton's view, sufferings alone cannot sanctify a life of wrongdoing. "Had he borrow'd *Davids* heart," instead of borrowing the mere rhetoric of David's penitential psalms, "it had bin much the holier theft" (III. 547). In the attempt to acquire David's character through his words, however, the easy-literature strategy backfires:

> Transported with the vain ostentation of imitating *Davids* language, not his life, observe how he brings a curse upon himself and his Fathers house (God so disposing it) by his usurp'd and ill imitated prayer: *Let thy anger I beseech thee be against me and my Fathers house, as for these Sheep what have they don.* For if David indeed sind in numbring the people, of which fault he in earnest made that confession, and acquitted the whole people from the guilt of that sin, then doth this King, using the same words, bear witness against himself to be the guilty person; and either in his soule and conscience heer acquitts the Parlament and the people, or els abuses the words of *David*, and dissembles grossly eev'n to the very face of God. (III.555)

Words exploited as self-witnessing bearers of truth may thus betray the exploiter – "the same words, bear witness against himself" – as well as deceive the idolater.

Like every idol, easy literature fails and betrays because the idolater complacently accepts the icon as truth rather than recognizing that all icons, verbal and otherwise, are themselves no more than mortal tools used in the continuing search for immortal, and therefore inexpressible, truth. If we expect to locate truth *in* the icon, we may gratify our senses, but the "streaming fountain" sickens and dies. As a fitting parody of the vital fountain of truth represented in scripture, Milton portrays the fountain that he believes *Eikon Basilike* offers its readers. The King's book would have us hold "our natural freedom by meer gift, as when the Conduit pisses Wine at Coronations, from the superfluity of thir royal grace and beneficence" (III.486). The civil idolater, without whom the King's image could never have turned idol, is set out by Milton's deft wine-transforming vulgarism to swill grace and beneficence as superfluous royal urine. Should the people desire to reject such a manifest, eminently expressible truth, they need only withdraw their approbation, "bethink themselves, and recover" (III.601).

Notes

1 The earliest known example of such displacement is the royal arms of Henry VIII at Rushbrooke in Suffolk. See John Phillips, *The Reformation of Images: Destruction of Art in England, 1535–1660* (Berkeley and London, 1973), p. 205, n.4. Phillips discusses the extended historical implications of Tudor icon manipulation on pages 204–5, in addition to the more immediate effects in chapters 3 and 4. Also, chapter 1 delineates the medieval Christian use of the arts as a "bridge" to the divine.

2 The line comes from Felltham's "Epitaph to the Eternal Memory of Charles the First . . . Inhumanely Murthered by a Perfidious Party of His Prevalent Subjects." William Lamont and Sybil Oldfield collect and discuss representative contemporary views on the public image of the executed King in chapter 5, "Charles I: Royal Martyr or 'Popish Favourite'?", *Politics, Religion and Literature in the Seventeenth Century* (London, 1975).

3 John Phillips discusses Bishop Gardiner's warnings about substituting royal images for religious ones in *Reformation of Images*, p. 194. The difficulty of determining what constitutes idolatry is a constant theme in Phillips' study, but see especially chapter 2 for Lollard mistrust of images as a species of self-love versus the Erasmian humanist view of the arts as instruments for educating and civilizing mankind; also, the Henrician doctrine of "things indifferent" as influenced by Erasmus and Melanchthon, pp. 51ff; "abused" versus "unabused" images, pp. 77–80; and "idolatrous" versus "commemorative" images, with Somerset's argument that idolatry inheres in what we make of images, not in the images themselves, pp. 88–91.

4 Roy Strong, *The English Icon: Elizabethan and Jacobean Portraiture* (New Haven, 1969), p. 29.

5 For a review of the troubled historical relations between figurative language and truth, see Mark Johnson's introductory essay in *Philosophical Perspectives on Metaphor* (Minneapolis, 1981).

6 Full elaboration of this argument can be found in my "Shuffling Up Such a God," *Milton Studies*, 21 (1985), pp. 3–33.

7 See my "Coupling Logic and Milton's Doctrine of Divorce," *Milton Studies*, 15 (1981), pp. 143–59.

8 Nigel Smith's essay in this volume explores *Areopagitica*'s truth as lying in the "choices made available" in "the divine pattern of education." See also Stanley Fish, "Truth and Indeterminacy in *Areopagitica*," in Mary Nyquist and Margaret Ferguson, eds., *Re-membering Milton: Essays on the Texts and Traditions* (New York and London, 1988), pp. 234–54.

9 II.554; compare II.528: "What ever thing we hear or see, sitting, walking, travelling, or conversing may be fitly call'd our book, and is of the same effect that writings are."

10 Philip A. Knachel, ed., *Eikon Basilike: The Portraiture of His Sacred Majesty in His Solitudes and Sufferings* (Ithaca, N.Y., 1966). The present quotation is on p. 11; subsequent page references (abbreviated *EB*) will appear in the text. Although *Eikon Basilike* was compiled and largely written by John Gauden, I discuss it as if entirely written by its putative author, King Charles. For a review of the authorship question and Gauden's actual role, see Hugh Trevor-Roper, "Eikon Basilike: The Problem of the King's Book," *History Today*, 1 (September 1951), pp. 7–12. In *Stuart England* (London, 1978), J. P. Kenyon characterizes *Eikon Basilike* as "a mixture of pietistic moralizing and shrewd historical revisionism" and regards it as a "seriously undervalued" book, second only to the Bible and Foxe's *Acts and Monuments* in its influence on the century (p. 165).

11 See Ernest B. Gilman, *Iconoclasm and Poetry in the English Reformation: Down Went Dagon* (Chicago and London, 1986) for a helpful study of Renaissance literary iconoclasm, especially as it relates to Milton's poetics. John Phillips points to the role of Reformation iconoclasm in the development of human consciousness in *Reformation of Images*, pp. 201ff. A related perspective is offered by J. J. Scarisbrick, *The Reformation and the English People* (Oxford, 1984), p. 68.

12 For a detailed discussion of theatricality and representation in *Eikonoklastes*, see David Loewenstein's *Milton and the Drama of History: Historical Vision, Iconoclasm, and the Literary Imagination* (Cambridge, 1990), chapter 3. Emphasizing the historical dimension of Milton's iconoclasm, Loewenstein argues that shattering the King's equivocal image and recasting it to display underlying corruption is itself an imaginative and theatrical gesture by which Milton intends to influence and dramatically reshape the course of English history.

13 "Icon and Iconoclast," *Left Hand*, pp. 160–84.

8

"Suffering for Truths sake": Milton and martyrdom

JOHN R. KNOTT, JR.

Readers of John Foxe's *Acts and Monuments*, the great work of Elizabethan martyrology, may be struck by an apparent contradiction between two characteristics of the martyrs he celebrates, their eager embrace of suffering as the Christian's means to victory over persecution and their militant resistance to the views of those who examine them and ultimately deliver them to the secular power to be burned as heretics. Foxe's martyrs are both willing victims, "as sheep for the slaughter" (Ps. 44:22) in a frequently invoked biblical phrase, and soldiers in Christ's army. Foxe himself saw no contradiction in this. For him, the constancy of martyrs to their vision of God's truth could manifest itself in defiance of their examiners in the name of truth and also in a willingness to suffer for it in prison and at the stake. Milton was significantly influenced by the *Acts and Monuments*, but his prose reveals a tension between the martyr as militant Christian and the martyr as victim, a tension not apparent to Foxe. In the prose, especially in the antiprelatical tracts and in *Eikonoklastes*, Milton appears much more willing to praise the combativeness of individual martyrs in the defense of truth than to dwell upon the fact of their suffering. While he acknowledges this suffering, and the triumph of weakness over strength that it represents, he appears uneasy with the emphasis traditionally placed upon suffering in the literature of martyrdom and skeptical about accounts of particular martyrdoms. It is not until his sonnet "On the Late Massacre in *Piemont*" and, especially, the later poetry that Milton focuses upon the suffering that Foxe presents as so critical to the experience of the martyr, and to that of the Christian in a frequently hostile world.

The view of martyrdom that one finds in *Paradise Lost* is more orthodox than that of the prose, and central to Milton's conception of Christian heroism. At the beginning of Book IX of *Paradise Lost*, Milton insists that his argument is "Not less but more Heroic than the wrauth / Of stern *Achilles*" (IX.14–15) and laments that his predecessors in the epic exercised their skills on the "long and tedious havoc" of wars, "the better fortitude / Of Patience and Heroic Martyrdom / Unsung" (IX.31–3).[1] Milton's prominent use of the idea of martyrdom here seems more understandable when Michael describes the crucifixion to Adam and subsequently explains how the faithful will be able to resist "*Satans* assaults" and "amaze / Thir proudest persecuters," fortified by "inward consolations" (XII.491–7). The heroes he offers Adam are those "who in the worship persevere / Of Spirit and Truth" (XII. 532–3) in the face of "heavie persecution." Adam does not see or hear of the sufferings of particular martyrs, but he grasps the principle underlying what has been called a theology of suffering:

> that suffering for Truths sake
> Is fortitude to highest victorie,
> And to the faithful Death the Gate of Life.
> (XII. 569–71)

The example of his "Redeemer ever blest" teaches him this, Adam goes on to say. It is the example of Christ's suffering that ultimately gives meaning to "Heroic Martyrdom" for Milton. Adam's response reminds us that all authentic martyrdom relates in some fashion to this act; the truth to which Christian martyrs bear witness (the literal meaning of the term "martyr") is that embodied by the life and teachings of Christ.

I

In much of Milton's commentary on martyrdom and martyrs in the prose, militancy in the defense of truth overshadows the sufferings whose importance emerges so clearly in *Paradise Lost*. Pathos is suspect except where it is associated with the generalized cause of truth or the sufferings of the true church. Milton's portrait of the true martyr emerges from his examination of abuses of the ideal of martyrdom, in older texts and in the contemporary example of *Eikon Basilike* (1649), which appeared shortly after the execution of Charles I and did more than anything else to establish the myth of the royal martyr.

Milton's view of martyrdom and of the Reformation was strongly colored by the *Acts and Monuments*, whose influence continued to be felt in the seventeenth century, yet he could respond to Foxe's zeal for reform and at the same time differentiate his ideal of the true church from Foxe's vision of a national church under Elizabeth.[2] Milton's celebration of the "bright and blissful Reformation" early in *Of Reformation in England* is very much in the spirit of Foxe, with its focus on the "returning Gospell" and the achievements of the martyrs: "Then was the Sacred BIBLE sought out of the dusty corners where prophane Falshood and Neglect had throwne it, the . . . *Martyrs*, with the unresistable *might* of *Weaknesse*, shaking the *Powers* of *Darknesse*, and scorning the *fiery rage* of the old *red Dragon*." Scripture, seen by both Milton and Foxe as the source of light and truth, is a key actor in the *Acts and Monuments*, and the martyrs who take their stand for God's truth as embodied in scripture are shown by Foxe as contending with the various forms of the "rage" of Satan (or Antichrist).

Milton resembles Foxe in seeing Wyclif as the progenitor of the Reformation and in attacking the worldliness and ceremonialism of bishops with a vigor that a modern reader is apt to find startling. Foxe was of course primarily attacking the vices he saw in the Roman Catholic clergy, embodied for him by the luxury of Wolsey, the cruelty of "bloody Bonner" and other persecuting bishops, and the idolatry that he found in the mass. Milton's anticlericalism was more fundamental, embracing prelacy in any form, and his iconoclasm extended to the *Book of Common Prayer* that Foxe championed. Milton's antiprelatical tracts owe much to Foxe's highly charged account of the struggles of an emerging Protestantism, in spirit and in substance, but his own reforming instinct was more deeply radical, pressing him toward a narrower and purer sense of the primitive church to be emulated. Where Foxe saw himself playing Eusebius to Elizabeth's Constantine, and celebrated the founding of a national church with the Elizabethan Settlement, Milton denounced Constantine for corrupting the church with wealth. His apostolic ideal of a poor and simple ministry gave little or no scope to the traditions of the early centuries of the church appealed to by those who spoke for the English church from Foxe's time to his own.

In *Animadversions* Milton represented Foxe's martyrs as "so hatefull to the *Prelates*, that their story was almost come to be a prohibited book" (1.678–9), alluding to the fact that Archbishop Laud had refused to license a new edition of the *Acts and Monuments* in 1637. Milton's own attitudes toward Foxe's book were more complicated than this taunt would suggest. Bishop Hall and other defenders of episcopacy traded on the aura of sanctity surrounding the bishops martyred by Mary and given heroic stature by Foxe: "*Remonst.* And why should I not speake of Martyrs, as the Authors and users of this holy *Liturgie?*" (1.678). Milton sought to discredit such claims by demonstrating the hostility of the episcopal establishment to Foxe's book, and, more bluntly, by devaluing the martyrs in question: bishops Latimer, Ridley, and Cranmer, the last the chief author of the *Book of Common Prayer*. He attacked Cranmer and Ridley as "halting and time-serving *Prelates*" (1.532), choosing to concentrate on the political fluctuations of their early careers rather than the triumphant martyrdoms that Foxe memorialized, although he could praise them for rejecting ceremony and vestments at the end, crediting their persecution with purifying them (1.803–4). Milton's uncompromising opposition to episcopacy forced him to distinguish between true and false martyrs in this case, appealing to the old argument that heretics have often claimed that martyrdom proved the truth of their position (1.533–5, 734–5, 912). To separate episcopacy from "the Heavenly Fortitude of *Martyrdome*" (1.536) he felt compelled to argue that Foxe's "*Prelat-Martyrs*" were "to bee judg'd what they were by the *Gospel*, and not the *Gospel* to be tried by them" (1.603), that is, judged by the Gospel he read, which gave no support for the modern institution of the bishopric and thus made it difficult for him to accept the idea that prelates of any kind could be true martyrs. Hall's claim that these bishops "subscrib'd the Gospell with their blood" is much closer to the spirit of Foxe's account.

Milton's ability to discount the suffering of Foxe's most prominent martyrs reflects more than his aggressiveness in the struggle against episcopacy. He shows considerably more skepticism than did Foxe toward individual martyrs, however he might honor the "glorious Name" (1.536) of martyrdom. Foxe was careful to dissociate himself from the *Legenda Aurea* of Jacobus de Voragine, with its credulous reporting of miracles surrounding the deaths of martyrs and their shrines. Both Foxe and Milton rejected the Catholic sense of a "potentia" lingering in the relics of saints and martyrs.[3] But where Foxe incorporated much from Eusebius' accounts of such celebrated early martyrs as Ignatius and Polycarp and dignified English martyrs by association with them, Milton proved less willing to credit accounts of early martyrdoms.[4] He objected to the use made of the tradition by those he saw as misleading credulous readers with "needlesse tractats stuff't with specious names of *Ignatius*, and *Polycarpus*, with fragments of old *Martyrologies*, and legends" (1.626–7). Milton's aim was to "recall the people of God from this vaine forraging after straw, and to reduce them to their firme stations under the standard of the Gospell" (1.627), or, as he put it elsewhere, to set God's word against "all the heaped names of Angells, and Martyrs, Councells, and Fathers urg'd upon us" (1.652).[5]

In *Of Prelatical Episcopacy* Milton sought to prove spurious the writings of Ignatius cited by his opponents, after citing him approvingly on the election of bishops in *Of Reformation*. The passages in the epistles of Ignatius to which he objects "must either be adulterat, or else *Ignatius* was not *Ignatius*, not a Martyr, but most adulterate, and corrupt himselfe" (1.639). With Ignatius, as with Latimer and Ridley, Milton was less interested in the fact of suffering than in the truth of the position taken. This emphasis was consistent with Augustine's principle for distinguishing between true and false martyrs: "*Martyrem non facit poena, sed causa*" (*Epist.* 89.2). Not the punishment but the cause makes a martyr. Milton could condemn Becket for his "insolencies and affronts to Regall Majestie" (1.581) and praise "the constant martyr St. Laurence" (1.611), who responded to the demand of a Roman prefect for the treasure of the church by presenting him with carts bearing the poor. Becket represented to him a Roman church greedy for secular power, St. Laurence a much earlier church striving to preserve apostolic ideals.

Milton challenged Irenaeus' claim that Polycarp was made bishop of Smyrna by the apostles, insisting that he was merely the most famous of the "*Smyrnian Presbyters*" (1.643) and offered "a light scruple or two" about miracles associated with his martyrdom. If Polycarp was really a prophet who foresaw his death by fire, how is it that the flames refused to touch his body and he had to be put to death by the sword? And why, when he was not only preserved from the flames but "exhaling such a sweet odour, as if all the incense of *Arabia* had bin burning," did his followers urge the executioner to make haste? Milton respected the holiness of Polycarp but, unlike Foxe, questioned the credulity and the tendency to veneration that he saw in Polycarp's admirers. He found similar attitudes in the disposition of members of the early church to be less interested in the writings of the apostles than in the stories of those who had known them and could say: "here hee taught, here he stood ... O happy this house that harbour'd him ... and that pavement bedew'd with the warme effusion of his last blood, that sprouted into eternall Roses to crowne his Martyrdome" (1.642). While they should have been studying the grounds of saving knowledge, "all their thoughts were powr'd out upon circumstances." That way superstition lay, and the sense of a magical power associated with martyrs that informed medieval martyrology. For Milton the meaning was not in the "circumstances," as it was for those who hung on the miraculous stories of the *Legenda Aurea* or even the detail of Foxe's grisly accounts of burnings,[6] but in the truth to which the martyrs witnessed. One of Milton's retorts to Hall is relevant here: "We also reverence the Martyrs but relye only upon the Scriptures" (1.912). This is a guarded reverence, wary of attributing too much to the heroic act and too little to the scriptural truth that motivated it.

One of the high aims for poetry that Milton announced in *The Reason of Church-Government* was "to sing the victorious agonies of Martyrs and Saints" (1.817). The phrase "victorious agonies" implies the familiar truth that suffering is the way to the martyr's crown. Yet Milton proved more interested in proclaiming the victory than in rendering the agony of martyrs, and, in the antiprelatical tracts, tended to see this victory more as a matter of actively defying evil than of patiently suffering the rage of persecutors. To have dwelt upon the agony would have been to portray the martyrs as victims, when he preferred to see them as soldiers in the wars of truth. Foxe labored to show his martyrs outspoken in the defense of biblical truth, but also focused on their suffering and the attitudes with which they met death, opposing their peace of mind to the "rage" of the enemies of the gospel and celebrating the joyfulness with which they endured their ordeals in the flames; to be "merry" in the fire was proof of one's faith and of God's support. Milton was more interested in branding persecutors and celebrating gestures of defiance, and he found enemies enough among the prelates who suppress sects, "persecute all knowing and zealous Christians by the violence of their courts" (1.784), and slit noses (1.894).

In one of his shrewdest thrusts, Milton played upon a comment in which the author of *A Modest Confutation* had accused him of blasphemy and called for those who loved Christ to "*stone him* [Milton] *to death*" (1.895). Milton readily embraced the role of the protomartyr Stephen, stoned to death by the Pharisees as a false prophet (Acts 6–7, 9), and, by associating his opponent with the high priest Caiaphas, identified with Christ as well, not the Christ of Galilee but the Christ who defied priests and was capable of speaking bluntly (1.895, 900). Calvin had commended "the vehemency of Stephen" before the

Sanhedrin and had characterized him as speaking God's truth while "beset round with raging enemies."[7] In justifying his own vehemence Milton protested that he could not see "how *Wickleffe* and *Luther*, with all the first Martyrs, and reformers, could avoid the imputation of libelling" (I.878). Milton was not simply being defensive. He prized contentiousness, even what he called "sanctified bitternesse against the enemies of truth" (I.901): "we may frequently reade, that many of the Martyrs in the midst of their troubles, were not sparing to deride and scoffe their superstitious persecutors" (I.903). One can imagine Milton relishing Philpot's abuse of Bonner in the accounts of his many examinations that Foxe reproduces, or the sarcastic taunts of some of Foxe's more obscure martyrs about the host – for example, that of Hugh Laverock of Colchester: "I cannot find in the Scriptures, that the priests should lift up over their heads a cake of bread."[8]

In the antiprelatical tracts Milton asserted a fundamental Christian truth that was to become centrally important for his major poetry, that weakness in the name of Christ can conquer worldly strength. He reminded prelates that God sent "Foolishnes to confute Wisdom, Weaknes to bind Strength, Despisednes to vanquish Pride" (I.824), appealing to Corinthians, and opposed "the mighty weaknes of the Gospel" (I.827) to an ecclesiastical establishment that he saw as built upon custom and tradition. Yet for all his appeal to weakness, and his identification with the persecuted defenders of a suffering church, the dominant note of the antiprelatical tracts is militancy in what he saw as "the fierce encounter of truth and falshood together" (I.796). His response to appeals for unity and concord was to welcome the tumults stirred up by the "renovating and re-ingendring Spirit of God" (I.703). It is not surprising to find Milton praising martyrs for their fierceness in condemning the "enemies of truth" or bestowing the name of martyr upon contemporaries combative enough to suffer for attacking episcopacy. In freeing Prynne, Bastwick, Burton, and others, "opening the prisons and dungeons," Parliament had "cal'd out of darknesse and bonds, the elect Martyrs and witnesses of their Redeemer" (I.925).

In *Areopagitica* Milton extended the language of martyrdom to the struggle for free expression that he saw as crucial to the advancement of Reformation in England. Suppressing books becomes "a persecution more undermining, and secretly decaying the Church, then the open cruelty of *Decius* or *Dioclesian*" (II.509); spilling the life of man preserved in books is "a kind of homicide ... sometimes a martyrdome" (II.493). Books become like Protestant martyrs for Milton in their "potencie of life," witnessing to God's truth and suffering their own kind of violence, as when the "expurging Indexes" of the Inquisition rake through the entrails of an author. In his brilliant adaptation of the myth of Isis and Osiris Milton made truth itself a martyr. The "deceivers" who arose after the death of the Apostles, like Typhon and his conspirators attacking Osiris, "took the virgin Truth, hewd her lovely form into a thousand peeces, and scatter'd them to the four winds." In the framework established by the figure, licensing becomes an assault upon piety: "Suffer not these licencing prohibitions to stand at every place of opportunity forbidding and disturbing them that continue seeking, that continue to do our obsequies to the torn body of our martyr'd Saint" (II.549–50). Milton plays upon the association of the "martyr'd Saint" with Christ, with whom truth came into the world as a "perfect shape" and upon whose return truth's "lovelines and perfection" will be restored, but the primary reference is to the "virgin Truth." He invested this figure with a pathos that he had not given to individual martyrs. Typhon becomes a particularly cruel and destructive version of the persecutor and truth herself, with her "torn body," a figure who suggests not only the violence done truth by its enemies but the state of the suffering church, often represented by the woman clothed with the sun of Revelation 12. Milton used the myth chiefly to represent the process of seeking knowledge, for him a matter of "still closing up truth to truth as we find it" (II.551), but he made it a powerful rhetorical tool by tapping the pathos evoked by the tradition of celebrating the suffering of martyrs for God's truth, often associated with the Passion itself. He could release such feelings about the "torn body" of truth, when he could not dwell upon the agony of an actual "martyr'd Saint," because to do the latter would have been to invite the kind of veneration that he abhorred in stories of martyrdom.

II

When Milton took up his commission to answer *Eikon Basilike*, he set out boldly to rescue Queen Truth from an image of King Charles that had captured the imagination of what he saw as an "inconstant, irrational, and Image-doting rabble" (III.601). The immense popularity of the "King's Book" made his task in *Eikonoklastes* all the more difficult; twenty English-language editions had appeared in England within a month and a half of the execution (there would be thirty-five by the end of 1649), and it had been translated into Latin and several European languages.[9] If Milton scorned the mob who worshiped at the new "Shrine," responding to the magical aura that attached to the "circumstances" of this supposed martyrdom, he felt a deeper contempt for those who manipulated their responses. The friends responsible for the frontispiece that fixed the image of Charles as the royal Martyr "would martyr him and Saint him to befool the people" (III.343). In claiming a victory through his meditations that he could not win otherwise, Charles was no more than a "politic contriver" to Milton. For him *Eikon Basilike* presented not the truth but a carefully wrought image of a Charles who discredited his claims to martyrdom by his self-conscious preoccupation with the wrongs done him: "Martyrs bear witness to the truth, not to themselves. If I beare witness of my self, saith *Christ*, my witness is not true. He who writes himself *Martyr* by his own inscription, is like an ill Painter, who, by writing on the shapeless Picture which he hath drawn, is fain to tell passengers what shape it is" (III.575).

Milton could accuse Charles of contriving a false image of himself as martyr and at the same time suggest that the language in *Eikon Basilike* sounded like that of "some houshold preist" (III.430) or "*Rhetorician*" (III.383), simultaneously holding Charles responsible for the work and questioning its authenticity. The matter of authorship was not resolved in Milton's day. It appears now that John Gauden, then Dean of Bocking in Essex and subsequently a bishop, worked from writings of Charles in fashioning the book and smuggled a draft to Charles in Carisbrooke Castle for revision and approval.[10] However this curious collaboration worked, Gauden and Charles did a brilliantly effective job of image-making, appropriating the language of martyrdom to ennoble what was at bottom a political conflict between King and Parliament. The famous frontispiece (Figure 1) created by William Marshall sets the tone for the work with its powerful image of the kneeling King, his actual crown cast aside, preparing to put on a crown of thorns and fixing his gaze on the crown of glory that is

1 William Marshall, frontispiece to *Eikon Basilike* (n.p., 1649)

the reward of the martyr.[11] In the background the emblem of a great rock rising from a turbulent sea expresses the fundamental characteristic of martyrs, constancy.[12] Its legend, "Immota Triumphans," points to the victory that the martyr can expect as a result of his patient suffering. The text of *Eikon Basilike* invests Charles with attributes of martyrs familiar from Foxe's martyrology (which he is thought to have read along with the Bible and devotional literature at Carisbrooke Castle),[13] most notably the sustaining faith that makes constancy possible and a corresponding peace of mind in the face of persecution and the threat of death. By endorsing the "Portraiture of His Sacred Majesty in His Solitudes and Sufferings" presented by *Eikon Basilike*, and by claiming on the scaffold that "I am the Martyr of the People," Charles sought to associate himself with the tradition of Protestant martyrs popularized by Foxe.

Unlike Foxe's persecuted reformers, however, Charles was a defender of the religious establishment, an irony that did not escape Milton: "no man could imagin . . . how a Martyrdom can belong to him, who therfore dyes for his Religion because it is *establisht*" (III. 575). Milton would not have acknowledged the further irony that the established church, rendered powerless by the ascendancy of Parliament and the army, was in a position to appropriate language used of the persecuted, "true" church by the early reformers. In the prayer that concludes the section of *Eikon Basilike* on church government, "Charles" identifies episcopacy with the apostolic church of the "*purest and most primitive times,*" and calls for God's mercy on "*Thy afflicted church*" (p. 112). A previous prayer ends with a reworking of the psalmist's plea (Ps. 25:22) to redeem Israel: "*Redeem Thy church, O God, out of all its troubles*" (p. 75). Milton had to destroy the image of a suffering church as well as that of a suffering king: "It was the fury of his own hatred to the professors of true Religion, which first incited him to persecute them with the Sword of Warr, when Whipps, Pillories, Exiles, and impris'nments, were not thought sufficient" (III.444). For Milton the appropriate identification of Charles was with the "Tyrant *Nero*" (III.439), that notorious persecutor of the early Christians. In *The Tenure of Kings and Magistrates* he had cited Christopher Goodman and other Marian exiles to justify resistance to tyranny, implicitly identifying Charles with "the bloudy persecution of Queen *Mary*" (III.251). Yet the most insidious and objectionable form of persecution to Milton was spiritual, the denial of liberty of conscience imposed by the "Antichristian tyranny" of the bishops. The "Church of God" had to appeal to Parliament "to remove [Charles'] force and heavy hands from off our consciences" (III.492). In *Eikonoklastes* Milton continued to sound Reformation themes that he had introduced in the antiprelatical tracts. His problem was the difficulty of reclaiming in the fall of 1649 the role of victim that he had given the "true" church he had championed in those tracts.

Anyone attacking the assertions of *Eikon Basilike* had to reckon with the aura of piety with which that work endows Charles. Florence Sandler has shown that this is a particular Anglican form of piety, nurtured by Donne's *Devotions* and Herbert's *The Temple* and also by James I's meditation on the scene in the narrative of the crucifixion in which the soldiers mock Christ.[14] *Eikon Basilike* skillfully reinforces the association with Christ established by the frontispiece and strengthened by numerous references in the text, especially to Christ's suffering ("they have mixed the gall and vinegar of falsity and contempt with the cup of my affliction" [p. 63], "I will rather choose to wear a crown of thorns" [p. 28]) and to Christ's charity ("forgive them, O my father, for they know not what they do" [p. 46]). This posture is closer to that of Archbishop Laud on the scaffold than to that of, say, Foxe's Latimer. Laud professed his forgiveness of his enemies and embraced the example of Christ: "I shall most willingly *drink of this cup* as deep as he pleases, and enter this Sea [of blood], yea and pass through it, *in the way that he shall lead me*."[15]

After his early, abortive poem on the Passion Milton avoided efforts to represent the pathos of Christ's suffering in his poetry, as Sandler and others have noted.[16] He would have seen the theatrical *imitatio Christi* of *Eikon Basilike* as a particularly egregious example of one of the excesses to which martyrologies were prone. In commenting upon Charles' vehemence against his accusers in his meditations upon death, Milton charges him with imitating not Christ "but his Grand-mother *Mary* Queen of Scots, as also in the most of his other scruples, exceptions and evasions" (III. 597). Where others saw Charles as assuming the dignity and constancy of a martyr, Milton could see only the influence of Charles' shifty, Catholic grandmother in the "most Martyr-like" of his words. To him the words and the gestures were calculated, all "Stage-work" (III. 530).[17]

Milton could not credit Charles' supposed piety because he was convinced of the falseness of the positions it was meant to validate. Charles exhibited not true piety but "Pietie grounded upon error" (III. 508). By the elaborate self-presentation of *Eikon Basilike*, he bore witness to himself rather than to the truth; unlike the genuine martyr, he sought to gain sympathy for a bad cause and a corrupted version of the true, apostolic church by presenting a false image of himself as helpless victim. Milton saw only outrageous hypocrisy in the claim that the "*chiefest Armes left him were those onely which the ancient Christians were wont to use against thir Persecuters, Prayers and Teares,*" observing with characteristic sarcasm that the Parliamentary armies faced real weapons purchased from the Dutch with the crown jewels: "Were Praiers and Teares at so high a rate in *Holland* that nothing could purchase them but the Crown Jewels?" (III.452). He is similarly scornful of Charles' pervasive appropriation of the language of the Psalms in order to portray himself as emulating David in repenting his sins, learning from his afflictions, and trusting in the mercy and protection of God. Charles' fate, in Milton's view, should be taken as "a warning to all Kings hereafter how they use presumptuously the words and protestations of *David*, without the spirit and conscience of *David*" (III.381–2). Such misuse of biblical language, in the effort to ally himself with David as with Christ, was blasphemous and a sign of the intrinsic falseness of Charles' position. Milton substituted his own biblical analogies, to such figures as Ahab and Herod, tyrants and persecutors rather than those who embodied the purifying or sacrificial character of suffering. He was willing to grant that Charles suffered, but he took the stern view that he suffered for his "own demerits" and by "his own doings" (III.418, 435). His real objection, of course, was to the manipulation of the image of the suffering King to sanction beliefs he found contemptible.

While most of Milton's energy went to the task of destroying the image of Charles as martyr and exposing what he labeled "the privat and overween-ing Reason of one obstinat Man" (III.416), *Eikonoklastes* offers glimpses of what Milton regarded as true martyrdom. These show an admiration for combativeness in the service of truth consistent with what one finds in the antiprelatical tracts. Milton justifies his attack on the King by appealing to biblical precedent: "nothing hinders us to speak evil, as oft as it is the truth, of those who in thir Dignities doe evil; thus did our Saviour himself, *John* the Baptist, and *Steev'n* the Martyr" (III.502). Milton focuses here on the Christ who accuses the scribes and Pharisees of hypocrisy and the Stephen who denounces his persecutors as "stiffnecked" (Acts 7:51) for resisting the Holy Ghost. This is the Christ Milton shows in the divorce tracts rebuking the Pharisees with "high and vehement speeches" (III.668).[18] He invokes Christ and Stephen as true martyrs in *Eikonoklastes* to offer an antithesis to the Charles of *Eikon Basilike*, self-portrayed as suffering victim, and to justify his own vehemence. Elsewhere he portrays as martyrs those who die defending Parliament against Charles' challenge to its authority to change the law against his will, "which tyrannous assertion forc'd upon us by the Sword, he who fights against, and dyes fighting, if his other sins overweigh not, dyes a *Martyr* undoubtedly both of the Faith and of the Common-wealth" (III.530). Here martyrdom takes on political dimensions more clearly than it had before for Milton. He is willing to grant those killed fighting for the parliamentary cause the honor of a double martyrdom. The constant is Milton's praise of readiness to defend the truth, to the point of dying for it.

III

Milton was to find his best contemporary examples of martyrdom in the Waldensians, in the event he commemorated in his powerful sonnet. The Waldensians figure in *Eikonoklastes* as exemplars of a faith not tainted by episcopacy and the other corruptions introduced into the church. Milton cites a source which claims "that those Churches in *Piemont* have held the same Doctrin and Goverment, since the time that *Constantine* with his mischeivous donations poyson'd *Silvester* and the whole Church. Others affirme they have so continu'd there since the Apostles" (III.514). Milton saw the Waldensians as "our first reformers," embodying the true church which held to the faith and practice of the Apostles. They provided an example he could cite to justify opposing tithes and taking up arms to resist tyranny.[19] He felt the violation of their "antient Fold" more acutely because they had demonstrated their constancy over many centuries ("Ev'n them who kept thy truth so pure of old / When all our Fathers worship't Stocks and Stones").

For Milton and European Protestants the "Piemontese Easter" presented a classic instance of the persecution of the true church. According to accounts circulated in England the troops of the Duke of Savoy had driven the Waldensians "out of their antient patrimonies and places of abode, in the midst of a sharp and terrible winter," and brutally murdered those they could track down in the mountains, with "no difference made of men, women, children, or sucking babes, dashing them against stones, some laying hold on them by the legges, and either dismembring them, or hurling them headlong into precipices" (Figure 2).[20] Milton captured the spirit of such accounts of the atrocities with his lurid image of the "bloody *Piemontese*" rolling "Mother with Infant down the Rocks." He could associate the murdered Waldensians with the martyrs under the throne of Revelation 6, evoked by the biblical echo of his opening line ("Avenge, O Lord, thy slaughter'd Saints"), because they embodied true faith and were "slain for the word of God" (Rev. 6:9). They were authentic martyrs because, unlike Charles, they died for their vision of the truth of the Word, unmistakably victims of religious persecution. Milton chose to focus on the helplessness of the Waldensians, portray-

2 Artist unknown, engraving from Samuel Morland, *The History of the Evangelical Churches of the Piemont* (London, 1658), p. 344

ing them as sheep slain in God's fold, when in fact some put up vigorous and initially successful resistance. He could evoke the pathos of their fate, where he had denounced efforts to evoke pathos in *Eikon Basilike*, because he thought them the true successors of the Apostles and also because he saw their suffering as that of a holy community. This was not a matter of celebrating an individual martyr, with the attendant risks of calling too much attention to the person or the circumstances. Nor was there any question of creating a shrine. The natural analogies in this case were with the Israelites, scattered by the enemies of God, rather than with the suffering Christ.[21] Milton would go on to celebrate the solitary defender of truth in *Paradise Lost* (the "one just Man") but along with an emphasis, in Michael's prophecy, upon the holy community of persecuted Christians who would persevere in the worship "of Spirit and Truth" (XII.533).

If Milton presented the Waldensians as helpless victims of Catholic violence, he also invested them with remarkable potency by insisting that their example would spawn an expanded community of the faithful, grown "A hunder'd-fold" and spread "O'er all th'*Italian* fields," committed to the continuing struggle for reformation. His allusion to the Cadmus myth, with its account of armed men sprung from the dragon's teeth sown by Cadmus, suggests the militancy of these spiritual heirs of the martyred Waldensians, but the sonnet looks to ultimate deliverance from papal power rather than to any temporal victory over it. The reference to flying the "Babylonian wo" recalls both the Old Testament prophecies of the deliverance of the Israelites from their Babylonian captivity and the prophecies of Revelation, commonly read by Protestants as promising divine vengeance on the Roman church. The sonnet transcends immediate efforts to condemn the action and secure relief for the dispossessed, placing the Waldensians in a perspective that includes New Testament martyrs, their predecessors among the faithful Israelites, and, in an imagined future, legions of new Italian Protestants.

The experience of the Waldensians is comprehended in Michael's prediction to Adam that the faithful will "amaze / Thir proudest persecuters" (XII.496–7), as is that of the Marian exiles, who "through all stormes and persecutions kept Religion from extinguishing, and deliverd it pure to us" (III.251). The ideal of "suffering for Truths sake" that Adam articulates looks chiefly to the future experience of members of the true church. As witnesses to God's truth among the enemies of truth, Abdiel, Enoch, and Noah illustrate both the vehemence that Milton admired and a constancy that in different circumstances would make martyrs.[22] The faithful Abdiel could serve as an emblem of constancy: "Nor number, nor example with him wrought / To swerve from truth, or change his constant mind / Though single" (V.901–3). Noah, like many of the Protestant martyrs celebrated by Foxe, admonishes the wicked "fearless of reproach, and scorn, / Or violence" (XI.811–12). Enoch and Noah, along with Abraham and Moses, can be found in the company of Old Testament heroes of faith enumerated by

Hebrews, the eleventh chapter of which begins with Abel and ends with nameless sufferers of affliction among the Israelites: "Others had trial of cruel mockings and scourgings, yea, moreover of bonds and imprisonment: They were stoned, they were sawn asunder, were tempted, were slain with the sword . . . they wandered in deserts, and in mountains, and in dens and caves of the earth" (Heb. 11:36–8). The broad definition of martyrdom that Milton gives in *De Doctrina Christiana* – the profession of true religion "when it leads to death or imprisonment or torture or disgrace" (VI.701) – embraces the Israelites who suffered for their faith (one of his proof texts is taken from the passage from Hebrews quoted above) as well as those persecuted for religious beliefs under Charles. The Waldensians were inheritors of the heroic tradition described in Hebrews and illuminated by numerous New Testament passages linking faith and suffering in the experience of early Christians; one observer described them, echoing Hebrews, as "poor banished men, who like the faithful of old, are wandering in the wilderness, in the Dens, in the Mountains and in the clefts of the earth."[23]

IV

In his sonnet on the Waldensians, Milton focused on the suffering of the righteous and their ultimate triumph in the imagined vengeance of God upon their enemies. Michael's prophecies to Adam predict the constancy under persecution of individual heroes of faith, and the triumph of all the faithful at the time of judgment, but with a darker sense of the future of the true church in this world: "Truth shall retire / Bestuck with slandrous darts, and works of Faith / Rarely be found" (XII.535–7). For the most fully-developed example of "suffering for Truths sake" in the later poetry one must look to Milton's portrayal of the Son in *Paradise Regained*. What Barbara Lewalski has called the "Jobean heroic pattern" of patient suffering[24] provides an important model for the Son's experience, but this experience also reflects Milton's mature understanding of the tradition of martyrdom: in the Son's blunt speaking of truth, in his constancy and his embrace of suffering, and in his demonstration of what Milton had called in *Of Reformation* "the unresistable *might* of *Weaknesse*" (I.524) to overcome satanic rage. In his bluntness and in his occasional denunciations of Satan, the Son recalls the vehemence with which Milton tended to associate martyrs in the prose. He appeals to the Word of God and turns aside subtle arguments in a fashion that recalls the more articulate of Foxe's martyrs in their dialectic with Catholic examiners, who embody for Foxe the deceit, the malice, and ultimately the rage of Satan. Yet the Son's grasp of the importance of suffering, and the constancy he illustrates by his calm endurance, reflects the fuller and more orthodox understanding of the significance of "Suffering for Truths sake" that one finds in the later poetry. The experience of the Son in *Paradise Regained* provides a clearer model than anything we actually see in *Paradise Lost* for those faithful who will persevere in the worship "of Spirit and Truth" (XII.533) under persecution.

In the desert the Son lays down the "rudiments" (the first principles as well as the beginnings) of the warfare in which he will conquer Sin and Death "By Humiliation and strong Sufferance" (I.160). While Satan is more tempter than persecutor in *Paradise Regained*, the dialectic of the temptations leads the Son to embrace his role as sufferer for truth:

> What if he hath decreed that I shall first
> Be try'd in humble state, and things adverse,
> By tribulations, injuries, insults,
> Contempts, and scorns, and snares, and violence,
> Suffering, abstaining, quietly expecting
> Without distrust or doubt, that he may know
> What I can suffer, how obey? who best
> Can suffer, best can do.
>
> (III.188–95)

Satan turns persecutor in the end, when he unleashes the violence of the storm in the hope of gaining by force what he could not by subtlety. The fact that the Son is "Unshaken," that he sits "unappall'd in calm and sinless peace" (IV.425) through the fury of the night, beautifully illustrates the constancy in the face of physical and psychological assault that explains how martyrs can endure suffering and triumph through it.

One of Milton's most telling epithets for the Son is "unmov'd" (III.386; IV.109). After the storm Satan confesses that he has found him "Proof against all temptation as a rock / Of Adamant" (IV.533–4). In a related simile Milton pictures Satan's assaults as "surging waves against a solid rock," which "Though all to shivers dash't, the assault renew, / Vain battry, and in froth or bubbles end" (IV.18–20). The image recalls the emblem from the frontispiece of *Eikon Basilike*, the rock battered by waves with its legend "Immota Triumphans." It can be seen as a further answer to the claims of martyrdom for a Christlike Charles, self-portrayed in the text of the work as constant to his faith and his principles in the face of popular tumults that are like "the raging of the sea" (p. 18). In the experience of the Son in *Paradise Regained* Milton set forth the "rudiments" of true martyrdom, showing in the pattern of humiliation and exaltation which takes shape in that work and points to the future experience of Christ what it is to be unmoved, and how it is that the Christian can expect to triumph through the power of God.

The power through which the Son triumphs in *Paradise Regained* resembles the "inward power" described in *Of Civil Power* rather than the divine power that erupts so violently in *Of Reformation in England*, in such images as that of the Protestant martyrs "shaking the *Power* of *Darknesse*, and scorning the *fiery rage* of the old *red Dragon*" (I.525). The apocalypticism of the antiprelatical tracts, with their vision of a host of martyrs in the vanguard of Reformation, has yielded to a quieter sense of divine power manifesting itself through the Holy Spirit working upon the conscience of the individual Christian, with acts of faith flowing from the "inward man." In *Of Civil Power* the role of persecutor has been taken over by Protestants determined to enforce church discipline ("How many persecutions then, imprisonments, penalties and stripes; how much bloodshed have the forcers of conscience to answer for, and protestants rather than papists!" [VII.253]), that of martyr by those who stand upon conscience rather than yield to force in matters of worship. If these are less obviously candidates for martyrdom than those the faithful Michael imagines resisting Satan's cruelties "to the death" (XII.494), they nonetheless belong to the company of those who must prove their faith by demonstrating their constancy to a vision of truth in the face of persecution. From the time of the antiprelatical tracts at least, Milton seems to have needed to see the defender of God's truth as embattled, "beset round with raging enemies" in the words of Calvin on Stephen. The difference in the later work, especially in the poetry, is that he identifies the faithful more clearly with the tradition of "suffering for Truths sake." The emphasis upon combativeness remains, but this is balanced by fuller attention to the reality and meaning of suffering. With the defeat of his hopes for reformation in England, Milton had to revise his sense of what kind of victory the faithful could expect, not the victory of the true church that he had seen the "victorious agonies" of the martyrs as heralding in the early 1640s but the victory of the individual Christian over death. He had learned that the true church was indeed a suffering church. We no longer hear of the "renovating and re-ingendring Spirit of God' transforming society, rather of the Spirit illuminating the solitary believer and fortifying him with "inward consolations." This believer is still prepared to defy the enemies of God but also, like the Son in *Paradise Regained*, to suffer the trials sent by God "Without distrust or doubt."

Notes

1 Milton may have been influenced by an analogous distinction made by Foxe in the prefatory piece on "The Utility of this Story" that first appeared in the 1563 edition of the *Acts and Monuments*. Foxe justifies his efforts by arguing that it is more fitting to preserve the lives and acts of martyrs than the wars that preoccupy the chroniclers. Martyrs, he insists, declare the "true Christian fortitude" of fighting under Christ (I.xxv). All quotations from Foxe are taken from *The Acts and Monuments of John Foxe*, ed. Josiah Pratt, 8 vols (London, 1877). Eusebius had offered a similar justification for his *Ecclesiastical History*, complaining that writers of historical works had concentrated on wars and the exploits of generals and soldiers and declaring his intent to record the struggles of "athletes of piety" who were "valiant for truth rather than for country." *Ecclesiastical History*, trans. Kirsopp Lake (London, 1926 and Cambridge, Mass., 1980), vol. I, p. 407.

2 On the influence of Foxe see William Haller, *Foxe's Book of Martyrs and the Elect*

Nation (London, 1963), chapter 7; William Lamont, *Marginal Prynne, 1600–1669* (London, 1963) and *Godly Rule: Politics and Religion, 1603–1660* (London, 1969), *passim*; Katharine R. Firth, *The Apocalyptic Tradition in Reformation Britain, 1530–1645* (Oxford, 1979), chapter 7; Paul Christianson, *Reformers and Babylon: Apocalyptic Visions from the Reformation to the Eve of the Civil War* (Toronto, 1978), pp. 172ff. See the essay by Janel Mueller in this volume for further discussion of the relationship between Milton and Foxe.

3 For an extended discussion of the "praesentia" and "potentia" associated with the saints in late antiquity see Peter Brown, *The Cult of the Saints* (Chicago, 1981), chapters 5 and 6.

4 Hall makes much of Ignatius and Polycarp, especially Ignatius, "so holy a bishop, so faithful a martyr, so true a saint"; see *Episcopacy by Divine Right Asserted*, in *Works*, ed. Philip Wynter (Oxford, 1963), pp. 216ff, 226, 280–1.

5 A comment in the *History of Britain* on St. Alban, martyred during the persecution of Diocletian, illustrates Milton's attitude toward the excesses of martyrology: "The story of whose martyrdom soil'd, and worse martyr'd with the fabling zeal of some idle fancies, more fond of Miracles, than apprehensive of Truth, deserves not longer digression" (V.111).

6 Foxe writes, in summary, of having recounted "the horrible troubles of persecution, the wonderful assistance of the Almighty in maintaining his truth, the glorious constancy of Christ's martyrs, the rage of the enemies." *Acts and Monuments*, vol. VIII, p. 754.

7 *Commentary upon The Acts of the Apostles*, trans. Henry Beveridge (Edinburgh, 1844), vol. I, pp. 311–12.

8 *Acts and Monuments*, vol. VIII, p. 141.

9 Philip A. Knachel, ed., *Eikon Basilike* (Ithaca, N.Y., 1966), pp. xivff.

10 This persuasive explanation of the conflicting testimony of contemporary witnesses was offered by Francis Madan, "A New Bibliography of the *Eikon Basilike*," *Oxford Bibliographical Society*, n.s., 3 (1950), pp. 126–63.

11 See Ernest B. Gilman, *Iconoclasm and Poetry in the English Reformation* (Chicago, 1986), pp. 154–8, for a discussion of the frontispiece and of Milton's attack on idolatry in *Eikonoklastes*.

12 Gilman (pp. 155, 216n.) notes that this is a version of an emblem used previously by George Wither and Henry Peacham. See Wither's *Emblemes* (London, 1635, p. 218), and Peacham's *Minerva Britanna* (London, 1612), p. 158. For Peacham the rock amid the waves signified "MANLIE CONSTANCIE of mind"; for Wither, "*True* Vertue" that "*whatsoere betides, / In all* extreames, *unmoov'd abides.*" Marshall may also have been influenced by another emblem of Wither's showing a halcyon's nest atop a rock buffeted by waves; Wither's verse commentary points to the ability of the church to withstand "the raging *Wave, / Of* dreadfull *Seas*" (p. 236). Those responsible for the frontispiece would have appreciated the irony of Marshall's transformation of the Puritan Wither's emblems.

13 According to Charles Carlton, *Charles I* (London, 1983), p. 347.

14 Florence Sandler, "Icon and Iconoclast," in *Left Hand*, pp. 160–84. See the essay by Lana Cable in this volume for further discussion of the parallels between Charles and Christ and also of the theatricality of *Eikon Basilike*.

15 *England's Black Tribunal*, 4th edn (London, 1703), p. 65. Charles resembled Christ, and often Josiah, for many of the preachers who commemorated the

martyrdom. Bishop Henry Lisle, in *The Martyrdome of King Charles* (The Hague, 1649), offered more than thirty parallels between Christ's suffering and that of Charles. For a discussion of commemorative sermons see Helen W. Randall, "The Rise and Fall of a Martyrology: Sermons on Charles I," *Huntington Library Quarterly*, 10 (1947), pp. 135–67.

16 Sandler, "Icon and Iconoclast," pp. 172, 183–4.

17 See David Loewenstein's book, *Milton and the Drama of History: Historical Vision, Iconoclasm, and the Literary Imagination* (Cambridge, 1990), chapter 3, for the best treatment of Milton's attack on theatricality in *Eikonoklastes* and for extensive discussion of Milton's iconoclasm. Loewenstein considers the way Milton remakes the image of Charles fashioned by *Eikon Basilike*, for example by associating him with a succession of biblical and secular tyrants.

18 Milton repeatedly characterizes Christ's speech as "vehement" in the divorce tracts (see III.282, 301, 644, 664) and stresses the severity of his responses to the Pharisees: "Christ administers here a sharp and corrosive sentence" (III.668). David Loewenstein, in chapter 9 below, comments on the aggressive stance of the Christ of the *First Defense*.

19 See *Hirelings* (VII.291, 302, 306, 308), on the opposition to tithes, and *The Tenure of Kings and Magistrates* (III.227) and *The Second Defense of the People of England* (IV.658) on resistance to tyranny.

20 J. B. Stouppe, *A Collection . . . Concerning the Bloody and Barbarous Massacres* (London, 1655), pp. 4, 24.

21 See my discussion of Milton's use of biblical allusions in the poem to reinforce the association of the Waldensians with the Israelites, "The Biblical Matrix of Milton's 'On the Late Massacre in Piemont,'" *Philological Quarterly*, 62 (1983), pp. 259–63.

22 See John M. Steadman's discussion of Abdiel, Enoch, and Noah, *Milton and the Renaissance Hero* (Oxford, 1967), pp. 66ff.

23 Stouppe, p. 43.

24 *Milton's Brief Epic* (Providence and London, 1966), p. 108. My argument is closer to that of John M. Steadman in "The 'Suffering Servant' and Milton's Heroic Norm," *Harvard Theological Review*, 54 (1961), pp. 29–43, and in *Milton and the Renaissance Hero*, chapter 2.

9

Milton and the poetics of defense

DAVID LOEWENSTEIN

As defender of the state, Milton exploited his creative powers in formidable ways. His controversial works written on behalf of the Commonwealth and the Protectorate of Cromwell reveal a writer self-conscious about his polemical discourse operating as a dynamic force in the sociopolitical process. The aggressive and violent rhetoric of the antiprelatical tracts, along with his vitalistic notion of the text in *Areopagitica*, had already demonstrated Milton's commitment to the power of his word and the Word to effect revolution in the church and state. Now as the official polemicist of the Commonwealth and the Cromwellian Protectorate, he finds his literary powers put to a new test: the process of defending and shaping the revolutionary ideals of the state becomes an enterprise of heroic and often mythopoetic scope. Even while Milton is undertaking this official task, especially in *Eikonoklastes* and his *Defenses*, he invests his polemical writing with an aesthetic dimension, which suggests how thoroughly his literary creativity informs his controversial prose works, with their emphasis upon active engagement in the political process.[1] Far from reflecting a period of "poetic inactivity," interruption, or delay, as one recent commentator has claimed,[2] the *Defenses* – especially the *Pro Populo Anglicano Defensio Secunda* (30 May 1654) – reveal precisely how deeply interconnected were Milton's aesthetics, his ideological commitments, and his achievements in prose. Written in response to Peter Du Moulin's anonymously published *Regii Sanguinis Clamor ad Coelum, Adversus Parricidas Anglicanus* (The Hague, 1652),[3] the *Second Defense* concerns Milton's capacity to engage creatively and decisively in the new social order – to help shape the state and its revolutionary program, as well as to respond to its political realities, through the poetics of his polemical discourse.

The achievements of Milton's *Second Defense* suggest that we should be wary of isolating his revolutionary polemics from his major poetry and of drawing a firm line between what we traditionally call Milton's literary writings and his "non-literary" discourses. His years as a controversial prose writer constitute a period of astonishing creativity – though it may be difficult to appreciate this adequately, so long as commentators continue to suggest that the prose works lack the imaginative dimensions of his poems.

Too often commentators have tended to regard great literary works as autonomous and non-occasional texts unsullied by the vicious and nasty activity of a polemical crisis; and yet this critical assumption has encouraged us to underestimate the aesthetic achievements of his political discourses, especially in relation to the achievements of his major poems.[4] Milton's state polemics, we need to recognize, were more than simply occasional works: they were also creative occasions – opportunities for Milton to employ his imaginative powers for political ends and to contribute to the social forces of his age.

The *Second Defense* is an especially rich text for this line of argument, since it brings to a culmination Milton's impressive skills as a controversial writer: its extraordinary integration of invective, panegyric, autobiographical writing, and mythopoetic vision underscores the convergence of the aesthetic and the political in Milton's revolutionary prose.[5] No other controversial pamphlet by Milton exploits such a variety of discursive modes and polemical postures to assert the power of the writer to operate creatively and forcefully in the social process. Indeed, more than any other work he wrote, the *Second Defense* turned out to be that poetic discourse "doctrinal and exemplary to a Nation" in which Milton presumes "to sing high praises of heroick men" (1.815, 890). Yet its remarkable virulency is no less a manifestation of his artistry in polemic – the poetic rhetor's capacity to engage aggressively in the sociopolitical process by singing discordant notes. Milton's trope of the polemicist as skillful musician in *An Apology for Smectymnuus* confirms that he understood the extreme modulations in his revolutionary discourse precisely in terms of his unusual powers of performance. When, having entertained "with some more pleasing fit," Milton suddenly shifts from the "smoother string" of his panegyric to Parliament back to the "harsh discord" and "jarring notes" of invective, he resembles "some Musicians [who] are wont skilfully to fall out of one key into another without breach of harmony" (1.922, 928). The term "fit," which refers to a "section of a poem or song" (*OED*, 1), reinforces the poetic and artistic nature of Milton's polemical discourse – whether in panegyric or invective. In no other prose work of his controversial career does Milton modulate keys quite so skillfully and dramatically as he does in the *Second Defense*.

Furthermore, as we shall see, if Milton is particularly conscious of the aesthetic and performative dimensions of his defensive discourse, he is no less conscious of the precarious social realities confronting the new Cromwellian regime. He exploits the power of his mythmaking and aggressive polemic to shape the ideological pressures of his revolutionary age, while boldly confronting the social contradictions and uncertainties generated by these pressures. Literary form and political discourse remain deeply interconnected in Milton's defense: not only did he channel his creative energies directly into his pamphleteering for the state, but this enterprise sharpened rather than thwarted his sense of social reality.[6]

I

What exactly did it mean, then, for Milton to write a polemical defense of the state, and what were the aesthetic and social implications of such a discourse? After all, he made no systematic definition of the concept of "defense," just as he made no systematic definition of his own poetics. Yet his defensive discourse had significant creative and artistic implications, as well as social ones. For Milton, the defense was an idiosyncratic and individualistic mode of discourse – a polemical form which was simultaneously rhetorical and sociopolitical, while also expressing deeply felt personal and poetic ideals. As a form of discourse, it not only guards and protects revolutionary ideals and power from polemical attack (suggested by the fact that Milton uses the term in the titles of his three Latin pamphlets); it also functions as a highly aggressive discourse, an essential means for the polemicist to assert his own power and authority in the social and ideological conflicts in which he finds himself heatedly engaged.

Milton's use of the term elsewhere in his writings helps to highlight some of its more distinctive implications for his state polemics. In *Comus* Milton had used defense to mean "guarding or protecting from attack; resistance against attack; warding off of injury; protection" (*OED*, III): thus the Attendant Spirit is dispatched for the "defense and guard" of the youths (line 42). The militant implications of this definition, however, would be developed more aggressively in the *Defenses*, as we shall see, and of course more extensively in *Paradise Lost* (see V.731, VI.337, 467). Later in the masque, when the Elder Brother is willing to put aside his charming neoplatonic philosophy for more heroic measures in defense of his sister's chastity, the concept acquires a somewhat different emphasis: "Defense is a good cause, and Heav'n be for us" (line 489) he remarks after his younger brother advises that they draw swords and stand guard.[7] Here the notion of defense assumes a specifically chivalric meaning, associated with the poetic ideals Milton expressed later in *An Apology*, where he notes his youthful reading in fables and romance about "the oath of every Knight": "From whence even then I learnt what a noble vertue chastity sure must be, to the defence of which so many worthies by such a deare adventure of themselves had sworne" (I.891). Milton had clearly outgrown this sort of youthful idealism by the time of writing the *Defenses*. Nevertheless, the chivalric notion of defense lingers in these polemics, such as when Milton writes proudly of his swordsmanship in the *Second Defense* – a gentlemanly stance which suggests how he sees himself defending the state – or when he includes on the title page of his *First Defense* the republican design of the shield with the cross, the coat of arms emblematic of St. George and Milton's own role as Commonwealth polemicist.[8] Indeed, Milton had already assumed a chivalric posture in his regicide polemic, when he claimed to make "no scruple" in taking up "[the] Gauntlet, though a Kings, in the behalf of Libertie, and the Common-wealth" (III.338).

As a mode of discourse, Milton's defense suggests the idea of defending by argument, as well as the idea of self-vindication (see *OED*, VI, 6b); in particular, it evokes a posture of righteousness on the part of the revolutionary polemicist. This is the same stance of fierce rectitude which enables the poet, who has himself helped to guide the ship of state, to "bear up and steer / Right onward," having lost his sight "In liberty's defense." In the "Preface" to *Eikonoklastes* Milton comments on those who "stand upright and stedfast in [God's] cause; dignify'd with the defence of truth and public libertie." Those who do the work of defense possess "a speciall mark of his favor" (III.348), a theme that recurs centrally in the *Second Defense*. Moreover, the appearance of this passage in *Eikonoklastes* reminds us that the righteous defense of truth may involve the astonishing vehemence and creativity of Milton's radical iconoclasm – his fierce "casting down of imaginations" (2 Cor. 10:4–5), an activity Milton continues in the violent polemics of his *Defenses*. After all, in 1649, negotiating and resisting "the world's vain mask" in the cause of liberty's defense would have meant nothing less than virulently dismantling the elaborate "Stage-work" (III.530) of *Eikon Basilike*.[9]

The defense was a highly active and often aggressive form of polemical engagement bound up with the sense of struggle and confrontation central to Milton's epistemological and aesthetic vision. The notion of defense as an active and energetic engagement in the social process is there already in *The Reason of Church-Government*: "the Church hath now overcom her late distresses after the unwearied labours of many her true servants that stood up in her defence" (I.805). And it is certainly there two years later in *Areopagitica*, when Milton – in a passage that conveys a sense of dynamic creativity – urges his audience to behold the wondrous "City of refuge," a metaphor for the nation as a whole: "the shop of warre hath not there more anvils and hammers waking, to fashion out the plates and instruments of armed Justice in defence of beleaguer'd Truth, then there be pens and heads there, sitting by their studious lamps, musing, searching, revolving new notions and idea's wherewith to present, as with their homage and their fealty the approaching Reformation" (II.553–4). Here the notion of defense refers not only to a process of energetic social activity; it refers especially to the active production of writing which generates and promotes ideological debate and social change in a revolutionary age. The idea of defense as a strenuous response engaging a writer's creative energies would prove equally essential to Milton's enterprise in the *Second Defense*, where he himself operates as an active, poetic ideologist "searching" and "revolving new notions" for the Protectorate, attempting, as we shall see, to engage and transform its political ideals and discourse. Commenting on sixteenth-century writers of literary defenses, Margaret Ferguson has recently observed that "their textual trials all manifest the wish to escape from the scene of trial itself, whether it is figured as a court, a battlefield, a prison, or a 'brazen world.'"[10] But for Milton the contrary seems true: he plunges himself into the scene of trial – we shall see that the experience of trial figured as a battlefield emerges prominently in the *Second Defense* – so that his defensive discourse becomes simultaneously an intensely energetic and mythopoetic means of responding to the personal and polemical controversies of his age.

II

The artistic dimension of Milton's defense is apparent from the striking way he conceives of his polemic as performance. Milton had achieved great fame as a polemicist in 1649–52, and the international reception of his *First Defense* – his text was burned in numerous European cities, yet also praised from Sweden to Greece – only increased Milton's self-consciousness as controversial writer, fuelling his sense of the power of his defensive discourse. In the exordium to the *Second Defense*, Milton finds that he "can scarcely restrain [himself] from loftier and bolder flights than are permissable" as he addresses "the entire assembly and council of all the most influential men, cities, and nations everywhere." Milton's posture here is not only oratorical: it recalls his ambition, passionately expressed in his early polemics, to sing "at high *strains* in new and lofty *Measures*" (*Of Reformation*, 1.616) and, when he imagines Zeale, "to soare a while as the Poets use" (*An Apology*, 1.900). Moreover, the trope of literary competition and over-reaching – of overshooting his ancient predecessors – is as apparent in this passage as it is in the opening invocation to *Paradise Lost*. The polemicist assumes a paradoxical stance: he expresses humility in relation to his predecessors (he cannot hope to match their eloquence and style) and yet he will take no "middle flight" in writing his adventurous discourse, as he searches for "a more exalted manner of expression" and outstrips "all the orators of every age in the grandeur of [his] subject and [his] theme" (IV.i.554; VIII.12). Much like Adam from the hill of history in *Paradise Lost* or Christ from the "Mountain high" in *Paradise Regained* (III.252), Milton seems "to be surveying from on high farflung regions and territories across the sea," as his eye takes in the powers of Europe captivated by his discourse – the manly Germans, the passionate Franks, the courageous Spanish, the magnanimous Italians. Fully intoxicated with his own rhetorical powers as state apologist and revolutionary liberator, Milton engages in a highly self-dramatic moment. He now imagines himself encompassed by an audience of multitudes – many greeting him with applause ("plausu") – as he himself brings back to Europe an exiled liberty:[11] "I seem to be leading home again everywhere in the world, after a vast space of time, Liberty herself, so long expelled and exiled" (IV.i.555; VIII.14).

Such is the power of his discourse, Milton believes, to command, like some extraordinary dramatic performance, the attention of all Europe. In *De Oratore*, Cicero had stressed the unique power of rhetorical discourse to move men to public action: "what other power [vis] could have been strong enough either to gather scattered humanity into one place, or to lead out of its brutish existence in the wilderness up to our present condition of civilization as men and citizens . . . [and] to give shape to laws, tribunals, and civic rights?"[12] Milton, however, has given the restorative power of his rhetorical discourse a distinctly mythic inflection, so that he even outstrips Triptolemus and the goddess Ceres in their fruitful powers as he disseminates "the renewed cultivation of freedom and civic life" throughout Europe (IV.i.556; VIII.14). The sense of excitement Milton expresses as he enters the polemical forum is unmistakable: writing his defense is an imaginative act, an occasion to interject his artistic powers into public controversy and to alter the ideological pressures of his revolutionary age. Milton's work fuses the imaginary and the polemic, literary art and social discourse; it becomes as difficult to separate these elements as it is for Psyche to separate out her various seeds.

Classical authorities like Cicero and Quintilian had acknowledged that the poet is a very near kinsman of the orator: thus in *De Oratore* Crassus observes that, like the orator, the poet "sets no boundaries or limits to his claims, such as would prevent him from ranging whither he will with the same freedom and license as the other" (I.xvi.70). Quintilian qualified the comparison, however, noting that "the orator must not follow the poets in everything, more especially in their freedom of language and their license in the use of figures [nec libertate verborum nec licentia figurarum]."[13] Yet even while Milton recognizes that orators may not enjoy the same license as poets (IV.i.656; VIII.192), his *Second Defense* does not conform to Quintilian's restriction: Marvell, after all, was struck by the dazzling way Milton's rhetorical and literary discourse employs tropes – by the way that, like Trajan's column, a monumental artifact, it "turns and rises with so many figures" as it operates on "the most compendious Scale . . . to the Height of the Roman Eloquence."[14] Through his figurative discourse Milton attempts not only to match the rhetorical power of his ancient predecessors, but to outstrip and soar – poetically – beyond theirs as well.

Indeed, Milton's polemical opponents were also aware of his state discourse as highly imaginative and rhetorical writing, though they were eager to deflate its dramatic power. In his address to the reader in the preface to the Hague edition of Milton's *Second Defense*, George Crantz accused Milton of being "a fabulist and a mere poet" ("Fabulator est et merus Poeta"), and in *Fides Publica*, Alexander More, the putative author of the *Clamor*, attacked Milton's exhilarating polemical performance as an illusory theatrical occasion embellished by his poetic imagination: "you imagine that you have painted [pinxisti] those things for eternity which you have only painted for a while, and, as you are drawn by four white horses, imagine that all nations everywhere are transfixed with admiration [admiratione] for you, that all the centuries applaud you. This is a vain delusion [vana delusus imagine], but a very agreeable ... deception."[15] The flamboyant rhetorical display of Milton's polemical writing elicited a mixed but passionate reaction from Peter Du Moulin, the real author of the *Clamor*, who simultaneously admired and condemned Milton's verbal powers: "wicked Books which say with a witty malice all that can be said for a bad cause, with a fluent and florid style are esteemed even by them that condemn them. . . . I had for my part such a jealousie to see that Traytour praised for his Language that I writ against him *Clamor Regii Sanguinis ad Coelum*."[16]

As such responses suggest, Milton's defensive discourse was a creative form of writing which skillfully exploited rhetoric, theatrics, and poetic vision. His was a politically engaged art in which he saw himself shaping social processes: a discourse which he believed had the power to effect "so great a reversal of opinion" (IV.i.557; VIII.16) as that of Queen Christina towards one of the most erudite and influential royal defenders in Europe – Claude de Saumaise. The *Second Defense* expresses Milton's assurance about his artistic and rhetorical powers in Latin polemic – his sense of his text as an aesthetic discourse capable of actively remaking the cultural and political forces of his age. Milton's state defense conflates poetic and rhetorical discourse: his *First Defense* opens with a passage resembling an epic invocation (he explicitly uses the verb "invocare") as he turns "to aid from on high" and calls upon "almighty God, giver of all gifts" to sustain his "elevated and splendid discourse" ("oratio . . . augusta atque magnifica") (IV.i.305; VII.6–8); and it closes with Milton comparing his heroic efforts in his Latin public discourse to those of Cicero (IV.i.536; VII.556). His *Second Defense* concludes by comparing Milton's polemical achievement to that of the epic poet ("poeta is qui Epicus vocatur") (IV.i.685; VIII.252), a remarkable passage we shall consider later.

One repeatedly senses that the *Second Defense* is a text centrally concerned with the role of literary discourse in the new social order – not just another polemical tract written in defense of the state. The other chief defense of the new regime which appeared in 1654, Marchamont Nedham's *True State of the Case of the Commonwealth*, is a highly skillful piece of revolutionary polemic justifying Cromwell's powers and prerogatives as Protector under the newly-established Instrument of the Government (16 December 1653). This particular discourse, however, displays nothing at all of the mythopoetic or figurative expression characteristic of Milton's polemic and self-presentation; nor does Nedham, for that matter, insert poetic texts as authorities to buttress his ideological views. Yet as early as *Of Reformation* – the revolutionary tract where he envisions himself singing "at high *strains* in new and lofty *Measures*" – Milton was citing poets like Dante, Petrarch, Ariosto, and Chaucer as authorities to reinforce his polemical assertions (1.558–60, 579–80, 595); and in *Animadversions*, he had aligned his vision with Spenser's pastoral critique of prelatical power in the May Eclogue (1.722–3). In the *First Defense* he likewise includes poets as authorities, along with orators, historians, tragedians, and philosophers (IV.i.439–46; VII.306–26). And in the *Second Defense* he insists that poets worth anything (he cites Buchanan as an example) have been aggressively hostile towards tyrants (IV.i.592; VIII.78), a view that recalls his reference in the *First Defense* to Alcaeus, "the prince of lyricists" cited by Horace (*Odes*, II.xiii.29–36) for pleasing the people by singing of tyrants banished (IV.i.441; VII.312). Milton's prominent use of poets as authorities in his controversial prose suggests that he not only wished to align his revolutionary discourse with theirs, but that he consciously attempted to use the aesthetic as a means to promote his polemical ideals.

His astonishing outbursts of vitriolic invective in the state polemics should likewise be understood as expressions of his creative engagement and performance in the revolutionary social process. Here Milton pushes to an extreme the traditional advice about those qualities in an ideal rhetor most effective for winning the support of an audience. Cicero's Antonius, for example, notes those moments when the effectiveness of the rhetor's performance depends upon his showing personal indignation and vehemence; yet Antonius also stresses that on many occasions the rhetor should display his upright and virtuous character by exhibiting a mild tone, gentle language, calmness, and a countenance expressing modesty, while avoiding vehemence, contentiousness, and harshness.[17] The impassioned and often violent rhetorical prose of Milton's *Defenses* (not to mention his other polemics), however, rarely conforms to Cicero's mild type of oratory: Milton's vituperative discourse aimed at Salmasius, More, and Vlacq is taunting, abusive, and vehement – its language anything but calm, gentle, or mild. His invective in the *Defenses* and other tracts exploits a rhetoric of extremity and aggression, an "art of powerful reclaiming" which Milton associates with therapeutic vehemence, such as Christ himself employed: "as the Physician cures him who hath tak'n down poyson," Milton observes in *Tetrachordon*, "not by the middling temper of nourishment, but by the other extreme of *antidote*, so Christ administers . . . a sharpe and corrosive sentence against a foul and putrid licence" (II.668). The Christ of the *First Defense* is likewise no meek and submissive figure, but rather an active and unyielding liberator who boldly censures, accuses, reproves, and warns his adversaries (IV.i.375, 377–8; VII.148, 154–6).

Vituperation was certainly the norm in the violent controversies of Milton's age, but Milton transforms it into a literary response which can assume poetic authority and force. It is worth recalling his discussion in *The Reason of Church-Government* regarding "things that are sharply spoken, or vehemently written": he places his remarks about "sharp" words in a prophetic context of divine inspiration (I.803–4), observing that such bitter denouncing was "[not] hid from the wise Poet *Sophocles*" in his portrayal of Tiresias. Milton, of course, places the justification of polemical vehemence only a few pages before the famous description of his poetic art and literary vocation – the autobiographical passage where he emerges as "an interpreter and relater of the best and sagest things among [his] own Citizens" (1.811–12). The most explicit expression of his poetics of vehemence, however, occurs in the Chariot of Zeale passage from the *Apology*, where Milton takes "leave to soare a while as the Poets use" in order to present an apocalyptic vision dramatizing "indignation," "derision and scorne" (1.900). Answering his polemical adversaries in "a vehement *scheme*" (II.664) – like the Christ of Milton's divorce tracts – involves an aggressive response that is simultaneously literary and destructive: Milton gives "scheme," a rhetorical figure of speech, a specifically textual emphasis. In the antiprelatical polemics Milton justifies his use of "a grim laughter" and "a rougher accent," since such vehement writing, he believes, "hath oft-times a strong and sinewy force in teaching and confuting" (*Animadversions*, 1.662–4). It is an active, vigorous, and strenuous discourse – didactic, aggressive, and poetic all at once. In *Pro Se Defensio* Milton again justifies the power and value of invective in his polemical writing: citing numerous precedents from classical, biblical, and Renaissance writers and texts, Milton asserts "that words unchaste and plain thrust out with indignation signify not obscenity, but the vehemence of gravest censure [gravissimae reprehensionis vehementiam]" (IV.ii.744; IX.108). As "the author both of purity and eloquence," he observes in a highly literary passage elsewhere, God Himself can speak in a "vehement character" (*An Apology*, 1.902). Milton thus regards vehemence as absolutely essential to the art of his polemics: through it he asserts his power and expresses his political activism. He would have been puzzled by the tendency of modern commentators either to apologize for or to deplore his extreme vituperation, and to disassociate it from his other literary and creative enterprises.[18]

Consequently, the claim that Milton's radical pamphleteering represents an extensive period of interruption in his creative and poetic development will hardly do at all. Milton, it seems, welcomed the strenuous activity of polemical controversy – even in its most heated, virulent, abusive moments – and appreciated its creative occasions. Indeed, his intensely abusive and combative *First Defense* was, in the words of Toland, nothing less than "his Masterpiece, his chief and favorite Work in prose, for Argument the noblest . . . for stile and disposition the most eloquent and elaborat, equalling the old *Romans* . . . and certain to endure while Oratory, Politics, or History, has any esteem among Men."[19] Furthermore, when Henry Oldenburg suggested that Milton might be wasting his talents composing a work like the *Second Defense*, Milton replied that "idle liesure" ("iners otium") never pleased him and that, despite his wish to pursue more delightful studies, he in no way regretted his engagement in polemics, since he was far from considering them inconsequential activities (IV.ii.866; XII.64). No matter how radical, offensive, or violent his ideological adversaries considered his writing for the state, he had never doubted at all that his revolutionary discourse "was right and true and pleasing to God" (IV.i.587; VIII.66). Unlike the poet of *Lycidas*, the state polemicist shows no reluctance in beginning his occasional enterprise, no anxiety about disclosing his literary powers prematurely. Instead, he appears energetic ("impiger") and active in his controversial engagement, giving it the full power of his mind and industry ("omne ingenium, omnes industriae vires") (IV.i.591, 622; VIII.74, 128). The vigor with which Milton dramatizes himself as a champion in the arena of polemical controversy, and as a mythic figure in the cultural crises of his time, suggests that he considered his engagement not only service in a righteous cause, but also an essential outlet for his imaginative powers. Public involvement and poetic assertion were not at odds in the career and writings of this radical polemicist: in the *Second Defense* we witness the convergence of Milton's creative energies and the social energies of his revolutionary age.

III

Milton's bold assertion of his presence and voice in the *Second Defense* is itself crucial to the artistry of his state polemic. In effect, he uses his powerful, idiosyncratic presence for rhetorical, political, and aesthetic purposes. His presence in the *Second Defense* is surely as distinctive as any in the revolutionary tracts – it underscores the sense of polemical performance throughout the work – and as strikingly individualistic in its way as the narrator's poetic voice in *Paradise Lost*. Milton's commanding presence and mythopoetic vision pervade his discourse, joining its various kinds of polemical postures and reinforcing its controversial arguments. Moreover, his is a hugely active presence, as he goes about vindicating, castigating, criticizing, praising, advising, and warning.

Milton's militant self-portrait underscores the notion of his defense as a highly aggressive mode of discourse. Quintilian had already noted the martial stance of the rhetor (in contrast to that of the poet, however, whose figurative expression is less direct and immediate): he "would have [the orator's weapons] shine with a splendour that shall strike terror to the foe, like the flashing steel that dazzles heart and eye at once" (*Institutio Oratoria*, X.i.30). In the *Defenses* Milton's martial characterization combines aggressive and chivalric qualities. Using the combative trope in the *First Defense*, Milton suggests that his defensive discourse places him among the greatest Protestant iconoclasts; he will confound and crush his opponent once he has "formed [his] battle line of Luthers, Zwinglis, Calvins, Martyrs and Paraeuses" (IV.i.396; VII.202). Especially proud in the *Second Defense* of his former skills with a sword – he practiced with it daily and wore it regularly – Milton thought himself "equal to anyone," and "fearless of any injury that one man could inflict on another" (IV.i.583; VIII.60). This posture of fearlessness is the posture of the controversial polemicist in the *Defenses* who himself bears arms, just like his revolutionary countrymen (IV.i.684; VIII.252); it is the posture of the "little *English David*" who alone, in the words of Edward Phillips, "had the Courage to undertake [the] great *French Goliah.*"[20] This man of learning and eloquence is also a national warrior, whose theater of operations extends beyond England to Europe itself. Milton himself suggests that his barbs may have killed Salmasius and speaks of waging a "posthumous war" ("bella ... posthuma") (IV.i.559; VIII.22); clearly enjoying this sort of self-dramatization, he writes proudly of his audacity in clashing with such an experienced polemical foe (IV.i.602–3; VIII.100) and of the fact that he "bore off the spoils of honor" after meeting his enemy in "single combat" (IV.i.556; VIII.14). As he puts it in *Pro Se Defensio*, there are occasions when it is proper "to venture into the sun, and dust, and field of battle, now to exert real brawn, brandish real arms, seek a real enemy" (IV.ii.795; IX.224): the defensive polemicist presents himself as a militant champion, engaging in a highly active, strenuous mode of confrontation no less hazardous, courageous, and aggressive than that of his warfaring contemporaries. But it is a warfare that he engages in by himself – a series of battles and skirmishes conducted within the privacy of his own walls, yet conceived as occasions for decisive forays into the world of public discourse. The wars of truth are thus as essential to Milton's defensive polemic – and to the distinctive nature of his performative and figurative discourse – as they were to his earlier tract on censorship.

Milton is never more self-dramatic than when he poeticizes his own career in his state polemic. Du Moulin had presented a scathing portrait of Milton in the *Clamor*: if Salmasius was presented as "the great prince of letters" and "our French Hercules," Milton was called a monstrous Polyphemus, a worm, a vain and vile adversary, a gallows-bird; and the savage invective written in Latin iambics and appended to the tract had characterized him as, among other things, a foul wretch, a vile buffoon, a dung-heap, an obscure ranter ("tenebricosus rabula") and hireling of commonplace origins.[21] Milton's compelling defense not only involved countering virulency with virulency; it also involved an intensely aesthetic reaction – his presentation of himself and his career as "a true Poem," to cite *An Apology*, "that is, a composition, and patterne of the best and honourablest things." This is not quite the same thing as asserting that the good poet or rhetor must be a good man:[22] rather, he who presumes "to sing high praises of heroick men" (I.890) must himself be nothing less than a good poem, a self transformed into a work of art, as the aesthetic terms "composition" and "patterne" suggest. Milton has redefined a common notion about the poet or rhetor, so as to underscore his commitment to the aesthetic as a shaping force in the sociopolitical process. The truly aestheticized self is not detached from the social world, but immediately and energetically engaged in it through discourses of "high praises," as well as things "vehemently written."

The conviction that the self should remain untainted and pure was already a deeply personal and vocational ideal in Milton's aesthetics going back to

Elegy VI, dramatized in *Comus*, and reiterated, as we have seen, in *An Apology*. In the *Defenses*, the poetic rhetor who wishes to remain unblemished and undefiled – his life "far removed from all vice and crime" (IV.i.611; VIII.118) – must defend himself not only through strenuous public involvement but through radically internal measures as well. As Milton explains in *Pro Se Defensio*, if the "good man" needs defense – after all, "he will be attacked not infrequently with envious detractions and slanders" – "he surrounds himself with his own integrity and the invincible knowledge of righteous deeds, by which, as if by the strongest bulwark and garrison [munimento atque praesidio firmissimo], he both receives the vain attacks of vicious men and frustrates their spears" (IV.ii.791; IX.214). As the military trope here suggests, the self becomes a kind of fortress capable of repelling the most aggressive and violent assaults. By aestheticizing the politically engaged poet or rhetor and by highlighting the internal dynamics of defense, Milton again underscores the convergence of his revolutionary polemic with his personal and poetic ideals.

Moreover, by presenting himself as a good man in the *Second Defense*, Milton presents himself as a sacred figure – in implicit contrast, I would suggest, to the sacred figure of Charles I skillfully fashioned in *Eikon Basilike*, and reiterated in posthumous defenses of the King made by Salmasius and Du Moulin.[23] In a sense, Milton continues the ideological program essential to *Eikonoklastes*: that of radically refashioning the powerful and highly effective representation of the King. He undermines the portrait of the Christlike martyr who has suffered terrible afflictions at the hands of his enemies by depicting the King not only as a rageful tyrant worse than his biblical paradigms, but as a mythical and theatrical figure elaborately fabricated by his ideological defenders (IV.i.646; VIII.172).[24] Yet in the *Second Defense*, Milton is generally less concerned with aggressively dismantling and recasting the invented icon of Charles (a polemical task Milton had executed passionately and at great length in *Eikonoklastes* and the *First Defense*); rather, here his creative response involves presenting an alternative sacred figure – that of the righteous, unreproachable, frugal poet–polemicist who is divinely favored and, like other blind men, "almost sacred." Blind to the external world though illuminated by "an inner and far more enduring light" (IV.i.590; VIII.72), this sacred poet-polemicist presents himself in implicit contrast to the sacred martyr of *Eikon Basilike* who beholds directly the light of the heavenly crown (in the famous frontispiece) and yet remains (in Milton's view) blind internally.[25]

In a sense, Milton's sacred portrait rivals the King's. *Eikon Basilike* had dramatized Charles asking for the comforts and mercies of David, after having endured afflictions comparable to those of the ancient King.[26] So Milton in his own extraordinarily bold way recalls David: he attributes his blindness to the protective shadow of heavenly wings – symbolic of God's defense of His sacred one (Ps. 17:8, 36:7, 63:7). In Milton's case, the analogy hardly evokes a posture of humility. Indeed, whereas Charles is presented in *Eikon Basilike* as a passive martyr who suffers, Milton presents himself in the *Second Defense* as an active figure energetically engaged in the ideological struggles of his revolutionary age. Aware of the continuing power of the royal icon and its fictional representation, Milton responds by offering his European audience a sacred image of the heroic defender of the state.

Nor is the issue of poetics insignificant here, since in the process of attacking the theatrical portrait of the King, Milton had sneeringly attacked the poetics of *Eikon Basilike*: "I begun to think that the whole Book might perhaps be intended a peece of Poetrie. The words are good, the fiction smooth and cleanly; there wanted onely Rime" (III.406). The King's book, his portrait, and his poetics are by implication inseparable – all contribute to the elaborate fiction and representation sustaining the ideology of Stuart court culture. Yet while Milton understands very well the poetics of fictional portraiture – and is anxious about its dramatic appeal even as he sneers at it – he also actively employs a poetics of self-portraiture in his own defense. In a way, the *Second Defense*, with its artful portrait of the sacred writer at its very center, is itself nothing less than "a peece of Poetrie" written in prose polemic – a continuation of Milton's creative responses to the art and politics of the King's portrait and book – by a writer who envisions himself as "a true Poem" and who dramatically asserts himself in his own text.

Indeed at times Milton very explicitly gives his career a mythopoetic dimension, such as when he compares himself to the wily Ulysses in his ability to circumvent a polemical opponent or when Milton aligns himself with Homer as he refutes Du Moulin's charge that his origins are uncertain (IV.i.595, 608; VIII.84, 112). And even when Milton says that he does "not covet the arms of Achilles" (IV.i.595–6; VIII.84), the intensely militant aspect of his self-portrait – not to mention the rage he often directs at his adversaries – reminds us that, as an active polemicist, he resembles that epic warrior as much as he resembles the more intellectual Ulysses. In any case, Milton does align his situation directly with the epic warrior's at another point in the text, when he rehearses how he chose to defend the state – his "most solemn duty" – at the expense of hastening his oncoming blindness. Milton recalls that hearing a divine monitor within reminded him of that moment in the *Iliad* when Achilles relates his two destinies brought back by Thetis from Delphi – either he dies fighting beside Troy and gains immortal fame or he returns home and loses glory, though his life will be long (IX.411–16). Milton could hardly dramatize himself as true poem more boldly: he resembles not only the epic poet, but the epic hero as well. Indeed, Milton's heroism supersedes the epic warrior's: his fighting in the polemical vanguard – a duty "more substantial [solidius] than glory" (IV.i.588; VIII.68–70) – has brought blindness, a mark of sacredness, rather than the brutal death of a Homeric hero.

Epic comparison, then, is one way Milton projects himself as a mythic figure, giving his polemical engagement a highly self-conscious literary dimension.

Furthermore, Milton's autobiographical digressions constitute a creative representation of the self: he presents his audience with a skillful *apologia pro vita sua* – confirming that his life and public involvement have been conducted as "a true Poem . . . a composition, and patterne of the best and honourablest things" – before he actually sings "high praises" of his revolutionary contemporaries. Milton gives an imaginative shape to his polemical career. His years of controversial engagement themselves assume a coherence as he reviews them – his revolutionary discourses all written in the service of ecclesiastical, domestic, and civil liberty (IV.i.624; VIII.130). On one level, Milton's self-portrait functions as ethical proof of his political commitments and his personal ideals. It also reveals Milton engaged in a literary process of actively interpreting his history as a writer – his means of creatively embedding his personal history and development within the history and conflicts of his culture.

His autobiographical discourse, then, concerns the making of Milton into the cultivated, poetic, and heroic revolutionary figure who has composed the *Second Defense*. His early life and passion for literary study, his years at Cambridge and Horton, his European tour, his return to England and settling in London, his engagement in political controversies, his work on the *History of Britain*, his appointment as Secretary for Foreign Tongues – all these stages and activities in Milton's life fall into a narrative configuration that is neither chaotic nor haphazard, but carefully organized by a writer who artfully reconstructs his polemical career as he invests it with aesthetic meaning. The concept of strength made perfect in weakness – the compelling interpretation based upon 2 Corinthians 12 which Milton uses to justify at great length his blindness in relation to his public involvement ("when I am weak, then I am strong") – would become nothing less than a crucial theme of his great poems. Having "lived free and untouched by the slightest sin or reproach" (IV.i.620; VIII.126) – like a true poem – the state polemicist exploits the rhetorical power of his autobiographical discourse for both aesthetic and social ends. He places his name and nationality boldly on the title pages of all three *Defenses*, and he is so ubiquitously present in his text – "What I am, I, for my part, openly admit [profiteor]" – that the poetics of self and the poetics of cultural history completely intersect in his work (IV.i.561; VIII.24).

IV

In writing the *Second Defense*, then, Milton was marshalling his extraordinary creative powers for the state and for God: there was no divorce at all in his imagination between literary and political discourse – political discourse *was* aesthetic. Revolution was thus less an interruption of Milton's poetic development than a series of occasions for Milton to rechannel his creative energies directly into polemic, to employ his literary and imaginative writing in the service of political activity. In effect, revolution stimulated his poetic creation, but in the medium of his flamboyant prose. We have already seen that Milton employed invective as an essential means of creative involvement in the sociopolitical process; autobiographical writing, as well as panegyric and advisory discourse, could function in a similar capacity. The *Second Defense* is astonishing for the mixture of postures and discourses the polemicist exploits – all of them informed by a sense of poetic and rhetorical engagement. As Milton remarks elsewhere, it is "not impossible" that Truth "may have more shapes then one" and that she "may be on this side, or on the other, without being unlike her self" (*Areopagitica*, II.563). The exceptionally versatile poet–polemicist of the *Second Defense* is rather like the figure of Truth here – he too can assume "more shapes than one," as he employs his creative energies in the name of God and the revolutionary state.

Thus Milton's panegyric on Bradshaw, who presided at the King's trial, is immediately preceded by a particularly savage passage condemning More's impurity, calling him "unmixed filth [meram spurcitiem], unmitigated crime," and stressing his brutish and devilish nature (IV.i.637; VIII.154). These "jarring notes" of invective (to recall the musical trope from *An Apology*) are an aggressive and dramatic means of setting off, by contrast, Milton's panegyrical discourse and the mythic figure of Bradshaw, who himself might qualify "to bee a true Poem." Bradshaw is everything his mythopoetic defender aspires to be – skillful and eloquent in his speech, tireless in his revolutionary activity, pure in his morals, "subservient to no man," sprung from a well-to-do family, steadfast and righteous in his dangerous cause, an embodiment of divine providence itself (IV.i.637–9; VIII.156–60). The aesthetic and political come together in Milton's discourse; his vision of this representative of the virtuous elite converges with his own poetic ideals as he now sings "high praises of heroick men." The other Commonwealthsmen he praises conform as well to this aesthetic vision of revolutionary culture: these men – outstanding for both their military and political skills – are cultivated, urbane, pious, courageous, accomplished citizens who have risen to their positions through merit, and Milton's "discourse is on fire to commemorate" their distinguished names (IV.i.675–8; VIII.232–4). Milton downplays differences among them, including those discontented with recent events: both Bradshaw and Bulstrode Whitelocke had opposed Cromwell's dissolution of the Rump, while Robert Overton had criticized Cromwell's Protectorate;[27] John Lambert, on the other hand – the most active supporter of the Protectorate – had drafted the Instrument of the Government and had urged Cromwell to accept the crown. If there is an attempt on Milton's part to reconcile these diverse figures – several, including William Sydenham and Edward Montague, were conservative in their political views – it is through his aesthetic conception of an elitist governing regime, as much as anything else. In any case, Milton was hardly troubled by

ideological schism among his compatriots: after all, "neighboring differences
... though they may be many," he had observed in *Areopagitica*, "need not
interrupt *the unity of Spirit*" (II.565). This unity of spirit – promoted by the
power of his mythopoetic discourse – is precisely what Milton aims to effect
in his revolutionary contemporaries.

Panegyric, then, is a means of both ideological persuasion and poetic
performance in prose: Milton musters his full rhetorical powers as his
discourse assumes a mythopoetic vision. In the case of his panegyric
addressed to Queen Christina, this may be taken to a rhetorical extreme, as
his highly self-conscious reference to "this digression" dramatizes: his
exuberant and unqualified praise of her "vigorous mind," "divine virtue and
wisdom," "magnanimity," and goddesslike powers (IV.i.603–6, 655–6;
VIII.104–8, 192) illustrates more than any other section of his work how, in
Kenneth Burke's words, "pure display rhetoric comes closest to the appeal of
the poetic in and for itself."[28] Using a trope from mineralogy, Milton
suggests that this "heroine" ("Heroina") embodies both a natural and
aesthetic perfection: her land, despite its "rough and unkind soil," has not
created in her anything "uneven or harsh"; rather, being "so rich in metals,"
it has, like a "kind parent," exerted all its power to make her "all gold"
("totam auream"). A sense of display and performance thus clearly informs
Milton's lavish panegyrics, though these passages usually operate even more
directly as a means of creative political engagement – as a mode of writing in
which the aesthetic does essential political and cultural work. For Milton
political and aesthetic discourse intersect: that fusion accounts for the figurative and rhetorical power Marvell immediately perceived upon reading the
Second Defense.

Milton manages to combine three essential functions – poet, prophet, and
spokesman for the new revolutionary order – in the *Second Defense*, and never
more effectively than in the addresses to Cromwell and the English people.[29]
He envisions Cromwell as a mythic figure whose deeds outstrip "the legends
[fabulas] of our heroes," his achievements almost soaring beyond the very
limits of Milton's own exceptional powers of mythopoetic representation:
"Your deeds surpass all degrees [modum omnem], not only of admiration,
but surely of titles too, and like the tops of pyramids, bury themselves in the
sky, towering above the popular favor of titles" (IV.i.672; VIII.222–4). Milton
thus self-consciously alerts his audience to the extraordinary achievement of
representing Cromwell within the confines of his discourse ("orationis
carceribus," VIII.214). Recalling the trope of literary over-reaching at the
beginning of his defense, Milton reminds his readers that he must again strive
for "loftier and bolder flights than are permissable." The effect is again
somewhat paradoxical: he acknowledges the limits of his own art and yet
implicitly attributes great power to it. Only a text capable of outstripping all
ancient and contemporary rhetorical discourses could possibly represent
Cromwell's exploits. Milton is making astonishing claims for his work: not

only does Cromwell excel all heroes, but Milton's heroic defense excels all rhetorical categories, achieving a level of expression – and mythopoetic representation – never matched before.

His representation of Cromwell combines historic and poetic ideals.[30] As *pater patriae*, Cromwell resembles a classical leader who embodies the political ideals of his nation. Milton extends this heroic analogy, moreover, by comparing Cromwell to such classical generals as Marcus Furius Camillus – called "parens patriae" after his triumph over the Gauls (Livy, Book v.xlix.7) – and Epaminondas, called by Cicero the greatest man in Greek history (*De Oratore*, III.xxxiv.139; Tusculan Disputations, I.ii.4). Yet Milton's Cromwell simultaneously embodies the spirit of the Puritan saint: this inward figure has fought the better fight within his own soul against "vain hopes, fears, desires" (IV.i.667; VIII.214) and has nourished a great spirit ("ingentem animum," VIII.212), while devoting himself to a purer mode of worship. Like the controversial polemicist in the fierce activity of defending the state, Cromwell is alone in his dangerous struggles; like the polemicist, he has endured and will continue to endure hardships, perils, and trials, even while he is divinely inspired in his righteous cause. Furthermore, like a seventeenth-century Aeneas, Cromwell will have his "pietas" and innermost self thoroughly tested as he takes upon himself the "heaviest burden" ("onus ... gravissimum") of his people (IV.i.673; VIII.226). Aligning his own heroic enterprise with that of epic heroes, Milton too claims to carry a genuine "burden" upon his shoulders (IV.i.596; VIII.84).[31] Cromwell combines within himself, again like the polemicist who praises him, both the textual and the political: Milton links Cromwell's authority – he is the very author of liberty ("libertatis auctor" [VIII.224]) – with the creativity of the revolutionary writer. Milton has written a poetics of revolution in the *Second Defense* and his panegyric involves nothing less than poetic mythmaking. This is no left-handed achievement: when Milton aligns his enterprise at the very end with the epic poet's and refers to the exploits of Achilles, Ulysses, and Aeneas (IV.i.685; VIII.252), his state polemic assumes a distinctly mythopoetic dimension with Cromwell and Milton himself as its great epic protagonists.

Milton is especially innovative – even more than critics have suggested – in his bold appropriation of epic vision to revolutionary polemic. His defense at the end does not focus at all on the world of the national heroic past, that essential subject of epic which, as Bakhtin has observed, makes its audience invariably conscious of "epic distance": "precisely because it is walled from all subsequent times, the epic past is absolute and complete. It is closed as a circle; inside it everything is finished, already over. There is no place in the epic world for any openendedness, indecision, indeterminacy." The great subject of Milton's epic performance, however, is the present and future: this epic discourse is taking place *right now*, unfolding dynamically before the very eyes of Milton's revolutionary contemporaries. As such, Milton's epic vision highlights the "possibility of activity and change" which the world of the epic past necessarily excludes, according to Bakhtin. Milton brings epic discourse immediately and dramatically into his contemporary world. It is not the past that is "the source of all authentic reality and value," to appropriate Bakhtin's words, but the present.[32] The "opportunity for doing the greatest deeds [maximarum rerum]" (IV.i.685; VIII.254) still lies before Milton's countrymen: the mythopoetic rhetor has interpreted the story of his culture in epic terms, but that story is ongoing, open-ended, and yet to be completed.

In addition to channeling his creative energies into the heroic vision of his defense, Milton also responds with exceptional acuteness to the fragile stability of the new political order. His defense of the Protectorate will not support the argument, made by a recent commentator, that Milton's tracts tend to absorb "social realities into imaginative patterns without confronting and assessing those realities on their own terms."[33] There is little doubt that Milton intends to win over his audience with his compelling vision of an imagined social order – a vision sustained by the rhetorical and mythopoetic power of his discourse to erect "a monument that will not soon pass away." And yet as Milton's defense turns from panegyric to advice and warning, his work directly confronts the slippery and precarious political realities threatening the new state. Fully aware that his hopes could easily be dashed, Milton already anticipates disappointment in his exhortation to his countrymen.[34] His text's conclusion is especially powerful, I suggest, because of the tension Milton generates by juxtaposing his exhilarating mythopoetic vision with his keen political realism.

If his defense exudes a sense of exhilaration and excitement about the new regime, it also projects a sense of caution and apprehension about a governing power that could very well prove transitory. Cromwell has reinvigorated the revolutionary state with his unparalleled achievements and leadership; nevertheless, Milton does not hesitate to stress precisely how ephemeral the power of that new state could turn out to be: if it "should miscarry, so to speak, and as quickly vanish" ("quasi aborta evanuerit"), he warns Cromwell, the nation would suffer terrible disgrace (IV.i.673; VIII.226). The metaphor of miscarriage conveys with great force Milton's fear and revulsion. No innocent idealist in the *Second Defense*, he faces political realities head on: men are too easily governed by personal interests and ambitions; tyranny becomes internalized so that peace itself proves the hardest war to win; a nation which "has delivered itself into slavery to its own lusts [libidinibus]" will find it more difficult than ever to establish and maintain political stability. Milton is only too aware that men may give in to "factions, hatreds, superstitions, injustices, lusts, and rapine against one another" (IV.i.684; VIII.250). These are hardly the warnings of an idealistic artist who possesses little grasp of concrete political realities or who neglects to confront them on their own terms. Indeed, if anything, the very urgency of Milton's warnings underscores his acute awareness that the political stability of a new social order too often exists in a delicate state of equilibrium. Even as he passionately celebrates the new regime, he anxiously envisions its potential demise.[35]

Moreover, the issue of representation is particularly crucial to Milton's response at this point. Representing godly power in regal forms, the new elite, he fears, might begin to ape the old.[36] By imitating the royalists – by slipping "into royalist excess and folly" ("in regium luxum atque socordiam") and chasing after royalist "vanities" ("inanitates") – his revolutionary contemporaries are in danger of becoming sons of a "meer artificiall *Adam*," to recall a resonant phrase from *Areopagitica* (II.527). Despised by other men, they would leave behind one "salutary lesson" useful to others, though not to themselves, a point Milton underscores by introducing the language of fiction and theater: "how great might have been the achievements of genuine virtue and piety, when the mere counterfeit and shadow of these qualities – cleverly feigned, no more [cum ficta et adumbrata, duntaxat belle simulando] – could embark upon such noble undertakings and through you progress so far towards execution" (IV.681–2; VIII.242–4). Here Milton himself makes the essential connection between *Realpolitik* and the aesthetic: he understands precisely how the power of representation operates in state politics – how seductive and precarious the artificial reality it creates and exploits may be. In effect, he warns his contemporaries not to establish a state that maintains its power by employing such fictions and representations. As a writer deeply committed to his own authority of representation, Milton remains both anxious about and fascinated by the intersection of the imaginative and the political. This conjunction in his discourse has hardly prevented him from confronting social reality: to the contrary, it has made him even more sensitive to the politics of aestheticizing state power.

Ten years earlier, in *Areopagitica*, he had imagined the architects of his revolutionary age harnessing their creative and social energies in order to construct the elaborate house of God, a figure for the godly nation itself (II.555); now in the *Second Defense*, Milton acknowledges – using one of those "many figures" Marvell appreciated – the possibility that this great superstructure of the new regime will be abandoned and left incomplete:

> If after such brave deeds you ignobly fail [deliqueritis], if you do aught
> unworthy of yourselves, be sure that posterity will speak out and pass
> judgment: the foundations [fundamenta] were soundly laid, the
> beginnings, in fact more than the beginnings, were splendid, but
> posterity will look in vain, not without a certain distress [non sine
> commotione], for those who were to complete the work, who were to
> put the pediment [fastigium] in place.   (IV.i.685; VIII.252–4)

Through counseling, encouraging, and inspiring, the state's defender has injected his creative energies into the dynamic process of social construction: this has been an active, heroic enterprise involving a full investment of his poetic talents. The novelty of the new state, however, has provoked Milton to respond simultaneously as mythopoetic visionary and social realist. Yet rather than diffusing the tension underlying this double stance, he has exploited its unsettling implications at the end of his defense. Milton's compelling challenge to the new age depends upon his highlighting this complex social vision – a vision combining the acute awareness of the realistic ideologist with the imaginative boldness of the creative artist. Fusing the aesthetic and the political, his discourse manages to probe the realities of social power, while promoting the power of his own mythopoetic text to shape the cultural forces of his age.

Notes

1 For a demonstration of Milton's artistry in his least examined state polemic, see Thomas N. Corns, "Milton's *Observations upon the Articles of Peace*: Ireland under English Eyes," chapter 6 above.

2 See Richard Helgerson, *Self-Crowned Laureates: Spenser, Jonson, Milton, and the Literary System* (Berkeley and London, 1983), pp. 242–3, 269, 273–80. His argument applies to the whole period of Milton's pamphleteering.

3 Translated selections appear in *CPW*, IV.i.1041–81; for a complete translation, see H. G. Merrill, III, "Milton's Secret Adversary: Du Moulin and the Politics of Protestant Humanism" (unpublished Ph.D. diss., University of Tennessee, 1959).

4 See e.g. the editor of the *Second Defense* in *CPW*: "His prose works in the main would have had little pertinence if they had been issued when the topics were subjects of current discussion. But Milton was realistic enough to know that his most lasting fame would come from poetry; here lay the real immortality, a matter he cannot discuss in the present polemic crisis" (IV.i.608 n.242). See also p. 554, n.27 on Milton's "left-handedness" and p. 632, n.358, on Milton's frustration at "the loss of leisure needed for the writing of greater works than tracts." *Cf.* Helgerson's remarks on "artistic autonomy" (*Self-Crowned Laureates*, pp. 273–6).

5 For a more general treatment of the discourse of the aesthetic in the period, see Michael McKeon, "Politics of Discourses and the Rise of the Aesthetic in Seventeenth-Century England," in *Politics of Discourse: The Literature and History of Seventeenth-Century England*, ed. Kevin Sharpe and Steven N. Zwicker (Berkeley and London, 1987), pp. 35–51. Also pertinent are remarks by Sharpe and Zwicker in their introduction, pp. 2–3, 18–20.

6 *Cf.* Helgerson: "What use a great poetic talent in an age that required prose?" (*Self-Crowned Laureates*, p. 280).

7 In the Bridgewater manuscript this chivalric stance is expressed even more militantly when the Elder Brother proclaims that he will "cleave [Comus'] scalp / Down to the hips"; see the variant for lines 608–9.

8 For further discussion of the Commonwealth insignia, see Joseph Anthony Wittreich, Jr., "Milton's Idea of the Orator," *Milton Quarterly*, 6 (1972), pp. 38–9.

9 The phrases in this paragraph are taken from the sonnet "To Mr. Cyriack Skinner upon his Blindness," lines 8–9, 11, 13.

10 *Trials of Desire: Renaissance Defenses of Poetry* (New Haven, 1983), p. 17. Ferguson

is interested in the defense as both "an interpsychic and a social phenomenon" (p. 193). See also Harold Bloom's illuminating psychoanalytic study, "Freud's Concepts of Defense and the Poetic Will," in *The Literary Freud: Mechanisms of Defense and the Poetic Will*, ed. Joseph H. Smith (New Haven, 1980), pp. 1–28.

11 *Cf. Prolusion* VI for a similar moment of self-dramatization in which Milton is aware of captivating his audience: "And so I entreat at the beginning of my entertainment the favour which actors beg at the end of theirs: give me your laughter and applause [Plaudite, et ridete]" (I.277; XII.226).

12 *De Oratore*, trans. E. W. Sutton and H. Rackham (Cambridge, Mass., 1942), I.viii.33; *cf.* I.viii.30, I.xlvi.202.

13 *Institutio Oratoria*, trans. H. E. Butler (London, 1922), X.i.28.

14 Letter from Marvell to Milton, 2 June 1654, in *CPW*, IV.ii.864.

15 For Crantz, see *The Life Records of John Milton*, ed. J. Milton French (New Brunswick, 1954), III.422; for More, see *CPW*, IV.ii.1109 and *Fides Publica, Contra Calumnias Joannis Miltoni* (The Hague, 1654), p. 71. *Cf.* pp. 15–16, 18; on pp. 73–4, More attacks Milton for concluding his defense "more poetically than prophetically" ("poetice magis quam prophetice").

16 *A Replie to a Person of Honour* (London, 1675), p. 40.

17 *De Oratore*, II.xlv.188–xlix.201, xliii.182–4.

18 See e.g. *John Milton: Selected Prose*, ed. C. A. Patrides (1974; revised edn Columbia, Mo., 1985): "The two *Defenses* and especially the third *Defense of Himself* (1655) are considerably marred by the frequently intemperate language which readers have often remarked, and as often deplored" (p. 36).

19 *Early Lives of Milton*, ed. Helen Darbishire (London, 1932), pp. 152–3.

20 *Ibid.*, p. 70.

21 On Salmasius, see *Clamor*, pp. 6, 16, 138; for abusive descriptions of Milton, see the dedicatory epistle, and pp. 8, 126, 129. For the invective in iambics, see *Clamor*, pp. 140–8.

22 *Cf.* Milton elsewhere in *An Apology*: "For doubtlesse that indeed according to art is most eloquent, which returnes and approaches nearest to nature from whence it came. . . . So that how he should be truly eloquent who is not withall a good man, I see not" (I.874).

23 For Du Moulin's unqualified admiration of *Eikon Basilike*, see *Clamor*, p. 66.

24 Du Moulin, however, asserted that the portrait of the martyred Charles was "not painted with false colors" (IV.ii.1067; *Clamor*, p. 66), and mocked the theatricality of the parricides (*Clamor*, p. 103). On Milton's response to theatricality in his state polemics, see my forthcoming book, *Milton and the Drama of History: Historical Vision, Iconoclasm, and the Literary Imagination* (Cambridge, 1990), chapter 3.

25 See *Eikonoklastes*, III.516: "whom God hard'ns, them also he blinds." *Cf.* Milton on More's inner blindness: IV.i.589; VIII.70.

26 *Eikon Basilike: The Portraiture of His Sacred Majesty in His Solitudes and Sufferings*, ed. Philip A. Knachel (Ithaca, N.Y., 1966), pp. 149–52.

27 I do not cite Algernon Sidney, the classical republican, among Cromwell's critics because it now seems more likely that the Sidney to whom Milton refers in the *Second Defense* is his brother, Philip, Lord Lisle, a staunch Cromwellian during the Protectorate. See William Riley Parker, *Milton: A Biography* (Oxford, 1968), vol. I, p. 444; *cf. CPW*, IV.i.677 n.524.

28 *A Rhetoric of Motives* (New York, 1950), p. 72; *cf.* p. 71.

29 For a contrary view, see Helgerson, p. 280.

30 I discuss the poetics of history in Milton's tract more extensively in *Milton and the Drama of History*, chapter 4.

31 *Cf. First Defense*, IV.i.305; VII.7.

32 *The Dialogic Imagination: Four Essays*, ed. Michael Holquist, trans. Caryl Emerson and Michael Holquist (Austin and London, 1981), pp. 16–18; *cf.* pp. 13–15, 19.

33 Keith W. Stavely, *The Politics of Milton's Prose Style* (New Haven, 1975), p. 2; *cf.* pp. 112–13. Stavely, however, examines only those prose works written in English. Elsewhere he qualifies his thesis in regard to Milton's responses to specific political situations, but notes that Milton's shrewdness "is not self-evident" (p. 129, n.1).

34 Even a classic assessment like E. M. W. Tillyard's seriously underestimates this aspect of Milton's work: "Behind his exhortation to the English people there is . . . no danger of his being disappointed by events going against his hopes. He has already faced the worst possibilities and his exhortation has the calm that belongs to the fulness of knowledge" (*Milton* [1930; revised edn London, 1966], pp. 164–5).

35 That Milton felt reservations about committing himself to the Protectorate is also confirmed by Austin Woolrych, "Milton and Cromwell: 'A Short But Scandalous Night of Interruption'?," *Left Hand*, p. 192.

36 On this phenomenon during the Protectorate, see Derek Hirst, *Authority and Conflict: England, 1603–1658* (Cambridge, Mass., 1986): "Oliver began to grant titles of knighthood . . . Lambert for one resided in palatial splendour at Wimbledon house" (p. 321); see also pp. 317–18.

10

Elective poetics and Milton's prose: *A Treatise of Civil Power* and *Considerations Touching the Likeliest Means to Remove Hirelings Out of the Church*

SUSANNE WOODS

Milton's pamphleteering was actively and consciously aimed at his own time and cultural circumstances, and our ability to retrieve its contemporary impact is limited. According to one of this century's notable appreciators of the pamphlet, George Orwell, the very genre has become alien.[1] For modern readers most subjects of Milton's pamphlets no longer carry passion or conviction, whether because Milton's position has been comprehended by Anglo-American culture (as divorce or an unlicenced press) or the historical imperative has receded (as monarchy versus a republic) or the religious controversies no longer contend on a field of commonly held beliefs.

Yet a central issue of our time as well as Milton's does get considerable attention in his pamphlets: human freedom and the range and meaning of human choice. Milton's views on the centrality of civil, domestic, and religious liberty to a free, responsible, and godly life were among the most radical in his culture, with many of the ideas he represents remaining vital today. Milton is also a poet conscious of his own radicalism and determined to reveal complex reality through language. In his prose, as in his verse, he presents himself as an artist aware of the subversive power of his own artistry. His ideas and linguistic strategies come together most instructively in what I call elective poetics, which can be found not only in the subtler reaches of his versifying but even in the very plainest of his prose: *A Treatise of Civil Power* (*Civil Power*) and *Considerations Touching the Likeliest Means to Remove Hirelings Out of the Church* (*Likeliest Means*), both written in the important political transition year of 1659. My present concern with these works is not primarily with the structure of their argument but with the way certain smaller strategies of syntax and diction advance a complex interconnection between author, text, reader, and the destabilization of cultural identity, specifically in its definition of liberty. I will be assuming throughout that Milton intends that destabilization and his texts resist conventional methods of deconstruction because they turn the tables on the reader – they invite readers to deconstruct their own cultural assumptions. This in itself is new. What is equally impressive is that Milton can do this in a Senecan as well as his more familiar Ciceronian style, and that a sophisticated poetics, or complex series of linguistic strategies, is evident in his plainest prose.

I

Elective poetics refers to constellations of technique and subject developed by essentially meritocratic English humanist poets from Spenser to Milton in order to present issues of freedom and choice. Not only are works such as Spenser's *Faerie Queene* and Milton's *Paradise Lost* fundamentally about choice, they enact the processes of choice on many levels. Generic mixture, for example, and the integration of classical and Christian materials involve obvious authorial choices. Christian humanism, embodied in such English treatises of the New Learning as Thomas Elyot's *Boke named the Governour* (1531) or George Puttenham's *Arte of English Poesie* (1589), assumed that generic choices were conscious and involved both a claim on the tradition and an assertion of individual freedom.[2] By transforming a received inheritance of epithalamic or epic materials, for example, an author can resituate a cultural past, claim its relevance to a contemporary present, and comment on the present through a (sometimes disingenuously skewed) lens of the past. Imitation in the Renaissance always included the desire to "overgo" that which was imitated, to assert both the author's right to claim a position within the cultural tradition and to change that tradition. Whether we choose to see these literary transformations in psychological terms (as, for example, Harold Bloom's challenge of literary sons to literary fathers), as part of a general cultural dialectic, or as inherent to an aesthetic of generic modeling, they are always emblematic of an author's freedom to choose.[3]

More subtly, encounters with entrenched or powerful attitudes, which meritocratic principles might subvert, lead authors toward ambiguities and disguises, paradox and contradictions, masks and indirection – all the techniques by which authors reveal by concealing. As David Norbrook has observed, Renaissance poets in service to powerful monarchs (or perhaps Parliaments and Lord Protectors) "of necessity fell in with the language of power; but far from regarding this process as 'natural', they developed elaborate strategies to try to preserve a degree of independence for their writing."[4] So Milton, from *Areopagitica* to *Civil Power*, purports to identify his interests with Parliament's and Parliament's with his, and to make deferential claims for parliamentary authority. But he always sets that deference in the larger contexts of divine purpose, human reason, and social contract. Any one of these has the potential, which Milton freely uses, to subvert the power relation essential to his rhetorical stance. Elective poetics often leaves readers to choose among multiple meanings, in part to protect the author from charges of subversion and in part to make subversive ideas available.[5]

A premise of this essay is that a writer who is concerned with issues of

human freedom will tend to invite reader choice as well as indicate consciousness of authorial choices available to a particular discursive medium. Thus the
Shepheardes Calendar's "Immerito," who is quick to invoke, and then alter,
models of Virgilian pastoral and Chaucerian dialogue, will also refrain from
heavily stated morals, give his debaters (such as Thomalin and Morrel or
Piers and Cuddie) a fair shot at each argument, will offer a variety of
metaphors, and will show a penchant for conditional or otherwise inconclusive language. This is not precisely a preference for writerly over lisible
discourse (as in Jonathan Goldberg's use of Roland Barthes' categories) or
dialectical over rhetorical, in Stanley Fish's terms, though it has some affinity
with the latter.[6] For a writer seeking to provoke a reader's sense of personal
freedom, the purpose of his or her poetics is not to create constant deferral but
to invite constant readerly attention and choice.

The invitation to judge or dispute the author's stated position, no matter
how apparently clear, is at the heart of elective poetics. The term is otherwise
fluid, not tied to particular techniques or conventions though more compatible with some than with others. Unlike classical models which ascribe
certain forms and approaches to certain subjects (low style for pastoral, high
for epic adventures), a poetics which seeks to define, assert, and provoke the
exercise of individual freedom will tend to be occasional and tied to
immediate political reality and contemporary aesthetic tastes. For one to
exercise personal freedom, there must be issues that seem compelling and
that require choices. An author who would deal with the power to choose
must tie into those issues in ways that will engage contemporary readers, and
at the same time invite choice by the techniques and methods appropriate to
the particular discourse. In Spenser's time eloquence, fable, and disguise were
not only prudent but fashionable. By the 1650s more open controversy on
topics involving civil and religious liberty, and a post-Baconian taste among
intellectuals for nonfiction and plainer writing (signified in part by their
preference for historical and biblical models over romance and allegory for
serious discourse), eventually helped to direct Milton's prose style, though
both eloquence and fable remained part of his repertoire. Elective poetics is a
function not of particular genres or styles, then, but of the way in which
certain public genres and recognizable styles and models may be most
profitably used in addressing a particular issue with implications for the
definition and exercise of personal freedom.

I claim the term poetics because works about freedom that tend to provoke
reader choice combine many of the elements usually associated with a more
formal poetic: a background of traditional models appropriate to the general
topic (though this is broad, including satire, oratory, and fable); a particular
view of the poet's relation to his subject (Milton as a free man because he is a
"knowing Christian," one who himself possesses and displays the Christian
liberty of which he writes); and the use of language in patterns that illustrate
certain assumptions about the nature of language itself (in Milton, language

conveys an emblem of the human mind, and therefore displays and invites either freedom or bondage). These are, in broad strokes, elements that become more formally refined in Milton's later poetry, where human choice, and election as a state of relation to God through liberty, are the central themes which the linguistic techniques of the poetry continually support – often by dislocating language and jarring the reader's assumptions, as well as those of Milton's central characters (including Adam, Samson, Jesus, and Satan).

An obvious example from Milton's earlier poetry is the pairing of *L'Allegro* with *Il Penseroso*. Attempts to decide which figure Milton preferred are largely beside the point. Each case is made on its merits, and a final decision on which is better, or a decision to hold both as valuable or as better in differing contexts, is left to the reader. The only sure invitation is for the reader to see and be engaged in evaluating alternatives, to exercise judgment and make choices. The poems offer both "The Mountain Nymph, sweet Liberty" (*L'Allegro*, line 36) and the neostoic freedom of "The Cherub Contemplation" (*Il Penseroso*, line 54), and, in sum, the exercise of free debate that Milton so eloquently extols in *Areopagitica*. Milton's early penchant for provoking readerly judgment can also be found in the densities of his developing style. A familiar example is the ambiguous "he" at the conclusion of *Lycidas*:

> At last he rose, and twitch'd his Mantle blew:
> To morrow to fresh Woods, and Pastures new.

The context describes the "uncouth Swain." The immediate referent is "the Sun," with the implicit "Son." The poem's preeminent rising and transcendence belong to the figure of Lycidas; the most notable rising above the pastoral environment belongs to that of the author. These varying and cohering referents for "he" in the penultimate line of the poem demand an active reader, one who recognizes a potential multiplicity of meaning and so rises to a richer consciousness and an interactive engagement with both the art of the poem and the continuing life to which it points.

Elective poetics, most simply, is an author's method for requiring and empowering reader choice, often to get the reader to enact the liberating and self-defining process of choosing that which a given text may be about or which an established power might find threatening. From early in his career Milton invites reader involvement, and continues to develop into one of the English-speaking culture's most explicit and emphatic champions of choice as the root of human liberty and the means for fulfilling the human side of divine election. Throughout his work he uses the terms "elect," "elected," and "elective" in religious, civil, and personal contexts that mirror his lifelong interest in divine, political, and individual liberty. Though Milton moves away from the hierarchical world view of Christian humanism, he is the fulfillment of its belief that learning and wisdom (more than birth) lead to virtue. Knowledge allows for informed and therefore right choice, and choice both is and leads to human freedom. As Milton says in the *Doctrine and Discipline of Divorce*: "God delights not to make a drudge of vertue, whose actions must all be elective and unconstrain'd" (II.342).[7]

Milton's poetry remains dense with concern for an invitation to human freedom, from early sophisticated efforts to the conclusion of *Samson Agonistes*, where election as vocation and election as free choice come together in Samson's understanding that the "rousing motions" in him are invitations to seize control of his own destiny, and so fulfill it. Like the Chorus, Manoa, and Samson himself, the reader is confronted with painful and contradictory evidence of Samson's godly call. Samson's bondage pervades the work, from his own cry of "impotence of mind, in body strong" (line 52), to the Chorus's "Thou art become (O worst imprisonment) / The dungeon of thyself" (lines 155–6), to Manoa's assumption that God must find glory through another champion (lines 472–8), and innumerable similar cries and assumptions through and after these.[8]

Only when Samson himself learns to weigh and judge the extent of both his call and his freedom, his election and his election, can the two come together and his work, and Milton's poetic work, be resolved: "Commands are no constraints. If I obey them, / I do it freely" (lines 1372–3). Even in *Samson*'s resolution the language remains, as here, conditional, or, as at the moment of Samson's great insight, ambiguous and prophetic:

> I begin to feel
> Some rousing motions in me which dispose
> To something extraordinary my thoughts.
> I with this Messenger will go along,
> Nothing to do, be sure, that may dishonor
> Our Law, or stain my vow of *Nazarite*.
> If there be aught of presage in the mind,
> This day will be remarkable in my life
> By some great act, or of my days the last.
>
> (lines 1381–9)

The will responds to the call. Samson is inwardly persuaded that to go with the messenger will fulfill his vocation. Yet it remains no clear heroism in even the biblical heroic tradition, and the truth of Samson's response remains between him and his God. The reader is left to judge the result, perhaps to gain "new acquist / Of true experience from this great event" (lines 1755–6), and certainly to learn from Milton's grand but nondirective style that God's call, the only true command, depends on an inner hearing. In *Samson*, human freedom comes through the choices mandated by the authority of individual conscience. This is also the principal theme of the prose.

II

Milton's polemical prose is more directive than his poetry. In overt argument he is less likely to use the subtleties that invite (rather than insist upon) the reader's agreement with an authorial point of view. Yet some of the techniques associated with elective poetics pervade the prose, and remain characteristic of his discourse on freedom and choice.

Areopagitica is an obvious instance, with its complex and disingenuous mode of address, its witty and eloquent use of metaphor, and its famous appeal to an active, risk-taking virtue. Similarly, the divorce tracts seek a feeling persuasion, and try as much to insinuate an unpopular libertarian position as to argue directly for it. Milton's situational interpretation of Christ's words on divorce, for example, invites the reader to perform similar complex hermeneutic acts and to make choices about context and content: "let us remember as a thing not to be deny'd, that all place of Scripture wherein just reason of doubt arises from the letter, are to be expounded by considering upon what occasion everything is set down; and by Comparing other Texts" (II.282).

What comprises "just reason of doubt" is itself a matter of interpretive choice. Milton is as likely to offer alternatives from metaphor as from logic:

> So heer he [Christ] may be justly thought to have giv'n this rigid
> sentence against divorce, not to cut off all remedy from a good man
> who finds himself consuming away in a disconsolate and uninjoy'd
> matrimony, but to lay a bridle on the bold abuses of those over-
> weening *Rabbies*; which he could not more effectually do than by a
> countersway of restraint, curbing their wild exorbitance almost into
> the other extreme; as when we bow things the contrary way, to make
> them come to their naturall straitnes.   (II.283)

Milton reminds his reader that rhetoric is situational and requires interpretation, a strategy that invites a continuing interpretive vigilance even of his own clearest prose.

Though Milton's prose is more directive and less invitational than the fictions and verses of his poems, it is often complex and eloquent. Yet if a measure of subtlety and complexity in prose, as in poetry, is the size and variousness of vocabulary, then the later pamphlets move away from the subtlety I have suggested as a feature of elective poetics. In particular, *Civil Power* and *Likeliest Means* are among the plainest of Milton's pamphlets, according to the statistical studies of Thomas N. Corns.[9] In general, later tracts have a more limited lexical vocabulary than earlier, with *Civil Power* and *Likeliest Means* having the smallest total vocabularies (826 and 873 words respectively) of any of the eleven tracts Corns examines (Table 1, p. 2); he uses numerous examples from both pamphlets to illustrate his contention that from the earlier to later tracts "flamboyance and linguistic innovation . . . is replaced by a more sober style, a plainer medium for exposition" (p. 65). Another sign of plainness is repetition. Corns cites *Civil Power* and *Likeliest Means* as preeminent examples of repetition and avoidance of synonyms, with, for example, "scripture" and "scriptures" appearing a combined twenty-five times in *Civil Power*, and "hire" and "hirelings" twenty times, "tithe" and "tithes" twenty-five times in *Likeliest Means* (p. 3).

This relative plainness is still very much a part of Milton's elective poetics, and an undervalued feature of his prose poetics generally. Keith W. Stavely and Allen Grossman are among those who find failure in Milton's political effort tied to the detachment of his prose from the world of political action, in favor of asserting an ideal.[10] The later pamphlets help show that Milton's view of politics was related to idea through language in ways not fully appreciated by his own time, or by ours. To define correctly was to choose truth, but the very process of choice was a political act in the direction of truth and in service to Christian liberty. As Barbara Lewalski has shown, Milton's commitment to Christian liberty was absolute, though his political strategies in 1659 shifted with the shifting situation.[11] By 1659 Milton no longer expects England to become the triumphant model of Christian liberty he envisioned in *Areopagitica*. *The Readie and Easie Way* is a last great effort to warn against the worst, but carries more desperation than conviction. Yet through 1659 he continues to be engaged in the world of political action, showing himself to believe ever more firmly that choice is Christian liberty and therefore the precondition for all godly action. It is no accident that the fundamental issue of both pamphlets is liberty of individual conscience, uncoerced by civil power.

Using devices such as repetition, litotes and other negative constructions, and the strategic use of tropes, Milton achieves a specifically prose elective poetics in these pamphlets, in which the appearance of plainness and simplicity is actually an invitation to enact liberty of conscience and fulfill individual vocation. Milton here uses expectations of lucidity and directness in plain style prose to achieve many of the effects of invitation and provocation I described earlier. The standard for Milton's plainness is scripture, which he claims is itself clear and "plane" on the separation of church and state, and whose model he invokes at the end of *Civil Power*: "Having herin the scripture so copious and so plane, we have all that can be properly calld the strength and nerve; the rest would be but pomp and incumbrance. Pomp and ostentation of reading is admir'd among the vulgar: but doubtless in matters of religion he is learnedest who is planest" (VII.272). Even in his use of rhetorical colors, Milton similarly asserts that he "shall only borrow a plane similie, the same which our own [Protestant] writers, when they would demonstrate planest that we rightly prefer the scripture before the church" (VII.248).

Milton goes on to extend past its common use the simile he then employs, but the posture of plain speaking is not entirely disingenuous. Like scripture, like God himself, Milton's plain clarity rather than the "pomp and incumbrance" of rhetorical force will invite the free assent of his reader. "How compells [God]? doubtless no otherwise then he draws, without which no man can come to him, *Joh.* 6.44: and that is by the inward perswasive motions of his spirit and by his ministers; not by the outward compulsions of a magistrate or his officers" (VII.261).

The job of Milton's artistry is to reach the reader's conscience, to incite the exercise of Christian liberty, and to invite the "inward perswasion" (VII.259) characteristic of the move from Old to New Covenant. The first and most basic technique of this elective poetics is, as the biblical model would suggest, verbal repetition. Corns might have looked beyond his own choices to notice that in *Civil Power* the word "free" appears alone or in variation twenty-eight times, "liberty" twenty-four times. In *Likeliest Means* versions of "free" appear forty-nine times, "liberty" ten times. Throughout each tract, but especially in *Civil Power*, which sets the tone for both, Milton rings changes on verbal leitmotifs that bring into question all the assumed cultural definitions and invite the reader to recast the meaning of language by rethinking their definitions, both connotative and denotative. In Saussure's terms, Milton would shift the *langue* by resignifying the *parole*. Other techniques mingle with devices of repetition throughout both works.

Civil Power begins by justifying the use of English: "natural dutie and affection hath confin'd and dedicated [this work] first to my own nation: and in a season wherin the timely reading therof, to the easier accomplishment of your great work, may save you much labor and interruption." The posture of accessibility assumes that a treatise written in Latin would have been too difficult for the Parliamentarians to slog through in time to make intelligent use of it. The reader is immediately the tutee, and not a very advanced one at that. Without talking down to any given reader, Milton underscores the simplicity and accessibility of what he will present as a central Gospel message. The techniques Milton-as-tutor will use are therefore suitably basic: repetition and definition. Words and phrases that appear in the dedication and set the tone for the treatise itself include "protestant," "Christian" ("the true protestant Christian religion"), "Christian libertie," "conscience," "power," and "freedom." From the beginning the tutorial tone is presented in service to the development and support of individual conscience and agency, even among Parliamentarians: "it will concern you while you are in power, so to regard other men's consciences, as you would your own should be regarded in the power of others; and to consider that any law against conscience is alike in force against any conscience, and so may one way or other justly redound upon your selves" (VII.239–40).

Another device central to *Civil Power* is the use of litotes and other negative constructions. These, too, appear immediately, in the dedication:

Of civil libertie I have written heretofore by the appointment, and *not without the approbation* of civil power: of Christian liberty I write now; which others long since having don with all freedom under heathen emperors, *I should do wrong to suspect, that I now shall with less* under Christian governors, and such especially as profess openly their defense of Christian libertie. (VII.240; my italics)

A double negative gives a positive assertion the appearance of balance, or of having been reached after weighing alternatives. The balanced stance sets the tone for the treatise proper, which claims "it can be *at no time* therfore *unseasonable* to speak of these things" (that is, of "force . . . restraining, and hire . . . corrupting the teachers" of "the church of God"). Milton's pamphlet will not only be timely, but "to the truth it will be at all times *no unneedfull testimonie*" (VII.241; my italics). Litotes necessarily invite rather than demand assent, since they risk displaying the proposition's negation. They may even encourage the reader to question a proposition. Under the "law" rather than "the gospel," for example, humanity was in a "state of rigor, childhood, bondage and works, to all which force *was not unbefitting*" (VII.259; my italics).

Though the language be "plane" and the syntax not particularly complex, it will be difficult for any reader to grasp these propositions without recognizing the need to think about them in more than one way. It is precisely this recognition that statements must be thought about in more than one way that engages the reader's own judgment, provokes choice, and models for the reader his or her freedom.

In another "plane" device that invites reader judgment, words repeated throughout the treatise accumulate connotation over the course of the work, with what is assumed about their definitions as important as what Milton makes explicit. "Protestant," for example, is linked with "scripture" and with "conscience" to make the three terms mutually defining. Each word assumes its own positive connotations, while the words' continuing association reinforces their individual power. With this assumed force in place, statements which define terms crucial to Milton's argument may be cast negatively, not only to give the appearance of disjunctive logic and balance, but also to invite the effort to reject Milton's premises, and so solicit more affective affirmation:

It cannot be deni'd, being the main foundation of our protestant religion, that we of these ages, having no other divine rule or autoritie from without us warrantable to one another as a common ground but the holy scripture, and no other within us but the illumination of the Holy Spirit so interpreting that scripture as warrantable only to our selves and to such whose consciences we can so perswade, can have no other ground in matters of religion but only from the scriptures. (VII.242)

To claim something "cannot be denied" is to invite denial, but the appeal to Protestantism and to scripture cannot in fact be denied by the Protestant Parliamentarian. The rejection of denial tends, then, to carry with it affirmation of the "illumination of the Holy Spirit" and set the case for individual conscience in the affective as well as cognitive realms. Yet the invitation to deny remains an invitation. Affirmation is also choice. By setting the argument in these terms, Milton involves the reader actively in the exercise of free assent.

Milton relies on scripture as both a source – he returns to it conscientiously throughout *Civil Power* – and a model for all argument as well as for his plain style. In one of the key passages of the work he uses biblical statements to confirm a definition of Christian liberty that he has been inviting throughout: the inviolability of the individual conscience:

> I have shewn that the civil power hath neither right nor can do right by forcing religious things: I will now shew the wrong it doth; by violating the fundamental privilege of the gospel, the new-birthright of everie true beleever, Christian libertie. 2 *Cor.* 3. 17. *where the spirit of the Lord is, there is libertie. Gal.* 4. 26. *Jerusalem which is above, is free; which is the mother of us all.* and 31. *we are not children of the bondwoman but of the free.* (VII.262)

Freedom is a gift of the spirit and characteristic of the regenerate. By linking free conscience solidly to the Gospel, Milton invites his reader to test not only the author's logic, but the reader's own sense of grace. As Milton makes the distinction between the legalism of the Old Testament and the evangelism of the New, he presents his view of Christian liberty as not merely right but, for the regenerate Christian, imperative:

> [God] hath not only given us this gift as a special privilege and excellence of the free gospel above the servile law, but strictly also hath commanded us to keep it and enjoy it. *Gal.* 5. 13. *you are calld to libertie.* 1 *Cor.* 7. 23 *be not made the servants of men. Gal.* 5. 14. *stand fast therfore in the libertie wherwith Christ hath made us free; and be not intangl'd again with the yoke of bondage.* (VII.263–4)

One may always reject God's call, and Milton's; one may always elect away from the path of the elect. But the interlinking of Milton's argument with the doctrine of election will be difficult for the Christian to reject without thought and the conscious choosing that already enacts the freedom Milton argues for.

Civil Power's simple diction along with relatively paratactic structure continue to invoke the authority of scriptural style, while Milton moves his reader through biblical passages to knowledge:

> What I argue, shall be drawn from the scripture only; and therin from true fundamental principles of the gospel; to all knowing Christians

undeniable. And if the governors of this commonwealth since the rooting out of prelats have made least use of force in religion, and most have favord Christian liberty of any in this Iland before them since the first preaching of the gospel ... they may, I doubt not, in this treatise finde that which not only will confirm them to defend still the Christian liberty which we enjoy, but will incite them also to enlarge it. (VII.241)

Key terms in this passage are "knowing Christians," which assumes the individual responsibility learning conveys, as well as the learning itself, and "incite them also to enlarge it," which assumes both that a compatible idea of liberty is already in the culture, and that the rhetorician's role is to provoke rather than demand assent.

Two things should be noted about Milton's appeal to the authority of scripture. The first is that scripture is brought in to give weight to an assent already invited on other grounds; it is the stamp on, not the precondition for, consent to Milton's definitions and emphases. Second, Milton uses scripture radically, to help him redefine cultural assumptions about liberty and freedom. What were traditionally words that defined a social condition (freedom versus slavery or citizenship versus villeinage) had by the sixteenth century become associated with the particular character of English citizenship, which gave social responsibility to a wide range of the citizenry.[12] Not until the English Civil Wars, however, were the terms "liberty" and "freedom" associated with dissent in any serious way. One need only compare the limited notion of freedom of speech in Elizabethan times with the one Milton expounds in *Areopagitica* or Gerrard Winstanley claims in *The True Levellers Standard Advanced* (1649).[13]

Both the view of freedom and the confirming use of scripture help set Milton's work against that of his opponents. Until the 1640s, freedom was the citizen's right to participate, under the law, in affirming and maintaining public order.[14] The idea of the law was central to English self-definitions as a free people, a point evident throughout *The Mirror for Magistrates* and *Faerie Queene* v. (Lucifera in *Faerie Queene* I.iv.12 is instantly identified as a tyrant, since she "Ne ruld her Realmes with lawes, but pollicie," or personal whim.) The appeal to law remained central to Sir Henry Spelman's *The Larger Treatise Concerning Tithes* (1647), one of several pamphlets supporting tithes to which *Likeliest Means* was a response. Probably written around 1628, when the Petition of Right became yet another major assertion of the free Englishman's belief in law, the pamphlet is introduced in 1647 by Jeremy Stephens, who underscores the legalistic argument in "To the Reader": laws enjoining tithing "being thus setled and confirmed, and thereby becomming fundamentall Laws of the Kingdome, they may, and ought to be enjoyed peaceably, without grudging, repining, alienation or spoil."[15] The pamphlet proper is legalistic in the most old-fashioned way, defining duties between man and God, between citizen and church, as forms of feudal hierarchical reciprocity: "we shall pay duelly unto him, all rights and duties, that belong unto his Seignory."[16] Spelman emphasizes the evolution of law from the law of nature (or "Morall" law) and from scripture and tradition ("Leviticall" law), and so reinforces traditional assumptions about hierarchy and authority (sig. N2). The issue of freedom of conscience does not arise, since Spelman's construct is a closed system of feudal reciprocity. God/Lord owns all; out of love he gives a portion to man/vassal, who from natural and legal duty and responsibility returns a portion (the tithe) to God/Lord, the gracious source of the gift.

The tone of Spelman's treatise is confident and assured. Its argument is explicit, with categories of discussion clearly announced and followed. He teaches from cultural authority, in a world where the dominant ideology is still (in the 1620s) unquestionably hierarchic and authoritarian, and the citizen's liberty tied to obedience to laws which are conceived on feudal property models. William Prynne, writing in 1653, illustrates in his pro-tithing pamphlet some of the breakdown in certainty into which Milton is able to place his rejection of traditional authority and to invite the free conscience to exercise judgment and choice. Prynne's long title says most of it: *A Gospel Plea (Interwoven with a Rational and Legal) for the Lawfulnes & Continuance of the Ancient Setled Maintenance and Tenthes Of the Ministers of the Gospel Proving, That there is a Just, Competent, Comfortable Maintenance due to all Lawfull painfull Preachers and Ministers of the Gospel, by Divine Right ... That the present opposition against Tithes, proceeds not from any reall grounds of Conscience, but base covetousnesse, Carnall policy, &c. and a Jesuiticall and Anabaptisticall designe, to subvert and ruin our Ministers, Church, Religion.* After this, there hardly seems any need to read the pamphlet.

Notice that in Prynne's title "Rational and Legal" are prominent, but parenthetical to the "Gospel Plea," and conscience is indeed a force, but one denied to the opponents of tithing, whose motives are impugned (one can't help but wonder what the "&c." after "Carnall policy" refers to) and whose "designe" is attributed to an odd lumping of the extremes of right and left wing as they were then perceived. If Spelman's style is calculatedly rational, Prynne's brims with enthusiastic indignation, in which groups (usually triads) of synonyms are designed to overwhelm the reluctant:

Hence it followes by necessary Consequences, (and let those who are guilty Consider it seriously in the fear of God with trembling and astonishment) that the opposing, oppressing, defrauding the Ministers of the Gospell in their deserved setled hire, wages; or the detaining all, or any part of their ancient, just, established Dues, Tithes, or Revenues from them (especially out of covetousnesse, spite, obstinacy, or malice against their very callings) is as great, as crying, as damnable a sin, oppression, unrighteousnesse; and will bring down as grievous curses,

plagues, judgements on all those who are culpable thereof; as the
defrauding, oppression of the hired servant or labourer, of or in his
hire, or detaining their wages from them, when due; as will
undeniably appear by *Deut.* 24.14, 15. *Levit.* 19.13. *Gen.* 31.7. *Mal.*
3.5. *Jam.* 4.1, to 5. Compared with *Mal.* 3.8, 9, 10, 11. *Nehem.* 13. 10.
11. and a sin against all these Scriptures; which all detainers of
Ministers Dues and Tithes, may do well to read and ponder.   (sig. B4)

Notice that as the lists of nouns and modifiers are lumped together to form
verbal bludgeons, biblical references are similarly grouped. This contrasts
with Milton's choice of interspersing pertinent biblical references with
specific arguments. There is no less reliance on the Bible, but Milton always
intertwines his authority with rational discourse and a variety of rhetorical
techniques.[17]

From Spelman to Prynne the terms of the debate have shifted, but *Civil
Power* and *Likeliest Means* respond both to the old legalistic and new
bombastic arguments with almost equal distance. Elective poetics eschews
both the hierarchical categorizing of Spelman's style and the relentless verbal
battering of Prynne's. Both Spelman and Prynne demand assent, the one by
tradition and reason, the other by force. Milton uses interrogative syntax,
litotes, clusters of association, and scripture to discredit tradition, and avoids
the rhetorical thundering and semantic diffusion of an appositional style. It
may well be the shrillness of his opponents, and indeed his own forays into
name-calling and bombast in the earlier antiprelatical tracts, that has led
Milton at last to the restraint, both in vocabulary and syntax, that Corns finds
in the later pamphlets (excepting, of course, *The Readie and Easie Way*).
Milton adds to his stylistic arsenal what Fish defines as the dialectical rather
than the rhetorical mode; this change in his prose style is consistent with
Milton's development of a poetics that depends on invitation and on the
invocation, if not the direct presentation, of multiple points of view.[18]

The intellectual battle to shift the meaning of liberty, from social responsibility and freedom from civic disorder on the one hand, to the right of
individual conviction on the other, was by no means won in Milton's time,
nor indeed immediately after it. His genius is to recognize that liberty of that
sort begins with and depends upon individual assent to its fundamental truth,
and *Civil Power* brings together argument, authority of scripture, and the
techniques of invitation fundamental to elective poetics, to begin the process
in the individual, if not in society (despite the nominal address to Parliament).

Likeliest Means completes Milton's case for the separation of church and
state, and continues his effort to invite redefinition of liberty. He reminds the
reader of the plan set out in *Civil Power*, that he would argue against "force on
the one hand restraining, and hire on the other side corrupting the teachers"
of truth, the former in the earlier pamphlet and the latter in this one. Of these
issues, "the latter . . . is by much the more dangerous: for under force, though

no thank to the forcers, true religion oft-times best thrives and flourishes: but the corruption of teachers, most commonly the effect of hire, is the very bane of truth in them who are so corrupted" (VII.277).

Litotes again help set the tone, again in a context that asserts individual liberty: "in these matters wherin every Christian hath his free suffrage, [it is] *no way misbecoming* [to] Christian meeknes to offer freely ... such advice as God shall incline him and inable him to propound" (VII.278; my italics). The double negatives nod at his opponents' concern about fallen human pride and self-assertion and at the issue of authority generally, but for Milton authority resides in the individual's relationship to God, and the interiority of that relationship ("incline ... and inable"), rather than on formal education or the trappings of patristic learning. Milton resumes his tutorial in this posture of accessible humility.

The structure of Milton's argument in *Likeliest Means* is also among his most direct and accessible. The teacher proposes that "we consider, first, what recompence God hath ordaind should be given to ministers of the Church; ... next by whom; and lastly, in what manner" (VII.280–1). Despite Milton's clear didactic mode, a central premise of *Likeliest Means* is that truth cannot be imposed from without but must be discovered, and the authoritarian regimes of state or even university sponsorship deflect rather than promote true ministry. The clarity of the pedagogical stance on the one hand, and the rejection of external authority on the other, make a delicate balance. The pamphlet's brilliance lies in the light touch it brings to the authorities it cites, from scripture (even this sparingly quoted for such controversies), to the early church fathers, to the Waldensian pre-reformation simplicities, to his readers' contemporary experience of homely church functions from baptism to preaching.

There are a good many parallels with *Civil Power*, including the argument that the change from old to new "dispensations" is a change from constraint to liberty: "under the law [God] gave [church-ministers] tithes; under the gospel, having left all things in his church to charity and Christian freedom, he hath given them only what is justly given them," which Milton asserts to be situational, not locked into a tithing system (VII.281). The minister's hire should be the ungrudging free gift of his congregation. As individual conscience must consent freely to doctrine and worship, according to the argument in *Civil Power*, so in *Likeliest Means* churches must gather freely and freely support their ministers, in what amounts to a Christian version of social contract. "The Christian church is universal; not ti'd to nation, dioces or parish, but consisting of many particular churches complete in themselves; gatherd, not by compulsion or the accident of dwelling nigh together, but by free consent.... Wheras if tithes be set up, all these Christian privileges will be disturbd and soone lost, and with them Christian libertie" (VII.292). Ministers should be maintained by those who choose them "for thir teacher ... wherin to ban them thir choise, is to violate Christian liberty" (VII.301).

Milton is strategically open about his appeal to radical Protestantism, especially in his frequent invocation of the example of "the *Waldenses*, our first reformers," whose ministry was supported by alms:

> If then by almes and benevolence, not by legal force, not by tenure or freehold or copyhold: for almes, though just, cannot be compelld; and benevolence forc'd, is malevolence rather, violent and inconsistent with the gospel; and declares him no true minister therof, but a rapacious hireling rather, who by force receiving it, eats the bread of violence and exaction. (VII.311)

The metaphor carries power in part because it is so unusual in this plain-style pamphlet and in part because it shakes the reader by its appeal to the authority of a freely-associating community rather than to patristic tradition and learned arguments.

The work's main authority, however, comes not from citation or any overt authorial claim, but from the simplicity with which radical ideas are assumed: "that the magistrate ... should take into his own power the stipendiarie maintenance of church-ministers or compell it by law, can stand neither with the peoples right nor with Christian liberty, but would suspend the church wholly upon the state, and turn her ministers into state-pension-ers" (VII.307). Milton here makes tacit what very few writers, himself most notably and most recently among them, have explicitly asserted – the profound separation between civil and divine ordination and governance. On one level it is argument by insinuation, but on another it is an invitation to an altered world view.

As in *Paradise Regained*, where Satan seeks to play off the assumption that human happiness resides in comfort, Hellenistic learning, and power, but is confronted in response by the simplicity of Christ's trust in God, so all the complex manipulations of Spelman and the powerful bombast of Prynne give way to the simple centrality of the individual conscience in its primary relationship with the divine. In *Civil Power* and especially in *Likeliest Means*, Milton has learned to present simplicity and directness as vehicles for choice. This is a lesson he carries with him to all the great poems, but especially to *Paradise Regained*.

Likeliest Means, then, has the virtues of good plain-style poetry that we tend to associate with Jonson and some of Herbert: simple diction, direct syntax, clear rhetorical structure, limited conceits. Rhetorical force comes precisely because the occasional metaphor is set against the apparently transparent language that surrounds it. So the passage that assumes separation between civil and divine goes on to invite emotional assent:

> And for the magistrate in person of a nursing father to make the church his meer ward ... her to subject to his political drifts or conceivd opinions by mastring her revenue, and so by his examinant

committies to circumscribe her free election of ministers, is neither just nor pious ... and upon her, whose only head is in heaven ... sets another in effect, and, which is most monstrous, a human on a heavenly, a carnal on a spiritual, a political head on an ecclesiastical bodie; which at length by such heterogeneal, such incestuous conjunction, transformes her oft-times into a beast of many heads and many horns.   (VII. 307–8)

These are techniques from a poet who had early thought of his prose as capable of "high *strains*" (I.616), and who has here set those strains into a subtle poetic of the middle kind.

With passages such as these, a reader who has been following the clear path of Milton's argument must pause and examine the intricacies of a denser rhetorical thicket. "Nursing father" demands from the outset a shifted perspective, sophisticated interpretation, and difficult semantic choices. From this image the pyrotechnic transformations of the carnal and political "head" to an image of the apocalyptic antichrist follow with an emotional logic that nonetheless demands intellectual understanding. Milton insists that merit is not coincident with a sophisticated education (VII.316–17), but the "knowing Christian" is one who can interpret contextually.

III

Milton was an effective rhetorician, whether in eloquent style or plain, and some of what I have called elective poetics may be found in any good poetic: subtlety, complexity, dialogic engagement with the reader. What is interesting about the later pamphlets is Milton's ability to manipulate those elements in even his most translucent prose and, in that context, show plainly how much he relied on his reader's ability to choose beyond current ideological assumptions. Milton creates distance between his text and cultural norms, and so at least initially between the text and the reader, in order to invite the reader to take a leap of faith toward redefinition. Once that leap is made, the reward is a mutual affirmation of the liberating principle of free choice. This is the special quality of elective poetics.

Repetition alone will not recast meaning, but persistent repetition in new or unexpected contexts breaks down old assumptions and invites new ones. As Milton repeats versions of "free" and "liberty" fifty-two times in *Civil Power* and fifty-nine times in *Likeliest Means*, in consistently alien contexts, he makes clear the distance these words have from traditional signification and he invites the reader to recast thought. Caught with Milton's words between traditional ideology and the affirmation of change, the reader is offered a choice between a constraining world view and Milton's liberating vision. The offer is a function of the convergence of topic, argument, diction, and the space between statement and authority – what Fish refers to as Milton's placing a subject before the reader "and going away."[19] It is not the text that is destabilized, but the reader and cultural ideology.

What Milton finally effects in *Civil Power* and *Likeliest Means* is a new union of three concepts – religion, conscience, and liberty: "Whence I here mean by conscience or religion that full perswasion whereby we are assur'd that our beleef and practise, as far as we are able to apprehend and probably make appeer, is according to the will of God & his Holy Spirit" (VII.242). "And where ought this equity [of free debate] to have more place, then in the libertie which is unseparable from Christian religion?" (VII.278). These equations between conscience and religion, liberty and conscience, religion and liberty, are implicit as well as explicit throughout both treatises. They are presented with such assurance that eventually liberty becomes routinely divine, routinely the single central calling for God's people. He who would be among the elect must choose liberty, and in so choosing exercise the liberty his calling requires.

Milton's elective poetics, plainly presented in these late pamphlets, prepare his readers for the central issues of *Paradise Lost*, *Paradise Regained*, and *Samson Agonistes*, which in each case are concerned with knowledge, choice, and vocation. Perhaps more importantly, they insist upon the primacy of individual choice, including the reader's interpretive choices in the face of textual authority. "If Christians would but know thir own dignitie, thir libertie, thir adoption ... thir spiritual priesthood, whereby they have all equally access to any ministerial function whenever calld by thir own abilities and the church," then the world truly would turn upside down. But without that willingness to trust conscience or "inward perswasion," to see religion in individual terms, and to accept the invitation to liberty that Milton's text offers, they "will be alwaies learning and never knowing, alwaies infants," instead of the "free men" they are called to be (VII.320).

As with the later poems, these pamphlets offer examples of the core paradox of Milton's poetic stance: the reader is invited to accept the truth and the authority of Milton's call to freedom, but only by rejecting authoritative pronouncements and only if the reader's conscience is persuaded to choose this truth. If we are left in *Paradise Lost* wondering at the dynamic of Satan's energy, or in *Paradise Regained* at the apparent passivity of divine self-knowledge, or in *Samson Agonistes* at the human complexity of the hero's motives, we are continually taught to think in new ways, trust our "assur'd" and "full perswasion," and be free.

Notes

1 *British Pamphleteers*, vol. 1, *From the Sixteenth Century to the French Revolution*, ed. George Orwell and Reginald Reynolds (London, 1948), "Introduction," p. 15.
2 See Ann E. Imbrie, "Defining Nonfiction Genres," in *Renaissance Genres: Essays on Theory, History, and Interpretation*, ed. Barbara K. Lewalski (Cambridge, Mass.,

1986), pp. 45–69. "For Renaissance writers, a literary intention is registered primarily in the choice of generic form" (p. 46).

3 Harold Bloom, *The Anxiety of Influence* (New York, 1973). T. S. Eliot's "Tradition and the Individual Talent" (1917) is the standard non-Marxist expression of cultural dialectic in literature. On generic transformation, see Rosalie Colie, *The Resources of Kind: Genre-Theory in the Renaissance* (Berkeley, 1973), and Alastair Fowler, *Kinds of Literature: An Introduction to the Theory of Genres and Modes* (Cambridge, Mass., 1982), pp. 9, 179–83, and *passim*.

4 David Norbrook, *Poetry and Politics in the English Renaissance* (London, 1984), p. 6.

5 Virginia Mollenkott has shown that Milton routinely presents his readers with multiple choices, though she does not focus on the freedom question:

> Milton's technique of multiple choice is an excellent symbol of the transitional age in which he lived, when many things no longer seemed as certain as they once had been. It is also an excellent archetype for the labyrinthine ambiguities of human experience in a fallen world. Sometimes Milton used multiple choice to avoid committing himself on issues where he himself was doubtful; sometimes to recognize the mysteries of the universe; sometimes to make his plot more intriguing; sometimes to create a bridge between Hebraic mythological exclusiveness and Hellenic richness; and sometimes to provide ironic commentary on the human condition. *But always the technique has the effect of drawing the reader into more active participation through choice.*
>
> ("Milton's Technique of Multiple Choice,"
> *Milton Studies*, 6 (1974), p. 111; my italics.)

6 Jonathan Goldberg, *Endlesse Worke: Spenser and the Structures of Discourse* (Baltimore, 1981); Stanley Fish, *Self-Consuming Artifacts: The Experience of Seventeenth-Century Literature* (Berkeley, 1971), pp. 1–4.

7 From *Complete Prose Works of John Milton* as noted at the beginning of this book. References to the poetry will be from *John Milton: Complete Poems and Major Prose*, ed. Merritt Y. Hughes (New York, 1957).

8 Joseph Wittreich summarizes the difficulties critics have had with *Samson*'s complexities and ambiguities, in *Interpreting Samson Agonistes* (Princeton, 1986), pp. x–xxiii and 3–52.

9 *The Development of Milton's Prose Style* (Oxford, 1982).

10 *The Politics of Milton's Prose Style* (New Haven, 1975), p. 113: "Form embodies abstract ideal to the detriment of concrete political meaning." Stavely goes on to quote Allen Grossman approvingly: "The limits of [Milton's] poetic style which Eliot saw very clearly and the limits of his rational apologetic are seen in the effort, which Marvell intuited in him, to exchange mind (as language) for world, rather than submit to the evidence of final complexity in historical experience" (p. 115).

11 Barbara K. Lewalski, "Milton: Political Beliefs and Polemical Methods, 1659–60," *PMLA*, 74 (1959), pp. 191–202.

12 The last villeinage case, against a man named Pigg, was tried in 1618. When Pigg was found free it effectively eliminated villeinage once and for all and confirmed the English subjects' long-standing cultural self-congratulation for being "free men" at all social levels. See Conrad Russell, *The Crisis of Parliaments: English History 1509–1660* (Oxford, 1971), p. 13.

13 In *The Mirror for Magistrates'* first "tragedy," that of "Robert Tresilian," free speech is assumed for parliamentary debate, but not otherwise; in the *Mirror's* "Poet Collingbourne" it is a privilege of fictive disguise. The "Diggers" that Winstanley represents based their essentially communist social and economic theory in part on more radical ideas of civil freedom and in part on a radical reading of the Bible's support for human equality: "not one word was spoken in the beginning, That one branch of mankind should rule over another . . . England is not a Free People, till the Poor that have no Land, have a free allowance to dig and labour the Commons, and so live as Comfortably as the Landlords that live in their Inclosures." In Orwell and Reynolds, *British Pamphleteers*, pp. 121, 125.

14 Joel Hurstfield, *Freedom, Corruption and the Government in Elizabethan England* (Cambridge, Mass., 1973), "Introduction: The Boundaries of Freedom," pp. 11–19, and "The Paradox of Liberty in Shakespeare's England," pp. 50–76. For a background to these attitudes, see Wallace MacCaffrey, *The Shaping of the Elizabethan Regime* (Princeton, 1968).

15 Henry Spelman, *The Larger Treatise Concerning Tithes* (London, 1647), sig. B4.

16 Spelman, sig. B2, mislabeled A2 in the 1647 edn.

17 Milton's perspective and style are of course much closer to those he admires, such as Sir Henry Vane. See, e.g., Vane's attack on episcopacy, *Speech in the House of Commons, at a Committee for the Bill against Episcopall Government . . . June 11. 1641* (London, 1641): "Thus have they not contented themselves with encroachments upon our spirituall priviledges, but have envied us our Civill freedome, desiring to make us grind in their mills, as the *Philistines* did *Sampson*, and to put out both our eyes" (sigs. B1–v). Even so, Vane's trust in a divinely guided theocracy is beyond Milton's trust in human magistracy, as in Vane's *The Retired Mans Meditations, or the Mysterie and Power of Godlines* (London, 1655): "Magistracy may be preserved in its lawful use and exercise, as a *faithful servant waiting for the coming of the Lord*; and the persons exercising that authority are to be accounted as the Ministers of God to us for our good" (sig. Aa3). Though Vane asserts the centrality of individual conscience and the importance of reason, his view of free will is less radical than Milton's.

18 Fish, *Self-Consuming Artifacts*, pp. 1–2; see also his chapter on Milton's "Reason in *The Reason of Church Government*," pp. 265–302. Fish has a different point to make in this chapter, but a number of his conclusions are compatible with my view of Milton's invitation to reader choice: "*The Reason of Church Government* . . . is a serious joke, which in the course of discrediting one kind of logic, makes use (almost surreptitiously) of another, a logic of association" (p. 271); one of Milton's statements about "Prelaty" "is less a statement than a strategy. Rather than passing judgment on Prelacy, it transfers the responsibility for judging to the reader by placing the defendant before him and going away" (p. 286).

19 Fish, *Self-Consuming Artifacts*, p. 286.

11

Milton's *The Readie and Easie Way* and the English jeremiad

LAURA LUNGER KNOPPERS

Milton's late prose tract *The Readie and Easie Way to Establish a Free Commonwealth* (1660) presents a number of critical cruxes. Milton argues that his proposed ready and easy way for a Commonwealth, now seasonably adopted, will preserve civil and religious liberty in England. But he writes on the eve of the Restoration of Charles II, and, as the certainty of Restoration increases, he revises, expands, and reissues the tract.[1] We have to ask, then, why does he write? What does he hope to accomplish? The question of purpose is complicated by Milton's own shifting assertions as to audience and aim, and by biblical allusion and imagery which seem counter to his persuasive end. Seen simply as an occasional argument, Milton's tract may seem ambivalent, futile, and even foolhardy. But a closer look at the generic complexity of the work reveals a more self-conscious and creative response to political crisis.

My argument is that Milton's voice, vision, style, and purpose in *The Readie and Easie Way* are clarified by recognizing the tract as a jeremiad, a prophetic lament over the apostasy of a chosen nation. Milton appropriates and boldly reworks the conventions of the genre, as developed in English jeremiads over the Good Old Cause of the Commonwealth in 1659. As a jeremiad, *The Readie and Easie Way* does not merely address the immediate situation to persuade the English to change their political course; it also gives meaning and value to that political crisis, providing a myth by which they can interpret the impending doom. Milton gives witness against the chosen nation; his jeremiad becomes uniquely self-authenticating, his final warning a performative utterance.

I

The conventions of the jeremiad in American Puritan writings have been defined by Perry Miller and revised and elaborated by Sacvan Bercovitch.[2] The jeremiad is a prophetic lament over the decline of a covenant nation. The speaker of the jeremiad assumes the authority and stance of the Old Testament prophets, looking to past ideal, present sin, and future judgment or blessing. The speaker depicts his nation by analogy, allusion, or metaphor as the new Israel, calling the nation to repent for violation of its covenant with God. Bercovitch sees in American jeremiads a distinctive duality: divine chastisement paradoxically attests not to New England's doom but to her election and errand.

Bercovitch's view that the jeremiad, thus defined, is unique to American Puritanism has been widely and uncritically accepted. But closer examination reveals that the jeremiad was also used by English Puritans in the period of the Civil War and Interregnum. In England, as in America, the jeremiad developed in response to crises. Preachers before the Long Parliament in the mid-1640s weep with Jeremiah, call for repentance, and see God's "covenant-avenging sword" in the Civil War.[3] In the late 1650s, supporters of the Good Old Cause extend the jeremiad mode to nonsermonic forms, politicizing the genre as they employ jeremiad rhetoric to advocate political actions. A closer look at the jeremiads of 1659 will establish the previously unexamined generic features which Milton draws on in his own distinctive jeremiad.[4]

Most relevant for Milton's late tract are the jeremiads written in support of the Good Old Cause of the Commonwealth. These jeremiads respond to the various political crises of 1658–60 which lead up to the Restoration – the death of Oliver Cromwell, the succession of Oliver's son Richard, the dissolution of the Protectorate and restoration of the long-banished Rump Parliament, and the various maneuverings of the army, Parliament, and General Monck.[5] The jeremiad mode can be found not only in sermons, but in a variety of writings – political tracts, proclamations for fasting, letters to the army and the Parliament. The republican writers use the language of the jeremiad to interpret the various political crises; by bringing typological categories to bear they try to persuade their audience to repentance, often allied with a particular political agenda. Milton writes in more desperate circumstances, when impending parliamentary elections, in the face of overwhelming public sentiment for the return of monarchy, seem certain to bring a pro-Royalist Parliament and the Restoration of Charles II. Reapplying the jeremiad language to this most extreme political situation, Milton writes not only to persuade and warn but to be a witness before God and man.

The speakers of the English jeremiads, like their American counterparts, look to the stance, style, themes, and tropes of the Old Testament prophets as literary models. Many of the writers of jeremiads on the Good Old Cause in 1659 identify and amplify their own voices by association with such alienated prophets as Jeremiah, Hosea, and Ezekiel. Employing biblical paraphrase and allusion, these jeremiad speakers depict themselves as "watchmen," "remembrancers," or "witnesses" who warn the English of their sins. Calling the nation to a fast in *A Declaration of the Lord Protector*, the restored Rump Parliament take it "as a duty incumbent upon us, who are set upon the watchtower, to declare what we see."[6]

The jeremiad speakers act as much out of duty to God as from hope that the people will listen. Echoing Ezekiel 2:5, the preacher of *The Cause of God and of these Nations* (1659) sets out his aim "to give my witness against the Present Apostacy, *whether this Generation will hear, or whether they will forbear*" (sig. B1). This speaker witnesses to the people, pointing out to them their sin. But the jeremiad can also witness to God, against the people. *Vox Dei: The Voice of God to the Officers of the Army* (1659) presents "some precepts which the Lord set upon the Heart of a Poor Creature to shew unto them; the which if they obey not, will be one witness for God against them, that he left them not without Remembrancers" (title-page). The prophetic warning to the nation can thus serve to justify God's ways in the impending judgment, since the audience is more accountable. Like the earlier jeremiad writers, Milton defines his own voice, audience, and purpose in *The Readie and Easie Way* through association with the prophet Jeremiah. But Milton's handling of voice becomes more complex than in these earlier jeremiads as he moves well beyond a single persuasive end, to tell the story of the covenant nation.

The jeremiads on the Good Old Cause exemplify certain themes and conventions which Milton extends. These writers, following Jeremiah and other prophets, remind their audience of an ideal past from which they have fallen, denounce present-day sins, call for repentance, and predict future judgment or blessing. Underlying these generic themes is the assumption that England is the new covenant nation, analogue of Old Testament Israel. The jeremiad in England, as in America, often strategically provides assurance by threat: divine chastisement, corrective not destructive, reaffirms the nation's covenant errand.

The English jeremiads, like the American, recall past blessings to denounce present sins, often using biblical language and allusive imagery. One recurrent trope for spiritual decline is the metaphor of going back to Egypt. A Postscript to *A Second Narrative of the Late Parliament* (1659) calls upon the "apostate" supporters of the Protectorate to repent, "lest the Judgments of the Lord break in upon you, as upon backsliding *Israel* of old, and your Carcasses fall in the Wilderness, &c. as theirs did, for making, and then dancing about the *Moulten* Calf, and their desiring to make a Captain to return to *Egypt*" (p. 44). The biblical allusion, about choosing a Captain to go back to Egypt (Numb. 14:4), recalls the murmuring Israelites under Moses, who for their lack of faith were condemned to wander and die in the wilderness, although their children did enter the promised land. The jeremiad writer hereby threatens his audience in typological language that attests to their elect status. *A Short Discourse Concerning the Work of God in this Nation* (1659) more explicitly uses the metaphor of returning to Egypt to reassure by threat: "the Lord in great goodness and wisdom (though also in judgment and displeasure) let some of us run back towards *Egypt* into the Wilderness, and chastened others by the strokes of their own Brethren; that thus he might shew us what was in our hearts" (p. 2). As we shall see, Milton draws on and extends this journey trope, but emphasizes, more pessimistically, the unstoppable rush and the irreversible consequences.

Like the biblical prophets, the jeremiad speakers for the Good Old Cause urge their audience to repent and reform of their many sins. One biblical metaphor they often use is that of repentance as a return to the good way, echoing Jeremiah 6:16, "Thus saith the Lord, Stand ye in the ways, and see, and ask for the old paths, where is the good way and walk therein, and ye shall find rest for your souls." *A Call to the Officers of the Army* (1659) pleads: "Be not displeased then, that we call upon you to stand in the good old way, and to return into that path, where the Lord met you and owned you, and displayed his marvellous loving kindnesses, and his triumphant excellencies before your eyes" (p. 50). Milton uses this jeremiad language in defining his ready and easy way, but, unlike the earlier jeremiad writers, he defines the way as a single political action – under circumstances in which it seems certain to fail.

Finally, these English jeremiads prophesy future blessing or judgment, contingent on the repentance of the people. Underlying the prophecy is the assumption of a conditional covenant between God and the nation, based on such texts as Jeremiah 18:8, "If that nation, against whom I have pronounced, turn from their evil, I will repent of the evil that I thought to do unto them." Sometimes this repentance is evinced by a particular political action, although the emphasis is on its moral and spiritual significance. *The Humble Representation of divers well-affected Persons* (1659) asserts that if the army restores the Rump Parliament, "the Lord will yet delight to dwell in the midst of you, and will make you a further blessing to this Commonwealth, and specially to his own peculiar People" (p. 5). But if "after all these shaking and stupendious Providences," the army fails to repent (and restore the Rump), God will "visit by some remarkable Judgment or other, for this perpetual Backsliding from Him and his Cause" (p. 5). Milton also prophesies future judgment or blessing, but with a shift in focus to the people's sin as its own punishment.

In looking to the future, the speakers of these late jeremiads, like the biblical prophets, hope for a saving remnant. The speaker of *The Cause of God* believes that "God hath a remnant among you, whom He will lead on to farther things; but it will be *with weeping and supplications*, with great brokennesse of heart, and poverty of spirit" (p. 28). The remnant depends on both human and divine action; there is an underlying duality or even tension in the jeremiad between the need for human action and its impossibility without divine aid. Milton's tract reflects this tension, as he stresses his own performative action, yet predicates his argument on past and future divine intervention.

The 1659 jeremiads attempt to explain the political and moral failure of England and yet maintain the ideology of the elect nation. These jeremiads continue and extend the politicizing of the 1640s Parliament sermons – deploying typological language to interpret the immediate political crises, to persuade not only to repentance but to political action. The jeremiad speakers are increasingly alienated and pessimistic, envisioning not general repentance but a saving remnant. Still, through explicit argument and biblical allusion they support the election of England and the continuation of her covenant mission. Stress falls on persuasion, and, indeed, the jeremiad tracts denouncing the Protectorate and calling for the return of the Rump did seem to have some influence on public opinion and even on political events.[7]

II

In early 1660 Milton writes alone, in greater personal danger, and seemingly with much less hope of influence than earlier jeremiad writers. Like his predecessors, he brings typological categories to bear on the immediate situation, to persuade his audience, and to interpret and universalize particular events. But his reworking of the style, subject matter, themes, and conventions of the jeremiad makes *The Readie and Easie Way* a far more pessimistic and threatening work, as well as one which seems finally more concerned to tell the story of the English people, than hopeful of preserving that people from destruction. Milton's shift in aim, from action to telling the story, brings a distinctively literary quality to his jeremiad.

In his exordium, Milton establishes through authorial stance and biblical allusion the generic context of *The Readie and Easie Way*. He first asserts that he writes "to remove, if it be possible, this noxious humor of returning to bondage, instilld of late by som deceivers, and nourishd from bad principles and fals apprehensions among too many of the people" (VII.407–8). Like earlier jeremiad speakers, Milton depicts himself as alienated from the people; but his isolation is even more complete in that, unlike them, he is now alone in opposing the "deceivers," or false prophets. Milton's allusive language, "returning to bondage," links his audience with backsliding Israel and himself with the Old Testament prophets. His audience initially seems to be the people and the Parliament they will elect. But his shifting rhetorical stance is indicated even in the exordium, when he gives a second, different aim for writing. He implies not persuasion but prophecy, a purpose fulfilled in the act of speaking: "If thir absolute determination be to enthrall us, before so long a Lent of Servitude, they may permitt us a little Shroving-time first, wherin to speak freely, and take our leaves of Libertie" (VII.408–9). His stance shifts from argument to the literary and prophetic aims of lament and farewell. His audience now seems to be fellow republicans ("us") and, implicitly, God, before whom he will confess. Milton indicates already in the exordium that his reasons for writing go beyond trying to change the immediate situation.

As a jeremiad speaker, Milton looks at past, present, and future to remind the chosen nation of her obligations; but he uniquely focuses on a single political agenda. Unlike many earlier jeremiad speakers, he denounces not a range of sins but a single political wrong – the desire to return to kingship – using the trope of return to Egypt to judge that desire as moral and spiritual apostasy. Milton uses the trope of backsliding in a more sustained and resonant way than the earlier jeremiads. He asserts that for England to disregard divine deliverance, "to fall back or rather to creep back so poorly as it seems the multitude would to thir once abjur'd and detested thraldom of Kingship . . . not only argues a strange degenerate contagion suddenly spread among us fitted and prepar'd for new slaverie, but will render us a scorn and derision to all our neighbours" (VII.421–2). Intensifying the backsliding metaphor with a number of vivid verbs, Milton underscores the rash, misguided backward movement. "Flying now to regal concessions," the English are "treading back again with lost labour all our happie steps in the progress of reformation" (VII.423–4). "Insensible and unworthie of those high mercies," they are "returning precipitantly, if he withold us not, back to the captivitie from whence he freed us" (VII.450). The accumulative force of these strong verbs and images, the impression of an irrational stampede, undermines any facile optimism about persuading the people. Milton's imagery reveals what he does not say: the near-impossibility of stopping the backsliding people.

Milton's use of the trope of backsliding, as he moves from present to future, conveys a new threat, rather than the implicit assurance we have seen in earlier jeremiads. Once returned to kingship, the English are "never like to attain thus far as we are now advanc'd to the recoverie of our freedom, never to have it in possession as we now have it, never to be voutsaf't heerafter the like mercies and signal assistances from heaven in our cause, if by our ingratefull backsliding we make these fruitless" (VII.423). Increasingly, Milton implies the difference between England and Israel. The "gentilizing Israelites" who clamored for a king "had thir longing, but with this testimonie of God's wrath; *ye shall cry out in that day because of your king whom ye shall have chosen, and the Lord will not hear you in that day*" (VII.450). In returning to kingship, the English have gone beyond the sin of the Israelites: "How much less" Milton warns, "will he hear when we cry heerafter" (VII.450). Milton's warning is not against divine chastisement (ultimately corrective), but against divine desertion.

Milton also extends the backsliding trope by emphasizing that the English are rushing to bondage and slavery, represented metonymically by the yoke. For the English, after winning their liberty, "basely and besottedly to run their necks again into the yoke which they have broken, and prostrate all the fruits of thir victorie for naught at the feet of the vanquishd" (VII.428), will bring unique shame and bondage. In going beyond Israel's sin, England also goes beyond Israel's assurance, and so their action will be irreversible. Having brought back the king, they "never shall be able . . . to free themselves from any yoke impos'd upon them" (VII.449).

Finally, Milton combines the images of backsliding and the yoke to castigate the multitude of sins incorporated in that single political action:

> Let our zealous backsliders forethink now with themselves, how their necks yok'd with these tigers of Bacchus, these new fanatics of not the preaching, but the sweating-tub, inspir'd with nothing holier than the Venereal pox, can draw one way under monarchie to the establishing of church discipline with these new-disgorg'd atheismes: yet shall they not have the honor to yoke with these, but shall be yok'd under them; these shall plow on their backs. (VII.452–3)

Milton draws on the castigating language of the prophets – sexual impurity, disease, animal yoking, prostitution, vomit – to create powerful satire and invective.

Milton's central proposal of a perpetual Senate is given in the jeremiad language of the good old way; here, however, he rewrites the call for repentance as a call for a certain form of government. This plan of government is far more detailed than any contained in previous jeremiads, which sometimes linked repentance to a particular action, but primarily stressed the "conscience of the thing." Milton suggests a "general councel of ablest men, chosen by the people to consult of public affairs from time to time for the common good" (VII.432). Going against prevailing sentiment, he argues that "the Grand or General Councel being well chosen, should be perpetual" (VII.433) and sets out election procedures, composition of the council, distribution of power, and various safeguards. Why does Milton present and expand this detailed plan, especially when it is almost certain to be rejected? A closer look at the jeremiad conventions, I believe, will clarify this continuing enigma.

While Milton is clearly addressing his political plan to the immediate situation, the rhetorical frame gives that plan broader significance – and indicates Milton's stance. Milton's allusive language links his proposal with Jeremiah's call to return to the good old way: "the way propounded is plane, easie and open before us" (VII.445) or "I say again, this way lies free and smooth before us; is not tangl'd with inconveniencies; invents no new incumbrances" (VII.445). In using this jeremiad language of the good way, Milton implies the moral and spiritual value of political action. But he does not, as did virtually all jeremiad writers in 1659, explicitly call the nation to repentance. This change might indicate that Milton no longer expects realistically that the situation will be reversed; the English may be past the point where repentance can save the Commonwealth. His detailed plan, however, makes the nation more accountable. Milton points out that this scheme "can have no considerable objection made against it, that it is not practicable: least it be said hereafter, that we gave up our libertie for want of a readie way or distinct form propos'd of a free Commonwealth" (VII.446).

Much of *The Readie and Easie Way* looks to the future to foretell judgment or blessing, contingent on the actions of the covenant people. Unlike the earlier jeremiad writers, Milton does not detail divine chastisement; rather, he shows that the sin itself – return to kingship – becomes the punishment. He imagines the restoration of monarchy as a time of confusion, loss of liberty, revenges, and recriminations: "But not to speak more of losses and extraordinarie levies on our estates, what will then be the revenges and offences rememberd and returnd ... accounts and reparations that will be requir'd, suites, inditements, inquiries, discoveries, complaints, informations ... if not to utmost infliction, yet to imprisonment, fines, banishment, or molestation" (VII.450–1). Milton extends the politicizing of the jeremiad by focusing on earthly and political rewards and punishments. But he does suggest a link between material and spiritual: establishing the Senate will bring "peace, justice, plentifull trade and all prosperitie ... even to the coming of our true and rightfull and only to be expected King, only worthie as he is our only Saviour, the Messiah, the Christ" (VII.445).

III

In the body of *The Readie and Easie Way*, Milton proposes a specific political plan and castigates a political sin, using the jeremiad language of backsliding, the yoke, and the good old way. His stance and aim in this extreme political crisis, however, seem ambivalent. In his moving and eloquent peroration, Milton develops and more clearly defines his prophetic witness, and both states and shows the dual purpose of his prophetic discourse.

He again employs the trope of return to Egypt, but now wholly transforms the typological link which in earlier jeremiads served to assure as well as threaten, by recalling a later time in Old Testament history when the Jews returned to Egypt:

> if lastly, after all this light among us, the same reason shall pass for
> current to put our necks again under kingship, as was made use of by
> the *Jews* to returne back to *Egypt* and to the worship of thir idol
> queen, because they falsly imagined that they then livd in more plentie
> and prosperitie, our condition is not sound but rotten, both in religion
> and all civil prudence.   (VII.462)

The precise context which Milton here recalls has not, to my knowledge, been previously identified.[8] England is now compared to Israel at her point of greatest crisis – the time of Jeremiah, just after the total destruction of Jerusalem.

Some of the Jews under Jeremiah responded to divine chastisement not with repentance but with despair; they returned to what they saw as the plenty and protection of Egypt, forcing the old prophet Jeremiah to accompany them. Back in Egypt, they openly defied Jeremiah:

As for the word that thou hast spoken unto us in the name of the Lord, we will not hearken unto thee. But we will certainly do whatsoever thing goeth forth out of our own mouth, to burn incense unto the queen of heaven, and to pour out drink offerings unto her, as we have done ... for then had we plenty of victuals, and were well and saw no evil. But since we left off to burn incense to the queen of heaven, and to pour out drink offerings unto her, we have wanted all things, and have been consumed by the sword and by the famine.

(Jer. 44:16–18)

Chastisement should have served to bring these Jews back to Yahweh, but they refused to repent and became apostate. Milton's reference to the idol queen, I believe, alludes to this queen of heaven, mentioned only in Jeremiah, and thereby points to this specific context. In Egypt the Jews fell into worship of the idol queen and, in doing so, abrogated their covenant with Yahweh, bringing upon themselves the covenant curse: "Behold, I will watch over them for evil, and not for good: and all the men of Judah that are in the land of Egypt shall be consumed by the sword and by the famine, until there be an end of them" (Jer. 44:27). Not even a remnant remained.

Milton hereby underscores the very tenuous position of the English nation: in going back to the idolatry of kingship, they face the danger that even the remnant will be wiped out. Earlier, *The Readie and Easie Way* depicted kingship as idolatry: "a king must be ador'd like a Demigod" (VII.425), the people will be "deifying and adoring" him for "nothing don that can deserve it" (VII.426), and a king wrongly assumes "extraordinarie honour and worship to himself" (VII.429). Now the backsliding trope is extended to link England's idolatry with Israel's in a dire prediction of destruction: in this, Milton is much more pessimistic than were the earlier English jeremiads.

In comparing England's return to kingship with the Jews' impious and disastrous return to Egypt in Jeremiah's time, Milton reminds his contemporaries of the curse involved in covenant abrogation. Like Israel under Jeremiah, the English falsely imagine that they will gain "more plentie and prosperitie" from kingship. He again uses the metaphor of return to point out that following the pattern of the backsliding Jews "will bring us soon, the way we are marching, to those calamities which attend alwaies and unavoidably on luxurie, all national judgments under foreign or domestic slaverie: so far we shall be from mending our condition by monarchizing our government, whatever new conceit now possesses us" (VII.462).

Milton now makes more explicit his prophetic attitude and mission. Like earlier jeremiad speakers he sets out his duty, his speaking in season, his forewarning: "with all hazard I have ventur'd what I thought my duty to speak in season, and to forewarne my countrey in time" (VII.462). He implicitly points to the generic context of the jeremiad by self-consciously identifying with the writers on the Good Old Cause: "What I have spoken, is the language of that which is not call'd amiss *the good Old Cause*" (VII.462). His willingness to be associated with this much disparaged term, and his subsequent acknowledgment that such language may now seem "strange," indicates that he recognizes the extremity of the situation: "if it seem strange to any, it will not seem more strange, I hope, then convincing to backsliders" (VII.462). Earlier Milton has stated that he writes not to convince those "who past reason and recoverie are devoted to kingship" but to "confirm them who yield not" (VII.455). Yet he is not necessarily disingenuous here; as a prophet he will hold them accountable, despite his dwindling hope. His rhetorical purpose is far more complex than the usual persuasion of backsliders found in the earlier jeremiads.

After all this, Milton seems to topple his entire rhetorical structure by indicating that, even if he had no audience to listen, he would still have spoken. Like Jeremiah, he would speak if only to the earth: "Thus much I should perhaps have said though I were sure I should have spoken only to trees and stones; and had none to say to with the Prophet, *O earth, earth, earth!* to tell the very soil it self, what her perverse inhabitants are deaf to" (VII.463–4).[9] In this context, we see the inadequacy of simply asking what Milton hopes to accomplish. He would have written, he implies, even if he had no hope whatsoever of preventing the restoration. But why, then, would he have written? Milton aligns himself with the later Jeremiah, who, appealing to the earth as witness, brings the divine judgment against a reprobate people who have rejected the prophetic call to the good old way (Jer. 6:16–17). Deferring to biblical authority, Milton establishes his own. He does not speak but points to Jeremiah's words of judgment: "Hear, O earth; behold, I will bring evil upon this people, even the fruit of their thoughts, because they have not hearkened unto my words, nor to my law, but rejected it" (Jer. 6:19). Milton makes clear in the peroration that rejection of his proposed ready and easy way will bring down the covenant curse. The threat of abrogation goes well beyond the chastisement envisioned in earlier jeremiads.

Acting as divine witness against the nation, Milton recalls the covenant curse. He then gives a second option, another possible end for writing beyond the practical and immediate situation. He says he would have spoken "though what I have spoke, should happ'n (which Thou suffer not, who didst create mankinde free; nor Thou next, who didst redeem us from being servants of men!) to be the last words of our expiring libertie" (VII.463). Here he shifts from prophetic curse to lament and prayer, in which his despair over man's actions is tempered by faith that a reversal will be brought about by God.

Milton recalls the generic tradition of the jeremiad and its traditional persuasive end. But then he sets out two other options by which his duty is fulfilled in the act of speaking – calling down the covenant curse or bidding his last farewell to liberty. In these senses, then, his tract is a performative utterance; it is accomplished even as he speaks. His message, as regards the backsliding majority, is almost surely going to be disregarded; but in that "failure" this jeremiad is self-authenticating.

Milton pleads for the English to avoid the covenant curse in the words that will constitute the curse if ignored. But the final status of *The Readie and Easie Way* is contingent upon the reactions of the audience. As a prophet, Milton pleads one more time, both to persuade and to make the nation more accountable. He holds out hope that within his audience a remnant may be found: "but I trust I shall have spoken perswasion to abundance of sensible and ingenuous men: to som perhaps whom God may raise of these stones to become children of reviving libertie; and may reclaim, though they seem now chusing them a captain back for *Egypt*, to bethink themselves a little and consider whether they are rushing" (VII.463). Milton's hope for a remnant reflects the duality or tension underlying his entire discourse. On one level, he pleads with "sensible and ingenuous men" to "bethink themselves"; on another level, he despairs over human action and hopes that God will "raise" a remnant from "these stones." The opposed descriptions – one positing human action, one divine – reflect a duality at the heart of prophetic witness: the prophet may despair over the people, but he must continue to call the nation to account. Milton again aligns England with Israel; "chusing them a Captain back for *Egypt*," the English may be like the Israelites under Moses who incur punishment, but are reclaimed. Or they may indeed backslide, as did the Jews under Jeremiah, to their own destruction. By once again alluding to the earlier biblical context (Numb. 14), Milton offers the English a last option: they may not be doomed to go back.

But while Milton's argument concludes with hope for a remnant, the imagery of the final paragraph conveys instead the force of the heedless, headlong multitude. We have seen earlier that the reiteration and accumulative force of the backsliding images give a sense of rushing to doom which undermines the assurances of easy correction. The backsliding trope culminates in a final image of the people as a raging torrent, just on the edge of a precipice. Milton concludes his tract by taking on the role of prophet directly, urging a remnant "to exhort this torrent also of the people, not to be so impetuos, but to keep their due channell . . . to stay these ruinous proceedings; justly and timely fearing to what a precipice of destruction the deluge of this epidemic madness would hurrie us through the general defection of a misguided and abus'd multitude" (VII.463). Although Milton concludes with a plea and exhortation, the metaphor itself undermines easy hope.

More pessimistic regarding the immediate political situation, Milton's jeremiad is also distinctive as a witness about the English nation. *The Readie and Easie Way* witnesses in that it tells England's story, testifying to and hence providing a mode of interpreting England's failure. Throughout the tract, Milton is concerned with England's reputation. He seems to fear the scandal that will come almost as much as the bondage. If the English reverse their own actions and bring back the King, they will become a "scorn and derision to all our neighbors" (VII.422). They will be mocked at and compared to the builders of the tower of Babel: "The foundation indeed they laid gallantly; but . . . have left no memorial of thir work behinde them remaining, but in the common laughter of *Europ*" (VII.423). Other aspiring republicans will be discouraged by the taunt "how sped the rebellious English?" or "how sped the rebels, your fathers?" (VII.449). Milton's jeremiad would justify the cause, while judging the nation. In threatening the English with covenant abrogation, Milton challenges the ideology underlying the genre itself: the assumption that England is – and will remain – elect.

The Readie and Easie Way is, then, a self-conscious performance which reveals Milton's awareness and bold reworking of the jeremiad genre. At length, Milton's jeremiad takes on a distinctively literary aim, to provide a myth of the nation, a story by which the English under the restored monarchy can interpret their tragedy. And he inscribes himself in that story as a prophet who is not only disregarded but in grave personal danger from "misguided and abus'd multitude." In this "failure" that legitimates and authenticates his prophetic identity, Milton is once again modeling himself upon the prophet Jeremiah.

Notes

1 My analysis is of the expanded second edition, which, I believe, intensifies rather than shifts to the prophetic mode. Stanley Stewart sees more of a change in aim between the two editions in "Milton Revises *The Readie and Easie Way*," *Milton Studies*, 20 (1984), pp. 205–24.

2 See Perry Miller, *The New England Mind: From Colony to Province* (Cambridge, 1953), pp. 27–39; Sacvan Bercovitch, "Horologicals to Chronometricals: The Rhetoric of the Jeremiad," *Literary Monographs*, 3 (1970), pp. 1–124; and Bercovitch, *The American Jeremiad* (Madison, 1978).

3 English jeremiads in the 1640s include Matthew Newcomen, *A Sermon Tending to Set Forth* (1644); John Whincop, *God's Call to Weeping and Mourning* (1644) and *Israel's Tears for Distressed Zion* (1645); John Arrowsmith, *The Covenant-Avenging Sword* (1642); and Cornelius Burges, *The Necessity of Agreement with God* (1645).

4 With a few notable exceptions, the subject of seventeenth-century English jeremiads has remained largely unexplored. On the 1640s sermons before Parliament as jeremiads, see James Egan, "'This is a Lamentation and shall be for a Lamentation': Nathaniel Ward and the Rhetoric of the Jeremiad," *Proceedings of the American Philosophical Society*, 122.6 (1978), pp. 400–10. James Holstun's astute and subtle treatment of *The Readie and Easie Way* as an anti-utopian jeremiad appeared too late for me to take it into account; see *A Rational Millennium: Puritan Utopias of Seventeenth-Century England and America* (Oxford, 1987), pp. 246–65.

5 For the political events of these years see Ronald Hutton, *The Restoration* (Oxford, 1985); Godfrey Davies, *The Restoration of Charles II, 1658–60* (San Marino, 1955); Austin Woolrych, "The Good Old Cause and the Fall of the Protectorate,"

Cambridge Historical Journal, 13 (1957), pp. 133–61; and Woolrych, *CPW*, VII.1–218. See Barbara K. Lewalski, "Milton: Political Beliefs and Polemical Methods, 1659–60," *PMLA*, 74 (1959), pp. 191–202 for discussion of *The Readie and Easie Way* in the context of the rapidly changing political situation and the pamphlet literature.

6 "A Declaration of the Lord Protector, and both Houses of Parliament, for a Day of Solemn Fasting" (May 1659), reprinted in *Somers Tracts*, ed. Sir Walter Scott (London, 1809–15), vol. VI, p. 506.

7 See Woolrych, *CPW*, VII.19–26, 66–73.

8 *CPW* suggests the Exodus account of the Israelites under Moses who desire to return to Egypt, identifying the idol queen as the Egyptian cow-goddess Hathor (VII.387). The idol queen is more likely, in my opinion, to be the "queen of heaven", *l^e malkat haššāmayim*, mentioned only in Jeremiah (44:17–19, 25). Milton refers to the queen of heaven in *Paradise Lost* and the "Nativity Ode," identifying her with Ashtoreth and the Phoenician Astarte.

9 In the first edition of the tract, Milton refers to Jeremiah's curse on Coniah, wicked and exiled king of Judah (Jer. 22:29–30). He says he would "tell the verie soil it self what God hath determined of *Coniah* and his seed for ever" (VII.388). In the second edition, he omits the curse on Coniah/Charles since the King's return is virtually assured. He testifies instead against the reprobate people who have disregarded his previous warning.

12

Citation, authority, and *De Doctrina Christiana*

REGINA M. SCHWARTZ

the truth . . .
Left only in those written Records pure
Though not but by the Spirit understood.
                    PL XII. 511–14 [3]

Discussions of Milton's *De Doctrina Christiana* – and there are not many[1] – typically begin by observing how little attention has been focused on Milton's "dearest and best possession." And so I will begin by asking why that has been the case. By his own account, Milton spent his lifetime in preparation and in labor over his Body of Divinity: he regards his early education in biblical languages, his subsequent attention to theological systems, his commonplace book where he grouped scriptural passages according to topics, and his reading in doctrinal controversies as preparatory; and if the first draft of his project was begun along with the composing of *Paradise Lost*,[2] it continued to be revised at various times using various scribes until his death. The effort is awesome, with at least four extensive revisions of the Picard manuscript, to say nothing of revisions in the hands of Amenuenses C, O, R, A, B, M, and N.[3]

Nonetheless, that long labor has been, with important exceptions, largely ignored; and Milton's own estimation of the crucial importance of his project has remained – sadly and ironically, for such a public figure – privately held. One reason is that *De Doctrina* has suffered from the contexts it has been assigned. When it is relegated to the theological arena – the thorny Reformation controversies – it becomes something of a curiosity. It was never as influential as the treatises of the so-called magisterial reformers, nor as controversial as the work of, say, Arminius or Béza. It simply could not have been, not only because Milton was a latecomer to many of these controversies, but because his own theological context was lost by the time the manuscript of *De Doctrina* was found. When *De Doctrina* was discovered in the Middle Treasury Gallery of the Old State Paper Office at Whitehall in 1823, it did not forge new consciences; instead, if it was read as serious theological speculation at all, it was only to be judged according to long-established biases. More often – and even more dismissively – its heresies were read as aberrations to be forgiven of a poet so deeply enshrined in "the Temple of Fame."[4] Subsequent efforts to retrieve *De Doctrina* have involved placing it in a different context – not Reformation theology, but literary history – where Milton's "dearest and best possession" became relegated to the status of a gloss for *Paradise Lost*.[5] However valuable that approach may be to students of the epic, Milton doubtless would have been disheartened. There is, however, another context. Not just as a curious relic of dated controversies or as a doctrinal key to the poetry, *De Doctrina Christiana* is important for its contribution to theoretical issues in literary studies, where an urgent question, as recent debates about the canon suggest,[6] is the authority of any text. As a "system of divinity," specifically a *catena*, *De Doctrina Christiana* is comprised of an assemblage of biblical citations and this incessant recourse to another text results in an exchange of authority, a "politics" of citation. Such chains of citations became standard after Aquinas's collection of excerpts, drawn from at least eighty sources, was published under the title *Catena aurea* in 1484. None the less, most systems of theology were structured differently from Milton's: a biblical verse was cited, and then it was glossed by the theologians. Milton reverses this relation, placing his own system of divinity in the authorized position, and turning the Bible into a gloss – on Milton.

I The dynamics of authority

Milton opens his introductory epistle to *De Doctrina Christiana* by assigning authority to the "original purity" of religion: "The process of restoring religion to something of its pure original state, after it had been defiled with impurities for more than thirteen hundred years, dates from the beginning of the last century" (VI.117; XIV.2). He proceeds to tell us that this purity was corrupted by the last thirteen centuries of interpretation – Milton thereby revokes authority from that unhealthy climate – and then he tells us that religion began to be restored recently, that treatises are now being published according to sounder principles; that is, Milton seems to be conferring some authority on contemporary theological treatises, only to revoke it finally on every count: these treatises are imperfect, and even if they were perfect, he still would not authorize them, for his only authority is himself.

> Since that time many theological systems have been propounded, aiming at further purification, and providing sometimes brief, sometimes more lengthy and methodical expositions of almost all the chief points of Christian doctrine. This being so, I think I should explain straight away why, if any work has yet been published on this subject which is as exhaustive as possible, I have been dissatisfied with it, and why, on the other hand, if all previous writers have failed in this attempt, I have not been discouraged from making the same attempt myself. (VI.117–18; XIV.2)

Already, in the first paragraph of the introduction to *De Doctrina Christiana*, Milton inscribes authority as a dynamic process; it is given, transferred, revoked, and re-given. He has also sought to simplify the terms of that process: Milton has cleared the ground between that authorized "original purity" and the authority of himself. Thirteen centuries are a blot, and the remaining ones not worth heeding. Henceforth, what will ensue will be a confrontation between the authority of the "original purity" – the scriptures – and the authority of John Milton. It will not always look like a confrontation. Rather, *De Doctrina* will be a testimony to Milton's drive to uphold the authority of the Bible even as he claims authority for himself. It is the dynamics of these rival claims for authority, scriptural and Miltonic, that I will explore.

To our ears, the following, also from Milton's prefatory epistle to *De Doctrina*, sounds like a contradiction: on the one hand, "the only authority I accepted was God's self-revelation," for "God has revealed the way of eternal salvation"; on the other (and this appears on the same page), "I made up my mind to puzzle out a religious creed for myself by my own exertions" ("habere mihimet ipsi") and so "I read and pondered [perlecta atque perpensa] the Holy Scriptures themselves with all possible diligence [quam diligentissime], never sparing myself in any way [quod mearum erat partium non omisso]" (VI.118; XIV.4). The terms describing Milton's own efforts to interpret suggest rigorous exertion on the part of the individual – "scrutinize," "ascertain for myself," "careful perusal and meditation" – and they seem at odds with the receptive passivity of "having taken the grounds of my faith from revelation" ("id fide non aliunde quam divinitus accepta"), where Milton seems to have received revelation as one would receive grace. On the one hand, he wrestles with the text, laboring to understand upon his own authority; on the other, he cannot help but understand, for his authority is divine.

The standard English translations make fascinating commentary on this potential conflict of authorities in Milton's prose. The Columbia edition emphasizes the contrast by using the "two-handed" division that I have, attributing it to Milton; the translation reads, "on the one hand, having taken the grounds of my faith from divine revelation alone, and on the other, having neglected nothing which depended upon my own industry" (XIV.5). The translation of the Yale edition glides over any sharp distinction between the authority of Milton and the authority of revelation:

> So I made up my mind to puzzle out a religious creed for myself by
> my own exertions, and to acquaint myself with it thoroughly. *In this*
> the only authority I accepted was God's self-revelation, *and accordingly* I
> pondered the Holy Scriptures themselves with all possible diligence,
> never sparing myself in any way.   (VI.118, my italics)

That clever "accordingly" – not explicit in the Latin – creates a causal relation between the authority of scripture and Milton's own efforts;[7] it seems that

Milton works so hard at puzzling out the text because it reveals itself to him. But the inherent contradiction between Miltonic authority and divine authority will not be so easily resolved. Milton remains preoccupied, soon offering a defensive disclaimer: "For assuredly I do not urge or enforce anything upon my own authority [auctoritate mea nihi suadeo, nihil impono]" (VI. 121; XIV. 10). And he offers his own method of interpretation as an example to others: no one should accept the opinions of others; rather he should wait "until the evidence of the Bible convinces him [vicerit] and induces his reason to assent and to believe" (VI. 122; XIV. 10). Milton's actively strenuous effort of interpretation is not so easily reconciled to the image of his reason being "induced" ("assensum"). The interpretation of scripture, indeed any interpretation, is an aggressive act of reconceiving and rewriting; even to cite a text is to commit essentially an act of violence, to dismember and rearrange parts. In *De Doctrina*, Milton is engaged in just such aggression, even as he is at pains to disguise it.

The result is not only an inconsistent representation of the act of interpreting, but a yoking together of radically opposed accounts: over and over, discussions that begin with the exertion of the interpreter conclude with his passivity, that begin with his authority and his control conclude with his disclaiming any authority or control. The twin urges are apparent in *Of Reformation*, where Milton explains that the scriptures are "protesting their own plainnes, and perspicuity," but they are also "requiring from [the reader] the ability of searching, trying, examining all things" (I. 566). In *De Doctrina*, his disclaimer that he urges nothing on his own authority because his "reason is induced" by scripture is followed by an even more defensive assertion: "I do not seek to conceal any part of my meaning [Latibula non quaero]" (VI. 122; XIV. 10). We might well wonder why he would suddenly speak of concealment here, amidst a discussion of the authority of scripture; given this context, what else could he be concealing but his own appropriation of that authority? Milton is hiding behind the Bible, filling *his* pages with *its* words, and in so doing, making its words his words; and the longer he cites the Bible and the more he appeals to its authority, the more it becomes clear that he is engaged, in *De Doctrina*, in an exercise of ventriloquism. Biblical authority *becomes* Miltonic authority.

My point is not that Milton is contradicting himself out of confusion, nor (a version of the same charge with the addition of culpability) that he is lying to the reader, pretending to rely upon scriptural authority when he knows full well how inventive he is, or conversely, that he is claiming independence when he knows how thorough his debt is. Rather, Milton's twin claims for his own authority and scriptural authority are hopelessly entangled for a good reason. The relation between these two authorities is not simply contradictory; rather, it is interdependent. Because Milton authorizes the Bible, the Bible in turn authorizes Milton. Authority does not inhere; it is assigned, by believers, by the very act of interpreting. None the less, to interpret a text is to appropriate authority from that text, from the very text the interpreter simultaneously authorizes by interpreting it at all. That means that interpretation is no stranger to the arena of power. The utter dependence of each of the elements in the power configurations of authority has been made graphic by Foucault:

> power must be understood in the first instance as the multiplicity of force relations immanent in the sphere in which they operate and which constitute their own organization; as the process which, through ceaseless struggles and confrontations, transforms, strengthens, or reverses them; as the support which these force relations find in one another, thus forming a chain or a system, or on the contrary, the disjunctions and contradictions which isolate them from one another.[8]

Canonization, the institutional authorization of a text, is marked by the same exchanges of authority, this time between the text and its community. "The emergence of the sacred text, then, occurs not as some natural (or supernatural) process but from an interplay of tradition and religious–political design ... a sacred text emerges through particular authoritative figures in a community of believers who work to lend a given text divine endorsement and thus render it sacred." Here again we see a circular exchange. "Texts become sacred because someone (or ones) manages to imbue them with an aura of divine authority, but conversely, their divine authority is accepted by the community because they have been persuaded that the text is 'sacred.'"[9] Like a commodity, authority is caught up in a system of exchange; its only life is relational.

II The politics of citation

The confusion of biblical and Miltonic authority in *De Doctrina* demonstrates that the ceaselessly ongoing exchange of authority also characterizes citation itself. Interestingly, before Foucault wrote of power as exchange, he wrote in the *Archeology of Knowledge* that the *statement* "is one of those objects that men produce, manipulate, use, transform, exchange, combine, decompose and recompose, and possibly destroy." These events in the life of the statement are not so much analogous to the reciprocity of power relations as they enact them. He continues: "Thus the statement circulates, is used, disappears, allows or prevents the realization of a desire, serves or resists various interests, participates in challenge and struggle, and becomes a theme of appropriation or rivalry."[10] When Milton quotes the Bible in his system of divinity, does he appropriate his source? rival his source? Or are these activities clearly distinct? It seems that Milton cites the Bible in order to authorize it and in order to *be authorized* by it, and the more insistently Milton cites the Bible, the more it becomes clear that he appropriates that authority he also grants.

In his opening epistle, Milton announces that while other commentators have indulged in writing their own opinions, "filling their pages almost entirely [totas fere paginas] with expositions of their own ideas," he is not guilty of such open accounts of his own opinions. (Only three sentences later he will offer a declaration of his right to "openly give opinions about doctrine and to write about it according to what he believes." And that in turn will be followed by a disclaimer that these arguments are based on – what else? – any authority other than scriptural authority.) Again, while others fill their pages with their own ideas, Milton has "striven to cram my pages even to overflowing, with quotations drawn from all parts of the Bible and to leave as little space as possible for my own words, even when they arise from the putting together of actual scriptural texts" (VI.122; XIV.10). The image of cramming the Bible to overflowing ("ingerentibus redundare") into Milton's own pages, leaving no room for Milton's own words is fascinating, first for its essential violence (*aggero* means to heap upon, and the root is used in the idiom for waging war) – Milton has ransacked the whole Bible and then crammed it, hardly a deferential approach to his sacred authority – but also because the idea of Milton's own words being squeezed out of his text is more than attenuated by his last qualifying clause: "even when they [his words] arise from the putting together of actual scriptural texts." Here, he depicts his own words as the product of combining (literally, being born from) actual scriptural texts ("ipso licet contextu scripturarum natis"). An unimportant addition, an afterthought, is suggested by that "even when" ("licet") construction, but what follows is a remarkable summation of the method governing *De Doctrina* as a whole: "my own words . . . arise from the putting together of actual scriptural texts." In his defense of scriptural authority, Milton has buried a profound insight into the nature of citation: to compose one's own words out of another's is to make them one's own. "Since, as often as not, the original text is deformed in my rendition, it no longer matters whose text it is," writes Arthur Cohen at the end of his recent notebook observations on literature and theology. "I try to make every quotation my own. If, after living with a text for a long time, I continue to remember its author, I give it back. It will never become mine and I have no use for it."[11] While Milton claimed that his commentary was so full of the Bible that the pages had no room left for his own words, in the end, the exiled author returns, stuffing his own pages – cramming them even to overflowing – with himself. In the end, the Bible's words become Milton's own.

III The contingency of the Spirit

The dynamics of authority are not confined to exchanges between the scripture and Milton. Milton complicates the dialectic by introducing further distinctions, and with them, further transfers of authority. First, he makes distinctions in the relative authority of the dispensations of law and grace, between the two testaments. Then, he makes distinctions between the authority of an external and internal scripture. Furthermore, just as he transfers authority from the first covenant to the second – "the covenant of grace . . . is much more excellent and perfect than the law" (VI. 521; XVI. 113) – so too he takes authority away from the external scripture altogether to confer it on the internal scripture.

The movement begins subtly, but it does begin at the very beginning of his discourse on the Holy Scriptures. Invoking the Lutheran doctrine of the perspicuity of scripture, Milton writes that "the scriptures are, both in themselves and through God's illumination absolutely clear" (VI. 578; XVI. 258). If the "vel/vel" construction (which could mean both/and as well as either/or) is meant to smooth over the difference between scripture's self-sufficiency and the necessity of the Spirit for divine illumination (much as the translation in the Yale edition easily joined scriptural to Miltonic authority), that difference will grow more insistent in subsequent pages until Milton deepens it explicitly. "Every believer is entitled to interpret the scriptures; and by that I mean interpret them for himself. He has the spirit, who guides truth; and he has the mind of Christ. . . . The rule and canon of faith, therefore, is scripture alone" (VI. 583–5; XVI. 264–6). Of course, that "therefore" ("itaque") is justified, for Milton means scripture without the mediation of tradition, but he proceeds to elaborate the *sola scriptura* doctrine on other grounds: "In controversies there is no arbitrator except scripture, or rather [aut saltem], each man is his own arbitrator, so long as he follows scripture and the Spirit of God" (VI. 585; XVI. 268). Here, Milton begins with the usual testimony to scriptural authority – for "arbitrator" we could read "authority" – but then he feels the need to amend his statement that scripture is the only arbitrator; and in his emendation, "each man" ("quisque") is *substituted* for scripture as the only authority. But Milton is not content to transfer authority from the text to the interpreter; he deems it necessary to return authority to the very scripture he took it away from, so that in the end he offers a circular exchange: "or rather [instead of scripture being the arbitrator] each man is the arbitrator" – so long as he consults scripture. Once again, authority is caught up in a relational configuration.

But a new term follows, a third term: the Spirit of God. The full, remarkably condensed sentence reads "Scripture is the sole judge of controversies; or rather, every man is to decide for himself through its aid, under the guidance of the Spirit of God." In Milton's formulation, the scripture and the Spirit are not synonymous, and authority will be distributed among all three: interpreter, scripture, and Spirit. The scripture will not be sufficient alone, for it is corruptible, the Spirit will be dependent on the authority of the scripture, and each man, the final arbitrator, will authorize both scripture and Spirit even as he is authorized by them:

> We have, particularly under the gospel, a double scripture. There is the
> external scripture of the written word and the internal scripture of the
> Holy Spirit which he, according to God's promise, has engraved upon
> the hearts of believers, and which is certainly not to be neglected.
>
> (VI.587; XVI.272)

Milton's recommendation that the *internal* scripture should not be neglected
soon becomes more forceful. His earlier characterization of the dynamic
interdependence of several authorized forces is suddenly replaced by a very
different structure, an absolute hierarchy:

> Nowadays the external authority for our faith, in other words, the
> scriptures, is of very considerable importance and, generally speaking,
> it is the authority of which we first have experience. The *pre-eminent*
> and *supreme* authority, however, is the authority of the Spirit, which is
> internal, and the individual possession of each man.
>
> (VI.587; XVI.274, my italics)

The external scripture that had been "the rule and canon of faith alone" only
two pages earlier is now only "of very considerable importance" ("max-
ima"); and the Spirit which was "not to be neglected" ("minime negli-
gendam") has become the "pre-eminent and supreme authority" ("summa
atque suprema"). The written text, which had been perspicuous and sufficient – along with some help from the Spirit and each man – is now only our
first experience of authority, to be supplanted by a greater one. Authority is
no longer relational, it is no longer a dynamic system of interdependence; it is
absolute, removed from all dependence, all contingency, and all corruption.

Milton will argue that the corruptions of scripture have induced this radical
shift:

> the external scripture, particularly the New Testament, has often been
> liable to corruption and is, in fact corrupt. This has come about
> because it has been committed to the care of various untrustworthy
> authorities, has been collected together from an assortment of
> divergent manuscripts, and has survived in a medley of transcripts and
> editions. But no one can corrupt the Spirit which guides man to truth.
>
> (VI.587–8; XVI.274)

And he will be frustrated that in his quest for an absolute authority he cannot
find an absolute original: "We possess no autograph copy: no exemplar
which we can rely on as more trustworthy than the others." There is no
"genuine, uncorrupted text, the indisputable word of God" (VI.589). But this
does not lead him to the deconstructive insight that there could be no absolute
original, no unmediated version; it does not enable him to be freed from the
rule of an absolute. Instead, it leads him to an internal principle that is not

subject to corruption and contingency:

> I do not know why God's providence should have committed the
> contents of the New Testament to such wayward and uncertain
> guardians, unless it was so that this very fact might convince us that
> the Spirit which is given to us is a more certain guide than scripture,
> and that we ought to follow it.   (VI.589; XVI.278)

Odd as it sounds, a corruptible text leads Milton straight to an absolute
Truth.

Just how independent is Milton's absolute, the Spirit, of the realm of the
corruptible and contingent? On what authority does Milton turn to this
principle? In an incredible maneuver, Milton makes the external scripture the
authority for denying itself authority. And the more he insists upon the
authority of the Spirit over the letter, the more he quotes the letter to do so,
once again authorizing (for to cite is to authorize) the very document he had
just painstakingly demonstrated to be corrupt. Among the citations that
proliferate:

> II Cor. iii.3: that you are the epistle of Christ, ministered by us,
> written not with ink but with the Spirit of the living God; not on
> tablets of stone, but on the fleshly tablets of the heart; Eph. vi:17: the
> sword of the Spirit, which is the word of God; I John ii.20: but you
> have an unction from the Holy One, and know all things, and ii.27:
> you do not need to be taught by anyone; but as the same unction
> teaches you about all things, and is truthful, not false, and as it has
> taught you, you shall remain in him.   (VI.586; XVI.270)[12]

Milton has made his independent authority dependent after all, upon the
authorization of the scripture – even though the external scripture has been
proven to be inferior to the far superior principle it authorizes, the internal
Spirit. Once again, despite his effort to erect an absolute authority, Milton
has created a network of authorizations and authorities. In doing so, he
violates the very principle he invokes in order to limit church authority: "the
writings of the prophets and of the apostles, which constitute the scriptures,
are the foundations of the church. Now the church is built on a foundation, it
cannot itself be the rule or arbiter of that foundation" (VI.585–6; XVI.268).
Milton builds his internal Spirit on the foundation of scripture, so that the
Spirit cannot possibly be the "rule or arbiter" of the scripture – and yet that is
precisely the role Milton assigns it, despite his awareness that the text is
corrupt, that the foundation is crumbling. In the Spirit, Milton's search for an
absolutely independent authorizing principle has not found a place of rest.

We are now in a position to understand that while the following doctrine,
introducing Milton's key chapter 27, "Of the Gospel and Christian Liberty,"
seems to echo commonplace formulas on the scripture and the Spirit, it is
fraught with tensions:

> The Gospel is the new dispensation of the covenant of grace, far more excellent and perfect than the law, announced first obscurely by Moses and the prophets, afterwards in the clearest terms by Christ himself, and his apostles and evangelists, written since by the Holy Spirit in the hearts of believers, and ordained to continue even to the end of the world . . .   (translation from Columbia edn, XVI.113)

The sense of progress could hardly be more explicit. What is new is more excellent than what came before; the movement from the covenant of the law to that of grace is clearly an advance. But that double structure quickly gives way to three stages of progress: from the writings of Moses, to the words of Christ and his apostles, to the inscription of the Spirit. And the principles of establishing their priority – and Milton is driven to prioritize his authorities – are slippery. The *clearest* terms (echoing the Lutheran doctrine of the perspicuity of scripture) are those of Christ, the apostles, and evangelists, that is, the external scripture; but the most recent and eternal inscription is written by the Holy Spirit in the hearts of believers – and we have this on the authority of a clear external scripture that seems to have been supplanted by an eternal internal one, or has it?

IV Political authority

In his demonstration that the Spirit and the scripture legitimize one another, Milton offers us a scheme in which authority must be given in order to be received. Nonetheless, he has not entangled these sources of authority to teach us a theory about the exchange of power. Rather, his discourse on authority encodes an urgent political crisis in authority created by England's Reformation. Distribution of authority in the ecclesiastical system was destabilized and redistributed in ways no one could predict. The distribution of authority in the state was destabilized and redistributed in ways that were scarcely imaginable. To say the least, this was an age when the locus and nature of authority were thrown open to question. Far from being removed from debates about state power and church government, the authority of scripture became the basis on which those reforms and revolutions rested. "The New Testament provided prime evidence on all religious questions, while the Old Testament was particularly valuable in delineating the relationship between the church and the commonwealth."[13] And the more urgently the traditional forms of church and state authority were questioned, the more insistently the authority of scripture was upheld: "whensoever the immortal God shall Command anything, and any Power on earth shall give it a Countermand, then must the Law of the earthen and morall God be rejected, justly."[14]

Amid this confusion, if the effort to unseat an ultimate authority seemed only to result in erecting a new one – now the Bible took the throne – it was with a key difference: the Bible shared that throne. Throughout the discourse of the reformers, twin authorities reflected one another in just the kind of interdependence Milton describes. Like Milton, William Whitaker sensed no contradiction in invoking two authorities:

> Now we determine that the supreme right, authority, and judgment of interpreting the scriptures, is lodged with the Holy Ghost and the scripture itself: for these two are not mutually repugnant. We say that the Holy Spirit is the supreme interpreter of scripture, because we must be illuminated by the Holy Spirit to be certainly persuaded of the true sense of scripture. . . . But this is only an internal persuasion, and concerns only ourselves. As an external persuasion, we say that scripture itself is its own interpreter; and therefore, that we should come to the external judgment of scripture itself, in order to persuade others: in which proceeding we must also use means.[15]

Far from feeling the tug of conflicting authorities, Richard Sibbes envisioned deep compatibility: "As the spirits in the arteries quicken the blood in the veins, so the Spirit of God goes along with the word, and makes it work." "The breath of the Spirit in us is suitable to the Spirit's breathing in the Scriptures; the same Spirit doth not breathe contrary motions."[16] And even Cromwell deems it necessary to attach the authority of the Spirit to the scripture: God "speaks without a written word sometimes, *yet according to it*" (my italics).[17]

Clearly, Milton has adopted conventional Protestant doctrines about the share the Spirit has in biblical authority. And yet that was neither the only, nor, for Milton, the obvious choice. His persistent distinction between the external and the internal and his valuation of the internal over the external – "And chiefly thou, O Spirit, who dost prefer/Before all Temples the upright heart and pure" – could have pointed him toward abandoning the external text altogether. After all, the Spirit that earlier inspired the scripture has *since* been written on the fleshly tablets of the heart. Whole epistles were lost, he tells us, and the apostles failed to record everything (XVI.270). When Milton's Spirit can offer the believer Truth in the event of missing texts and textual corruption, why not simply rely upon the inner light? Illumination by that light alone was sufficient for spiritualists like Müntzer or Sebastian Frank; why did Milton refuse to give up the biblical text? Or, to rephrase the question in the terms of this discussion, if Milton is really only citing the Bible in order to authorize himself, why not simply abandon the ventriloquism and speak in his own voice (that is, the voice dictated by the Holy Spirit)?[18] Why not abandon, that is, the interdependence I have characterized as Miltonic authority? What does Milton gain by an *exchange* of authority, rather than a one-way appropriation of it?

Whitaker offers a key. The Holy Spirit persuades us; the scripture helps us to persuade others. Milton was not interested in appropriating authority for

its own sake, but in order to persuade others, and that battle, like all the
Reformation battles, had to be waged on two fronts. The church and state
needed to be dismantled on some authority, but individual freedom of
conscience needed to be protected on some authority, as new competing
systems of government and divinity laid claim to authority. Perhaps Milton
needed one authority to dismantle the old, and another to preserve his
independence in the face of the new. The external text offers him "a common
ground," in Whitaker's term, the "means" for persuading others, a hedge
against the charge of complete individualism, while the Holy Spirit guarantees the rights of individualism, ensuring freedom of conscience, for it is
based upon the infusion of the Holy Spirit.[19] Authority becomes the instrument to de-authorize: if Scripture liberated men from the church, the Holy
Spirit liberated men from other men.

The authority of the scripture and the Spirit have precisely these functions
in *Of Civil Power*. Milton begins predictably enough:

> First it cannot be deni'd, being the main foundation of our protestant
> religion, that we of these ages, having no other divine rule or autoritie
> from without us warrantable to one another as a common ground
> but the holy scripture, and no other within us but the illumination
> of the Holy Spirit so interpreting that scripture as warrantable only to
> our selves and to such whose consciences we can so perswade, can
> have no other ground in matters of religion but only from the
> scriptures.   (VII.242)

Here, it sounds as if the Holy Spirit, empowering us to interpret scripture,
also enables us to persuade others even though the final ground is scripture.
That reading works only out of context. The sentence that follows shows
Milton at pains to maintain that familiar balance of power between scripture
and spirit: there can be no other ground but the scriptures, but they cannot be
understood without the Spirit:

> And these [the scriptures] being not possible to be understood without
> this divine illumination, which no man can know at all times to be in
> himself, much less to be at any time for certain in any other, it follows
> cleerly, that no man or body of men in these times can be the infallible
> judges or determiners in matters of religion to any other mens
> consciences but thir own.   (VII.242–3)

It is the conclusion of this sentence that rings with political urgency: the
illuminating Spirit protects the individual's freedom of conscience. Milton
will reiterate the point: "what can there els be nam'd of more autoritie then
the church but the conscience; then which God only is greater, I *Joh.* 3.20?"
(VII.243), and "if apostles had no dominion or constraining power over

faith or conscience, much less have ordinary ministers" (VII.245).

De Doctrina Christiana, Milton's "dearest and best possession," was no anomaly in his political career. This was the labor of the Spirit interpreting the scripture. This was that ground which enabled him to stand apart from the claims of other authorities, "searching the scriptures daily, to try, to judge these things for himself." This was the judge that allowed him to accept neither "traditions, councels nor canons of any visible church, much less edicts of any magistrate or civil session" (VII.243). *De Doctrina Christiana* was the labor of a lifetime spent authorizing the scripture so that it authorized him: to reject the authority of anyone else. The external/internal scripture, *De Doctrina*, authorized that life, even as, according to Milton's own logic, that life authorized/authored *De Doctrina Christiana*. Leaning with all the weight of his doctrine of scriptural authority on these verses, Milton cites Galatians 6:4–5. "let every man prove his own work, and then shall he have rejoicing in himself alone, and not in another: for every man shall bear his own burden." Surely these words became Milton's own.[20]

Notes

1 The only book-length study of the *De Doctrina* itself was published in 1939 by Arthur Sewell, *A Study in Milton's Christian Doctrine* (London). Theological issues have been treated in the essays collected by William B. Hunter, C. A. Patrides, and J. H. Adamson, in *Bright Essence: Studies in Milton's Theology* (Salt Lake City, 1971); other brief studies include those of Gordon Campbell, "Alleged Imperfections in Milton's *De Doctrina*," *MQ*, 12 (1978), pp. 64–5, and "*De Doctrina Christiana*: Its Structural Principles and its Unfinished State," *MS*, 9 (1976), pp. 243–60; Dayton Haskin, "Milton's Strange Pantheon: The Apparent Tritheism of the *De Doctrina*," *Heythrop Journal*, 16 (1975), pp. 129–48, and William Shullenberger, "Linguistic and Poetic Theory in Milton's *De Doctrina*," *ELN*, 19 (1982), pp. 262–78.

2 The Picard draft is dated *ca*. 1658–*ca*. 1660 in J. H. Hanford, "The Date of Milton's *De Doctrina Christiana*," *SP*, 17 (1920), pp. 309–19.

3 *CPW*, VI.35. "Even before Picard left his employ, Milton sought to improve not only such minor matters as diction and style but also larger aspects of his treatise … [Then, he] gave the Picard manuscript at least four further and extensive revisions. Picard's, however, was only the first of several later revisions" (VI.34).

4 See the *Quarterly Theological Review*, 3 (1826), p. 65. The brief discussion of the critical reception of *De Doctrina* in the Yale edition should also be consulted.

5 The classic is by Maurice Kelley, *This Great Argument: A Study of Milton's "De Doctrina Christiana" as a Gloss Upon "Paradise Lost"* (Princeton 1941); other studies include those of B. Rajan, *"Paradise Lost* and the *De Doctrina"* in *"Paradise Lost" and the Seventeenth-century Reader* (London, 1947), pp. 22–38; Gordon Campbell, "The Son of God in *De Doctrina* and *Paradise Lost*," *MLR*, 75 (1980), pp. 507–14; Campbell, "Milton's Theological and Literary Treatments of the Creation," *Journal of Theological Studies*, 30 (1979), pp. 128–37; and Nasseb Shaheen,

"Milton's Muse and the *De Doctrina*," *MQ*, 8 (1974), pp. 72–6.

6 A good introduction to this vast literature is the collection of essays drawn from two issues of *Critical Inquiry*, *Canons*, ed. W. T. J. Mitchell (Chicago, 1985).

7 Milton is willing to make that causal connection explicit elsewhere; in another construct, scripture is plain and perspicuous, "whence it follows that" we can scrutinize it. "Ex quo rursum sequitur, scripturas a quibusvis esse perscrutandas" (XVI.258).

8 Michel Foucault, *History of Sexuality* (New York, 1978), vol. I, p. 92.

9 Robert Deitweiler, "What Is a Sacred Text?," in *Semeia*, 31 (1985), p. 215.

10 Michel Foucault, *The Archeology of Knowledge*, trans. A. M. Sheridan Smith (New York, 1972), p. 105.

11 *Prooftexts*, 7.2 (1987), p. 121.

12 See also chapter 27 on the authority of the letter, devoted to the superiority of grace over law, faith over the letter.

13 J. P. Sommerville, *Politics and Ideology in England 1603–1640* (London, 1986), p. 189.

14 Thomas Morton, *A Sermon Preached before the Kings Most Excellent Maiestie* (Newcastle upon Tyne, 1639), pp. 13–14.

15 William Whitaker, *A Disputation on Holy Scripture*, trans. and ed. William Fitzgerald (Cambridge, 1849), p. 415.

16 *The Complete Works of Richard Sibbes*, ed. Alexander B. Grosart (Edinburgh, 1862–4), VII.193; V.427.

17 Oliver Cromwell, *Letters and Speeches*, ed. Thomas Carlyle (London and New York, 1908), III.65–87.

18 See Derek Hirst, *Authority and Conflict: England, 1603–1658* (Cambridge, Mass., 1986), p. 72. See also G. F. Nuttall, *The Holy Spirit in Puritan Faith and Experience* (Oxford, 1946).

19 *Disputation*, p. 415.

20 For discussions of Milton's debt to the Bible and the appropriation of it in his poetry, see my "From Shadowy Types to Shadowy Types: The Unendings of *Paradise Lost*," *Milton Studies* 24 (1988), pp. 123–39, and *Remembering and Repeating: Biblical Creation in Paradise Lost* (Cambridge, 1988).

13

The History of Britain and its Restoration audience

GARY D. HAMILTON

In times when speaking out might be dangerous, it would seem that writing histories could be a relatively safe alternative. In his 1698 biography of Milton, John Toland called attention to this premise while defending the truth of his account against what was "commonly seen, that Historians are suspected rather to make their Hero what they would have him to be, than such as he really was; and that, as they are promted by different Passions, they put those words in his mouth which they might not speak themselves without incurring som danger."[1] The hazard involved in speaking one's mind becomes an especially pertinent topic when reading Toland's account of the problems that Milton the historian faced when presenting his *History of Britain* to the world in 1670: "yet we have it not as it came out of his hands; for the Licensers, those sworn Officers to destroy Learning, Liberty and good Sense, expung'd several passages of it wherin he expos'd the Superstition, Pride, and Cunning of the Popish Monks in the *Saxon* Times, but apply'd by the sagacious Licensers to *Charles* the Second's Bishops."[2]

Given Toland's awareness of the suspicions of his age regarding the writing of histories, one would have wished from him some speculation about Milton's motives in publishing the *History*. Were the censors justified in their suspicions, or was Milton merely doing what Toland assured his readers that he as Milton's historian was doing, giving the truth as best it could be determined? Did Milton attempt to address the political realities of the Restoration when he readied his work for publication, or did he present materials that remained unchanged since he had worked on them two decades before?[3] Instead of dwelling on these issues, Toland turned to reflect on how valuable the *History* might have been had it been finished, thus providing a rationale for neglecting and isolating the work that has been adopted by later Miltonists as well. Yet if the *History* is to become more integrated into the canon, the questions about which Toland did not speculate might well be the ones we can least afford to ignore. One of the ways of bringing this work into a closer relationship with Milton's other prose works, and his major poems as well, is to consider his account of ancient British history as itself an historical event. We need, in other words, to place the text and the author in a 1670 context, "situating," as J. G. A. Pocock puts it, "the author's performance

241

... in the midst of conditions and circumstances that will help us understand" what was, and how it was being, performed.[4]

Largely unexplored in past discussions of the *History* is the relationship between the writer's ideology and his manner of presenting materials on Britain's ancient past. In particular, the manner in which Milton encouraged his seventeenth-century readers to think about their contemporary story needs attention. In the Yale edition, for example, the standards used to evaluate Milton's achievement do not allow a serious consideration of the politics of the *History*. It is Milton's art of economy, "his preoccupation with the *manner* of the narrative, his insistence that the historian ... 'be able to throw off a great deal in few words' " (v.xlvi), that French Fogel finds most admirable about the work. What is most unsatisfactory is "Milton's insistence that common features of life and politics bound ancient Britons and contemporary Englishmen in some significant sort of comparison" (v.416). Placing heavy emphasis on the 15 July 1657 letter to Henry de Brass, where Milton contrasts the historian's use of materials to that of the orator and political writer,[5] Fogel isolates the *History* from works in which Milton utilized historical materials as an "effective means of persuading and moving to action." In contrast to such utilizations, which "could hardly be said to rest on a purely objective examination of the historical facts," the *History* sets out "to present the facts and leave judgment to the reader" (v.xxix).

Even if it were possible to produce a history that presented "a purely objective examination" of the facts, the ideologically self-conscious Milton would have been among those writers least likely to attempt it. As recent studies have pointed out, writing history in seventeenth-century England was a way of addressing the arguments of the Stuart crown concerning the basis on which it ruled.[6] By producing an account of the past that could be held up against the unhistorically grounded propositions of their opponents, historians were, in effect, carrying on an argument. What distinguished history writing from other political writing was not motive, therefore, but the relative absence of rhetorical pressure. The argument was made indirectly, or was left unstated, to be articulated by any reader familiar with the opponent's position. Viewed in this setting, the *History* might differ from some of Milton's other presentations of history not so much in rhetorical purpose as in rhetorical strategy. At least as relevant as Fogel's art of economy, therefore, might be what I shall term Milton's "art of indirection."

The art of indirection is involved whenever history writing presents an ideological argument implicitly. There are two different contexts in which this art can be examined, however, both of which are alluded to in Toland's brief remarks on historiography. First of all, the rhetorical effectiveness of an argument based on history depends, of course, on a perception that what is being given *is* true – a perception more likely to occur if the narrator of events *seems* to be interested only in presenting the facts and letting readers judge them for themselves. And indeed, a remarkable feature throughout the

History is Milton's apparent commitment to the truth, a commitment so strong that he frequently calls into question the truth of the "facts" that he presents – a point to which I shall return later.

The other setting in which the art of indirection can be profitably explored is the interpretative situation that Annabel Patterson defines in her discussion of the hermeneutics of censorship, a situation readers anticipate (as do Toland's projected readers) and thus respond to (as do Milton's Restoration censors) by producing the meaning that the writer dares not take responsibility for saying directly.[7] Here the writer's art entails not so much the conveying of one's commitment to truth as it does the signaling to the reader that this story be *used* to create the other story that cannot be told. If this activity seems strangely inappropriate for a writer who boasted, in the *Second Defense*, of his boldness in the face of "the toils and dangers" involved in "the glorious task of defending the very defenders" of "the excellent cause" (IV.1.552–4; VIII.8–12), we need only be reminded that boldness in one battle can be foolhardiness in another, particularly if one's goal is getting one's words into print.⸮

I

In the *History*, as in other works where an art of indirection may be present, the reader's challenge is that of detecting *when* this art is operating. Though this task sometimes involves having to decide whether personages or actions are there to signal contemporary events, it also entails knowing when those "universal" truths that seem to transcend the particular concerns of contemporary politics might be profoundly implicated in them. If this latter consideration is relevant in any way to the art of the *History*, it is because Milton does not merely present a long parade of facts about kings, battles, alliances, and invasions. Sometimes he pauses briefly to comment on the moral lessons to be gained from the outcome of specific actions, lessons that are at times taken directly from his sources. At other times, however, the commentary is more extensive, suspending the narrative as it elaborates on the pattern manifested in the events that are being related.

Not atypical of Milton's handling of this suspension of narrative is his account of the downfall of the Saxons in the beginning of Book V: they were

> now under the power of one man; and him one of the worthiest, which, as far as can be found in good Authors, was by none at any time here before unless in Fables; men might with some reason have expected from such Union, peace and plenty, greatness, and the flourishing of all Estates and Degrees: but far the contrary fell out soon after, Invasion, Spoil, Desolation, slaughter of many, slavery of the rest. (V.257)

As is the case in Book XI of *Paradise Lost*, where Michael refers to "one rising, eminent / In wise deport" and "The one just Man alive,"[9] the "worthiest" is not identified by name at this point in the *History*. By recalling the last section in Book IV of the *History*, we can easily confirm that Egbert is the "one man," but this confirmation seems rather beside the point. It is the pattern of events, not the particular king, that Milton features as he proceeds with his sometimes "wearisom" recitation of "bare and reasonless Actions" (v.239).

The pattern to be seen in the ensuing narrative is a familiar one; the story of the Saxons is to illustrate the falling away from an ideal, and the reasons for that fall. It is to be read as another version of losing paradise, the external enemy being the Danes – whom Milton links genealogically with the Normans – and the internal enemy being factionalism and "luxurie and sloth, either secular or superstitious." Nor is this pattern new in the *History* itself; Milton also asked his readers to see the design in the fall of the Britons, whose story featured a different external enemy but similar internal ones. The historian completes his description of this pattern by clarifying how the effects of this fall relate to a divine scheme in which "God hath decreed servitude on a sinful Nation, fitted by thir own vices for no condition but servile" (v.259). As he does in *Paradise Lost*, Milton offers, in this work, a "vision of history" that attempts to justify God's ways toward men.

How to respond to that "vision" in the *History* is the issue at hand. Most discussions suggest that it is the work's main source of interest, both for those who wish to trace Milton's intellectual development and for those who would establish a motive for his writing the work. Attempting to fill a gap in our understanding of Milton's life, William Riley Parker uses this "vision" to confirm Milton's mental restlessness in the 1646–8 period, a time when Milton printed no tracts. For Parker the *History* reveals "a cynical and disillusioned view of the national character, a view unquestionably influenced by the confusion of his own times and the general atmosphere of pessimism in 1648."[10] For Fogel, who believes that Milton took up writing this work, probably in 1648, in order to re-evaluate his conception of history, it confirms Milton's "disillusionment with the pattern of history by which he had *thought* he discerned the meaning of the past and the hope of the future."[11] There is, of course, an alternative to this kind of biographical reading of the work, one which responds to Milton's "vision" not as the product of his stepping back to contemplate his world but as a strategy employed in his ongoing dialogue with it. This approach demands an interrogation not only of assumptions about Milton's motives, but also of certain conclusions about dating the work.

What twentieth-century discussions of the *History* illustrate most clearly is that the questions that are asked of the work are tied to the interests they are designed to serve, and that any argument for dating tends to be circular. Surely there are substantial problems in using the *History* to write anything about the stages of Milton's intellectual development. The biographical conclusions for the 1646–8 period, for example, tend to rely heavily on a 1648 dating of that added (or deleted) section of the *History*, the Digression, the early dating of which Austin Woolrych has rightly called into question.[12] Furthermore, the arguments rest on the questionable assumption that Milton's conception of the *History* did not change from the moment he began working on the project, a position that few would think of taking with *Paradise Lost*, the dramatic version of which Parker believes Milton was also working on but then dropped during this period.

Yet the alternative assumption, that parts of the *History* were written at various stages of Milton's life, does not simplify the problem of charting his intellectual progress; for there is no easy way to determine if and when the various sections were reworked before publication. Granted, it is not difficult to reconcile certain aspects of the *History* with the ideological positions of *The Tenure of Kings and Magistrates* and *Eikonoklastes*, the works between which Milton indicates that he wrote the first four books. The "facts" that are presented in the *History* indeed support an argument about the origins of kingship that Milton makes directly in *The Tenure* and the later regicide tracts. In the *History*, some kings are good and some are bad; some kings are elected by their people, some force themselves upon their people, and some are deposed by the people. However, other aspects of Milton's presentation of facts – such as those moments when he suspends his narrative to comment gloomily on the backsliding of the Britons and the Saxons – are not so readily illuminated in the context of his writings of this period, where his interest was in defending those among his contemporaries whose destruction of monarchy could be celebrated as an action positively affecting the course of English history.

The sections of commentary on backsliding might fit more easily into the canon at the point at which Woolrych puts the Digression, in the context of the second edition of *The Readie and Easie Way*, where, on the eve of the Restoration, Milton projected with dread the consequences of England's backsliding. Indeed, the Digression, which Woolrych dates shortly after the Restoration, is a supporting, contemporary example of that pattern of events on which Milton elaborates extensively in commentaries throughout Book III, the book in which the Digression was to appear. It might even be argued that commentaries on backsliding in the *History* are interruptions that differ from the Digression more in degree than in kind. For these generalizing statements are not always easy to reconcile with the narratives preceding or following them. At times, for example, Milton presents good kings and noble actions well after his guiding commentary would lead us to expect none. Perhaps the apparent discrepancy between the gloomy pattern identified in the commentary and some of the "facts" in the narrative surrounding it could be explained in terms of different stages of composition; some of the generalizing commentary could have been added to materials composed earlier according to standards more consistent with the de Brass letters. Establishing a 1670 perspective on the function of these "interruptions" is more to our purposes, however, than speculating on when each section was written or revised.

There are two ways of accounting for Milton's pessimistic vision in the *History*. Either Milton became disillusioned, as Parker would have it, or he decided it would be a good rhetorical strategy to present such a view. On the one hand, the issue is when Milton came to believe as he did, and on the other, when and how this view might have been politically useful to express. In focusing on the latter option we might do well to consider the pessimism of the *History* alongside Milton's *Of Reformation*, a work which, though printed nearly three decades earlier, recounts a pattern of failures in England's past in such a way as to communicate little cause for optimism. The gloom that Milton allows to cloud the brightness of the Reformation in the antiprelatical tract functions to enforce the notion that as long as bishops exist in England there is little reason to be hopeful; reformation without the removal of bishops is not to be equated with progress. Pitted against the historical overview of failure, however, is that magnificent prayer, at the end of the work, beseeching God to aid the nation. By invoking the apocalyptic rhetoric being used by the most strident critics of prelacy, this petition would seem to endorse their stridency as it suggests that they are the instruments through which God might cause the nation to cast "farre from her the *rags* of her old *vices*" (1.616). If this work challenges conventional optimism about the Reformation in order to emphasize the need for casting off those rags, the *History* uses its gloom for somewhat different effects, ones appropriate to a different time and audience. *Of Reformation* ends by holding out "the *darkest* and *deepest Gulfe* of HELL" only to those who impair and diminish "the true *Faith*" (1.617). The *History*, though ostensibly incomplete, conveys a sense of completion by pushing ever forward to a supreme punishment for a whole nation – the Norman Conquest, an event that represented to many critics of the Stuarts the beginning of the abhorrent notion of king as feudal landlord.[13]

In a Restoration reading of the *History*, the rhetorical usefulness of the pessimistic view of the national character would seem to be self-evident. Milton's strategy might best be explained by setting the *History* alongside Dryden's *Annus Mirabilis* (1667), and that body of Restoration royalist millenarian rhetoric that Michael McKeon has demonstrated lies immediately behind Dryden's work.[14] In contrast to Dryden's secularized vision of a New Jerusalem that England, through imperialist expansion, will help create in the world, Milton presents his readers with the prospect of another Norman Conquest: "If these were the Causes of such misery and thraldom to our ancestors, with what better close can be concluded, than here in fit season to remember this Age in the midst of her security, to fear from like Vices, without amendment, the Revolution of like Calamities" (v.403). Milton's vision of history presents no happy endings; there are only repetitions of failure. It predicts not peace but continued suffering and future punishment. For the Restoration critic of Stuart monarchy, the experience of reading the ending of Milton's *History* in 1670 might have been not unlike our confronting that narrative moment at the beginning of Book IV of *Paradise Lost*, where the narrator cries, "O For that warning voice" that might prevent what the reader understands has already occurred. For some 1670 readers, the future that Milton warned against had already come to be; the past (the fall of the Britons and Saxons due to factionalism and slothful clergy) was but an image of England's recent history, a point which Milton's suppressed Digression would only have made more explicit.

II

If a Restoration reading of the *History* allows that work to convey ideas that challenge the image of Milton as the aloof exile contemplating eternal verities, it also encourages us to consider ways in which we might expect a continued dialogue with his traditional political enemies to be carried out – indirectly, under cover, and as his new political situation required, by telling one story by means of another. We can find that dialogue taking place not only in his commentary on the "facts" that he narrates; it is present in his manipulation of some of the narrative materials as well.

From the perspective of the ideology of Milton's history writing and the art of indirection employed in its service, one of the most fascinating aspects of the *History* is Milton's self-presentation, particularly as it involves the issue of the truth of his account. Rather than being able to vouch for the accuracy of what he writes, Milton presents himself as one whose interest in truth forces him constantly to interrogate the authorities on whom he must rely, and to expose, at times, their ideological biases. Indeed, he often presents himself in the *pose* of questioning his sources, sometimes discarding their accounts outright, and at other times having to choose the most probable version among contradictory accounts. By conveying a sense of the difficulty of his task, Milton gives his efforts a heroic dimension. Like Psyche, this historian always must be busy sifting truth from error, and like Samson, he must be "his own deliverer" from the bondage of his predecessors. By focusing his efforts so intently on establishing accuracy, Milton avoids any appearance of being the infamous polemicist that his political enemies once knew. He adopts for himself, instead, the image of a trustworthy guide through the mazes of half-truths and forests of improbabilities offered in previous accounts.

Milton's posture here is important for more than simply establishing the truth of his history writing, of course. It also serves as a poignant reminder of his own political situation in 1670. Much of the hardship that Milton must endure in his pursuit of a true account in the *History* is due to the monks, whose records he must use after Book II, where his Roman sources run out. He presents the untrustworthiness of these churchmen as not just another case of ideologically corrupted history writing, however; they are identified more specifically as an example of the corruption that takes place when the church interferes in state affairs. "In civil matters," Milton tells us, the monks are "dubious Relaters"; they write history "to the best advantage of what they term holy Church, meaning indeed themselves: in most other matters of Religion, blind, astonish'd, and strook with superstition" (v. 127). Though Milton will not unquestioningly follow their lead, he acknowledges, in a marvelously ambiguous manner, the realities of his situation: "these Guides, where can be had no better, must be follow'd" (v. 128). Milton's manipulations of the materials of his authorities in the *History* might readily be seen as a lively image of his subtle maneuverings in the face of the political authorities with which he, as Restoration exile, must deal.

Of particular interest in this respect is Milton's initially bold handling of Augustine, the missionary monk and archbishop whose story Milton uses in Book IV to convey the courage and plight of nonconformists. According to Milton, "*Austin* laboured well among Infidels, but not with like commendation . . . among Christians," requiring the "*Britan* Bishops . . . to conform," which "they refused to do" because he sat "pontifically in his Chair" (v. 192). Milton refuses to follow Bede in his attempt to "excuse *Austin*" from blame for the massacre of "1200 [nonconformist] Monks" on the grounds that he was not alive at the time. According to Milton's calculations, he was still "sitting Archbishop" when this "slaughter" occurred. No sooner does the reader grasp that this arithmetic is being used to indict the archbishop, however, than Milton backs away from where he seemed to be headed. He is concerned with correcting Bede's facts, not with condemning his failure to assess proper blame. Indeed, Milton can find no weighty authority to charge Augustine with these crimes: "Other just ground of charging him with this imputation appears not, save what evidently we have from *Geffry Monmouth*, whose weight we know" (v. 194–5).

Obviously Milton is using his sources here not simply to establish a true account but to get his readers to think about the political realities with which he and they must live.[15] Besides raising the topical issue of persecution for nonconformity, Milton's presentation of Augustine also seems to acknowledge the impossibility, in a church-dominated state, of bringing to justice those responsible for persecution. For without the weight of authority to condemn the archbishop, there is no way he can be called to account for the bloodshed. Milton says none of these things, of course. Earlier he encouraged readers "who can judiciously read" their own times in his narrative (v. 129); he now "appears" to be interested merely in the facts.

The technique of introducing materials from his sources in such a way as to prompt the reader to think about contemporary issues is evident also in Milton's presentation of another national hero, King Edgar. Unlike his account of Augustine, Milton opens his narrative of Edgar with profuse praise, but he delivers it with self-conscious wit. As Milton's sources testify, Edgar "had no War all his Reign; yet allways well prepar'd for War, govern'd the Kingdom in great Peace, Honour, and Prosperity," and was "much extoll'd for Justice, Clemency, and all Kingly Vertues." Yet Milton cannot continue with these accolades without calling attention to the sources with which he must deal. Edgar, he adds, is extolled "the more, ye may be sure, by Monks, for his building so many Monasteries; as some write, every year one" (v.321). What is of most relevance here, however, is the way in which Milton closes his account by relating Edgar's faults.

Again one of the fascinations of this concluding section of Edgar's portrait is Milton's self-presentation. The first of the two stories of Edgar's faults is of special interest to students of Milton because he once used it as the subject of a projected tragedy featuring the consequences of the King's pride and lust. It tells of how Edgar murdered his future wife's husband, who had fallen in love with this woman while supposedly pursuing her on behalf of the King. In the *History*, Milton sharply dissociates himself from those who "censure this act [of Edgar's] as cruel and tyrannical," for "consider'd well," he adds, "it may be judg'd more favourably, and that no man of sensible Spirit but in his place, without extraordinary perfection, would have done the like: for next to life what worse treason could have bin committed against him?" (v.326). It is both amusing and jarring to find Milton sympathetically siding with a king against his detractors. If readers are to pass judgment on Edgar, they must take issue with this unexpected defender of a king.

The second story of Edgar's faults, though also about lust, is a more light-hearted tale. The plot features a bed trick played on the youthful King, who "yet unmarried . . . abstain'd not from Women." In this case, the maid who substituted for her lady's desired daughter tells the King of the trick, and there is a happy ending. Instead of being angry at the maid, the King "advanc'd her above her Lady, lov'd her and accompanied with her only, till he married *Elfrida*" (v.327).

That Milton included this story is the most intriguing aspect of it. Ostensibly it is here because it provides another illustration of the King's faults. Milton is not able to endorse its truth, however; he calls it "fitter for a Novel then a History; but as I find it in *Malmsbury*, so I relate it" (v.327). Yet it is hard to believe that he includes it merely because Malmesbury did. To be sure, the story fits well into an aesthetic scheme; a tragedy about lust is balanced by a comedy about lust, thus ending the portrait of a good king on an appropriately positive note. But for a Restoration audience it could prompt other, less purely aesthetic responses. In addition to what it may add to the lengthy portrait of Edgar, this tale of a lusty king's exploits is capable of forging an amusing link between an ancient national hero and a contemporary one. If there were no other similarities, Charles II at least shared his faults with this great king. Whatever else the Restoration monarch deserved to be known for, his combination of lust and kind pity toward lower-class maidens, and his proclivities for elevating them to ladies, were among his best-known accomplishments. Again, Milton, refusing even to attest to the truth of the story, is silent, leaving the reader to draw the parallel. He is but a relayer of the accounts of others, and a good-natured accepter of the human frailties of kings.

As in Milton's Restoration poems, the silences in the *History* – those moments when Milton allows readers to say things for themselves – are as central to its art as are the words that he utters. Of the numerous places where Restoration readers might have been prompted to make their own utterances, there is no more engaging example of Milton's art of indirection than the story of Tosti, Earl of Northumberland. Like the account of Edgar's faults in Book v, this narrative, told in Book vi, features a combination of "truth" and "fable." Indeed, Milton relates two different extended versions of this story, the second of which he does not accept as true. The lack of economy of Milton's method leads Fogel to exclaim "it is somewhat surprising to find Milton devoting so much space to a story he does not believe, when his usual practice is to condense to the limit" (v. 389). But does Milton's failure to condense his materials demonstrate a nodding-off of his artistic judgment here?

In both versions of the story, Tosti is an earl who is banished for his crimes. Involved in the discrepancies between the two versions – though Milton does not call attention to this point – is whether Tosti was banished because of crimes against the people or crimes against the King. In the first account, which relies heavily on Simeon, Milton focuses on an insurrection of the Northumbrians against the earl, who is portrayed as guilty of "treachery... intolerable exactions and oppressions." Milton relates "a tumult at York," in which the Northumbrians "beset the Palace of Tosti their Earl, slew more then 200 of his Souldiers and Servants, pillag'd his Tresure, and put him to flie for his life." When the King sent Duke Harold "to pacifie the Northumbrians," "the whole Country" came "to complain of their grevances" against Tosti, laying "op'n the cruelty of his Government, and thir own birth-right of freedom not to endure the tyranny of any Governour whatsoever, with absolute refusal to admit him again, and Harold hearing reason, all the complices of Tosti were expell'd the Earldom. He himself [was] banish't" (v. 388).

The version of the story that Milton rejects is taken from Huntingdon, and it features Tosti's envy of his younger brother, Harold, whose preparations for an entertainment for the King are interrupted when Tosti violently murders some of Harold's followers: "lopping off Hands, Armes, Legs of some, Heads of others, [Tosti] threw them into Butts of Wine, Meath, or Ale, which were laid in for the Kings drinking." In Huntingdon's account, it was "for this barbarous Act [that] the King pronounc't him banish'd," and it was only then that the Northumbrians, "taking advantage at the Kings displeasure and sentence against him, rose also to be reveng'd of his cruelties done to themselves" (v. 389).

There can be no doubt which of the two accounts of Tosti's banishment is more compatible with Milton's own political views. The first version credits the Northumbrians with initiating an insurrection and with forthrightly presenting their grievances. The second one presents them following the lead of their king, and getting their revenge only when it was expedient for them to do so. In the interest of economy, Milton could have given the "true" version only. That he includes the second version, the politically safer story he is rejecting, not only permits the reader to grasp more easily the political import of the story he is accepting. It allows Milton the opportunity both to reproduce the political options from which he as an Englishman has had to choose, and to reaffirm, under cover, the validity of his choice. The reason that Milton gives for rejecting the second version of his story clarifies none of these points, however. But what he does say is equally interesting.

The rationale offered for rejecting the second version of the Tosti story is perfectly consistent with Milton's presentation of himself as a seeker after truth. Its plot does not make sense of the facts as we know them: "but this no way agrees, for why then should *Harold* or the King so much labour with the Northumbrians to re-admit him, if he were a banish'd man for his Crimes done before?" (v. 389). As a response to the lengthy second account, this remark cannot be faulted for lack of economy. It quickly gets to the heart of a matter that Milton mentioned in his first account but did not touch upon in the second version – the pressure put upon the Northumbrians by the King's party to readmit Tosti as their ruler. Milton interrogates the logic of the plot of the second story because it makes the party that Tosti had wronged the same party that wanted him readmitted.

But the logic that seems faulty in Milton's second story is precisely the logic that was not making sense, for Milton and others, in the early months of 1660, when pressure had been mounting for the King's return. Though Milton does not encourage the drawing of parallels with contemporary events in this section of his narrative, he effectively focuses the reader's attention, at the end of the Tosti account, on restoring power to someone who has previously done crimes; and he does it in such a way as to make restoration the issue at stake in deciding between the two versions he tells. Milton prefers the first version because those who were wronged, the Northumbrians, refused to readmit the criminal, despite pressure from the King's party. A story about a wronged party inviting back to power the doer of that wrong is a story that seems too illogical to be true.

What Restoration readers would or would not have seen as they confronted the *History* would have depended a good deal no doubt on what they expected to find there. If they turned to the work to learn the "facts" of ancient British history, they might have been impressed by the care with which this historian diligently sifts through the conflicting materials at his disposal. On the other hand, if readers had turned to the work in the spirit of Toland's projected readers, suspecting that historians presented "facts" as they would have them be, not as they really were, they would have found little in the *History* to alleviate those suspicions. But neither would they have found a simple case of a writer using the mouths of others to express his own opinions. What they could have found instead is an author well equipped with subtler devices capable of getting them to formulate those opinions for themselves.

As the above examples would seem to demonstrate, one of the most interesting of these devices is the image that Milton presents of himself; and one of the most engaging aspects of the way in which that image functions is the extent to which our response to it depends on our *prior* knowledge of this historian. As is the case in our time, most of the readers who confronted this work in 1670 undoubtedly did not pick it up simply for the history lesson; they read it because they were acquainted with the author. And thus their expectations were shaped not only by suspicions about how historians manipulate history, but also by knowledge of Milton's own history. They were reading a work written by a man who had a past to live up to, or to live down, as the case might be.

In the *History*, as in *Paradise Lost*, Milton presents himself in ways that invite readers to recollect other accounts – presented by both Milton and his enemies – of who the author is, or was.[16] It is this recollection of Milton's own history that will allow them to respond in ways not directly prompted by the "fact-oriented" historian in the *History*, and that will allow them, both here and in *Paradise Lost*, to begin the process of thinking metaphorically about the stories they are reading, a process that Paul Ricoeur aptly defines when he says, "to see *the like* is to see the same in spite of, and through, the different."[17] In the *History* Milton's self-presentation both is and is not like images of him they have encountered elsewhere. On the one hand, Milton's constant search for truth amidst the accounts of his monkish authorities presents a familiar picture of what Milton wanted to stand for throughout his writings. But on the other hand, Milton's failure to condemn a king for lust and murder, as in the case of Edgar, or to press charges vigorously against an archbishop for his forcing of consciences, as in the case of Augustine, is so at odds with other images of Milton that his readers must conclude either that the author has mellowed, or that he has created for himself a protective facade, one that allows him to raise controversial issues without appearing to have a polemical interest in them. Compatible with the latter option is Milton's method of using history in the great Restoration poems, where his task was obviously not to create situations exactly parallel with his contemporary world but to shape his stories in such a way as to "make [the] discourse" of that world outside the work "appear."[18]

Of the various ways in which we could position the *History* in the canon, one of the easiest might be by means of the kind of self-portrait that Milton creates in this work. We might relate this image to two other Miltonic characters, Abdiel and Samson, whose speeches reverberate richly in the presence of the knowledge we bring about the author who created them.

Abdiel is the bold and aggressive champion of God, the pre-Restoration Milton of the *Second Defense,* who fearlessly attacks the enemy and even causes him to lose his balance. On Day One of the battle, he and his cohorts force the enemy to flee, but on Day Two, when the enemy unexpectedly returns to the battle, Abdiel and his companions are on the defensive, and though they fight bravely, they do not make any headway. Abdiel's tactics, which worked better on Day One than on Day Two, are not operating in the *History.*

Then there are the tactics of Samson. For all of the complicated things that Milton may be trying to convey through this story and this character, few would refuse to acknowledge that the blind and haughty Samson is there to project and reject and modify various images of Milton himself. We might readily connect Samson to the historian of the *History* by relating the latter's statement about monks – "these guides, where can be had no better, must be follow'd" – to Samson's equally ambiguous reply to the officer: "Masters' commands come with a power resistless / To such as owe them absolute subjection" (1404–5). The officer finds in Samson's reply a welcome compliance. Indeed, he will see that Samson is "fresh clad / To appear as fits before th'illustrious Lords" (1317–18). It is in this appropriate dress of "thir state Livery" (1616) that Samson unsuspiciously pretends to be "overtired" so that he might "lean a while" (1632). If Samson is Milton's fantasy of having made a difference in the world, the *History* shows the author himself unsuspiciously (to some at least) tugging at the pillars.

Notes

1 *The Early Lives of Milton,* ed. Helen Darbishire (London, 1932), p. 84.
2 *Early Lives,* p. 184. Toland's account is more specific than that of Milton's nephew, Edward Phillips, who reports, "some Passages . . . being thought too sharp against the Clergy, could not pass the Hand of the Licencer" (p. 75).
3 For a discussion of pre-Restoration dating of the work, see French Fogel's introduction to his edition: v.xxxvii–xliii.
4 "Texts as Events: Reflections on the History of Political Thought," in *The Politics of Discourse: The Literature and History of Seventeenth-Century England,* ed. Kevin Sharpe and Steven N. Zwicker (Berkeley and London, 1987), pp. 24–5. Pocock's insistence that the historian give a "third-person reconstitution" of an action being performed at a particular time, rather than describe the work in terms of what was apparent to the author in the process of writing it, could perhaps have more than usual relevance for the *History,* a work which was probably composed over many years.
5 Milton writes:

> For I do not insist on ornate language; I ask for a historian, not an orator.
> Nor would I favor injecting frequent maxims or judgments on historical
> exploits, lest by breaking the chain of events, the historian invade the
> province of the political writer; if, in explaining plans and narrating deeds,

he follows to the best of his ability not his own invention or conjecture but the truth, he truly fulfills his function. (VII.501; XII.94)

In his 16 December 1957 letter to Henry de Brass, Milton also explains that "the functions of rhetorician and historian are different . . . just as the arts themselves are different from each other" (VII.506; XII.102).

Without explicitly denying that historians might have political motives, Fogel strongly suggests there is a difference in motive between historians and political writers when invoking the de Brass letters to condemn the Digression as "one of Milton's less successful ventures into historical analysis, one in which his depth of political conviction . . . diverted him temporarily from his task as historian and led him to 'invade the office of the Political Writer'" (v.435).

6 See especially Quentin Skinner, "History and Ideology in the English Revolution," *Historical Journal*, 8 (1965), 151–78; and Martin Dzelzainis, "The Ideological Context of Milton's *History of Britain*" (unpublished Ph.D. dissertation, University of Cambridge, 1983).

7 *Censorship and Interpretation* (Madison, 1984), p. 48 and *passim*.

8 Obviously boldness and aggressiveness were not always Milton's polemical strategies. See Christopher Hill, *Milton and the English Revolution* (London, 1977), p. 157, for a relevant discussion of Milton's "tactical concessions" in *Areopagitica*.

9 Lines 665–6, 818. All references to Milton's poetry are from *The Student's Milton*, ed. Frank Allen Patterson (New York, 1957).

10 *Milton: A Biography* (Oxford, 1968), vol. I, p. 327.

11 Fogel, "Milton as Historian," in F. R. Fogel and H. R. Trevor-Roper, *Milton and Clarendon* (Los Angeles, 1965), pp. 8, 10.

12 For the argument for the early dating of the Digression, see Fogel's introduction to this piece: v.426–35. However, the Digression can just as readily be seen as an *indirect* discussion of the causes of the Restoration. When the secluded members of the Long Parliament were restored on 21 February 1660 and proceeded to remove the obstacles to the restoration of monarchy, that body ceased to be of use as a symbol of resistance to monarchical tyranny and thus could be portrayed as an accomplice in the final destruction of Milton's "Free Commonwealth." Also, Milton's attack on Presbyterian failure to resist tyranny was surely as relevant in 1660 as it was in 1648. See Woolrych, "The Date of the Digression in Milton's *History of Britain*," *For Veronica Wedgwood These: Studies in Seventeenth-century History*, ed. Richard Ollard and Pamela Tudor-Craig (London, 1986), pp. 217–46, for an extended argument for a late 1660 dating. I am not comfortable with Woolrych's assumption that the Digression was added to a work already completed. That it might have been part of an extensive Restoration revision of old materials is a possibility that needs to be taken more seriously. Whether it was suppressed by the censors or withheld by Milton himself in 1670 seems impossible to determine.

13 On the place of the Norman Conquest in oppositional historiography, see Skinner, "History and Ideology in the English Revolution," pp. 152–3.

14 *Politics and Poetry in Restoration England: The Case of Dryden's "Annus Mirabilis"* (Cambridge, Mass., 1975), pp. 231–57.

15 For a relevant account of the strong role Archbishop Sheldon was to play in suppressing nonconformity, see Ronald Hutton, *The Restoration: A Political and*

Religious History of England and Wales 1658–1667 (Oxford, 1985), pp. 176–7, 194, 200, 214, 235–6.

16 My point here is that in a political reading of Milton's Restoration works images of the writer must inevitably be read rhetorically, as answers to images of the writer that have been presented previously by Milton or by others. For a contrasting formulation of Milton's relationship to his persona, see John Guillory, *Poetic Authority* (New York, 1983), p. 104: "Milton's habitual stance, both in his poetry and in his prose, is to present himself as he is, or believes himself to be."

17 "The Metaphorical Process as Cognition, Imagination, and Feeling," *Critical Inquiry*, 5 (1978), p. 148.

18 *Ibid.*, p. 144.

14

The poetics of engagement

JAMES GRANTHAM TURNER

Breaking out of critical separatism – the polarization of Milton's *œuvre* that thrusts his prose into the underclass – involves abandoning certain engrained assumptions: that the aesthetic is timeless; that the persuasive–instrumental text must be inferior to the pure literary text, where language becomes an end in itself; that occasionality diminishes artistic quality, and polemic destroys it entirely. Even Sartre, the philosopher of *engagement*, assumes that "poetic language rises upon the ruins of prose," that prose is end-directed and poetry the reverse, and though he claims to be defining only the modern era, his use of an example from Homer suggests that he considers this antithesis universal.[1] The antiseparatist camp, which seeks to reestablish literature as an active partner in the political discourse of its own age, finds a strong ally in Shakespeare's Hamlet, who tells the players that art must "shew . . . the verie Age and Bodie of the Time his forme and pressure" (III.ii). The separatist position finds an apparently incontrovertible champion in Milton himself, however. Milton repeatedly contrasts the distasteful and violent task of polemic with the poetic career interrupted by "these tumultuous times," particularly in that famous passage of *The Reason of Church-Government* where he complains of being limited by "the cool element of prose," where "knowing my self inferior to my self . . . I have the use, as I may account it, but of my left hand" (I.807–8).

No one doubts that, for better or worse, Milton's life-work demonstrates (in Hamlet's words) the "pressure" of the revolutionary age. The question of historically–determined "forme" is more difficult, however. When Milton promises "high *strains* in new and lofty *Measures*" to match the coming age of national regeneration (I.616) he seems to assume a direct equivalence between literary form and the state of England, a direct relationship between the godly times and the highest inspiration; but this claim relates to his future, not his present performance, and he makes it in a form dissociated from lofty status, disqualified by virtue of its very suitability to the times. Separatism continues to divide Milton's output into the rough illegitimate forms of prose, contaminated by the body of the age, and authentic poetic forms: the superficial prose/verse dichotomy becomes the sign of a deeper distinction, between pure art and polemic non-art. Even in the seventeenth century, political conservatives would cleanse Milton of his fanatical taint by praising the magnificent verse and raging against the "seditious prose," product of a "mercenary pen" and thus by definition anti-art (*MCH* I. 122–3). The young Addison lamented: "Oh had the Poet ne'er profan'd his pen, / To varnish o'er the guilt of faithless men!" (I. 105–6). (In later years he would write an immensely detailed appreciation of *Paradise Lost* without once mentioning the prose.) In one sublime poem, set in the celestial regions shortly after the death of Dryden, the shade of Milton confesses that the Laureate's "smoothness" and loyalty to the crown made him by far the better poet. Only by virtue of a formal distinction, a separation of the literary and the political that Dryden would have thought strange, did Milton himself squeeze in to Heaven: "'twas verse alone / Did for my hideous crimes atone" (I. 124). By 1700, then, God Himself was a separatist.

An alternative reception-history structured and valued Milton's *œuvre* quite differently. For his nephew Edward Phillips, Milton is "the Author (not to mention his other Works, both in strict and solute Oration...) of two Heroic Poems, and a Tragedy"; the minor poems and prose tracts are classed together as rhetoric, and (though they cleave the sentence with a parenthesis) all bear witness to his status as Author. For his friend Thomas Ellwood, the hierarchy is still clearer: *Eikonoklastes*, the *Defenses* and the epics are listed in triumphant sequence to prove the general thesis that "Great his undertakings were ... / Invention never higher rose / In poetic strains, or prose." Questions of form are subordinated to the heroic quality of the assertion.[2] We should recall that Milton's own claim in *Paradise Lost* – to write "Things unattempted yet in Prose or Rhyme" (I. 16) – simultaneously isolates the epic and brackets together all previous attempts, prose as well as verse. When morning hymns are sung in Paradise, "Prose or numerous Verse" cannot be told apart; the value of discourse lies not in postlapsarian artistic categories, but in "rapture" and "unmeditated" authenticity (V. 145–52). A similar assumption, deriving likewise from the nonconformist hatred of set forms, underlies John Toland's attempt to reinstate Milton's prose at the highest level of literature: "the best Books," whatever the form, have been "oppos'd to the prevalency of the contrary opinion" and stimulated by personal suffering and oppression, in contrast to "the Writings of unconcern'd and retir'd Persons," which are mere amusements or exercises, "pitiful Declamations without any Force, Experience, or Vivacity." Toland evolves a kind of oppositional aesthetic: he promotes energetic and experiential criteria over formal ones, and links discursive achievement directly to political controversy.[3]

Even conservative critics would recognize the intimate relation between Milton's radical political energies and his distinctive poetic grandeur. For one reader, to be made aware of the prose (by Toland's edition) actually contaminates his experience of *Paradise Lost* ("thy seditious prose... soils the beauties of thy brightest page"), but this horror is then equated with what is most sublime in the poem, the sudden plunge into "the dread abyss beneath" (*MCH* I.122–3). Milton is thus identified with his own rebel angels both politically and aesthetically. Addison, as we have seen, praises the sublime poetry and deplores the political profanity, but the terms of his praise unwittingly recombine them: poetic description itself is a kind of rebellion; Addison's Milton is a Satanic activist driven by "hallow'd rage," who "Spurns the dull province of mortality, / Shakes heav'ns eternal throne with dire alarms, / And sets th'Almighty thunderer in arms" (I.105–6). Bishop Warburton makes the association explicit, recognizing sublimity in the prose as well as in the epic, and identifying it, not as an isolated exception, but as a direct product of radical puritanism:

> What was fanaticism and cant in the rest of his party shows itself in him in a prodigious spirit of poetical enthusiasm; and he frequently breaks out into strains as sublime, or if possible more so, than any in his higher Poetry. (*MCH* II.92)

"Or if possible more so . . ." The current volume does not claim so much, but it is glad to acknowledge this tribute to the integration of poetry and prose, the literary and the political.

I Achievements of the left hand?

How did Milton himself understand the relation of the two "forms," prose and verse? In *The Reason of Church-Government* prose is not only a less ornate mode of expression but the polar opposite of poetry, earthbound and phlegmatic: "sitting here below in the cool element of prose" contrasts dramatically with the "Poet soaring in the high region of his fancies with his garland and singing robes about him" (I.808). Elsewhere, however, this conceptual hierarchy could be shaken or even reversed. Milton's earliest letters reveal simultaneously a reverence and a contempt for poetry: he praises the "truly Poetical Majesty and Virgilian Genius [ingenium]" of Alexander Gil's ode – a topical political poem, interestingly enough – but refers to his own Vacation Exercise as a trifle, delegated to him by someone with more important things to do. Writing to Thomas Young, the influential tutor who would later draw him into prose controversy, he confesses his pleasure in quitting the manacles of verse and writing *soluto stylo*, a "free Oration" that allows him to attempt "an Asiatic exuberance of words." (Phillips' "solute Oration" seems to echo his uncle's own vocabulary.) Even earlier than this (while still at St. Paul's) Milton had apologized for this tendency to "Asiana exuberantia" in his own discourse, but in the letter to Young it is heartily embraced: conceptual space, creative freedom, and fine excess are associated with prose, constraint with verse.[4]

This juggling of alternative hierarchies is not just a juvenile confusion of Milton's. Hatred of the bondage of rhyme rings out in the preface to *Paradise*

Lost (though "Asiatic exuberance" has now been transferred to the barbarous aesthetic of Satan).[5] *Eikonoklastes* reserves its most virulent contempt for Charles I's "Poetical" garb, for his "straines that come almost to Sonnetting" – though Milton himself longed for the "high *strains*" and "singing robes" of the poet, and wrote sonnets throughout the crisis-period; as Lana Cable points out in chapter 7 above, he dismissed the *Eikon Basilike* as "a peece of Poetrie," lacking only rhyme (III.406, 420). And in *Of Education*, the most orderly exposition of Milton's intellectual program, the position of poetry is doubly ambiguous. Firstly, in a curriculum where the sequence of subjects is all-important, Milton fumbles at the crucial moment: logic opens into rhetoric, "to which Poetry would be made subsequent, or indeed rather precedent, as being more simple, sensuous and passionate" (II.403). Secondly, it becomes unclear what he means by "Poetry." It is certainly not "the prosody of a verse," a rudimentary skill which should be taught much earlier (II.404). The context suggests that he is thinking of literature itself, the "new and lofty *Measures*" of *Of Reformation* or the mighty program of epics, tragedies, lyrics, and satires outlined in *The Reason of Church-Government*, that would "imbreed and cherish in a great people the seeds of vertu and publick civility" (I.816). But in fact the "sublime art" proposed here in *Of Education*, the famous "sensuous and passionate" discourse, is not creative writing but literary theory, not poetry but poetics. High literary enterprise is always Milton's ideal, whether the "Carmina grandia" praised in his friend Gil or the "glorious and magnificent Use [that] might be made of Poetry" in *Of Education* (II.405–6). But he seems uncertain whether prose or verse is the best vehicle, or whether poetics is related to prosodic form at all.

Given this conceptual slippage, we should look more closely at the "left hand" passage that twentieth-century critics often read as a deprecation of the entire prose enterprise.[6] What are the principles that differentiate "this manner of writing" from the great future work, and thereby alienate Milton from himself? His complaints are all interrelated, but they can be schematized as follows. Prose is a "cool element" incompatible with his own "genial power" and his natural tendency to "soar." The readers of polemic are "of no Empyreall conceit" and have neither the erudition nor the leisure to give his work the proper attention. Consequently, formal excellence must be sacrificed to expediency, "art" to mere "solidity": "it were a folly to commit any thing elaborately compos'd to the carelesse and interrupted listening of these tumultuous times." Could he have chosen his own subject and production schedule, on the other hand, he could have brought his work to a high finish, "pencill[ing] it over with all the curious touches of art, even to the perfection of a faultlesse picture." These failures – each matched to an individual criterion of discursive excellence – are all symptoms of a larger problem: the "necessity and constraint" imposed by the urgency of the crisis.

It is my contention that every one of these complaints is circumvented or exploded, either in *The Reason of Church-Government* itself or in closely-related polemical works. Take, for example, Milton's lament that prose allows him only "solidity" and not the "art" he longs to produce. In the rapturous account of his literary plans – that is, what he *should* be doing if not prevented by the sordid task of writing this pamphlet – he identified "solid and treatable smoothnesse" as the distinguishing gift of the poet. And his definition of "art" comes close to what he universally condemns: "verbal curiosities" (dismissed in this very section of *The Reason of Church-Government*), superadded ornament, a style that is "beautified" rather than beautiful, the "swelling Epithets thick laid / As varnish on a Harlot's cheek" that Christ denounces in *Paradise Regained*, the poetical "garb" that Charles I wraps around his deformities.[7] Stanley Fish's point (chapter 2 above) about "supplementarity" in Milton's hermeneutics – that he is forced simultaneously to condemn it and to display it – applies also to his verbal aesthetics. Milton extols scriptural plainness and associates ornate prose with depravity and heresy, denouncing the "knotty Africanisms, the pamper'd metafors, the intricat and involv'd sentences . . . the fantastick and declamatory flashes, the cross-jingling periods" of Patristic Latin (1. 568). But in so doing he describes his own style perfectly. The passage in front of us provides an example of this "Asiatic" loquacity and "African" ornateness: after admitting the folly of exposing his art to the common reader and the frustration of working only with the left hand, he goes on "and though I shall be foolish in saying more to this purpose, yet since it will be such a folly as wisest men going about to commit have only confest and so committed, I may trust with more reason, because with more folly, to have courteous pardon." Just as he inscribes this higher folly over the lower one, cancelling his earlier disavowal, so he "pencils over" his deprecatory text with ornate and "cross-jingling" rhetoric. Is this "precedent" or "subsequent" to Poetry?

This display of artifice has a tactical purpose, of course. At the mid-point of his tract, Milton is tendering a "petition" to a new class of reader, "intelligent and equal . . . elegant and learned." This petition is immediately granted, since he goes on to do exactly what he complained he could not do: he gives us an elaborate literary autobiography. Though he presents this as only a temporary change of focus, the entire tract actually appeals to – and thus constitutes – this higher reader, while expelling the opposing kind.[8] Milton here presents his opponents as back-street warehousemen ("hollow antiquities sold by the seeming bulk") and packhorses who "la[y] ye down their hors load of citations and fathers at your doore . . . let any gentle apprehension that can distinguish learned pains from unlearned drudgery imagin what pleasure or profoundnesse can be in this, or what honour to deal against such adversaries." The quality of the polemic enterprise thus depends on the status of one's opponent, and status is determined by class. The scrivener's son objects to Joseph Hall's satires, for example, not because they are aggressive or topical, but because they are timid, grovelling and hence plebeian: true satire ought "to strike high, and adventure dangerously at the most eminent vices among the greatest persons, and not to creepe into every blinde Taphouse that fears a Constable more than a Satyr" (1.916). The nobility of liberal or leisured activity is opposed to the loathsome servility of wage labor – precisely the duality used by Royalists to separate Milton's sublime art from his "mercenary" prose. Enforced marital copulation is revolting for Milton because it is analogous to labor (as Annabel Patterson shows in chapter 4 above), and opposition to divorce is branded in *Colasterion* as the work of a cast-off servant, a peasant, a "mechanic," a boar, a solicitor or legal scrivener incapable of "gentle breeding" (11.724–57 *passim*). In this context, his general dismissal of "this manner of writing" should be understood to refer, not to the prose format, but to the drudgery of response to opponents who soil his page.

The left-handed preface to Book 11 of *The Reason of Church-Government* thus becomes, if not quite a self-consuming artifact, then certainly a self-invalidating modesty topos. "Time servs not now" to describe his literary ambitions, which are then promptly described; one might almost say that the occasion serves *mainly* to empower this revelation.[9] And by thus representing "the mind at home in the spacious circuits of her musing" in the medium of prose, Milton abolishes restrictions allegedly intrinsic to that medium, so inhospitable to the "Poet soaring in the high region of his fancies." Just as the free movement of prose vanquishes the restriction of verse in the early letter to Young, so here the constraining properties of prose are localized and transcended, not by deferring all hopes to an unattainable poetic vision, but by reconstituting spaciousness in the prose itself.

This reassertion of *auctoritas* seems at first to be undermined by the lament that he cannot choose his topic for himself; he presents himself in *Paradise Lost*, after all, as "long choosing, and beginning late" (1x.26). But we must be careful not to miss a subtle shift in emphasis from *choice* to *self*. "If I were wise only to mine own ends, I would certainly take such a subject as of it self might catch applause" – the phrasing reminds us that Milton has put public spirit over private interests, and associates the latter with careerism and cheap theatricality. Such art would bear witness only to itself, an idolatrous condition that Milton denounced in his Royalist opponents (as John Knott and Lana Cable remark in their essays for this volume). In any case, the issue of choice is over before it begins, because Milton has just made the far larger claim that God Himself has "command[ed him] to take the trumpet and blow a dolorous or a jarring blast." His own will, consequently, dissolves into a higher authority.

Indeed, so many of the "high" criteria are fulfilled in the passage that disclaims them (artistic elaboration, audience refinement, erudition, warmth, divine sanction, triumph over restraint) that when he refers to his early achievements in "prosing or versing, but chiefly this latter," we are momentarily uncertain whether he refers to poetry or to "this" specimen of the higher prose. The effect of hierarchy dissolves as soon as it is made.

Though verse is "chiefly" favored, both forms are conceived as valid uses of the one talent that is death to hide, and both are marked by "vital signes." Milton constantly invokes evaluative hierarchy, of course; his main concern, however, is not the hierarchy of verse over prose but that of vitality over deadness, the high text defended in *Areopagitica* ("the pretious life-blood of a master spirit") as opposed to the trash he is forced to attack in *Animadversions* or *Colasterion*. And this deep dichotomy in Milton's criticism cannot be assimilated to the polarity of aesthetic *versus* functional or literary *versus* political; he uses the same terms to praise the life blood threatened by censorship and the "life blood Lawes" trampled by the bishops (I.592, II.493, 557). The issue is whether the text manifests an intrinsic vigor and authority, not whether it is formally or intentionally poetic. On this scale of values, the text-in-the-world, the committed and end-directed text in whatever form, wins out over the text of aesthetic disengagement, sporting with Amaryllis in the shade.

II Dust and heat

At one point, however, Milton definitely ascribes an intrinsic property to prose: it is a "cool element." This complaint runs parallel to the fear that the colder climate of England endangered Milton's inspiration – mentioned here together with "the fate of this age" (I.814), as well as in *Mansus* and *Paradise Lost*. Since the poem embodying this confession stands as proof that the poet *can* overcome "cold / Climate" and "evil days," we should see *The Reason of Church-Government* as a rehearsal for performative transcendence; the clamminess of his discursive environment is evoked as a potential danger, not an absolute limitation. Prose need not be considered "cool" at all, since it is the vehicle for impassioned Philippics and biblical prophesy. Milton himself identifies the loftiest passages in scripture as "hymns in prose," and applies the phrase directly to a fervent and aggressive passage in his own *Animadversions* (I.704–7, 930). The opening pages of *The Reason of Church-Government*, however, seem to associate prose (more conventionally) with temperance and rational persuasion, mental operations that involve the colder humors of the brain.

By equating Milton's intentions with "conventional expectations" of rationality ("the standards we usually apply to controversial prose"), Fish discovers an absolute contradiction between the ostensible goal of this tract – "Reason" manifested in calm and logical argument – and its actual effect: irrationality, stasis, passionately aggressive coercion.[10] But if we look closely at the opening paragraph, we see that Milton does acknowledge the passionate and extra-rational component of persuasion. *Reason* in the title is not merely expounded but *Urg'd*. "Hearts" must be "season'd"; the author must "incite, and in a manner, charme" the reader into the lifelong embrace of Truth. Eloquence is a matter of "colours and graces," operating not directly on reason but on "those inner parts and affections of the mind where the seat of reason is"; this idea expands into a remarkable scene in Book II, where Milton (driven by "the ardency of my mind") explains that he must work through "the severall Affections and Desires," "sensual mistresses" who control access to Queen Truth.[11] The "sensuous and passionate" *differentiates* poetry from rhetoric in *Of Education*, but here it is an essential part of prose persuasion.

This suggests that Milton is already putting into practice the poetic program that allegedly must wait for some future period. The whole point of this program is to reach the epicurean upper classes and bring them back into leadership. *Of Education* is extraordinarily sympathetic to that segment of the gentry "of a more delicious and airie spirit," who retire from public life "to the enjoyments of ease and luxury"; given the corruption of their culture, theirs is "the wisest and the safest course" (II.376). The new regenerate poetry proposed in *The Reason of Church-Government* will appeal "to those especially of soft and delicious temper who will not so much as look upon Truth herselfe, unlesse they see her elegantly drest"; he explicitly targets "our youth and gentry" (I.817–18). But the intended reader of this tract is already "elegant" (in Book II) and susceptible to passionate seduction (in this preface), needing to be "incite[d]" and "charme[d]" into an erotic love of Truth. Though Milton refers ostensibly to "the multitude" here, his inviting attitude is quite different from his usual antipopulist contempt, and effectively incorporates the common reader into that refined and "passionate" élite.

Prose thus claims the energetic–impulsive and seductive power sometimes ascribed to poetry alone. By undertaking to "incite and charme," Milton aligns his polemic with the "charming pipe" of the divorce tracts and with the "conversation" that can "cherish and re-incite" the sexual life of the married couple (II.241, 740). The new poetry will "imbreed and cherish" the "seeds" of civil virtue, but the generative function need not be deferred until then: the preachers defended in *Animadversions* "procreate a number of faithfull men, making a kind of creation like to Gods, by infusing his sprit and likenesse into them"; Milton himself, though writing explicitly as a "Rhetorician" and confining himself to the "outward" political sphere, aspires "with a kind of Promethean skill to shape and fashion" a human figure (I.721, 835). Even in the dullest exposition and compilation Milton could discover a supplement of exotic charm; when he admits that the "desert Authors" of *Moscovia* "yet with some delight drew me after them" (VIII.475), he echoes the Song of Solomon: "draw me, we will run after thee" (1:4).

Milton's self-conception in the prose departs from the "cool" ratiocinative model in three significant ways. One depends on sensuous warmth – the incitement and charm promised (though hardly delivered) in *The Reason of Church-Government*, or the "gentle stroking" of the divorce tracts, "cherishing to man's life" (II.240). The second, and most prominent, is the vehement and vituperative mode associated with the biblical prophets. The third, that most impressed conservatives and radicals alike during the following decades, is the display of sublimity, energy, and power. These strategies are exemplified in the celebrated "chariot of Zeale" passage in the *Apology for Smectymnuus*, often singled out by critics even when they deny the artistic quality of the prose works in general (1.899–900). The context is nothing less than a genealogy of religious discourse itself, tracing its different modes back to a single fountainhead. Christ represented the origin and totality, being "Lord to expresse his indoctrinating power in what sort him best seem'd." (The expression of power, we notice, is assumed to be the highest function of the text.) After Christ's departure "what was all in him" was divided among many followers, each specialists in a particular tone. The different styles are linked to the various physiological tempers of the audience, and produce effects hardly less physical: they "check," make "cheerefull," "draw to salvation," "strengthen with . . . revivings." Rationality is only one among these rhetorical modes, and certainly not the highest:

> Some also were indu'd with a staid moderation, and soundnesse of argument to teach and convince the rationall and sober-minded; yet not therefore that to be thought the only expedient course of teaching, for in times of opposition when either against new heresies arising or old corruptions to be reform'd this coole unpassionate mildnesse of positive wisdome is not anough to damp and astonish the proud resistance of carnall and false Doctors, then (that I may have leave to soare a while as the Poets use) then Zeale whose substance is ethereall, arming in compleat diamond ascends his fiery Chariot . . .

"Coole" ratiocination is dull compared to the hot and passionate modes, which come closer to Christ's power and higher in the scale that leads back to His primal authority. The "times of opposition" demand, not a deferral, but an unleashing of high poetic aspiration. And this soaring is performed within the text itself, as the chariot–sentence rolls inexorably over reasoners and prelates alike, "brusing their stiffe necks under his flaming wheels." Milton *enacts* the rise of zeal rather than just describing it, so that when he continues "Thus" did the prophets of old and "Thus" did Christ Himself – steering back to the origin from which the paragraph unrolled – he refers to the impact of the immediately preceding sentence, the self-actualizing of the text itself.

This passage is not an isolated "Poetic" interlude or digression, as separatist critics contend. Firstly, it belongs to a proenergetic and antirationalist tendency that runs throughout the controversial prose. Secondly, Milton's self-conscious raising of the tone, his petition to "soare a while as the Poets use" inserted dramatically between two "thens," equates the complete tract with poetry, not this single moment. Poets do not soar continually, but rise to climactic moments in the course of their work, as in the "paulo majora canamus" of Virgil or the Zealous ecclesiastical speech in *Lycidas* that "shrinks" the stream of conventional pastoral. The war-chariot of Zeale is drawn, in fact, by two creatures who represent precisely the qualities considered most unpoetic by separatist critics: scorn and indignation.[12] Rather than assuming that vituperation "mars" the text and disqualifies it as literature, Milton assigns it an intense uplifting power.

The poetic status of denunciation was not a new idea; Averroes, for example, assumed that "all poetry consists in vituperation or praise [in vituperandi vel laudandi]."[13] But Milton invests it with his own peculiar "ardency of mind." David Loewenstein shows (in chapter 9 above) how fully it sustained Milton's self-justification in the *Defenses*, and how he conceived denigration as an artistic effect, a musical modulation. The future poetry outlined in *The Reason of Church-Government* will not just celebrate the good, but will perform medical cures (associated with caustics and purgatives) and "deplore" the backsliding of once godly nations (1.816–17, and cf. 846–8). Verbal abuse provides Milton with an extra-rational energy and bodily presence in the text, the "strong and sinewy force" of derision in *Animadversions* or the "vis demonstrativis" explicitly claimed for his "vituperatio" in the *Pro Se Defensio* (1.664, IV.ii.795; IX.222). It also matches his view of literature as a high and dangerous combat, as chivalric–aggressive "Assertion" – a model that develops as he passes from the frigid purity of the 1630s to the confrontational ethics of *Areopagitica*, where the "dust and heat" of controversy is welcomed as the authenticating mark of commitment, a battle-scar for one who did not take the field in person. "Assertion" is a key word in Milton's self-presentation, a bridging concept that suppresses the formal distinction of prose and verse; it is applied equally to the divorce tracts, to the denunciation of hirelings, and to *Paradise Lost* itself, whose purpose is to "assert Eternal Providence."[14]

Finally, the polemic combination of praise and vituperation may rest on an intuitive analogy between literary and cosmic creation. The creative moment is always opposed, implicitly or explicitly, to a revolting counterpart which must be expelled: the "infusing" procreation of godly preaching is contrasted to the reptilian spawn of the bishops, the imagined expulsion of the bad wife in the divorce tracts reenacts the "divorcing command" by which God first brought the universe out of chaos (1.720; II.273). The impure composite texts of controversy allowed Milton to gather together all the modes that had been scattered after the departure of Christ – celebratory, analytic, vituperative, monitory – and to achieve "a kind of creation like to Gods," driving out the foul adversary and establishing the laws and tokens of obedience that will guarantee the future. Is it too much to suggest that Milton adopts a divorcive and expulsive model of creation *because* of his experience in revolutionary polemic, *because* of the self-empowering discovery of a true vein of aggressive eloquence, first in the tracts of 1641–5 and then in the *Defenses*? Political *engagement* may then have generated rather than aborted Milton's epic vision; in the words that Dryden applied to Charles II, "crisis" may have *"authorized"* his skill.[15] Embracing a contaminating descent, creating and expelling the demonic Other (hirelings, bishops, wives, Presbyters, Royalists), valorizing activity, energy, and contrast – all this must have contributed to the cosmic and moral design of *Paradise Lost*. When Raphael recreates the original shaping of matter, telling how God

> vital virtue infus'd, and vital warmth
> Throughout the fluid Mass, but downward purg'd
> The black tartareous cold Infernal dregs
> Adverse to life,[16]

the language of epic description alternates with the language of Zeale, heated, seething and excessive.

III The poet's time

Milton's chief complaint, however, is not contamination but interruption. The list of works that claim to have been impaired by diversion ranges from the first letter to Thomas Young (cut short by "urbana diverticula") through *Moscovia* to the *Defensio Secunda*, which "snatched me to itself against my will [ad se rapuit invitum]" from more delightful tasks. He would never "divide thus, or transpose my former thoughts" to write *Of Education*, if his friend Hartlib had not forced the subject on him; diversion means the dispersal of his powers, the dismembering of Truth in his own person.[17] In some cases the crisis of England is squarely blamed. *The Reason of Church-Government* echoes *Lycidas* in bewailing the "necessity and constraint" that make him leave his studies for the world of "interrupted listening," the "urgent reason" that has "pluckt" his autobiography "by an abortive and foredated discovery"; the unripe berries of the earlier poem have now become a damaged foetus (1.807, 814, 820, 823). (He is wrong, of course, since the emergency should make him suppress rather than expose his more leisurely plans.) "The fate of this age," along with the cold climate, may even ruin those future poetic achievements that are to compensate for the present catastrophe. In each case a greater work has been set aside, with traumatic consequences.

Given that Milton laments the interruption of a self-motivated and self-paced cycle of studies which should mature into literature, critics have been eager to equate the abortive work with the prose and the greater work with the major poems that emerged in the 1660s, after he had been mercifully freed from politics. Even the radical Toland, promoting Milton's prose works to the highest rank, falls into the assumption that "religious Controversy" in his youth and "Affairs of State" in his mature years were obstacles, "Interruptions," distractions from his true epic vocation (*MCH*, 1.119–20). But Milton cannot be forced into a polar opposition between poetic quality and occasionality. The first important complaint is, after all, a major poem: *Lycidas* certainly begins by equating "occasion" with constraint and unripeness, but it rises to a sublime denunciation of the current condition, and it ends by superseding the "uncouth swain" with a voice of calm satisfaction and accomplishment. The modesty-topos may express genuine anxieties, but it is cancelled by the actual poetic achievement – an achievement empowered by precisely the occasionality it blames. By 1645, Milton could single out the passage written "by occasion" for special mention in his headnote. This revaluation is anticipated, typically, in the future poetry section of *The Reason of Church-Government*: if he were not struggling in the toils of occasion, he would be producing not only epics and tragedies, but sublime lyrics – "if occasion shall lead" (1.815).

The antiprelatical tracts, like *Lycidas*, appeared on the eve or threshhold of the crisis, before the outbreak of civil war; they are caught uneasily between an aesthetics of detachment and leisurely "elaboration," and an ethics of militant commitment. Like *Lycidas*, they seek to undo their own abortiveness and antitemporality, and in so doing they move from a natural–individual model of time – the poet has his own "seasons," out of step with the violent age – towards what we might call revolutionary time. "Occasion" obstructs, but it may also lead. When God's zeal has brought on the Last Days, or when corruption has washed away every vestige of national character, then the poet must take the stage:

> Then is the Poets time, 'tis then he drawes,
> And single fights forsaken Vertues cause,

as Marvell proclaimed in 1650.[18] *Of Reformation* anticipates the day of Christ's coming, when "some one" will be able to create a new and lofty poetry. *Animadversions* likewise begs Christ to finish his apocalyptic transformations of England, so that "he that now for haste snatches up a plain ungarnish't present as a thanke-offering to thee, which could not bee deferr'd ... may then perhaps take up a Harp, and sing thee an elaborate Song to Generations" (1.706; the pun on "present" is presumably intentional). But in each instance the gap between now and then, "ungarnish't present" and future song, is closed in the very act of opening it. In the words of Milton's most revealing letter, he "run[s] into a reciprocall contradiction" by "do[ing] that which I excuse myselfe for not doing" (1.320).

These prayers to Christ are as rhetorically "elaborate," dextrous, and impassioned as the poetry they supposedly cannot reach, and they *enact* the apocalypse whose deferral supposedly prevents them from rising to such heights. As Janel Mueller suggests in chapter 1 above, Milton turns the Song promised in *Of Reformation* from a celebration of Christ's coming into an agent of it, a means "whereby" the godly nation will be stirred up and the Last Days accelerated. Then, to conclude his tract, he brings on (or "prevents"?) the Day of Judgment in his own text, expelling the foul matter, damning the bishops in person to the lowest depths of Hell, sharing the savage glee of the slavemaster commanding *"Slaves* and *Negro's."* Having envisioned the joy and fragrance that "must needs rush into the bosome" at the moment of true reformation, and having hinted that Christ should come "sudden and swift . . . speedy and vehement," Milton now starts without Him. He expropriates the power that Marvell would later ascribe to Cromwell, the power to "fore-shorten Time." The text performs a kind of deconstruction in reverse, demolishing its own statements of absence, division, and deferral. This self-empowering, moreover, is conceived in literary/stylistic as well as in polemic/political terms. The great prayer in *Animadversions* is there called an "ungarnish't present" that suffers from not being deferred, but when the Modest Confuter attacked it (quite rightly) as *"theatricall,"* this false disclaimer vanishes immediately: far from being inartistic and hasty, Milton explains, the passage was a fully-realized "hymne in prose," an even higher genre than prayer. Consequently, "the stile was greater."[19]

These slightly desperate attempts to heal the cleaving mischief of untimeliness suggest that the political crisis had injected a new urgency into a traditional problem, the relation between Time and Truth. In *Of Prelatical Episcopacy* Milton strives to separate the spotless robe of Truth from the "verminous and polluted rags" of Time, and in *Doctrine and Discipline* he tries to downplay the traumatic hostile reception of the first edition by demoting Time from mother to "Midwife" of Truth, arrogating the whole female-procreative function to himself. Milton's anxiety about temporality is "pencilled over" but not obliterated by these touches of metaphoric art, and *Areopagitica* is full of such visible *pentimenti*. Truth must not be caught and bound, for then – the opposite of Proteus – she "turns herself into all shapes, except her own, and perhaps tunes her voice according to the time, as *Micaiah* did before *Ahab."* But immediately Milton/Truth becomes a Proteus again: Micaiah in fact *did* speak the unpalatable truth to King Ahab, and Truth actually *"may* have more shapes than one." We have lost the whole notion of an extra-temporal basis for epistemology, a hierarchy that separates pure transcendent essences from the tangled and bloody mass that we call "the times." What should be a scandal comes across as an empowering moment, an *occasion*:

> And now the time in special is, by priviledge to write and speak what may help to the furder discussing of matters in agitation. The Temple of *Janus* with his two *controversal* faces might now not unsignificantly be set open. (II. 561)

Agitation begets privilege. Significance is generated rather than dispersed by crisis. To the extent that Milton feels part of the accelerated movement of history, he embraces this oppositional theory of truth that undermines his most idealistic beliefs. In *Eikonoklastes*, in a passage used as the second epigraph to this volume, hermeneutics itself must bend to the needs of revolution: "For in words which admitt of various sense, the libertie is ours to choose that interpretation which may best minde us of what our restless enemies endeavor, and what wee are timely to prevent."[20]

"Prevent" is a Janus-faced term, however, which means both anticipation – foreshortening of time by supreme achievement – and annihilation. Milton remained profoundly uncertain whether revolutionary violence dispersed or concentrated his literary gifts. In *The Reason of Church-Government* he laments the "feaver" of the body politic, the "interrupted listening," the "troubl'd sea of noises" that makes literature impossible; tumult means the breakdown of proper reading and the destruction of a civilized model of authorship (1.748, 807, 821). But this complaint is swallowed up in the larger context of Book II, the claim to a prophetic vehemence answerable only to God, that disregards the fire and destruction it visits upon the world. The argument seems to lead away from this Old Testament model towards Renaissance humanism, when he describes his future plans in terms of the classical literary genres. Shortly afterwards, however, the terrible prophetic mode is firmly re-established as the highest plane of inspiration: the great work must not be "obtain'd by the invocation of Dame Memory and her Siren daughters" – little better than the sex and wine that produce Royalist libertine verse – but rather "by devout prayer to that eternall Spirit who ... sends out his Seraphim with the hallow'd fire of his Altar to touch and purify the lips of whom he pleases" (1.820–1). And the notorious "left hand" image, the central evidence for the separatist condemnation, actually reinforces the equation of high authorship with combat. Like generals defeated in a guerilla war, Milton protests that he does not perform with full vehemence because his sword-hand is tied.

It is natural to correlate this excuse for half-heartedness with the fear of division and dispersal ("knowing my self inferior to my self"), the halving of his resources, the feebleness of the child born "out of mine own season" (1.807). Elsewhere, however, he admits that he did throw all his resources into these controversial tracts. In the prefatory remarks to *Of Prelatical Episcopacy*, for example, he explains how

> it came into my thoughts to perswade my selfe, setting all distances and nice respects aside, that I could do Religion and my Country no better service for the time than doing my utmost endeavour to recall the people of GOD from this vaine forraging after straw, and to reduce them to their firme stations under the standard of the Gospell. (1.627)

Milton equates himself with Moses at his most militant and with a heroic general who saves the battle, and he will commit his "utmost endeavour" to the task, not just his left hand. Internal divisions and "distances" prompt rather than inhibit the textual enterprise, just as the psychomachia of accusing voices or "stories" in his conscience generates *The Reason of Church-Government*, which is both a left-handed travesty and the trumpet-voice of God

Himself. Summarizing these tracts in the *Defensio Secunda*, he claims to have "transferred all my genius [ingenium] and all the force of my industry" to them, contradicting his own complaint at the time that his "genial power" was thwarted. Now they represent not a fatal interruption, "out of mine own season," but the deliberate working out of a rational idea. He thus attempts to bring his internal self-generated program into step with the national emergency, and to match his achievements of the 1640s with those of the 1650s, which he described in 1658 as a "fruit" now fully "enjoyed," the "highest task I have ever set myself" and a payment to his country of "the highest I possessed."[21] The voice of ripe satisfaction that closes *Lycidas* rings out again, amplified tenfold. The first two *Defenses*, in Milton's own view, are simultaneously the products of "haste" and interruption, a "snatching away" of the passive author, and a supreme achievement that not only satisfies his earlier promise of a national epic, but is itself a heroic act of liberation, the single-handed salvation of a whole people.[22] It is all the more striking, then, that by 1659 he could refer to the Protectorate as "a short but scandalous night of interruption" (VII.274).

Milton never entirely escaped the dialectic of wholeness and division, contemplation and action, self-satisfaction and self-deferral. In 1633 we find him agonizing over his "belatednesse" and fearing that the contemplative life leaves him "cutt off" and "unweapon'd" for combat or procreation (I.319–20); nine years later he is bemoaning his earliness, his premature ejaculation into the world of action, the distance between his current task and his future ideals. But at some point in the crisis he firmly embraced revolutionary time, and spoke as an integrated *auctor* already fulfilling his literary promise. The *Defenses of the English People* are so wholeheartedly confident that they run the risk of bearing witness only to themselves – an accusation often levelled by his Royalist enemies; even when he complains of the interruption in a private letter, he conjoins a scornful remark on *otium* and thus attacks the principle (beloved of separatist critics) that only calm and detachment can produce art (IV.ii.866; XII.64). In many ways Milton's prose polemics fit the criteria of "future poetry" better than his verse does. The *Defenses* "imbreed and cherish" the seeds of national pride, vituperate the enemy, and combine "medicine" and "doctrine" with their celebration of God's special favor to England. They are consistently "elaborate" and "magnificent," rising to epic and monumental claims: when Milton compares the *Defensio Secunda* to an epic poem, he does so by directly imitating an epic simile and thus dissolving analogy into identity (IV.i.685; VIII.252). Above all, they are "self-crowning," Richard Helgerson's requirement for artistic maturity. Yet Helgerson interprets the prose as an artistic disaster; the poetic promise made in *The Reason of Church-Government* had to wait "a quarter of a century" for fulfilment.[23]

We have seen the early prose tracts straining towards a state of heroic self-actualization that leaves behind the need to apologize for divided powers, or to separate the functions of art and polemic. *Of Prelatical Episcopacy* aspires to be such an "utmost endeavour," but (as Fish shows in chapter 2 above) it is a self-incapacitating text, still foraging after straw to build its bricks. The critical moment of fusion occurs not (as one might expect) in the 1650s, when his epic Latin polemics gained him a European reputation, but at the most intense "time of opposition," when civil war was raging and Milton's personal disturbance rose to match that of the nation. The complaints of interruption in *Of Education* are quite different from those in *The Reason of Church-Government*, for the great work is now located in "the present": those "assertions," which promise to bring truth, "honest living" and "peace," suggest the divorce tracts – more precisely the later divorce tracts and *Areopagitica*, prepared to counter the savage assault on the *Doctrine and Discipline* during the first half of 1644. The "poetic" status of *Areopagitica* is universally acknowledged, particularly by those most eager to prove the separatist position (and *Of Education* made the cross-over in Milton's lifetime, being printed with the poems in 1673). The divorce tracts should now be recognized as a pivotal text of Milton's "poetic" career, both in terms of narrative sophistication (demonstrated by Annabel Patterson in chapter 4 above) and as works of self-authorizing rhetoric.

The addresses to Parliament in *The Doctrine and Discipline of Divorce* and *The Judgment of Martin Bucer* are high points in Milton's crisis rhetoric, utterly confident in their authorial presence, intensely dramatic when describing (that is, fabricating) the urgency of the moment:

> Yee have now, doubtlesse by the favour and appointment of God, yee have now in your hands a great and populous Nation to Reform; from what corruption, what blindnes in Religion yee know wel; in what a degenerat and fal'n spirit from the apprehension of native liberty, and true manlines, I am sure ye find: with what unbounded licence rushing to whordoms and adulteries needs not long enquiry. (II.226–7)

Pressure *becomes* form; Milton *becomes* the Body of the Time. He no longer "borrows Authority" for his Promethean self-fashioning (I.835), but declares himself quite free from influence and dependency, "running equal and authentic" with the Reformation fathers he translates (II.437), a wholly self-activating figure whose creative autonomy, though produced only in the dramatic moment of the text, guarantees him the right to command and coerce a whole nation:

> Ye are now in the glorious way to high vertue, and matchless deeds... Dare to be as great, as ample, and as eminent in the fair progress of your noble designes, as the full and goodly stature of truth and excellence it self. (II.438)

If the nation now takes on the *amplitudo* and sublimity of the body of truth – that is, of these very lines – then the gap is closed between political "designes" and artistic achievement, "poetical enthusiasm" and godly Zeale; Britain will then have fulfilled the command made earlier in *Of Reformation*, to "be the *Praise* and the *Heroick Song* of all POSTERITY" (I.597).

Milton takes in *Bucer* the stance that Helgerson finds only in the later poetry, "at once apart and engaged": he is both the crest of a revolutionary wave and the solitary watchman, appealing to Parliament whether "any thing generous, any thing noble, and above the multitude, were left yet in the spirit of England," and announcing, as he would do later at the end of the *Second Defense*, that "there livs yet [one] who will be ready" to fight the wars of truth (II.435, 440). This solitary hyper-activism, Milton fondly dreams, is a sign that he has been singled out by God, that he is not active at all but a passive instrument of unmediated divinity. And as in the later claim to tackle "Things unattempted yet in Prose or Rhyme," the self-pronounced courage of the enterprise implies the self-evident quality of the text. God Himself has prompted him "to take in hand and maintain [this] assertion ... God, it seems, intended to prove me, whether I durst alone take up a rightful cause against a world of disesteem, and found that I durst" (II.433–4). The higher poetics depends on the higher engagement.

Notes

1 *Qu'est-ce que la littérature?* (Paris, 1948), pp. 45–7.
2 *MCH*, I.84, 85–7 (emended from "high").
3 *A Complete Collection of the Historical, Political, and Miscellaneous Works of John Milton* (London, 1698), vol. I, pp. 126–7.
4 I.311–17, 1039; XII.4–10, 290.
5 Blank verse cannot of course be *equated* with prose, but it might be seen as a way of reconciling the two impulses that conflict in the early letters. One of the first appreciators and imitators of Milton's blank verse, the Earl of Roscommon, did collapse the distinction: "Have we forgot how *Raphaels* Num'rous Prose / Led our exalted Souls through heavenly Camps?" (J. E. Spingarn, ed., *Critical Essays of the Seventeenth Century*, vol. II [Oxford, 1908], p. 308; *cf. MCH*, I.91, where Shawcross substitutes "out" for "our" and thus reduces the involvement of the reader).
6 Unless otherwise specified, quotations in this section come from the preface to Book II of *The Reason of Church-Government*, I.801–23. J. Max Patrick warns us not to take Milton's disclaimer too seriously, in his edition of *The Prose of John Milton* (New York and London, 1968), p. xxvi; he follows Edward Le Comte's "Milton as Satirist and Wit," in A. P. Fiore, ed., *Th'Upright Heart and Pure* (Pittsburgh, 1967), p. 56.
7 *CPW*, I.590, 805, 811, III.406; *PR*, IV.343–4. Milton uses "beautified" for Laudian church ornament and the vain poetry he might have produced if he had kept aloof from controversy. When he complains that Charles wore "a garb somwhat more Poetical than for a Statist" he is using the separation of art and politics to score a political point; Milton's enemies in turn accused him of giving the Cromwellians "a Counterfeit Majesty with the Roabs of Eloquence" (*MCH*, I.91).

8 The Yale edition suggests, however, that the "intelligent and equal" reader is quite distinct from the "elegant" one (1.807n). For "equal," see *Bucer*, cited on p. 272 below.

9 This is close to Fish's argument in *Self-Consuming Artifacts* (Berkeley, 1972), pp. 298–301, that the "digression" is not a digression at all but a heroic self-display that anticipates the Abdiel episode.

10 *Artifacts*, pp. 266, 290.

11 1.746–7, 830–1; despite this sensual presentation of the affections (they are also heavily made-up "inchantresses"), the Yale edition identifies them as higher faculties quite distinct from the passions (1.747n). *Cf.* John Huntley in *Left Hand*, pp. 101–2 and Lana Cable's essay above, which stresses the extra-rational in Milton's persuasion.

12 C. A. Patrides, for example, cites it to show a profound connection between rhetoric and truth that runs through both the prose and the poetry, but still assumes that Zeal and art are entirely incompatible; by promoting calm, rational and "transcendent" effects over passionate or "enthusiastic" ones, Patrides precisely reverses Milton's scale of discursive value (*John Milton: Selected Prose*, revised edn [Columbia, Mo., 1985], pp. 44–5 and *passim*; *cf.* Kerrigan, discussed in Introduction above). The fullest treatment of the Chariot passage is Michael Lieb, "Milton's 'Chariot of Paternal Deitie' as a Reformation Conceit," *Journal of Religion*, 65 (1985), pp. 364–9.

13 Cited in Guido Morpurgo-Tagliabue, *Anatomia del Barocco* (Palermo, 1987), p. 18.

14 *PL*, 1.25. The prose and verse concordances reveal many examples of the word, to which one can add "asserenda" in the letter to Oldenburg defending the *Defensio Secunda* (IV.ii.866; XII.64), and Moses Wall's reference to "your Assertion of that storied voice that shold speak from heaven [denouncing hirelings]," which may echo Milton's lost letter; neither of the published passages cited in the Yale edition use the word (VII.512 and note).

15 *Astrea Redux*, line 178; Charles is compared to a wise physician who waits for the most efficacious moment.

16 VII.236–9; in chapter 3 above Stephen Fallon links this passage to the divorce tracts.

17 1.312, II.363 (and *cf.* 549), IV.ii.866; XII.6, 64. *Moscovia* drew him "to the Walls of Cathay," but "From proceeding further, other occasions diverted me" (VIII.475). Note that, in Milton's tortuous account, Hartlib thinks he can urge *Of Education* on Milton because he (Hartlib) has found himself "prest and almost constrain'd" by the pleasure of his (Milton's) conversation.

18 *Tom Mays Death*, lines 65–6. Milton is surprisingly fond of this conservative "last remnant" model; *cf.* his theory of satire (pp. 261–2 above), his stance in *Bucer* (p. 273 below), and the figures of Abdiel and the "one just man" in *Paradise Lost*. One eighteenth-century reader assumed that Abdiel was Milton's portrait of a brave Royalist – one instance where his allegiance to poetry overcame his abominable politics (*MCH*, 1.258–9). It might be argued that the ode "Ad Joannem Rousium" reverts to a separatist position; the Muses have almost deserted Britain because of the tumults of civil war. Even here, however, he makes poetry out of "occasion" (the theft of his book) and political confrontation, launching an attack on two fronts – against the disgusting "vulgus," and against the Royalist snakes and harpies whose degenerate luxury caused the war in the first place.

19 I.524, 602, 616–17 (and *cf.* 707, "Come forth . . . for now the voice of thy Bride calls thee"), 930; Marvell, *The First Anniversary of the Government under O. C.*, line 139. I am grateful to Charita Ford for drawing my attention to the racial implications of 1.617.

20 I.639, II.225, 561–3, III.342. I would like to thank Robin Harders and Wendy Motooka for drawing my attention to these passages.

21 I.808, IV.i.537, 622–5; VII.558, VIII.128–34. *Cf.* the end of *Likeliest Means*: "I . . . have borne my witnes *not out of season* to the church and to my country" (VII.321, my italics).

22 IV.i.306, 536, 685, ii.866; VII.8, 554–6, VIII.252, XII.64. The *Defensio Secunda* has often been recognized as a true (or in some critics a misguided) fulfilment of the future poetry covenant made in the early 1640s; *cf.* Sir Herbert Grierson, *Milton and Wordsworth* (New York, 1937), p. 72, and Annabel Patterson, "The Civic Hero in Milton's Prose," *Milton Studies*, 8 (1975), pp. 71–101.

23 *Self-Crowned Laureates* (Berkeley, 1983), pp. 245–51. My thesis is that the prose (from the divorce tracts onwards) fulfils most of Helgerson's criteria for poetic success – a reconciliation with Time, a sense of victorious self-empowerment, a stance "at once apart and engaged."

Index